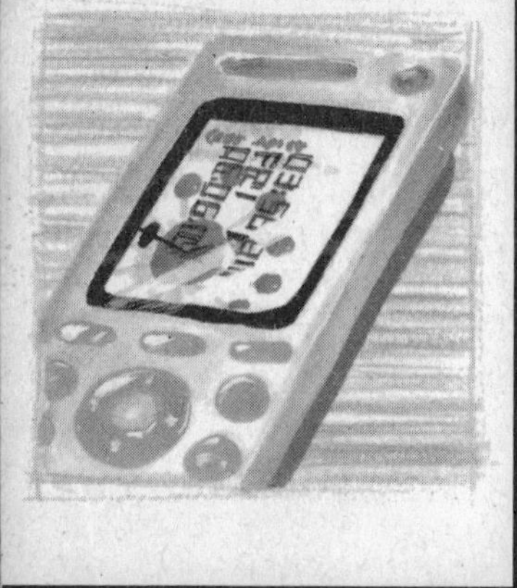

It's been four years since I've worked with my first editor, yet his is still the first name in my address book. I'm surprised just how little my social life has changed in the last four years. My resolution for this year is to make a new friend whose name will come before "Asada."

-Tite Kubo

BLEACH is author Tite Kubo's second title. Kubo made his debut with *ZOMBIEPOWDER.*, a four-volume series for *WEEKLY SHONEN JUMP*. To date, *BLEACH* has been translated into numerous languages and has also inspired an animated TV series that began airing in the U.S. in 2006. Beginning its serialization in 2001, *BLEACH* is still a mainstay in the pages of *WEEKLY SHONEN JUMP*. In 2005, *BLEACH* was awarded the prestigious Shogakukan Manga Award in the *shonen* (boys) category.

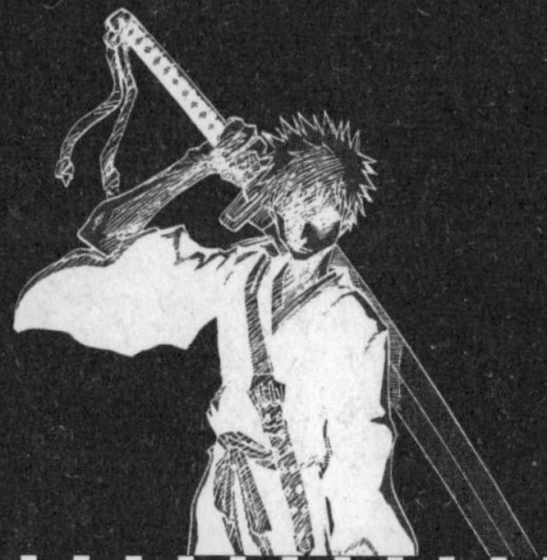

BLEACH
Vol. 23: ¡Mala Suerte!
The SHONEN JUMP Manga Edition
This volume contains material that was originally published in SHONEN JUMP
#63-65. Artwork in the magazine may have been altered slightly from what is
presented in this volume.

STORY AND ART BY
TITE KUBO

English Adaptation/Lance Caselman
Translation/Joe Yamazaki
Touch-Up Art & Lettering/Mark McMurray
Design/Sean Lee
Editor/Pancha Diaz

Editor in Chief, Books/Alvin Lu
Editor in Chief, Magazines/Marc Weidenbaum
VP of Publishing Licensing/Rika Inouye
VP of Sales/Gonzalo Ferreyra
Sr. VP of Marketing/Liza Coppola
Publisher/Hyoe Narita

Printed in the U.S.A.

Published by VIZ Media, LLC
P.O. Box 77010
San Francisco, CA 94107

SHONEN JUMP Manga Edition
10 9 8 7 6 5 4 3 2 1
First printing, June 2008

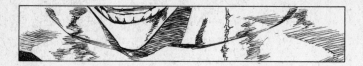

We are the fish in front of the waterfall.
We are the insects inside the cage.

We are the ruins of the billows,
The skull on the crosier,
The force of the torrent and the whale that drinks it.

We are the five-horned bull.
We are the fire-breathing monster.
And the screaming children.

Oh, we are poisoned by the moonlight.

BLEACH 23 ¡MALA SUERTE!

Shonen Jump Manga

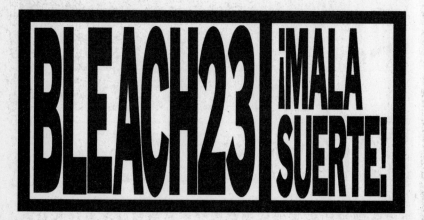

STARS AND

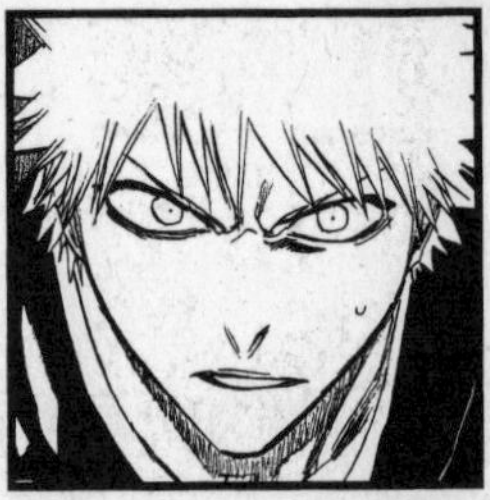

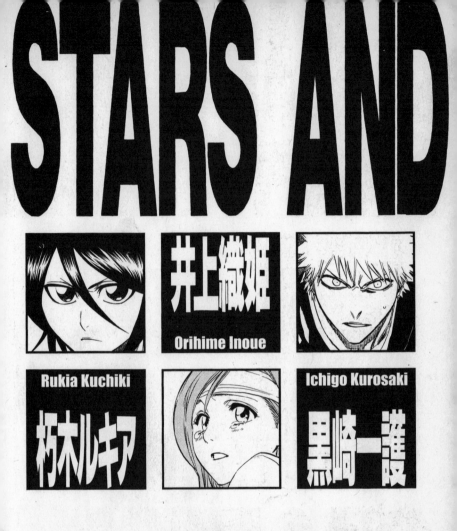

井上織姫

Orihime Inoue

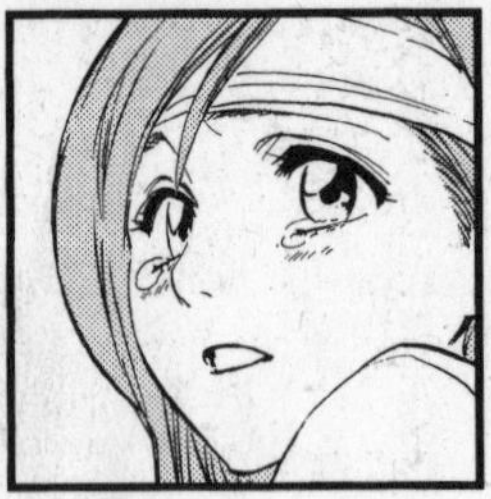

Ichigo Kurosaki

黒崎一護

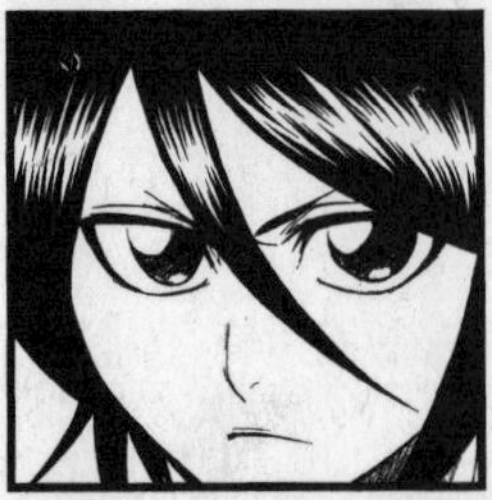

Rukia Kuchiki

朽木ルキア

plot

When Ichigo Kurosaki meets Soul Reaper Rukia Kuchiki, his life is changed forever. Soon Ichigo is a Soul Reaper himself, cleansing lost souls called Hollows, and even traveling to the strange world of the Soul Society in order to rescue Rukia.

Now back in the world of the living, Ichigo has his hands full once more cleansing Hollows. But when Chad and Orihime are injured by Arrancars, the Soul Society sends a team to help fight this deadly new threat, and Rukia is with them. She wastes little time in giving the disheartened Ichigo a much-needed dose of tough love. And meanwhile, in another world, Aizen and his minions plan their next move.

BLEACH ALL

斑目一角

Ikkaku Madarame

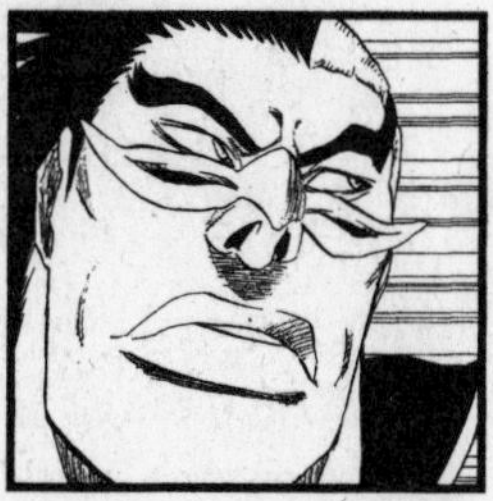

茶渡泰虎

Chad Yasutora

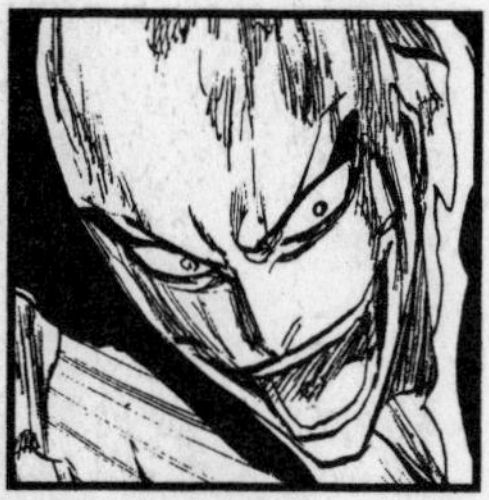

Edorad

エドラド

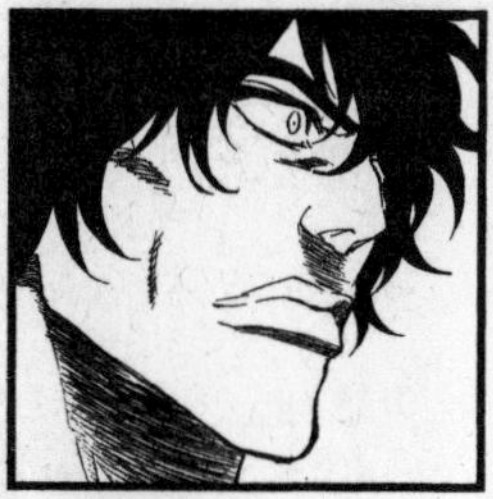

STORIES

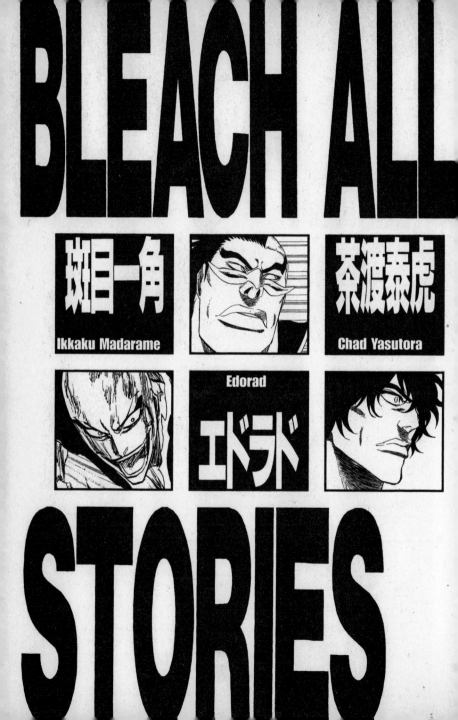

BLEACH 23

¡MALA SUERTE!

Contents

198.	The Icecold Discord	7
199.	Ugly	27
200.	Night of Sledgehammer	47
201.	Wind & Snowbound	67
202.	¡Mala Suerte!	91
203.	¡Mala Suerte! 2 (El Monstruo)	111
204.	¡Mala Suerte! 3 (Monstruo Sangrienta)	131
205.	¡Mala Suerte! 4 (Tempestad de La Lucha)	155
0.	side-A the sand	177
0.	side-B the rotator	187

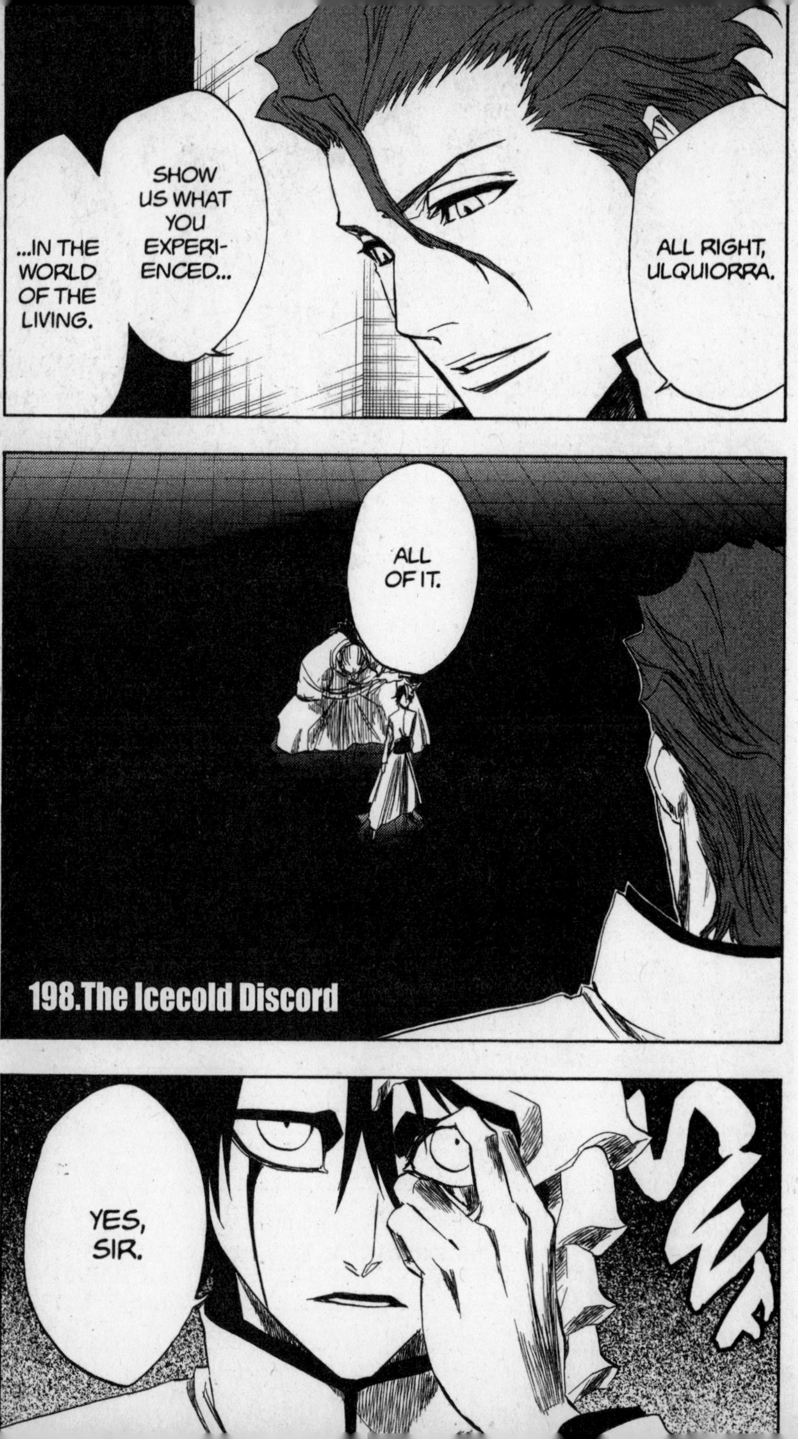
ALL RIGHT, ULQUIORRA.
SHOW US WHAT YOU EXPERIENCED...
...IN THE WORLD OF THE LIVING.
ALL OF IT.
198.The Icecold Discord
SWF
YES, SIR.

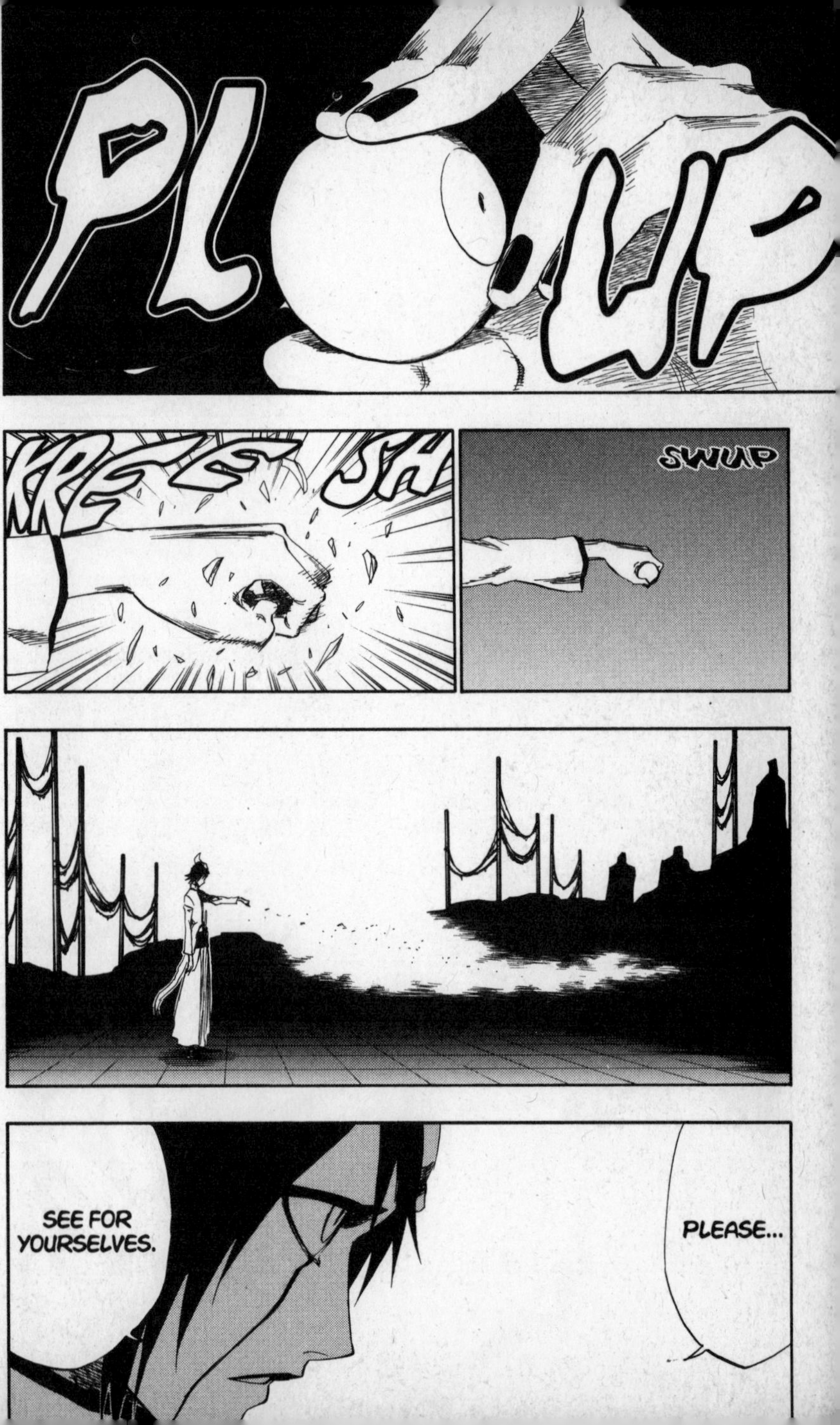
SWUP
PLEASE...
SEE FOR YOURSELVES.

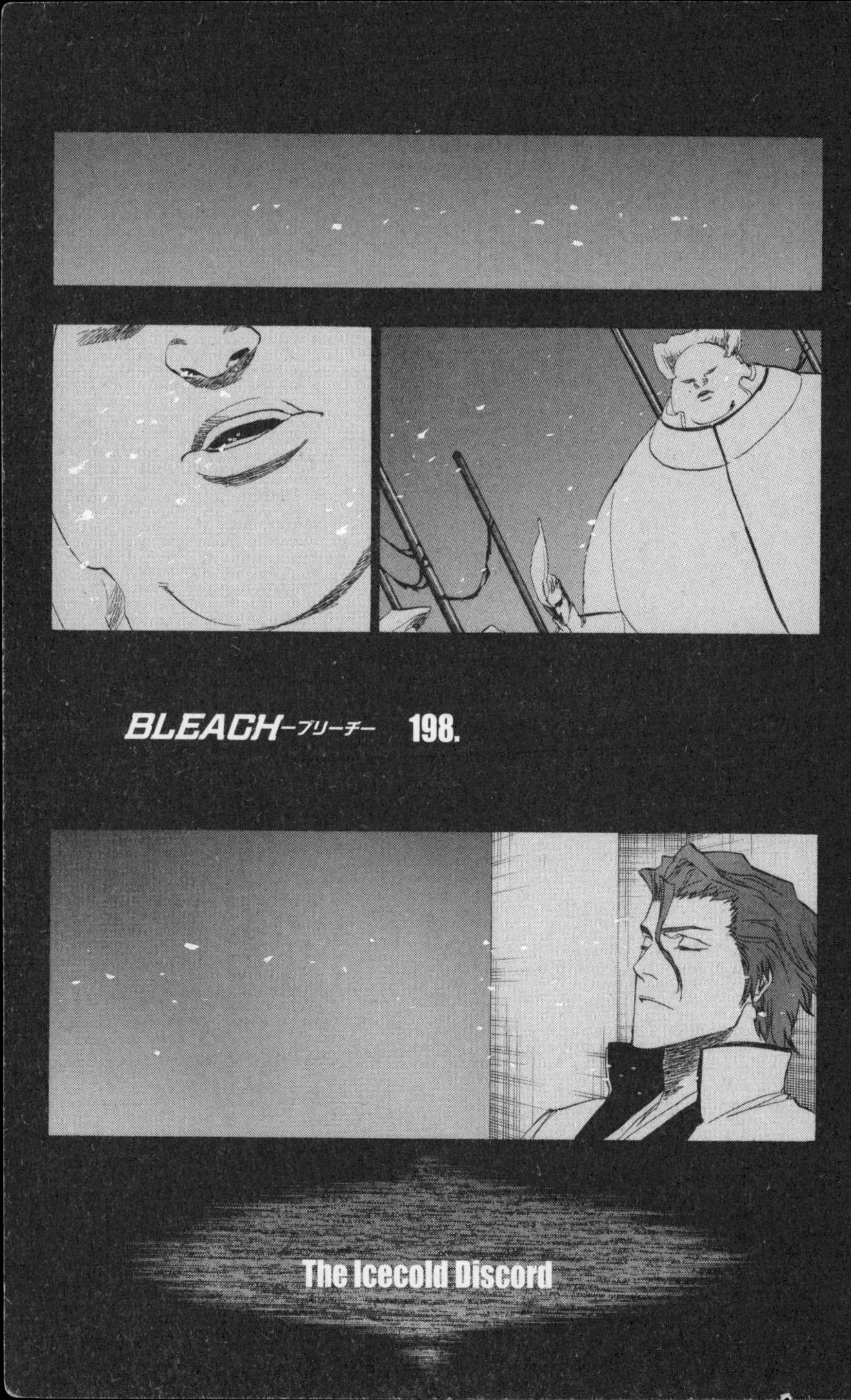
BLEACH-ブリーチ- 198.
The Icecold Discord

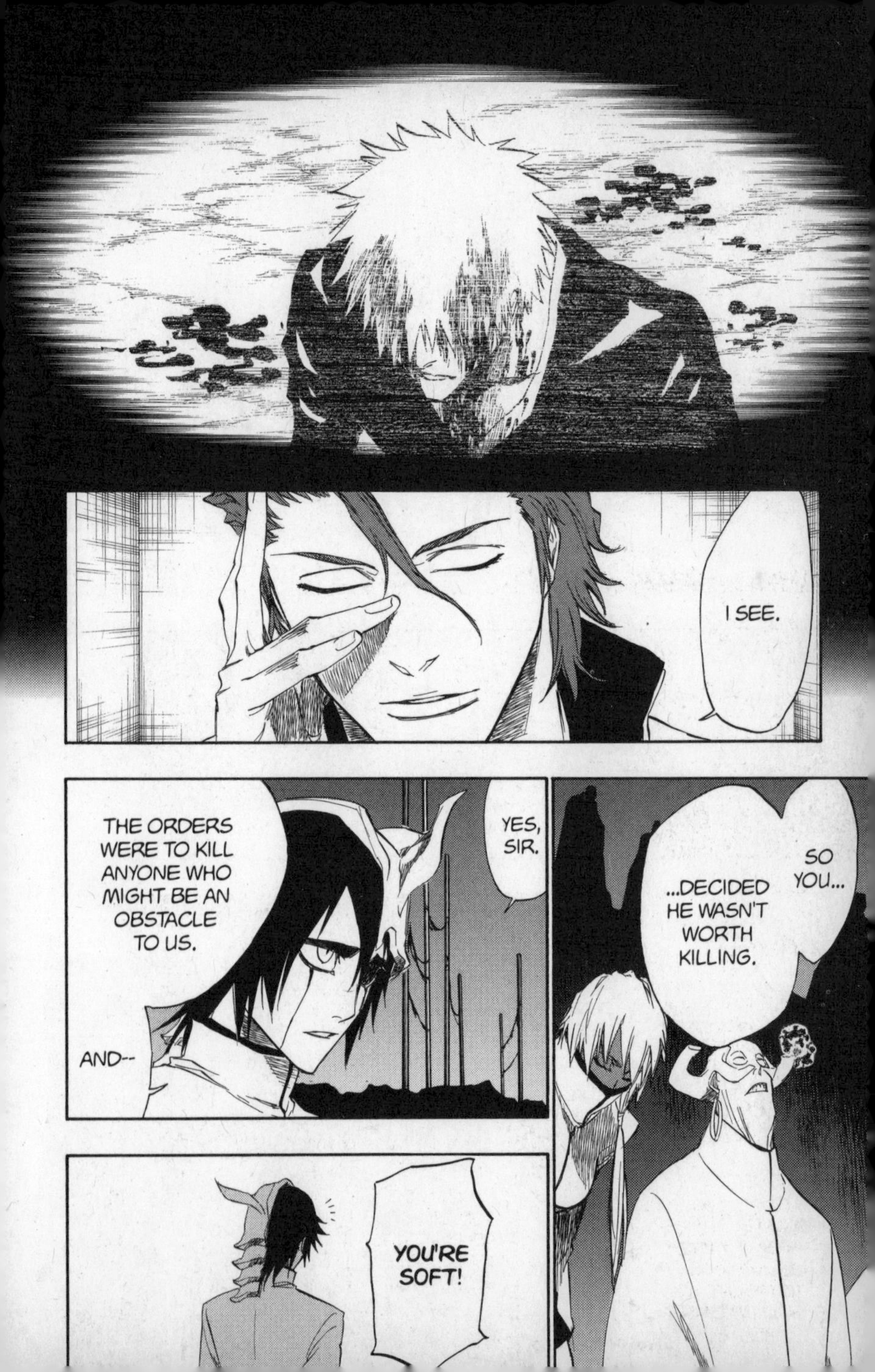
I SEE.
SO YOU...
...DECIDED HE WASN'T WORTH KILLING.
YES, SIR.
THE ORDERS WERE TO KILL ANYONE WHO MIGHT BE AN OBSTACLE TO US.
AND--
YOU'RE SOFT!

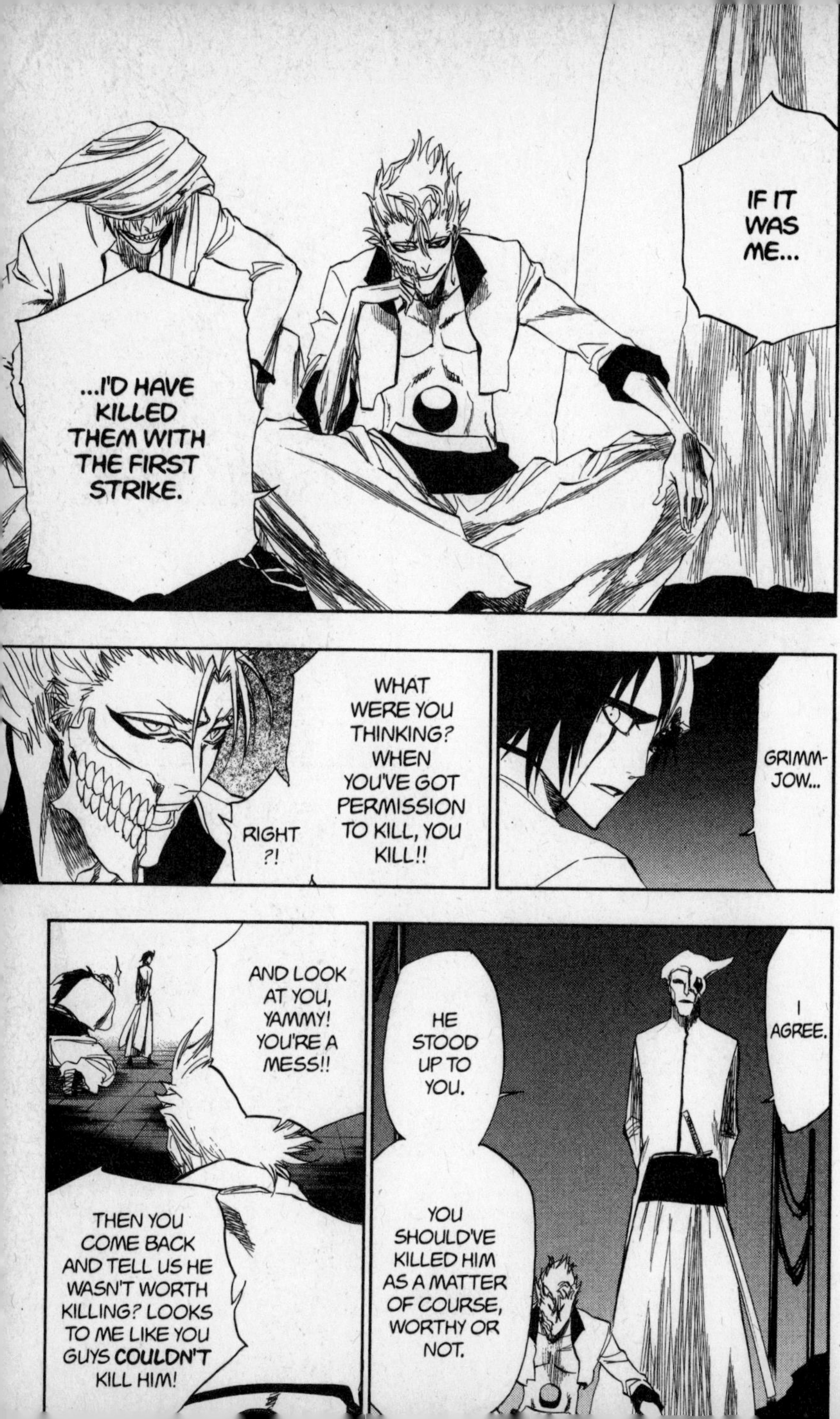
IF IT WAS ME...
...I'D HAVE KILLED THEM WITH THE FIRST STRIKE.
GRIMM-JOW...
WHAT WERE YOU THINKING? WHEN YOU'VE GOT PERMISSION TO KILL, YOU KILL!!
RIGHT ?!
I AGREE.
HE STOOD UP TO YOU.
YOU SHOULD'VE KILLED HIM AS A MATTER OF COURSE, WORTHY OR NOT.
AND LOOK AT YOU, YAMMY! YOU'RE A MESS!!
THEN YOU COME BACK AND TELL US HE WASN'T WORTH KILLING? LOOKS TO ME LIKE YOU GUYS **COULDN'T** KILL HIM!

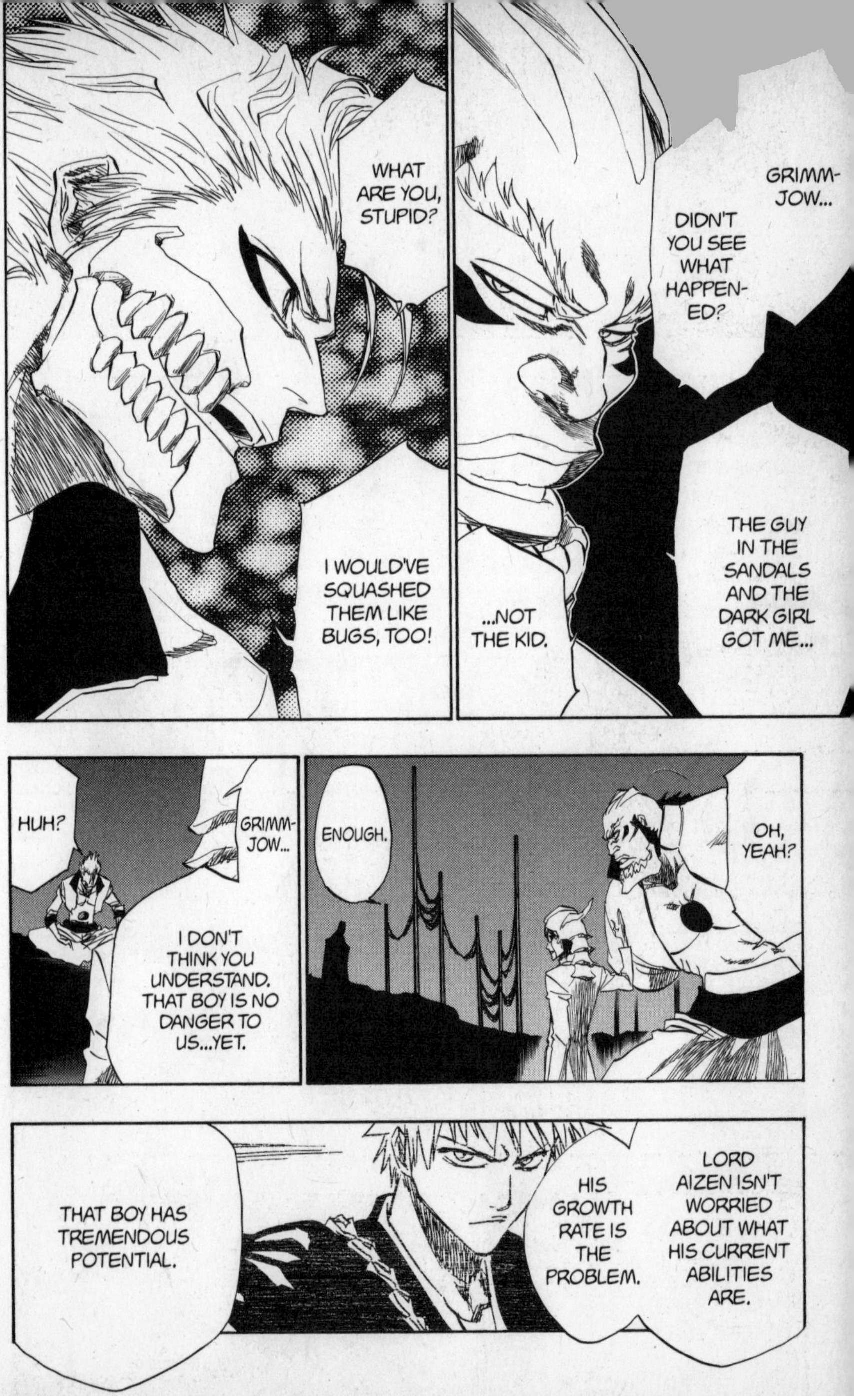
GRIMM-JOW...
DIDN'T YOU SEE WHAT HAPPEN-ED?
THE GUY IN THE SANDALS AND THE DARK GIRL GOT ME...
...NOT THE KID.
WHAT ARE YOU, STUPID?
I WOULD'VE SQUASHED THEM LIKE BUGS, TOO!
OH, YEAH?
ENOUGH.
HUH?
GRIMM-JOW...
I DON'T THINK YOU UNDERSTAND. THAT BOY IS NO DANGER TO US...YET.
LORD AIZEN ISN'T WORRIED ABOUT WHAT HIS CURRENT ABILITIES ARE.
HIS GROWTH RATE IS THE PROBLEM.
THAT BOY HAS TREMENDOUS POTENTIAL.

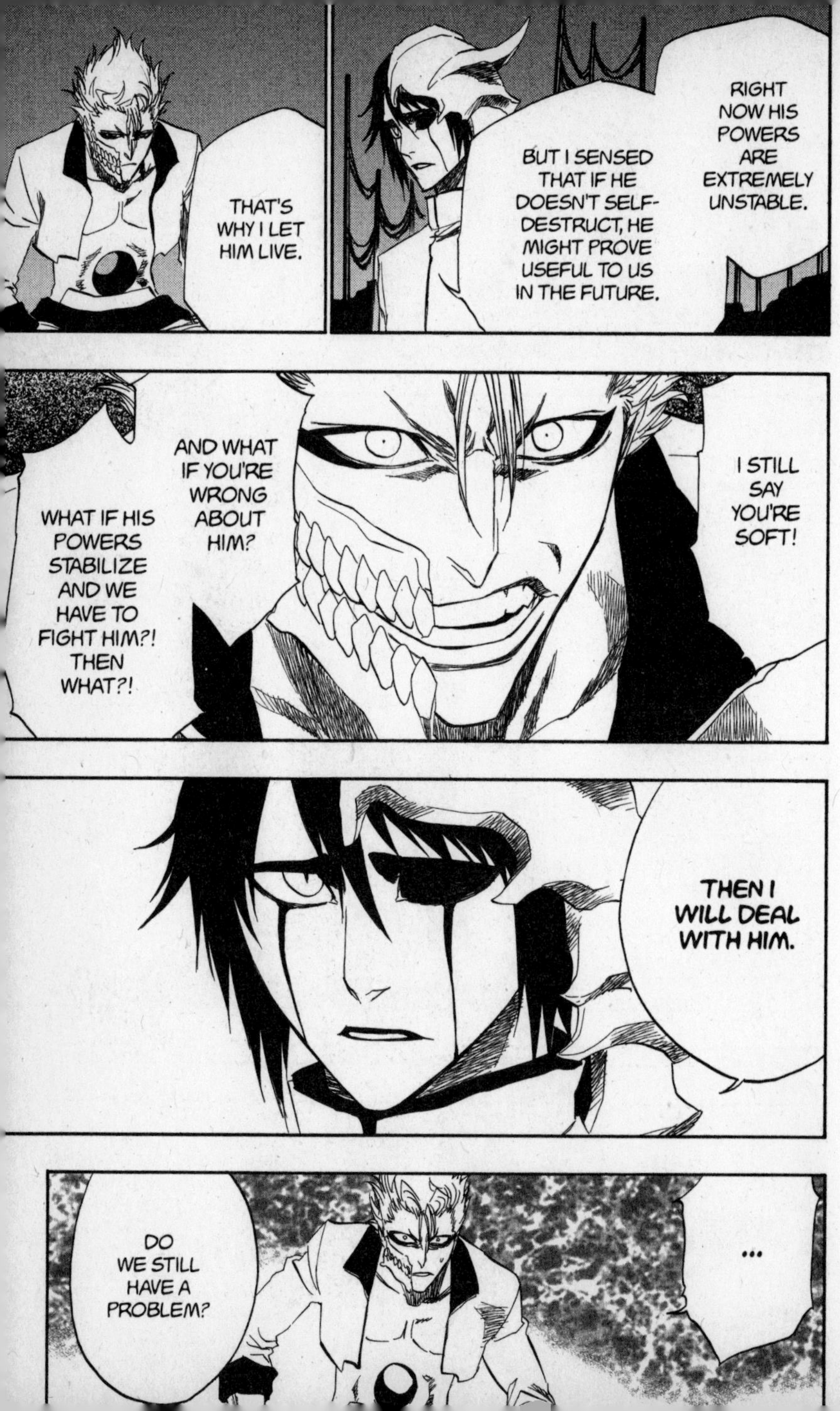
RIGHT NOW HIS POWERS ARE EXTREMELY UNSTABLE.
BUT I SENSED THAT IF HE DOESN'T SELF-DESTRUCT, HE MIGHT PROVE USEFUL TO US IN THE FUTURE.
THAT'S WHY I LET HIM LIVE.
I STILL SAY YOU'RE SOFT!
AND WHAT IF YOU'RE WRONG ABOUT HIM?
WHAT IF HIS POWERS STABILIZE AND WE HAVE TO FIGHT HIM?! THEN WHAT?!
THEN I WILL DEAL WITH HIM.
...
DO WE STILL HAVE A PROBLEM?

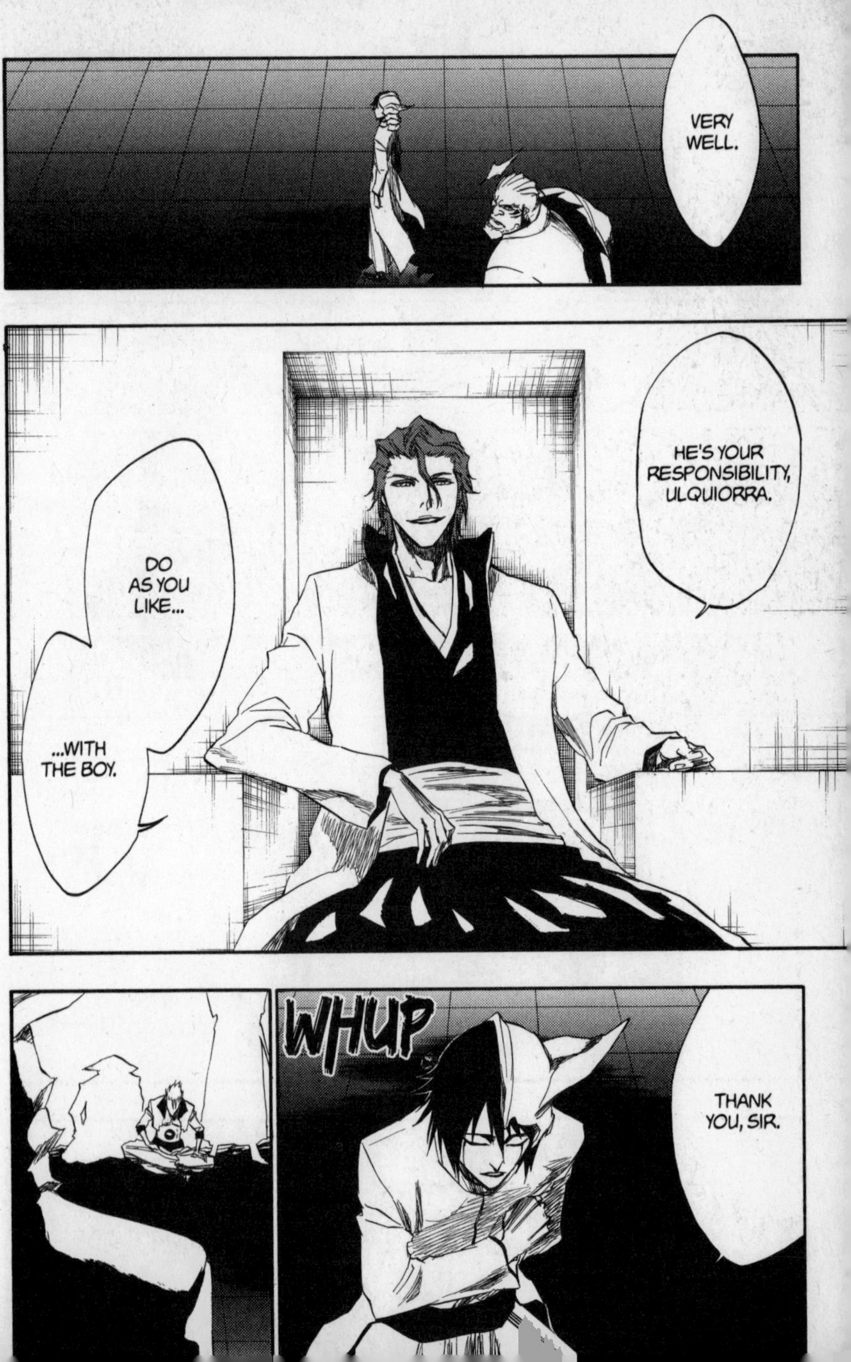
VERY WELL.
HE'S YOUR RESPONSIBILITY, ULQUIORRA.
DO AS YOU LIKE...
...WITH THE BOY.
WHUP
THANK YOU, SIR.

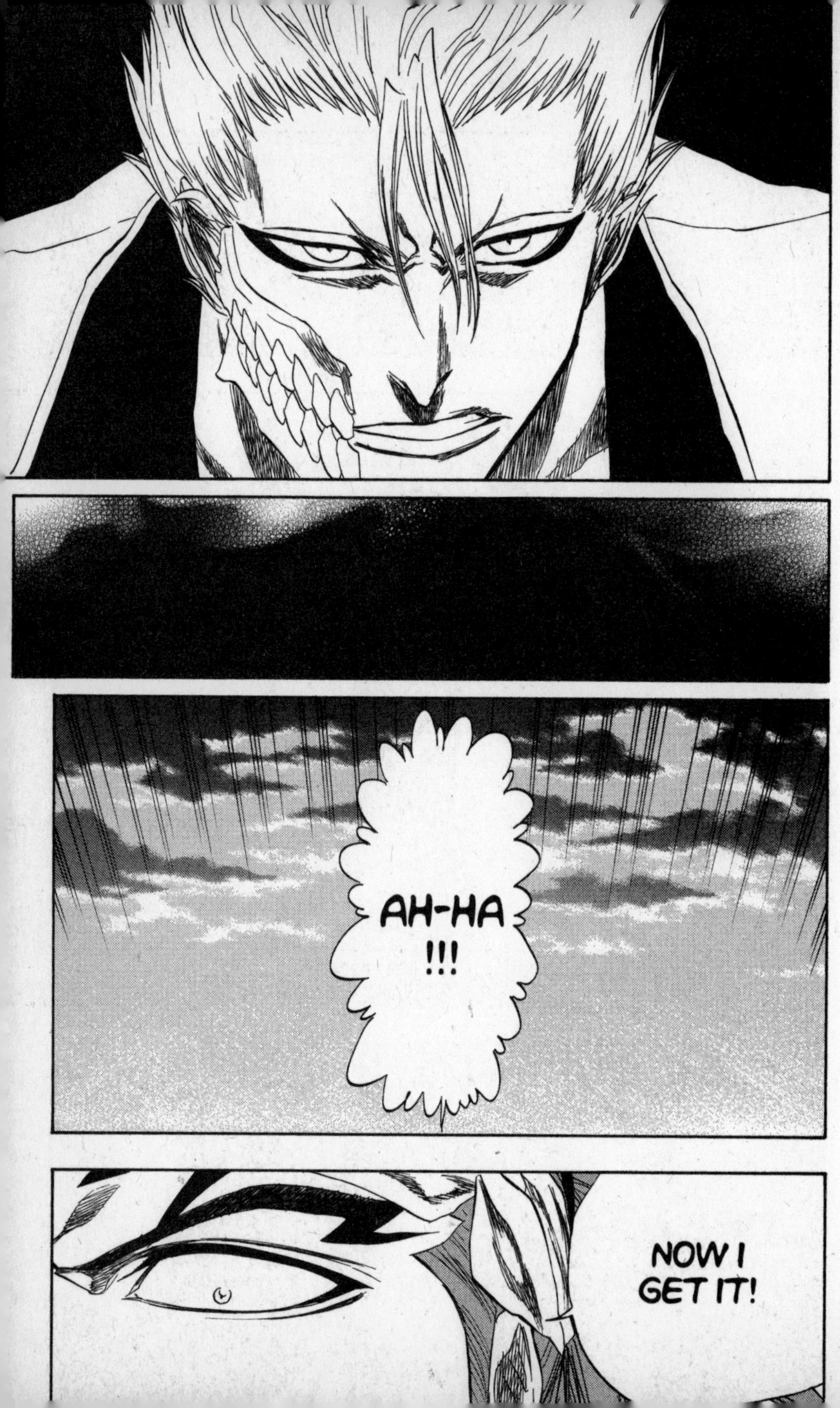
AH-HA !!!
NOW I GET IT!

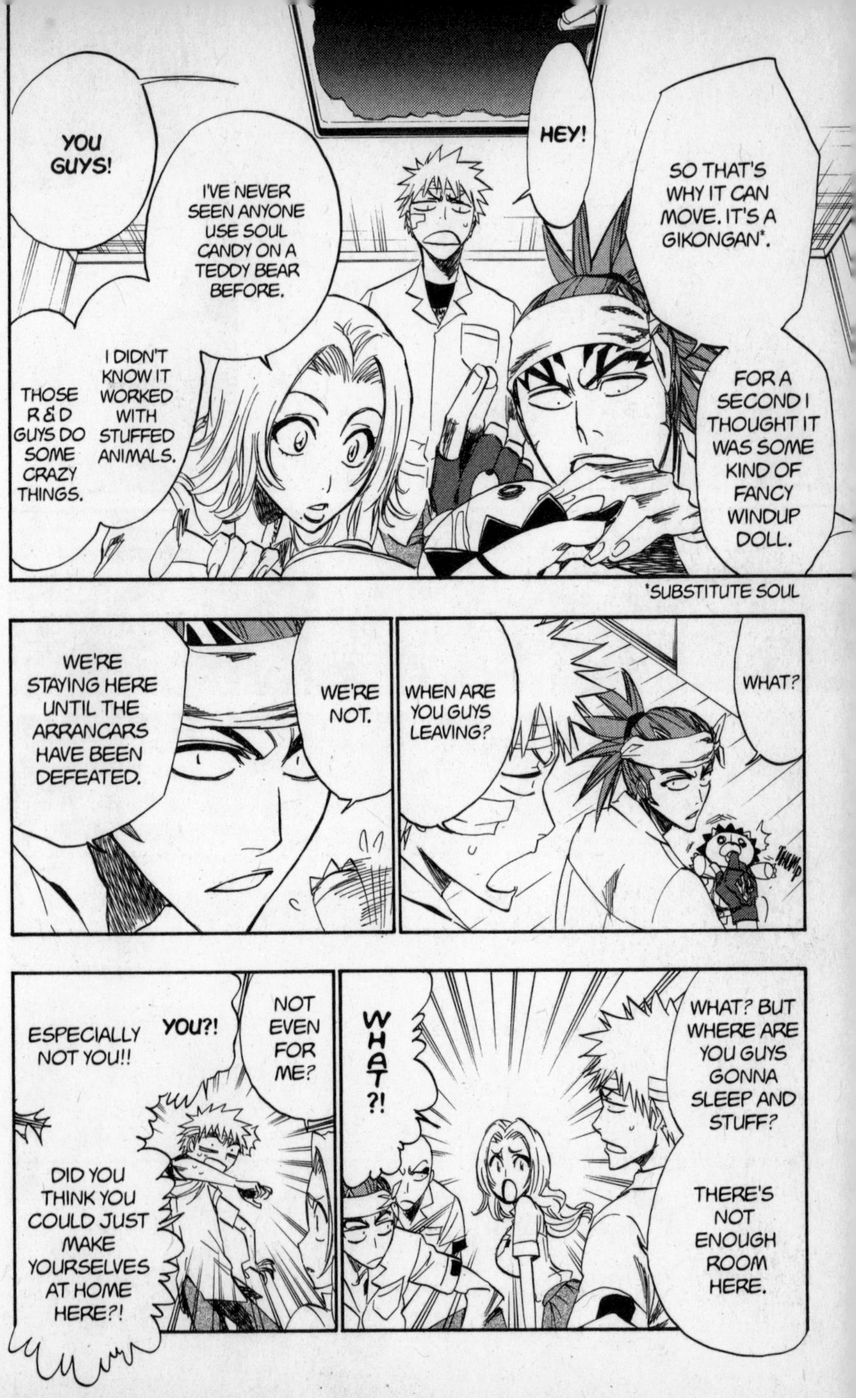
HEY!
SO THAT'S WHY IT CAN MOVE. IT'S A GIKONGAN*.
YOU GUYS!
I'VE NEVER SEEN ANYONE USE SOUL CANDY ON A TEDDY BEAR BEFORE.
FOR A SECOND I THOUGHT IT WAS SOME KIND OF FANCY WINDUP DOLL.
I DIDN'T KNOW IT WORKED WITH STUFFED ANIMALS.
THOSE R&D GUYS DO SOME CRAZY THINGS.
*SUBSTITUTE SOUL
WHAT?
WHEN ARE YOU GUYS LEAVING?
THUMP
WE'RE NOT.
WE'RE STAYING HERE UNTIL THE ARRANCARS HAVE BEEN DEFEATED.
WHAT? BUT WHERE ARE YOU GUYS GONNA SLEEP AND STUFF?
THERE'S NOT ENOUGH ROOM HERE.
WHAT?!
NOT EVEN FOR ME?
YOU?!
ESPECIALLY NOT YOU!!
DID YOU THINK YOU COULD JUST MAKE YOURSELVES AT HOME HERE?!

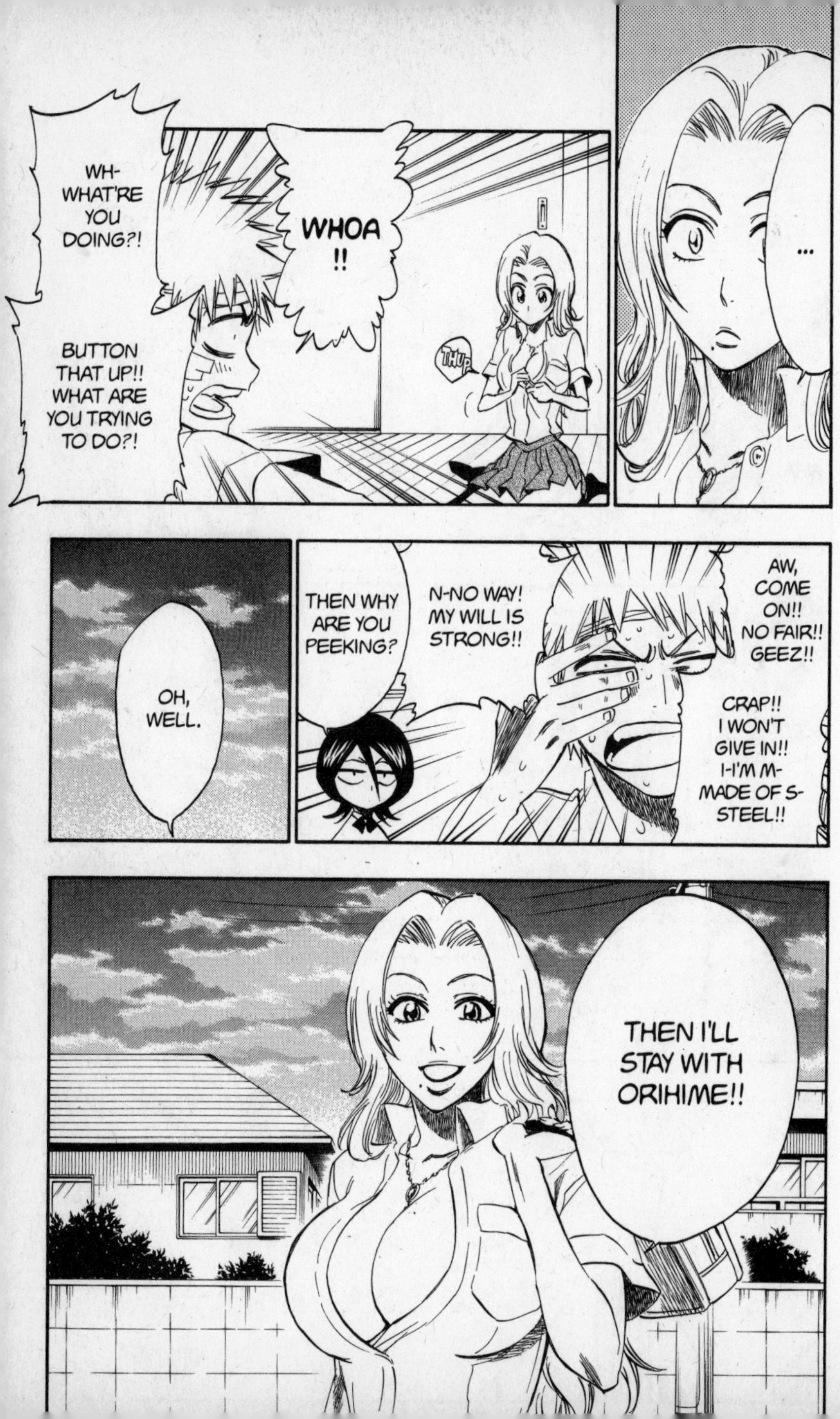
...
WHOA!!
WH- WHAT'RE YOU DOING?!
THUP
BUTTON THAT UP!! WHAT ARE YOU TRYING TO DO?!
AW, COME ON!! NO FAIR!! GEEZ!!
CRAP!! I WON'T GIVE IN!! I-I'M M- MADE OF S- STEEL!!
N-NO WAY! MY WILL IS STRONG!!
THEN WHY ARE YOU PEEKING?
OH, WELL.
THEN I'LL STAY WITH ORIHIME!!

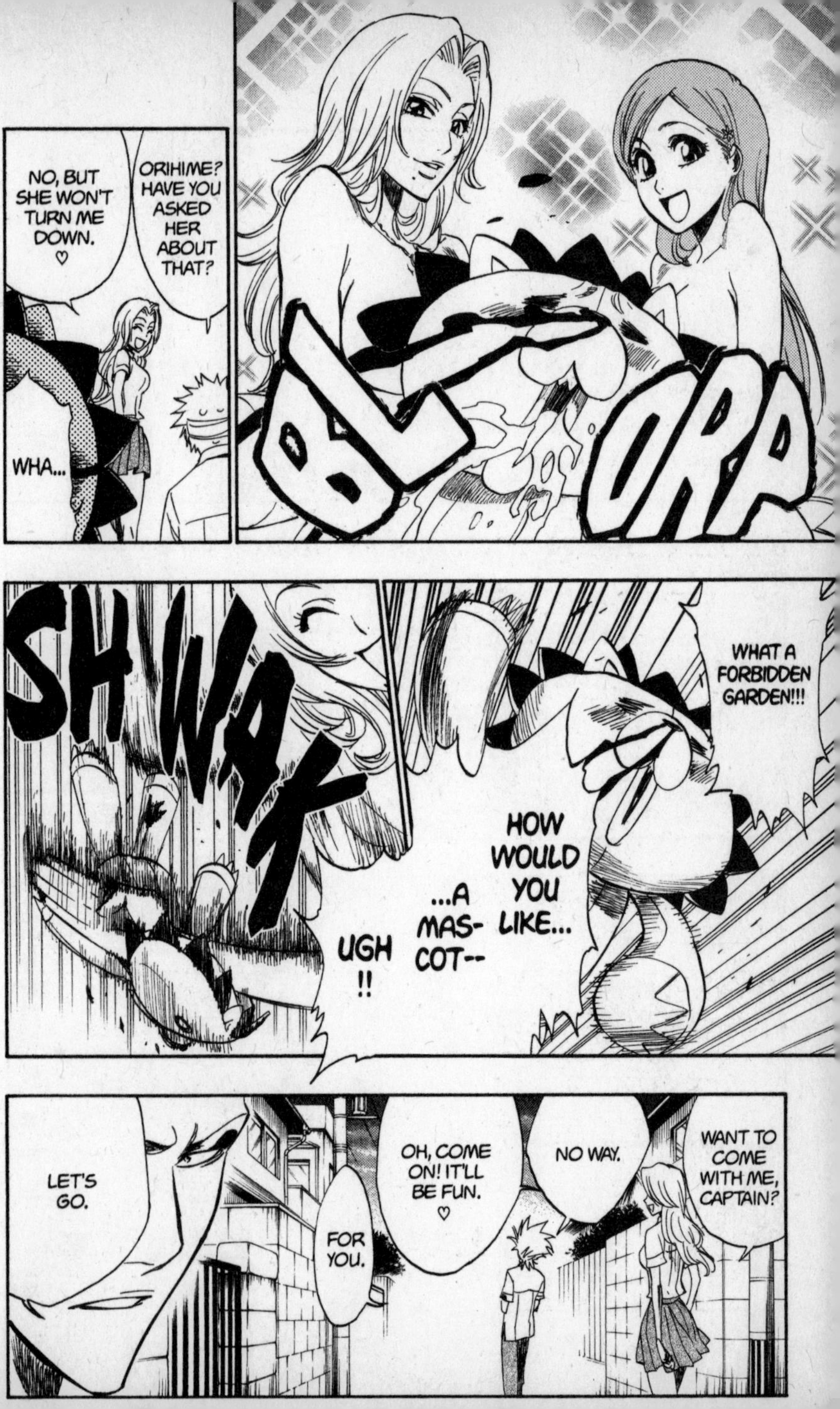
BLORP
ORIHIME? HAVE YOU ASKED HER ABOUT THAT?
NO, BUT SHE WON'T TURN ME DOWN. ♡
WHA...
WHAT A FORBIDDEN GARDEN!!!
HOW WOULD YOU LIKE...
...A MAS-COT--
UGH !!
SHWAK
WANT TO COME WITH ME, CAPTAIN?
NO WAY.
OH, COME ON! IT'LL BE FUN. ♡
FOR YOU.
LET'S GO.

READ THIS WAY

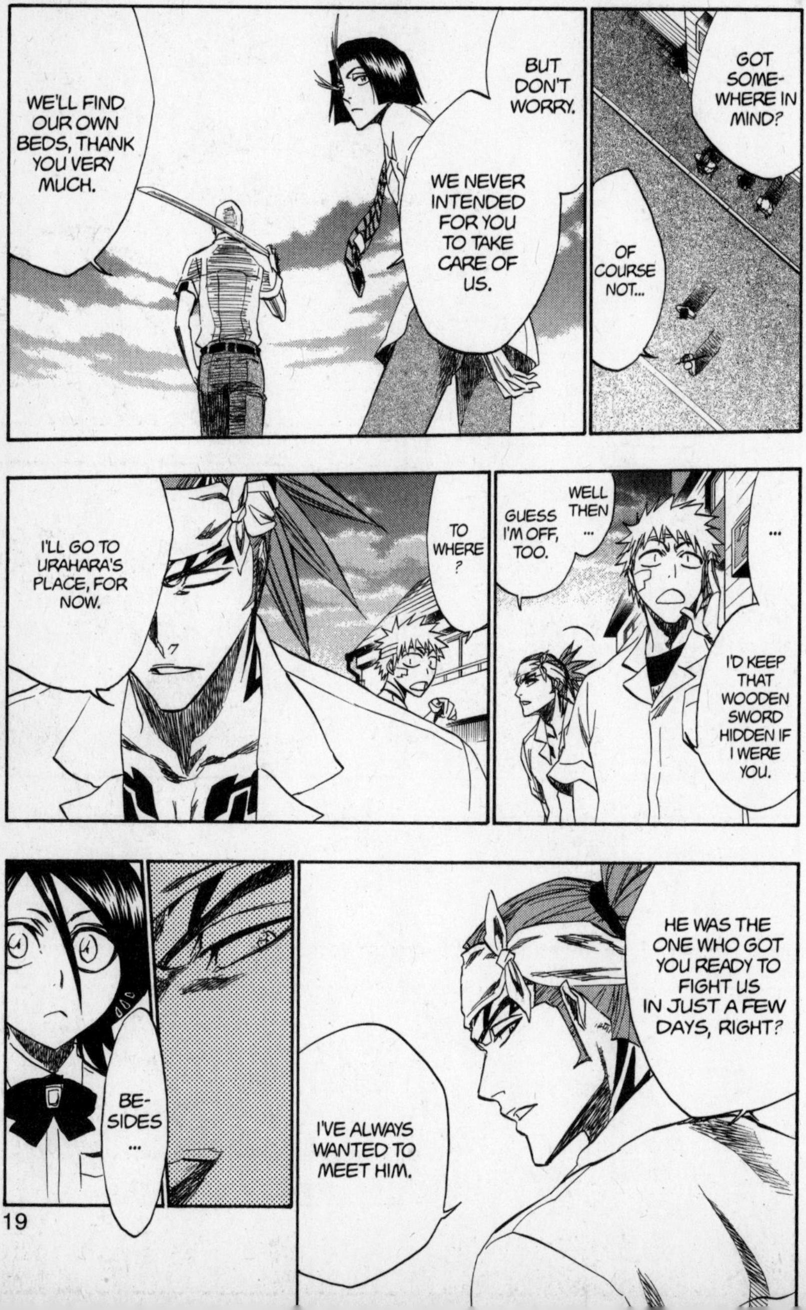
GOT SOME-WHERE IN MIND?
OF COURSE NOT...
BUT DON'T WORRY.
WE NEVER INTENDED FOR YOU TO TAKE CARE OF US.
WE'LL FIND OUR OWN BEDS, THANK YOU VERY MUCH.
...
WELL THEN ...
GUESS I'M OFF, TOO.
I'D KEEP THAT WOODEN SWORD HIDDEN IF I WERE YOU.
TO WHERE ?
I'LL GO TO URAHARA'S PLACE, FOR NOW.
HE WAS THE ONE WHO GOT YOU READY TO FIGHT US IN JUST A FEW DAYS, RIGHT?
I'VE ALWAYS WANTED TO MEET HIM.
BE-SIDES ...

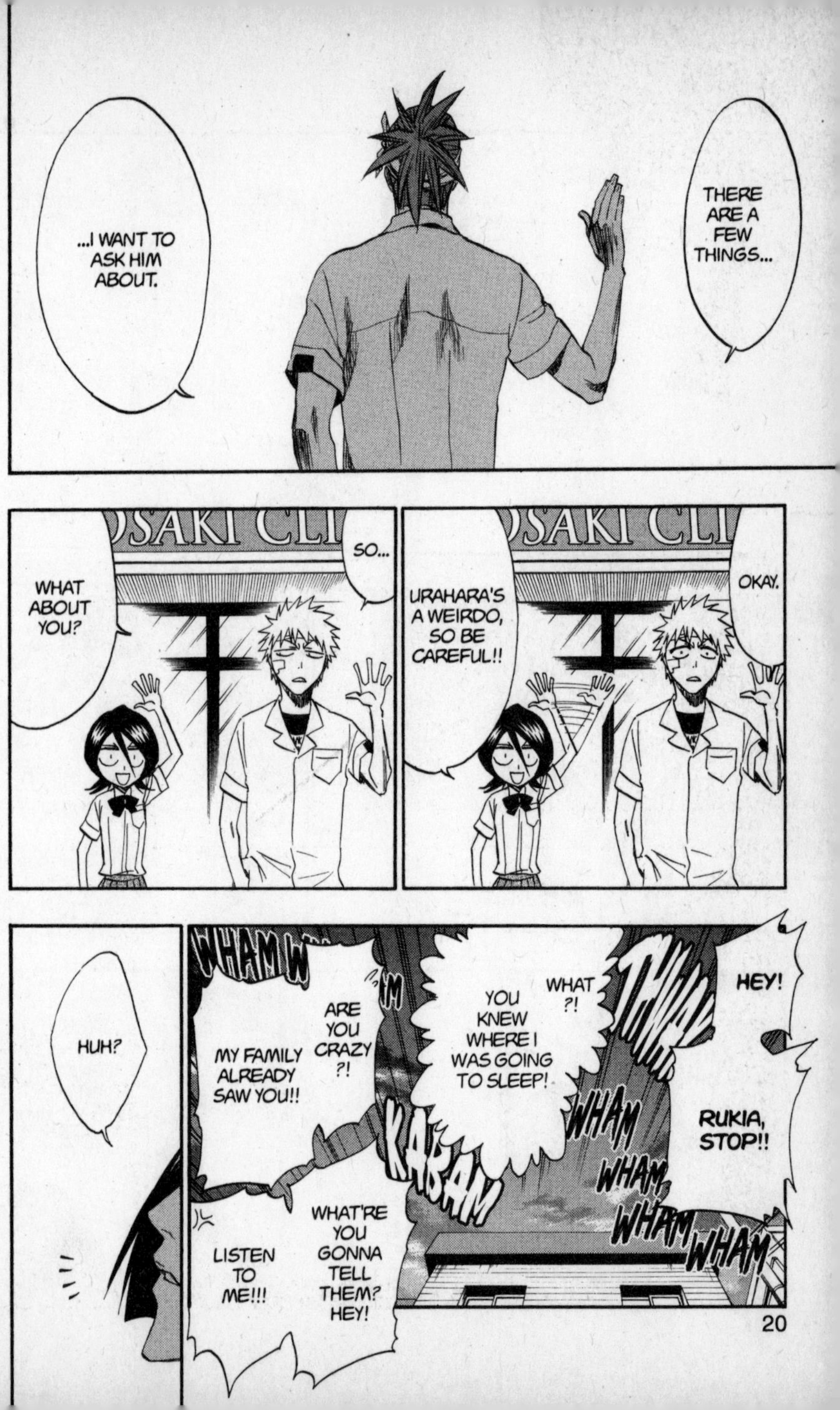
THERE ARE A FEW THINGS...
...I WANT TO ASK HIM ABOUT.
OKAY.
URAHARA'S A WEIRDO, SO BE CAREFUL!!
SO...
WHAT ABOUT YOU?
HEY!
WHAT ?!
YOU KNEW WHERE I WAS GOING TO SLEEP!
RUKIA, STOP!!
WHAM WHAM WHAM WHAM
KABAM
ARE YOU CRAZY ?!
MY FAMILY ALREADY SAW YOU!!
WHAT'RE YOU GONNA TELL THEM? HEY!
LISTEN TO ME!!!
HUH?

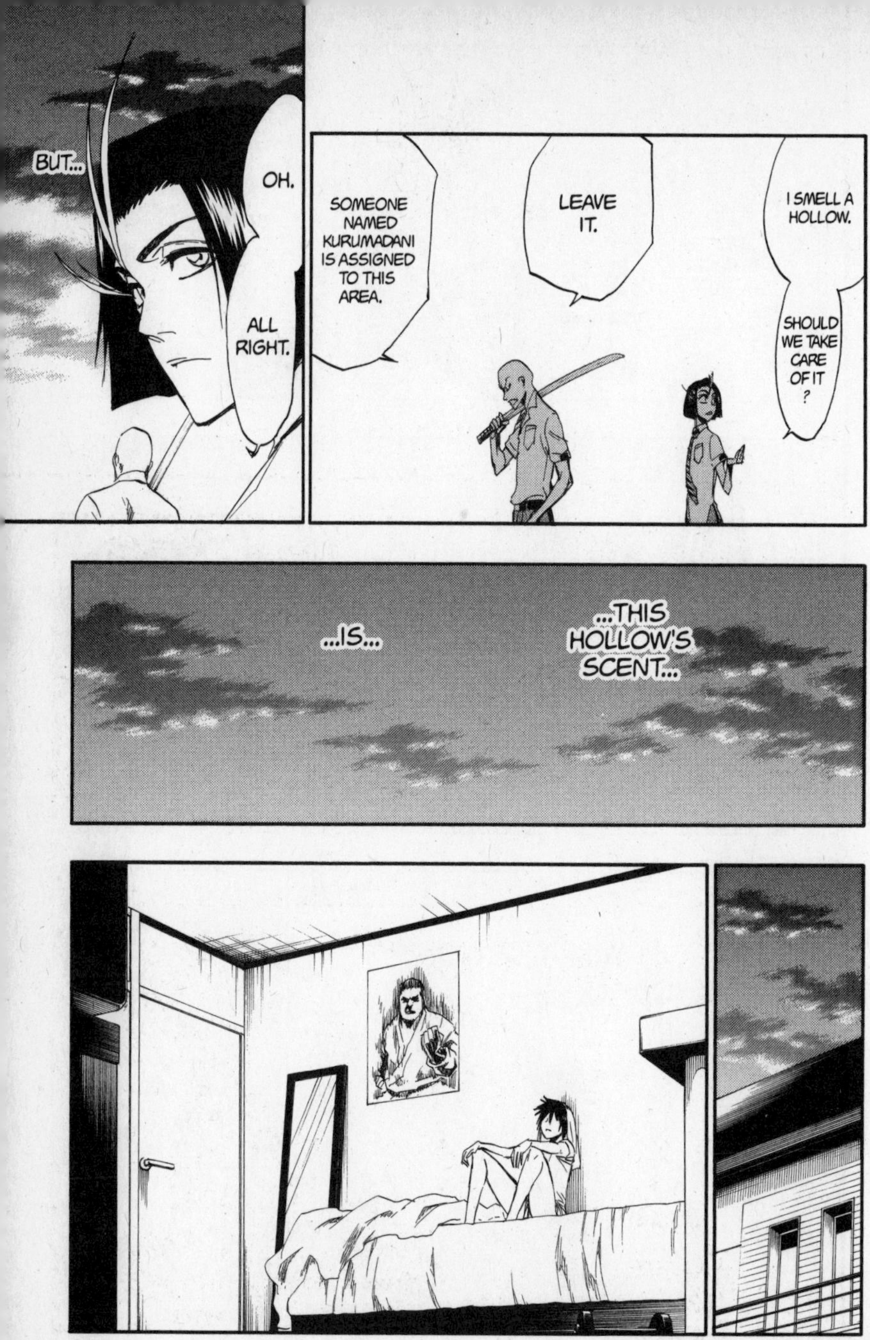
I SMELL A HOLLOW.
SHOULD WE TAKE CARE OF IT?
LEAVE IT.
SOMEONE NAMED KURUMADANI IS ASSIGNED TO THIS AREA.
OH.
ALL RIGHT.
BUT...
...THIS HOLLOW'S SCENT...
...IS...

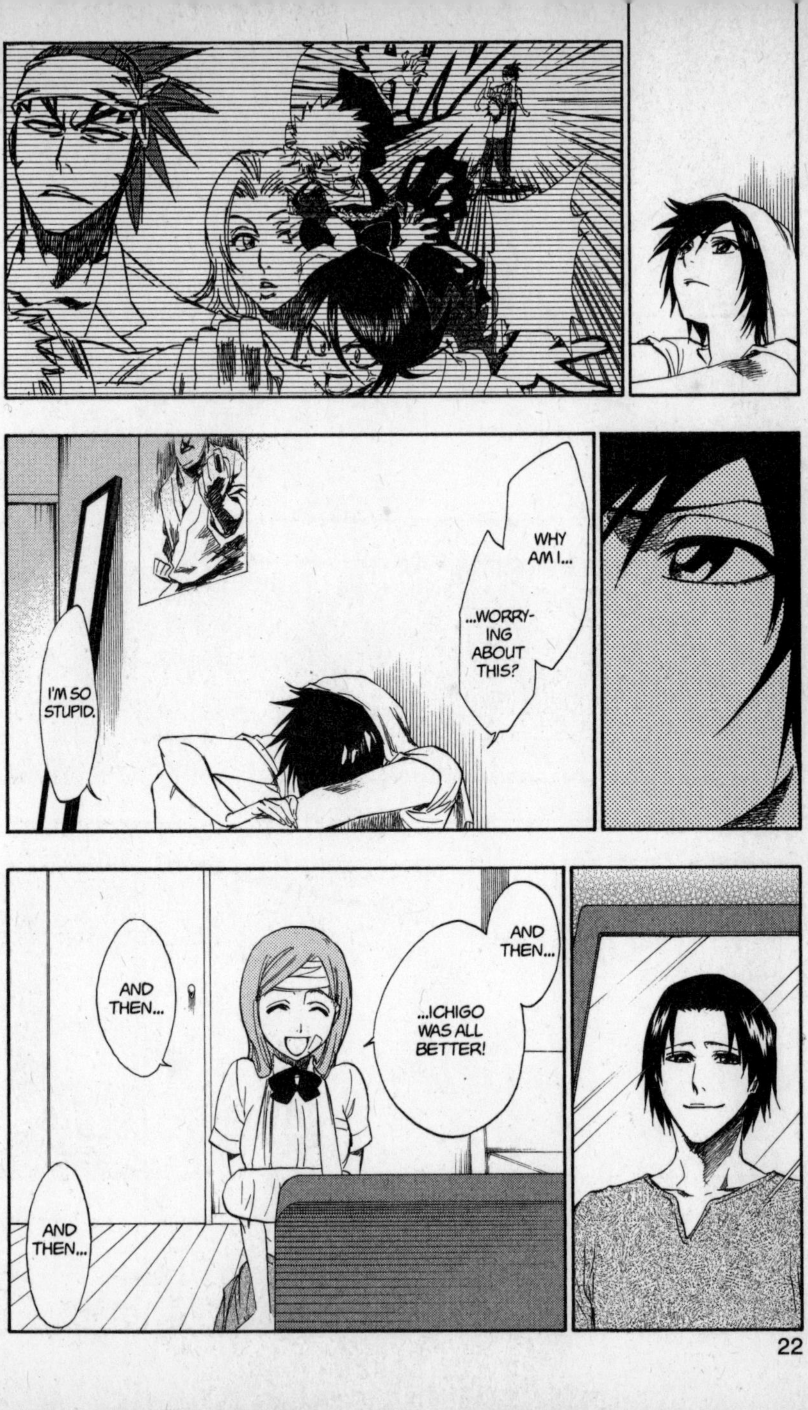
WHY AM I...
...WORRY-ING ABOUT THIS?
I'M SO STUPID.
AND THEN...
...ICHIGO WAS ALL BETTER!
AND THEN...
AND THEN...

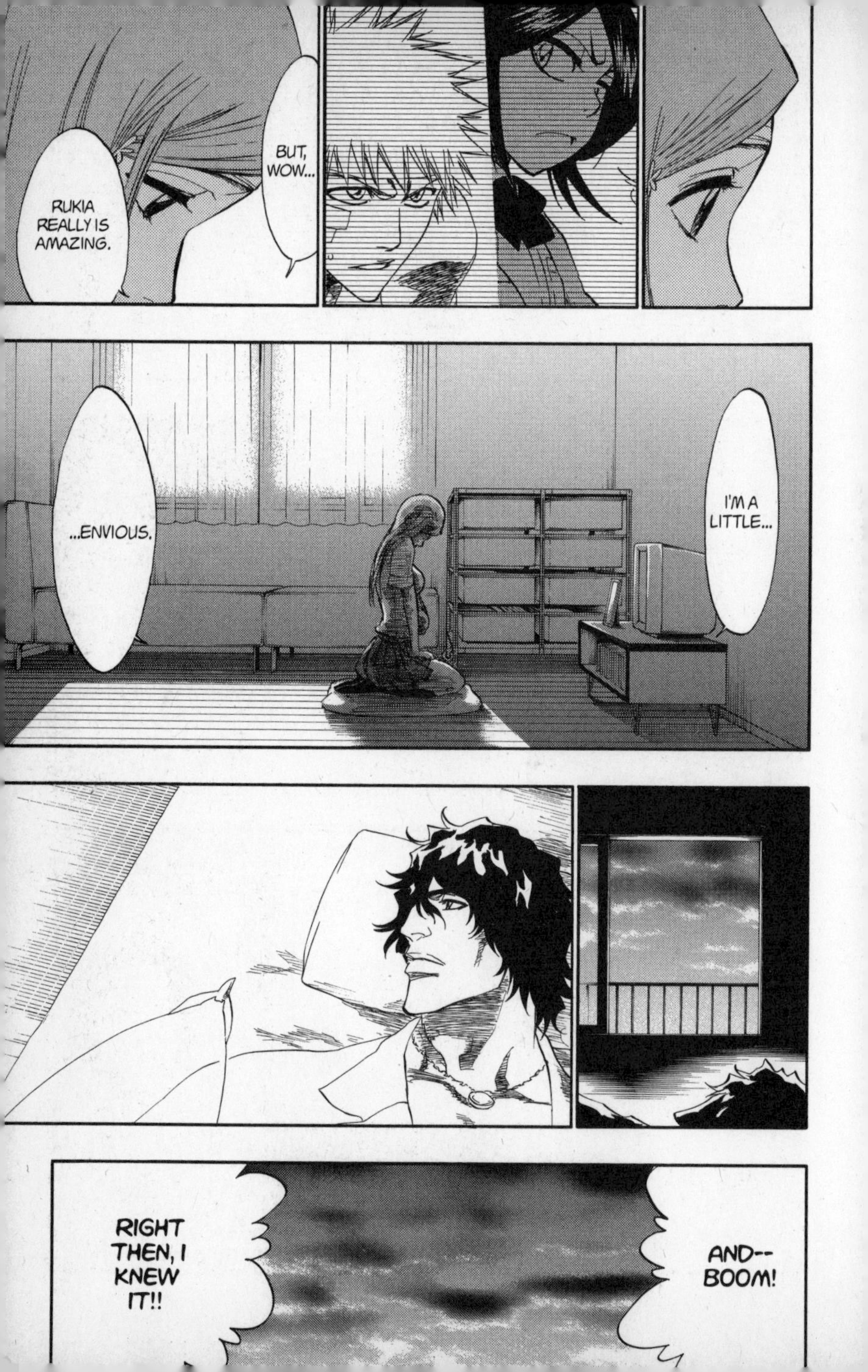
BUT, WOW...
RUKIA REALLY IS AMAZING.
I'M A LITTLE...
...ENVIOUS.
AND-- BOOM!
RIGHT THEN, I KNEW IT!!

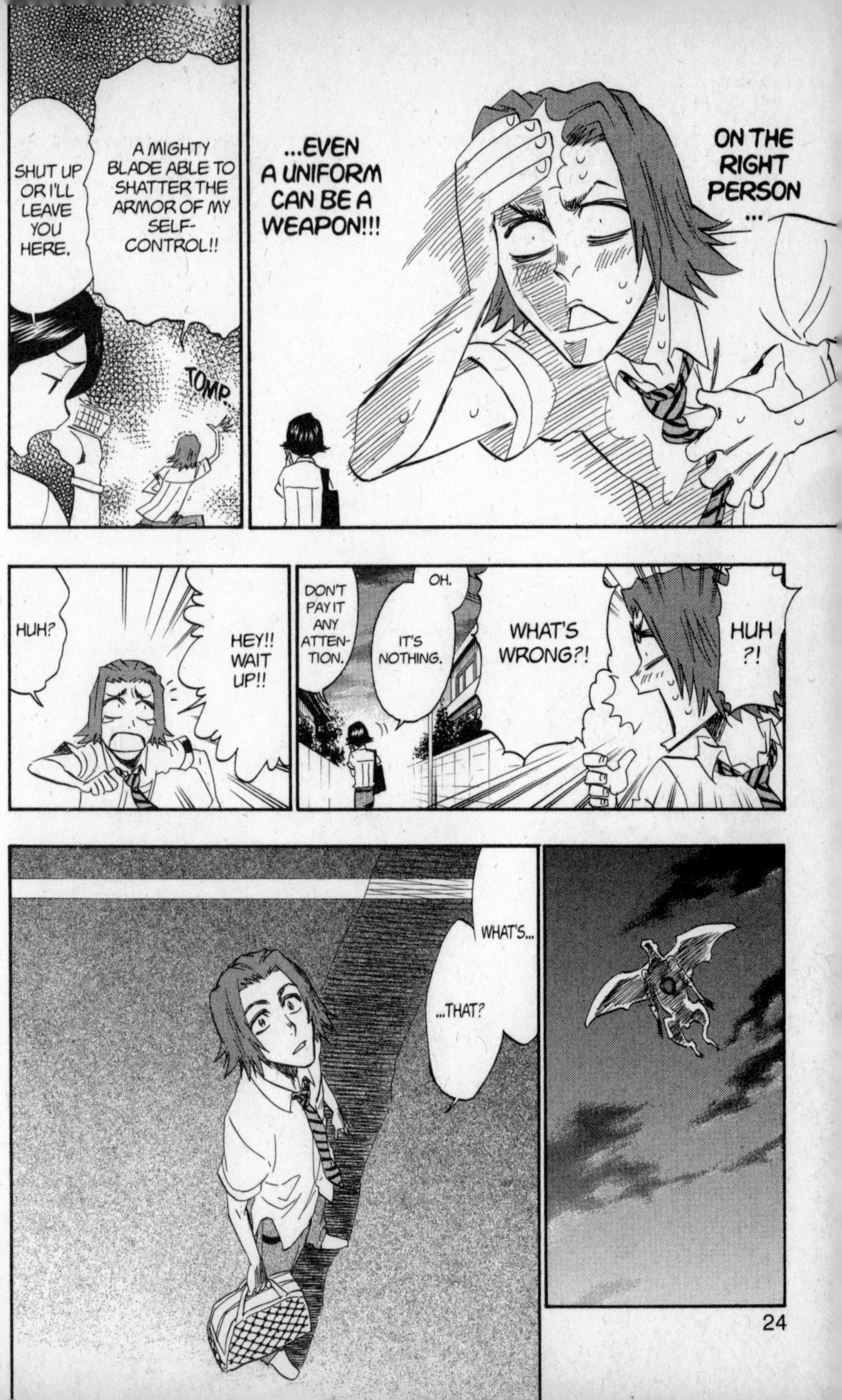
ON THE RIGHT PERSON ...
...EVEN A UNIFORM CAN BE A WEAPON!!!
A MIGHTY BLADE ABLE TO SHATTER THE ARMOR OF MY SELF-CONTROL!!
SHUT UP OR I'LL LEAVE YOU HERE.
TOMP...
HUH ?!
WHAT'S WRONG?!
OH.
IT'S NOTHING.
DON'T PAY IT ANY ATTENTION.
HEY!! WAIT UP!!
HUH?
WHAT'S...
...THAT?

READ THIS WAY

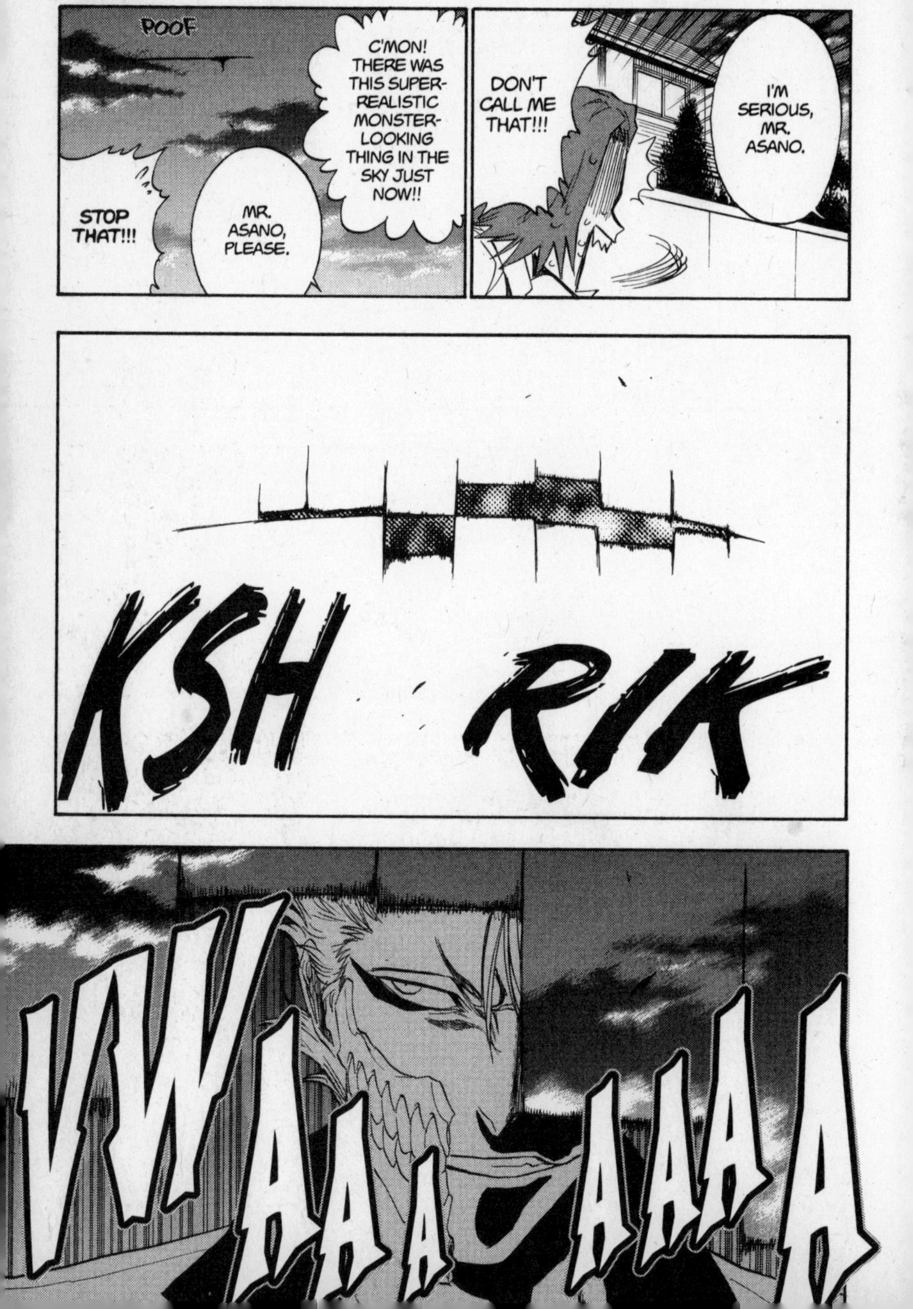
I'M SERIOUS, MR. ASANO.
DON'T CALL ME THAT!!!
C'MON! THERE WAS THIS SUPER-REALISTIC MONSTER-LOOKING THING IN THE SKY JUST NOW!!
POOF
MR. ASANO, PLEASE.
STOP THAT!!!
KSH RIK
VWAAAAAAA

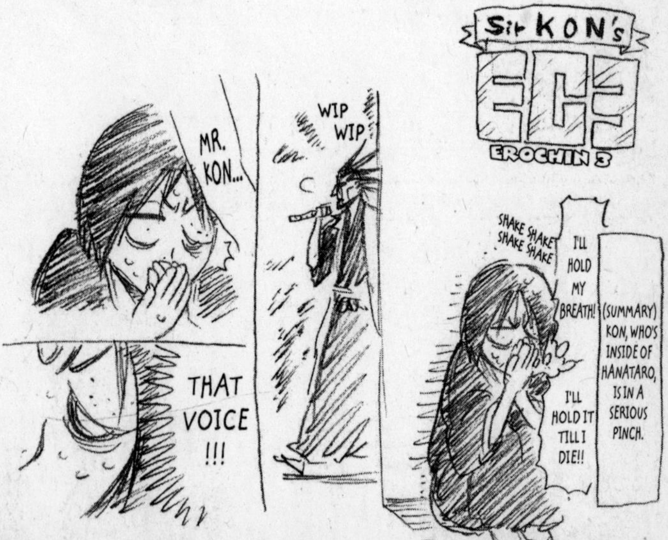
Sir KON's
EC3
EROCHIN 3
(SUMMARY) KON, WHO'S INSIDE OF HANATARO, IS IN A SERIOUS PINCH.
I'LL HOLD MY BREATH!
SHAKE SHAKE SHAKE SHAKE
I'LL HOLD IT TILL I DIE!!
WIP WIP
MR. KON...
THAT VOICE!!!

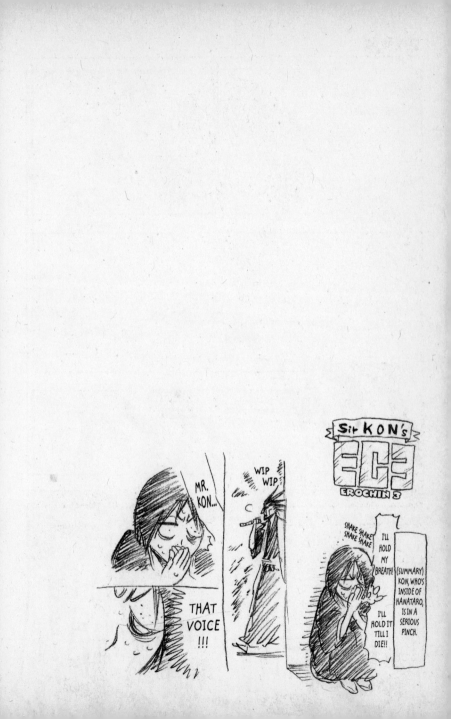

199. Ugly

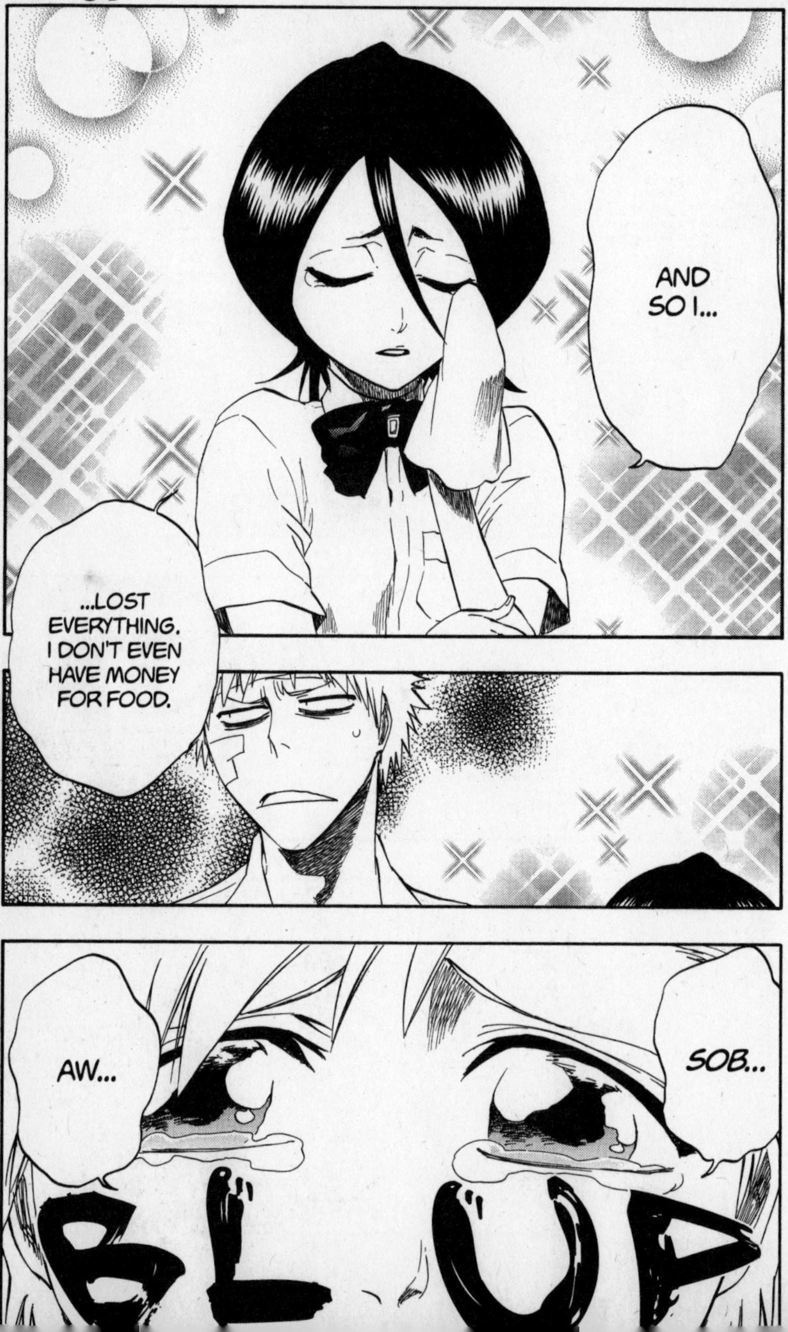

AND SO I...
...LOST EVERYTHING. I DON'T EVEN HAVE MONEY FOR FOOD.
SOB...
AW...
BLUA

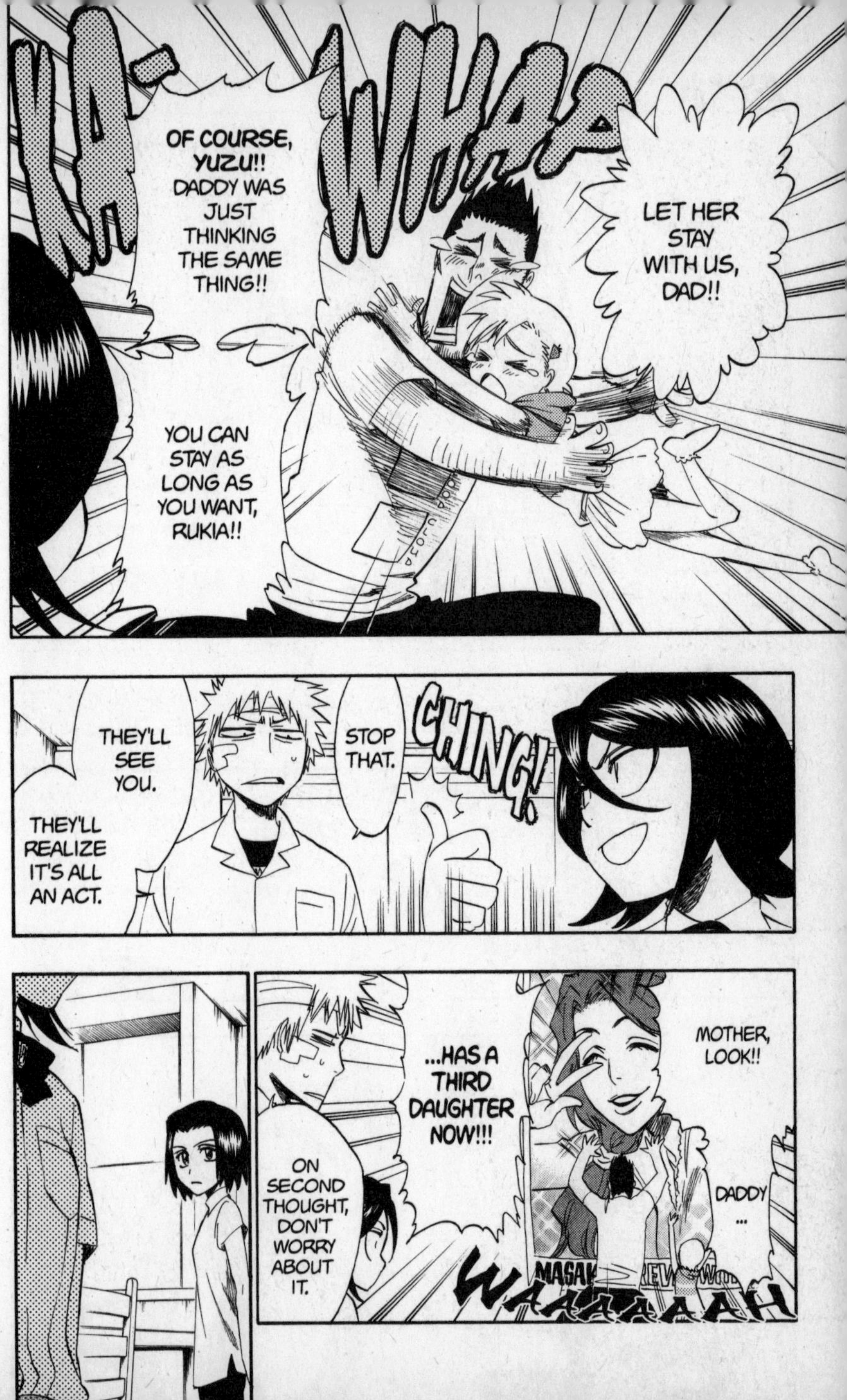

LET HER STAY WITH US, DAD!!
OF COURSE, YUZU!! DADDY WAS JUST THINKING THE SAME THING!!
YOU CAN STAY AS LONG AS YOU WANT, RUKIA!!
CHING!
STOP THAT.
THEY'LL SEE YOU.
THEY'LL REALIZE IT'S ALL AN ACT.
MOTHER, LOOK!!
DADDY ...
...HAS A THIRD DAUGHTER NOW!!!
WAAAAAAH
ON SECOND THOUGHT, DON'T WORRY ABOUT IT.

READ THIS WAY

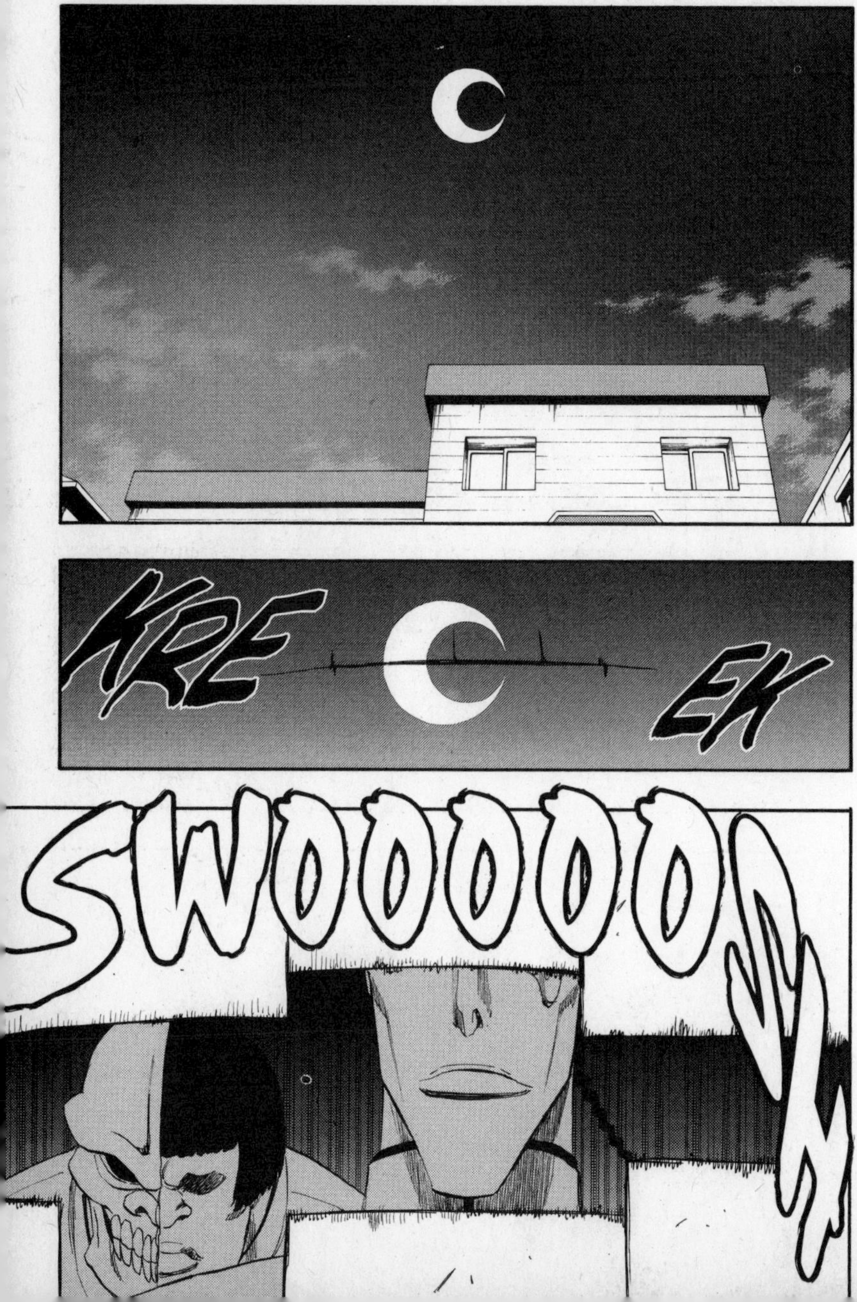
KRE
EK
SWOOOOOSH

BLEACH ーブリーチー 199. Ugly

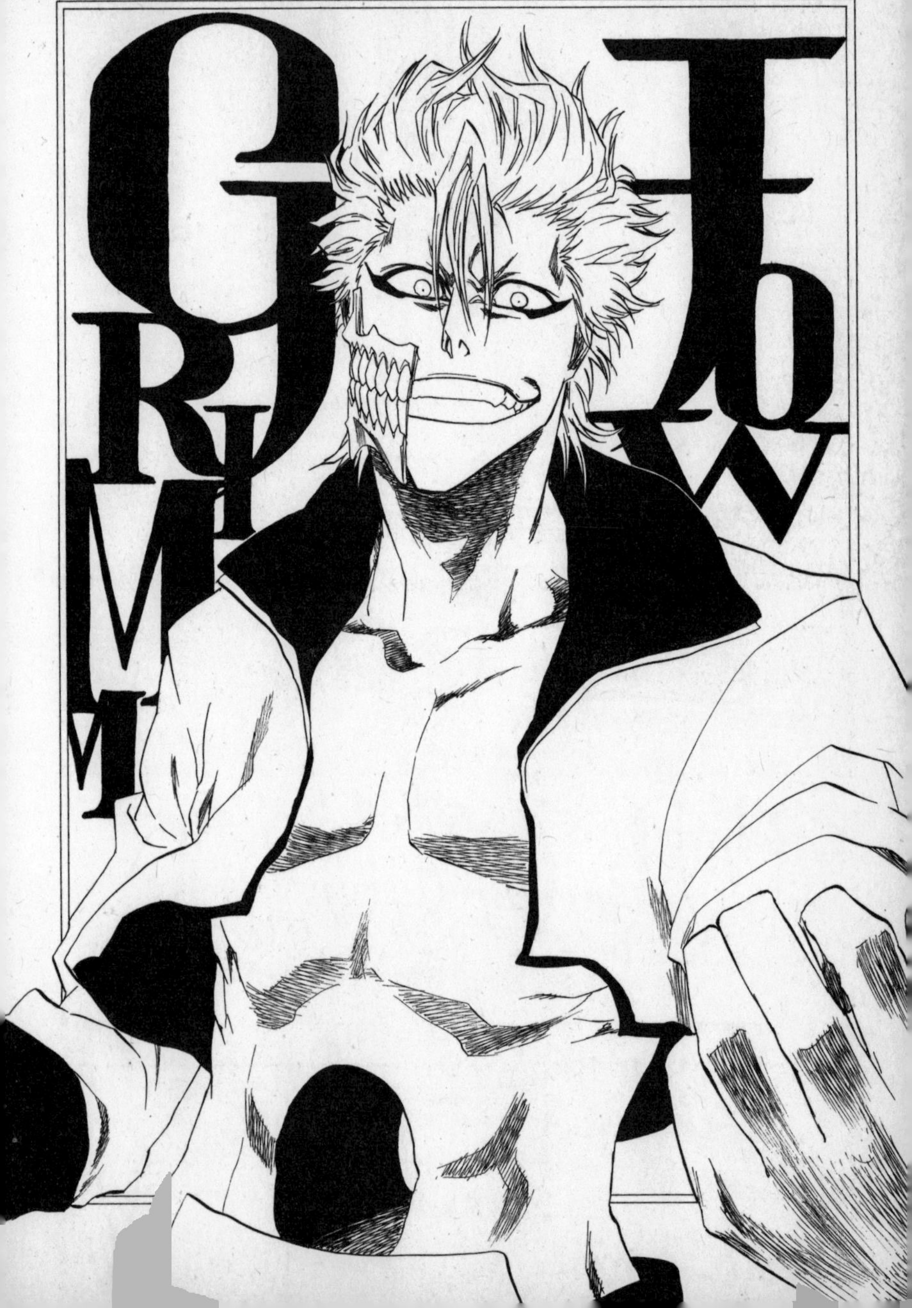
GRIMMJOW

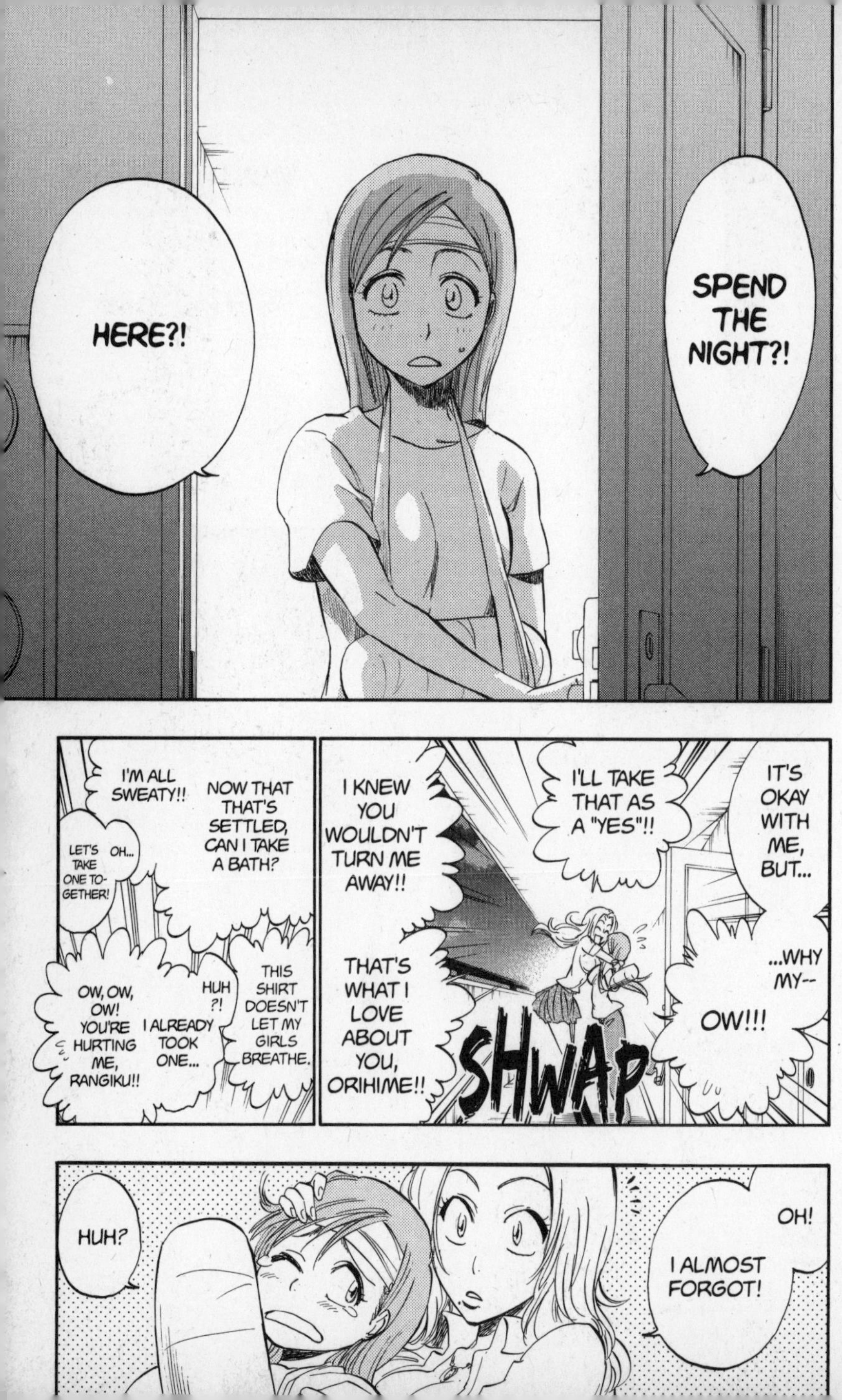
SPEND THE NIGHT?!
HERE?!
IT'S OKAY WITH ME, BUT...
I'LL TAKE THAT AS A "YES"!!
I KNEW YOU WOULDN'T TURN ME AWAY!!
...WHY MY--
OW!!!
SHWAP
THAT'S WHAT I LOVE ABOUT YOU, ORIHIME!!
NOW THAT THAT'S SETTLED, CAN I TAKE A BATH?
I'M ALL SWEATY!!
OH...
LET'S TAKE ONE TO-GETHER!
THIS SHIRT DOESN'T LET MY GIRLS BREATHE.
HUH ?!
I ALREADY TOOK ONE...
OW, OW, OW! YOU'RE HURTING ME, RANGIKU!!
OH!
I ALMOST FORGOT!
HUH?

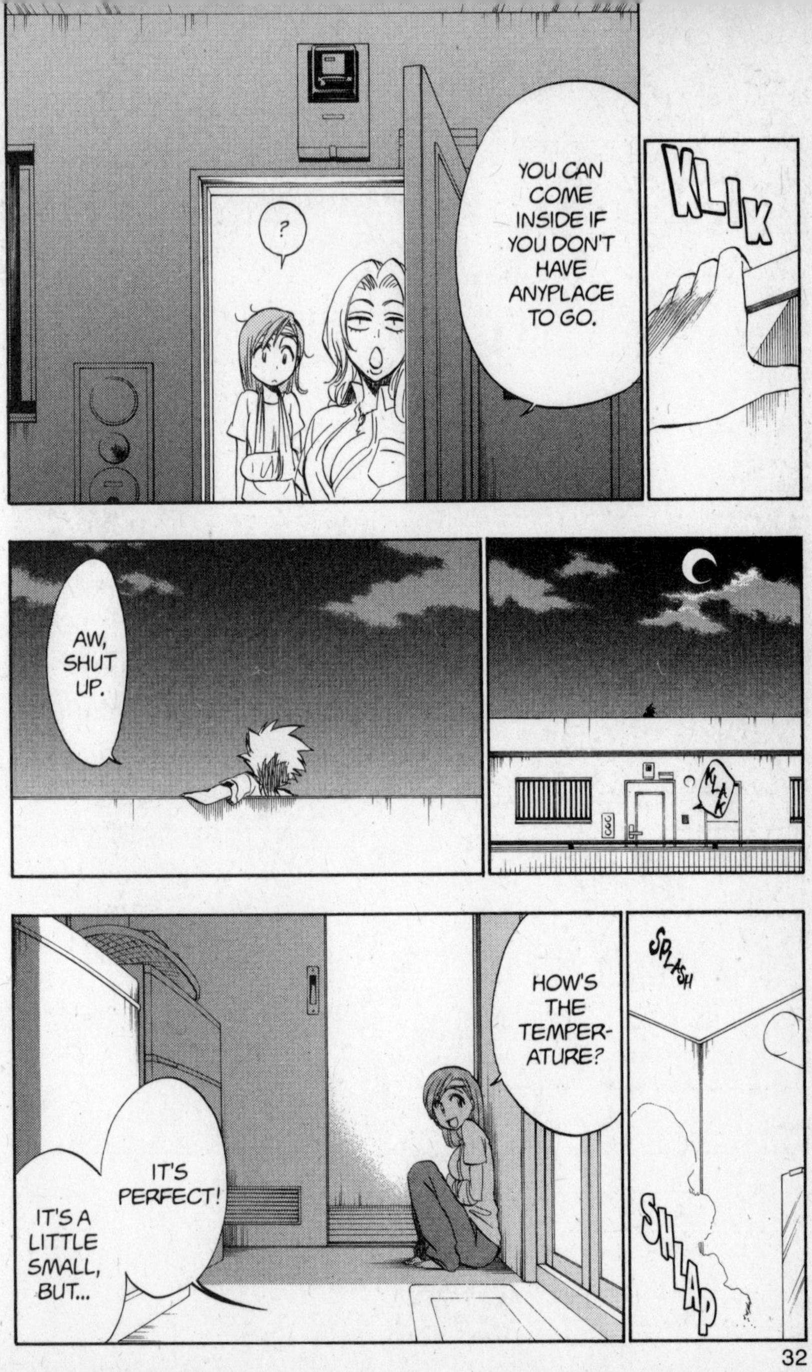
KLIK
YOU CAN COME INSIDE IF YOU DON'T HAVE ANYPLACE TO GO.
?
KLAK
AW, SHUT UP.
SPLASH
SHLAP
HOW'S THE TEMPER-ATURE?
IT'S PERFECT!
IT'S A LITTLE SMALL, BUT...

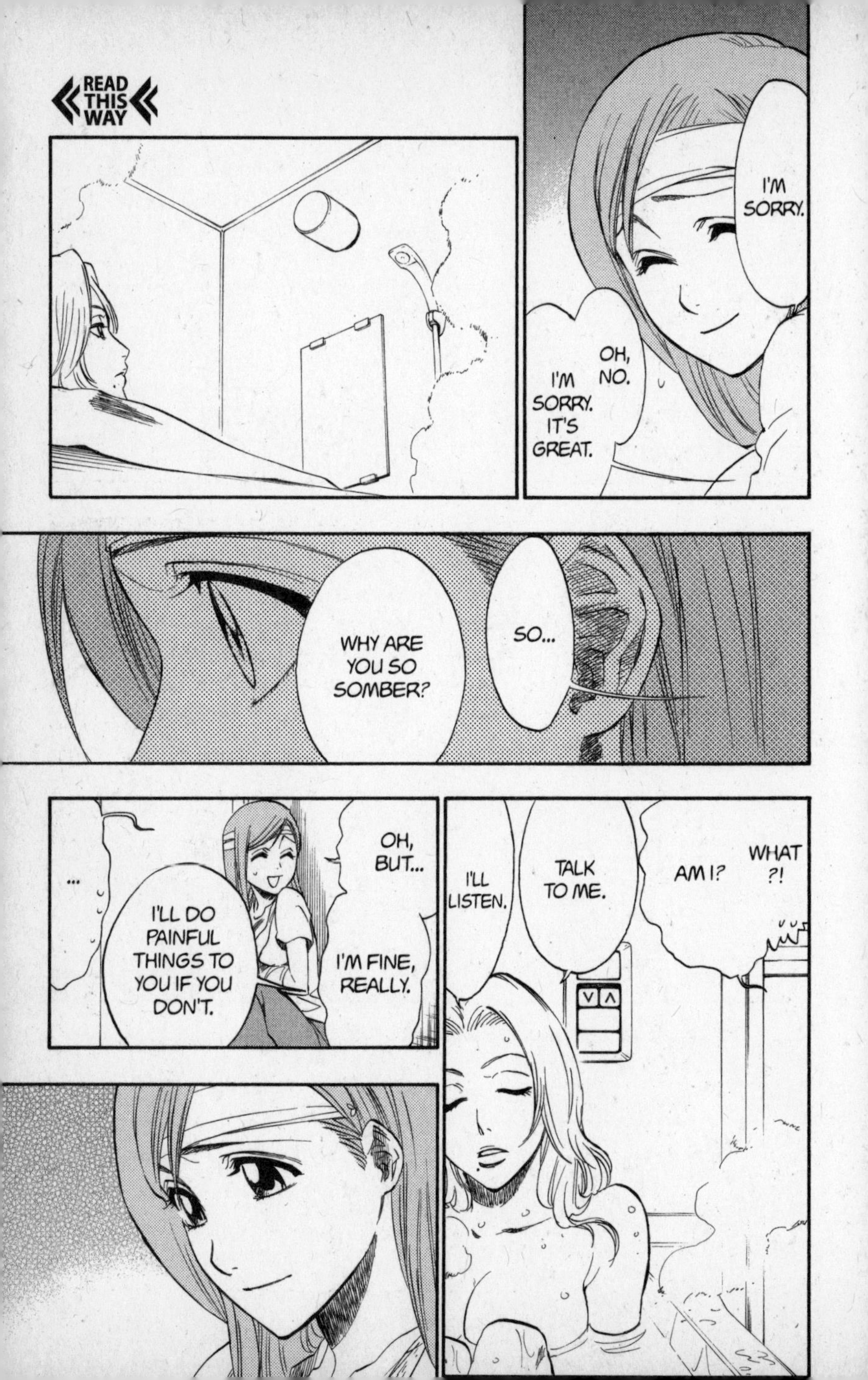
READ THIS WAY
I'M SORRY.
OH, NO.
I'M SORRY. IT'S GREAT.
SO...
WHY ARE YOU SO SOMBER?
WHAT?!
AM I?
TALK TO ME.
I'LL LISTEN.
OH, BUT...
I'M FINE, REALLY.
I'LL DO PAINFUL THINGS TO YOU IF YOU DON'T.
...

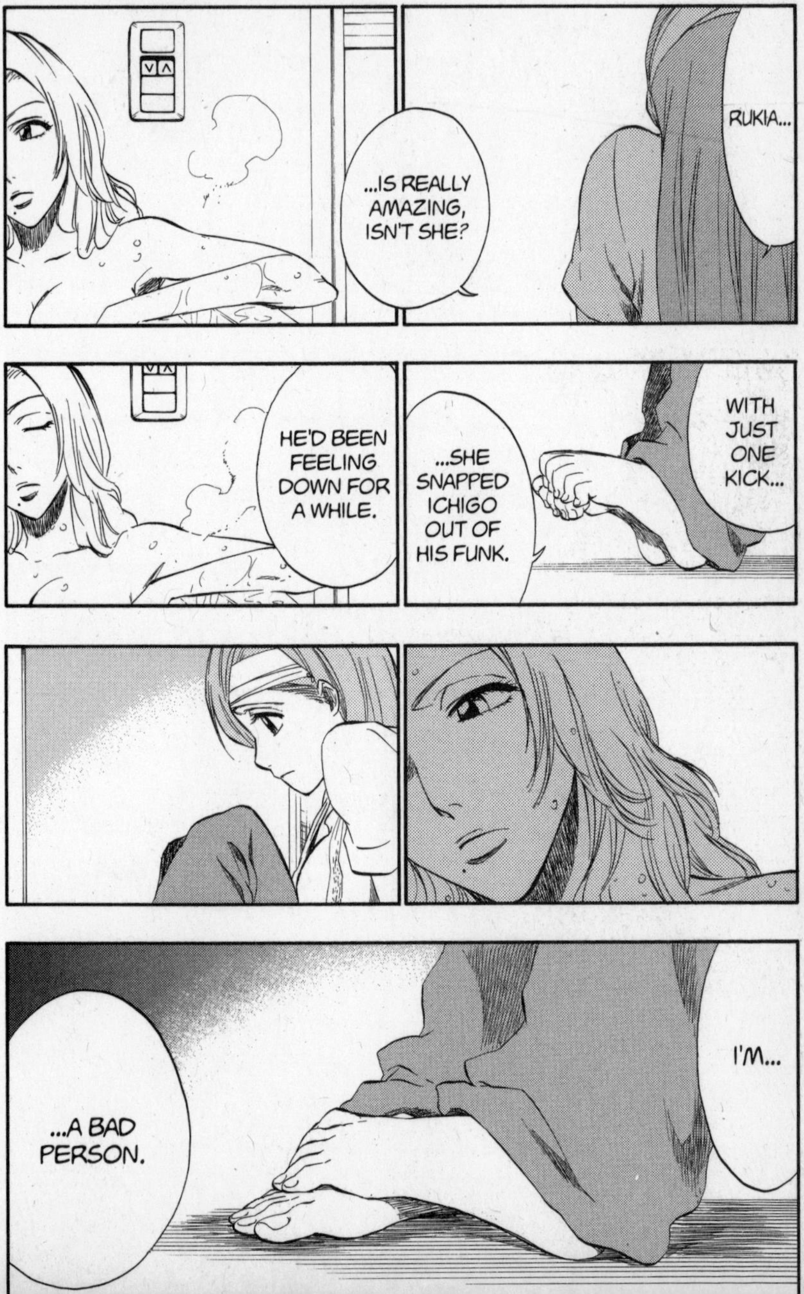
RUKIA...
...IS REALLY AMAZING, ISN'T SHE?
WITH JUST ONE KICK...
...SHE SNAPPED ICHIGO OUT OF HIS FUNK.
HE'D BEEN FEELING DOWN FOR A WHILE.
I'M...
...A BAD PERSON.

READ THIS WAY

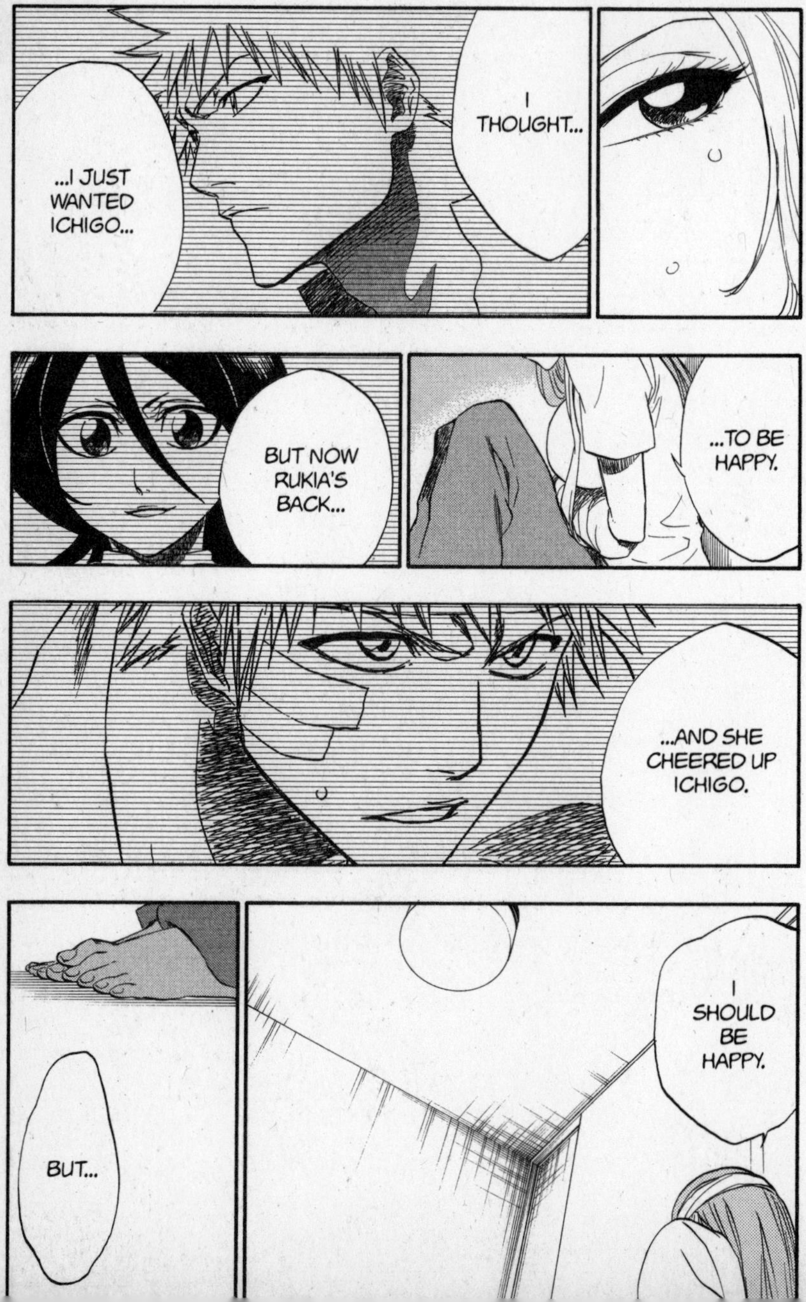
I THOUGHT...
...I JUST WANTED ICHIGO...
...TO BE HAPPY.
BUT NOW RUKIA'S BACK...
...AND SHE CHEERED UP ICHIGO.
I SHOULD BE HAPPY.
BUT...

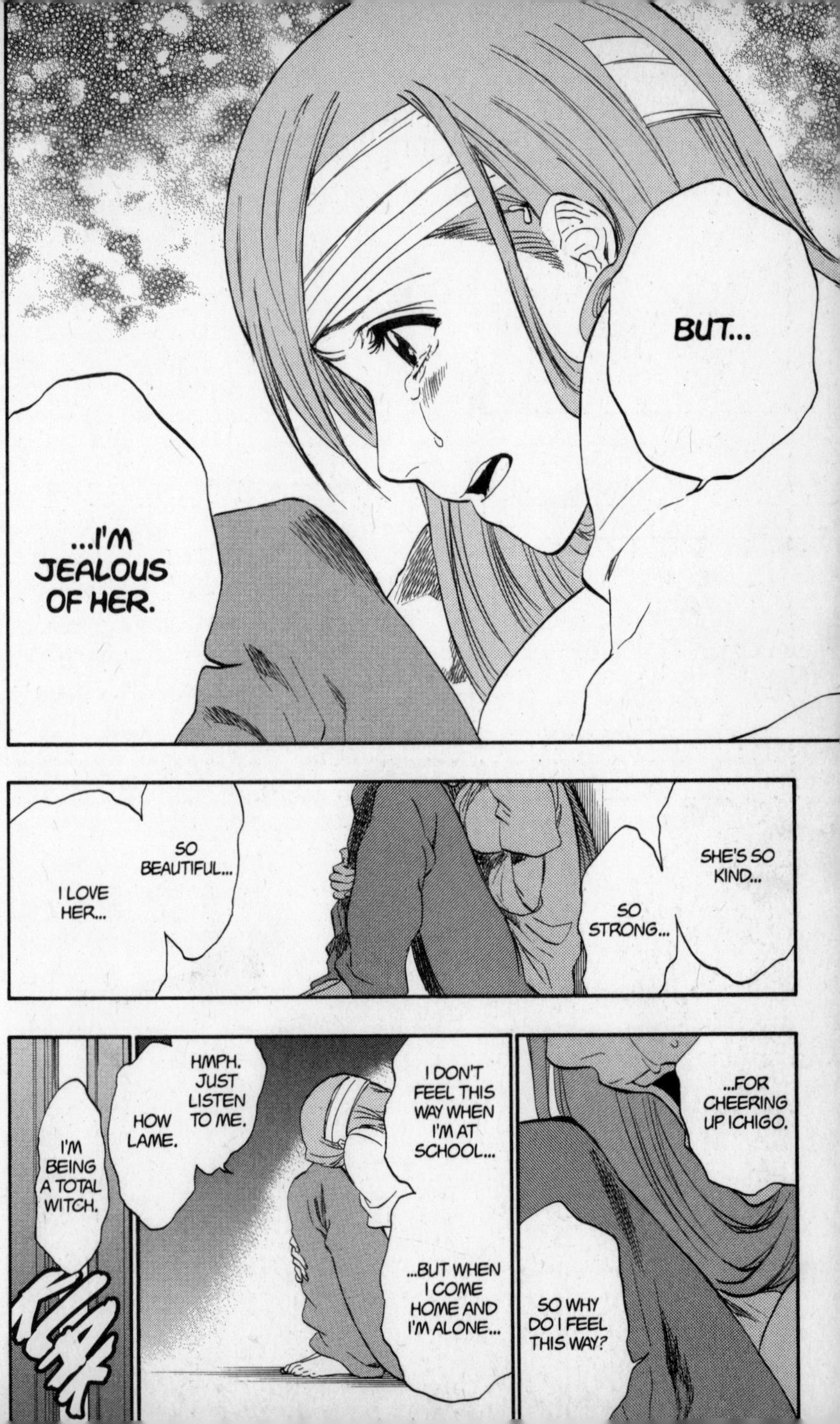
BUT...
...I'M JEALOUS OF HER.
SHE'S SO KIND...
SO STRONG...
SO BEAUTIFUL...
I LOVE HER...
...FOR CHEERING UP ICHIGO.
SO WHY DO I FEEL THIS WAY?
I DON'T FEEL THIS WAY WHEN I'M AT SCHOOL...
...BUT WHEN I COME HOME AND I'M ALONE...
HMPH. JUST LISTEN TO ME.
HOW LAME.
I'M BEING A TOTAL WITCH.
KLAK

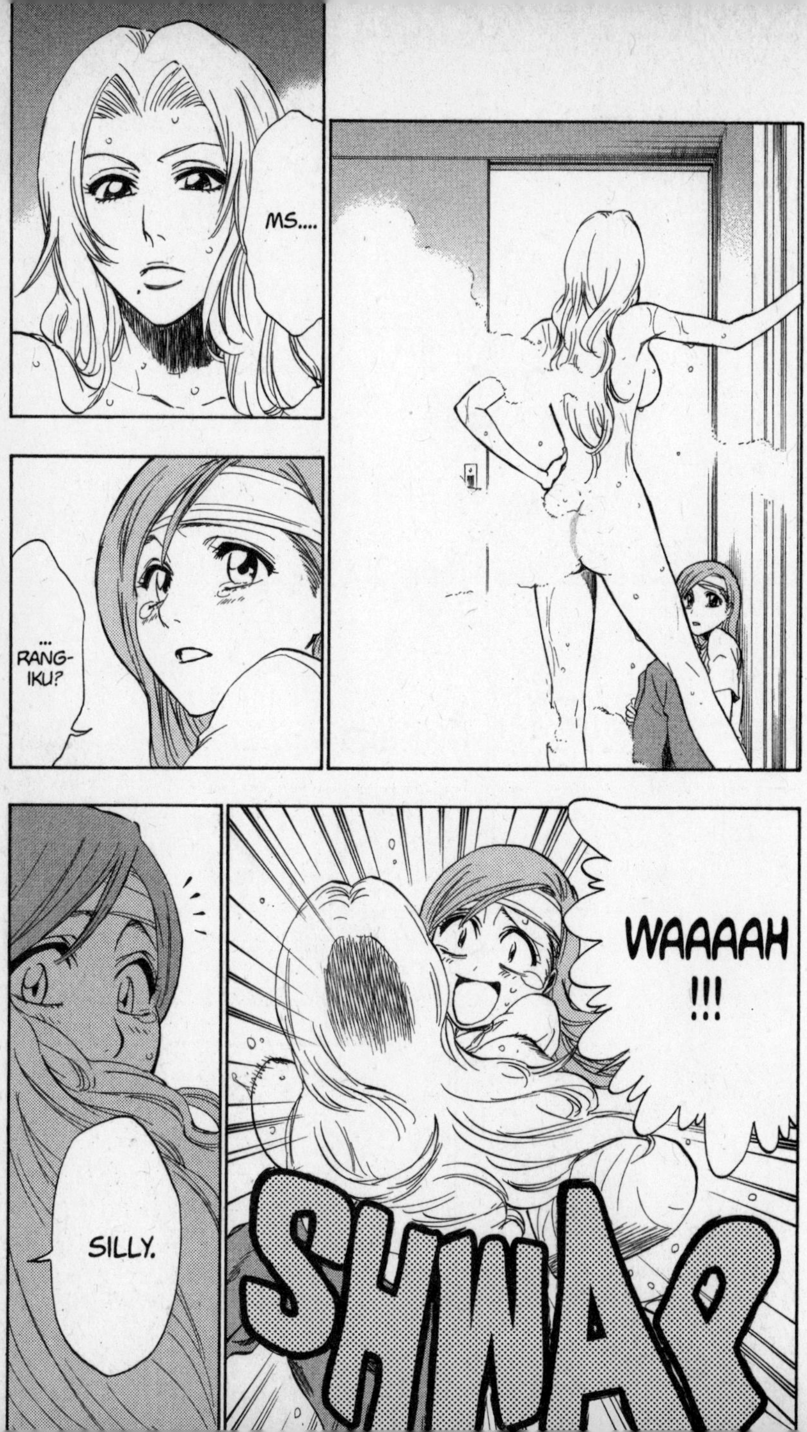
MS....
... RANG-IKU?
WAAAAH !!!
SHWAP
SILLY.

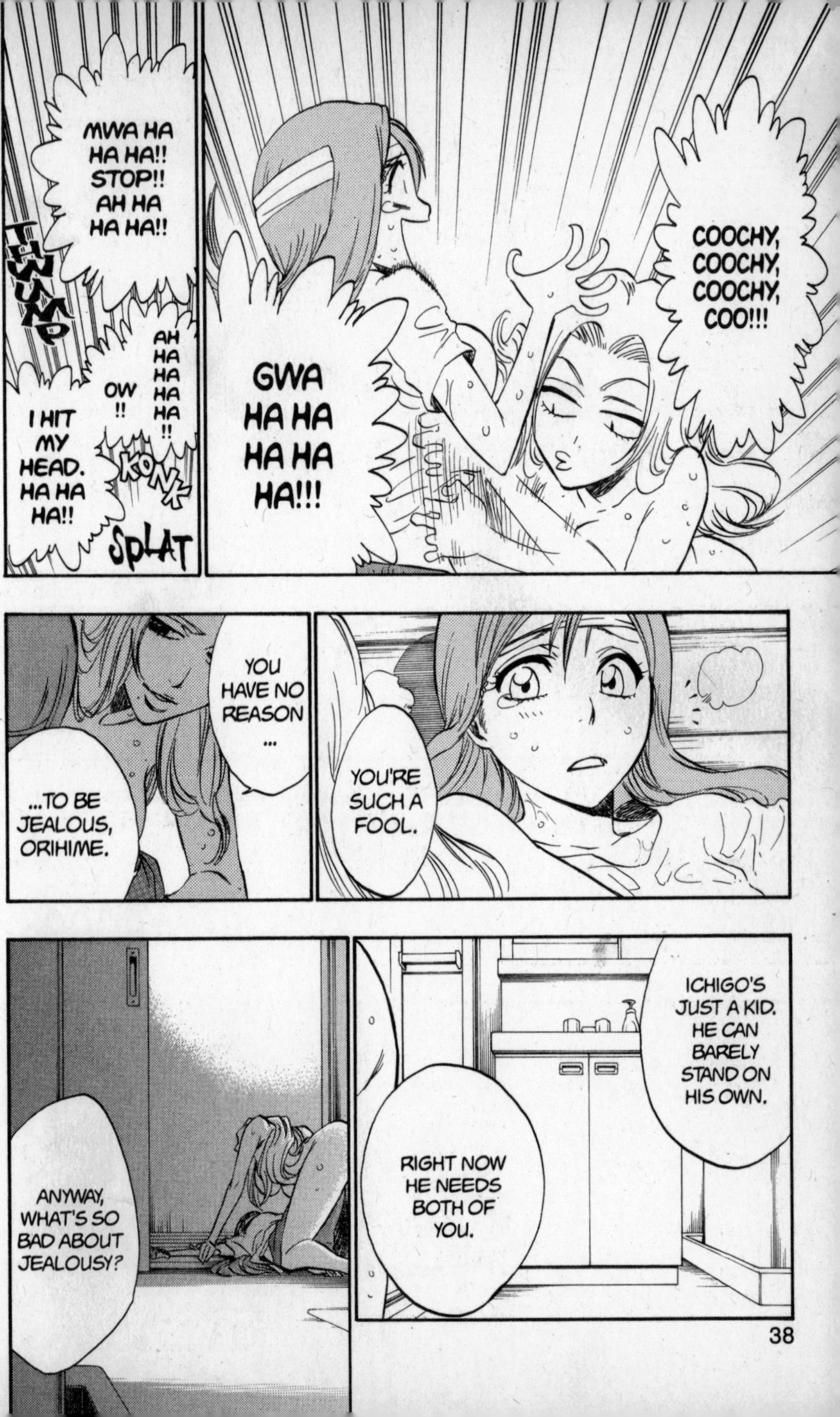
COOCHY, COOCHY, COOCHY, COO!!!
GWA HA HA HA HA HA!!!
MWA HA HA HA!! STOP!! AH HA HA HA!!
THWUMP
AH HA HA HA HA!!
OW!!
KONK
I HIT MY HEAD. HA HA HA!!
SPLAT
YOU'RE SUCH A FOOL.
YOU HAVE NO REASON...
...TO BE JEALOUS, ORIHIME.
ICHIGO'S JUST A KID. HE CAN BARELY STAND ON HIS OWN.
RIGHT NOW HE NEEDS BOTH OF YOU.
ANYWAY, WHAT'S SO BAD ABOUT JEALOUSY?

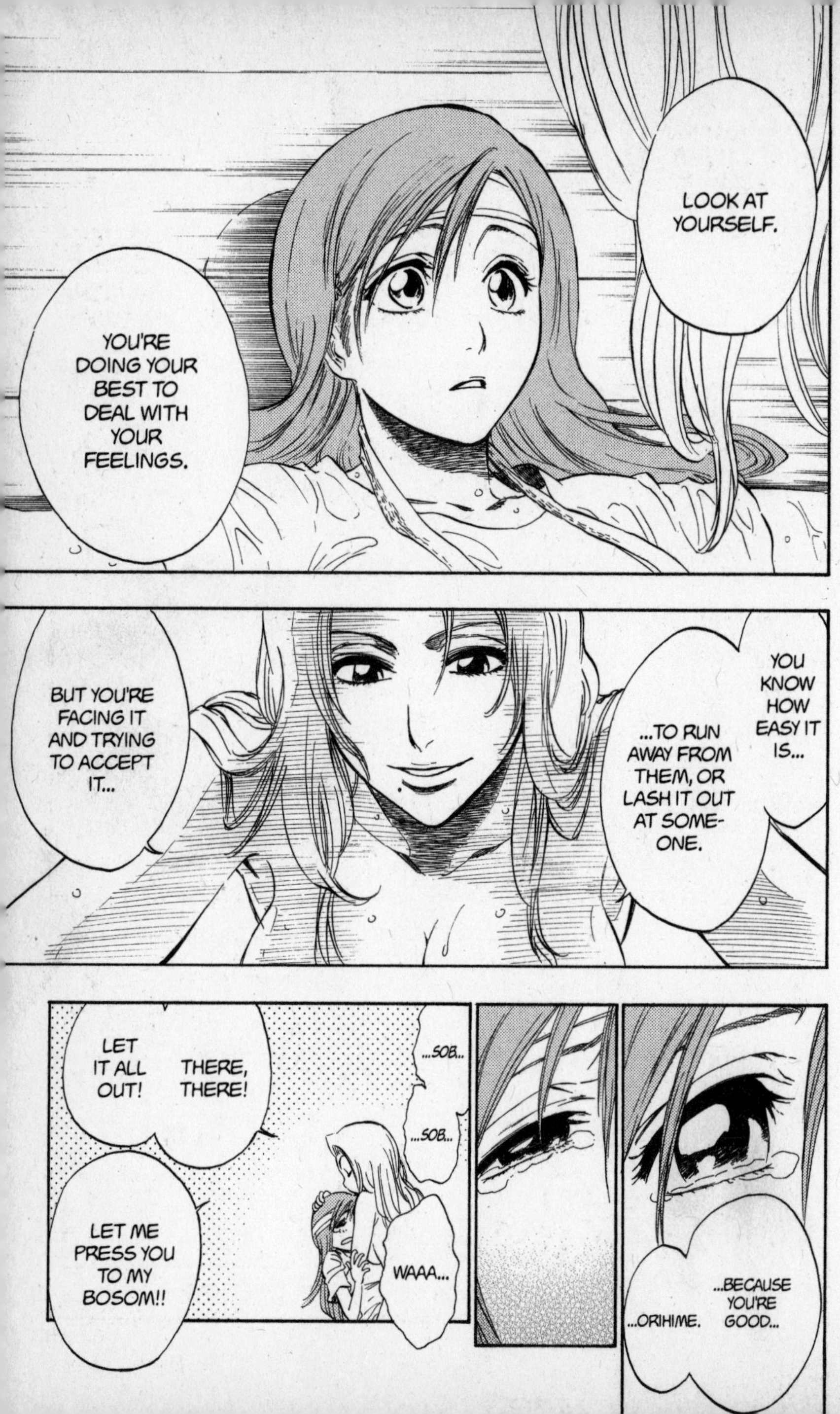
LOOK AT YOURSELF.
YOU'RE DOING YOUR BEST TO DEAL WITH YOUR FEELINGS.
YOU KNOW HOW EASY IT IS...
...TO RUN AWAY FROM THEM, OR LASH IT OUT AT SOME-ONE.
BUT YOU'RE FACING IT AND TRYING TO ACCEPT IT...
...BECAUSE YOU'RE GOOD...
...ORIHIME.
...SOB...
...SOB...
WAAA...
THERE, THERE!
LET IT ALL OUT!
LET ME PRESS YOU TO MY BOSOM!!

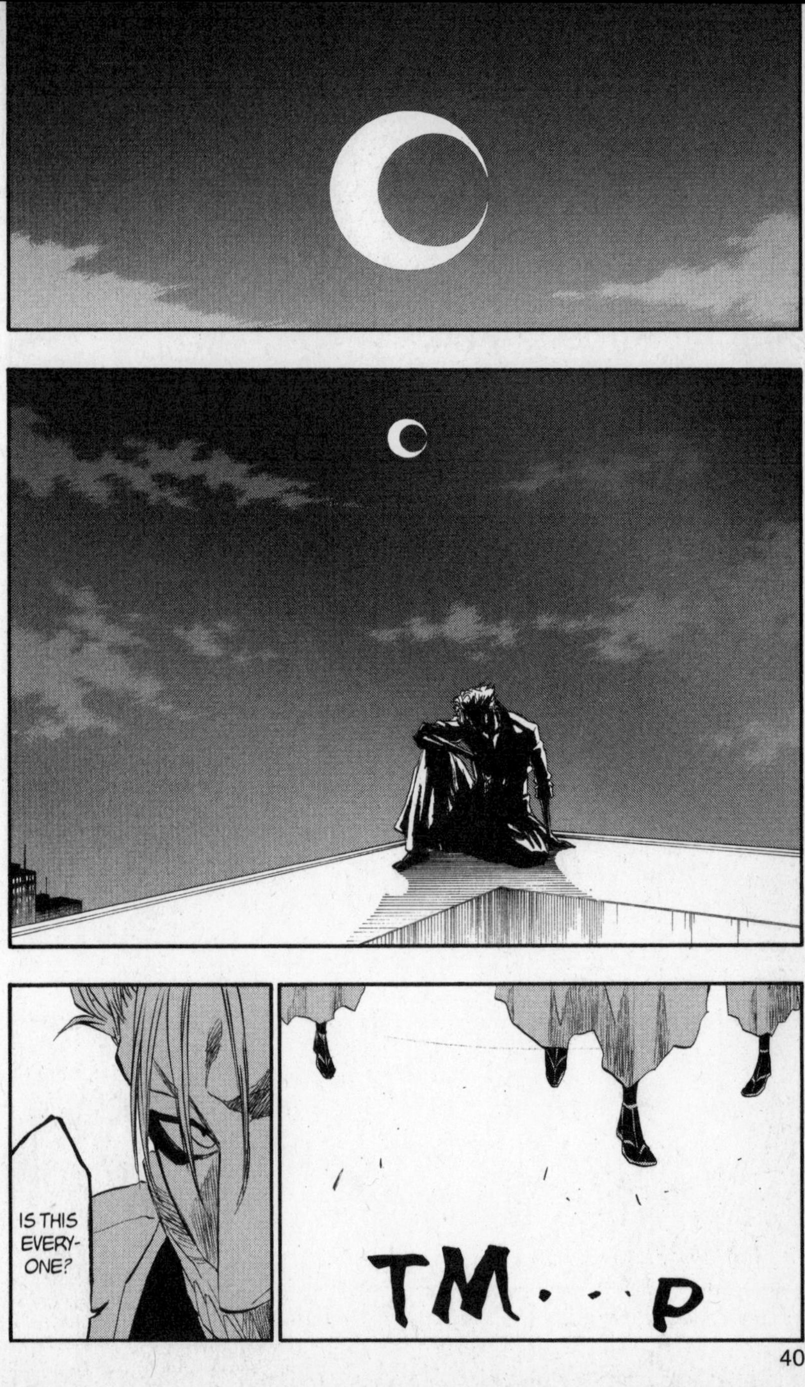
TM··P
IS THIS EVERY-ONE?

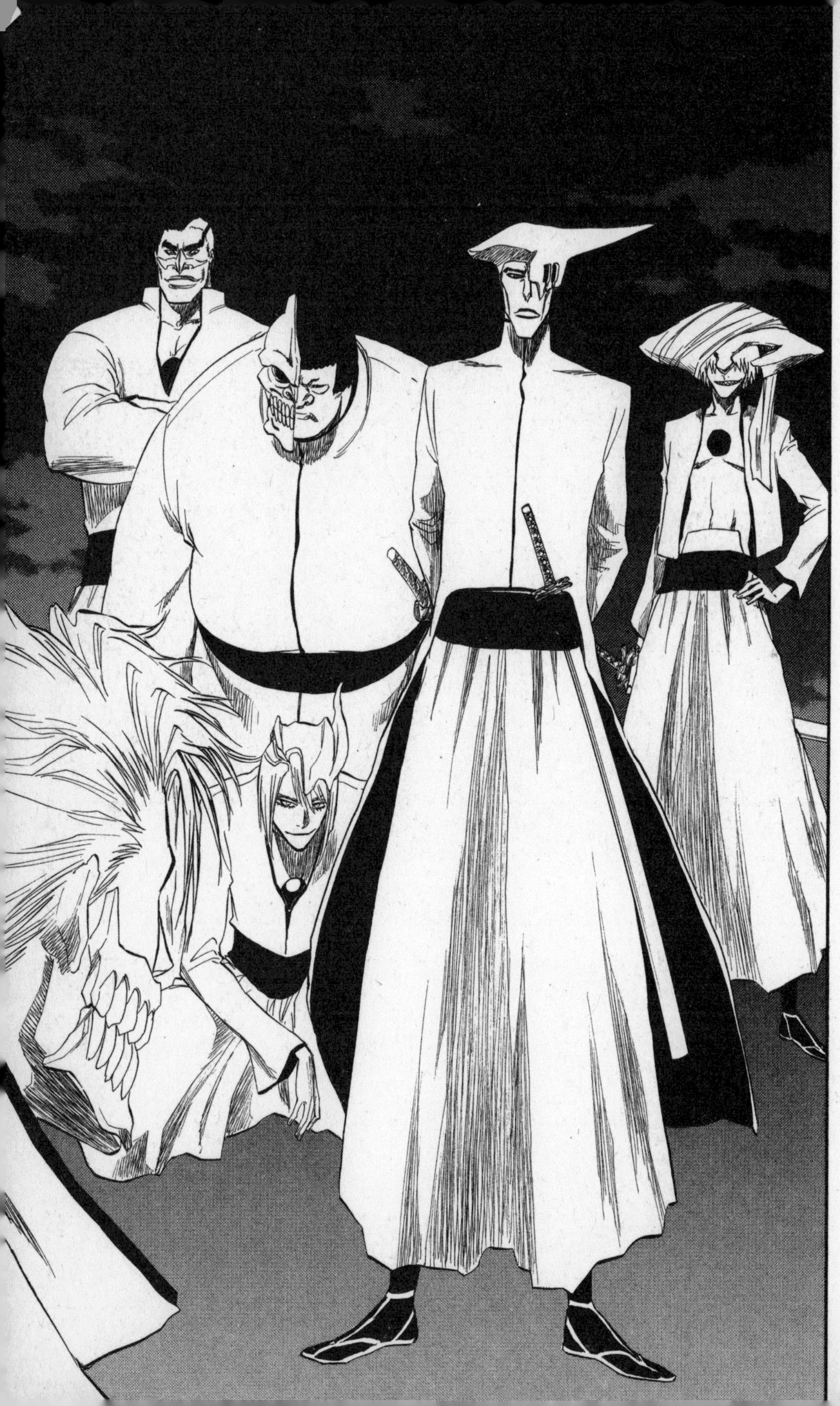

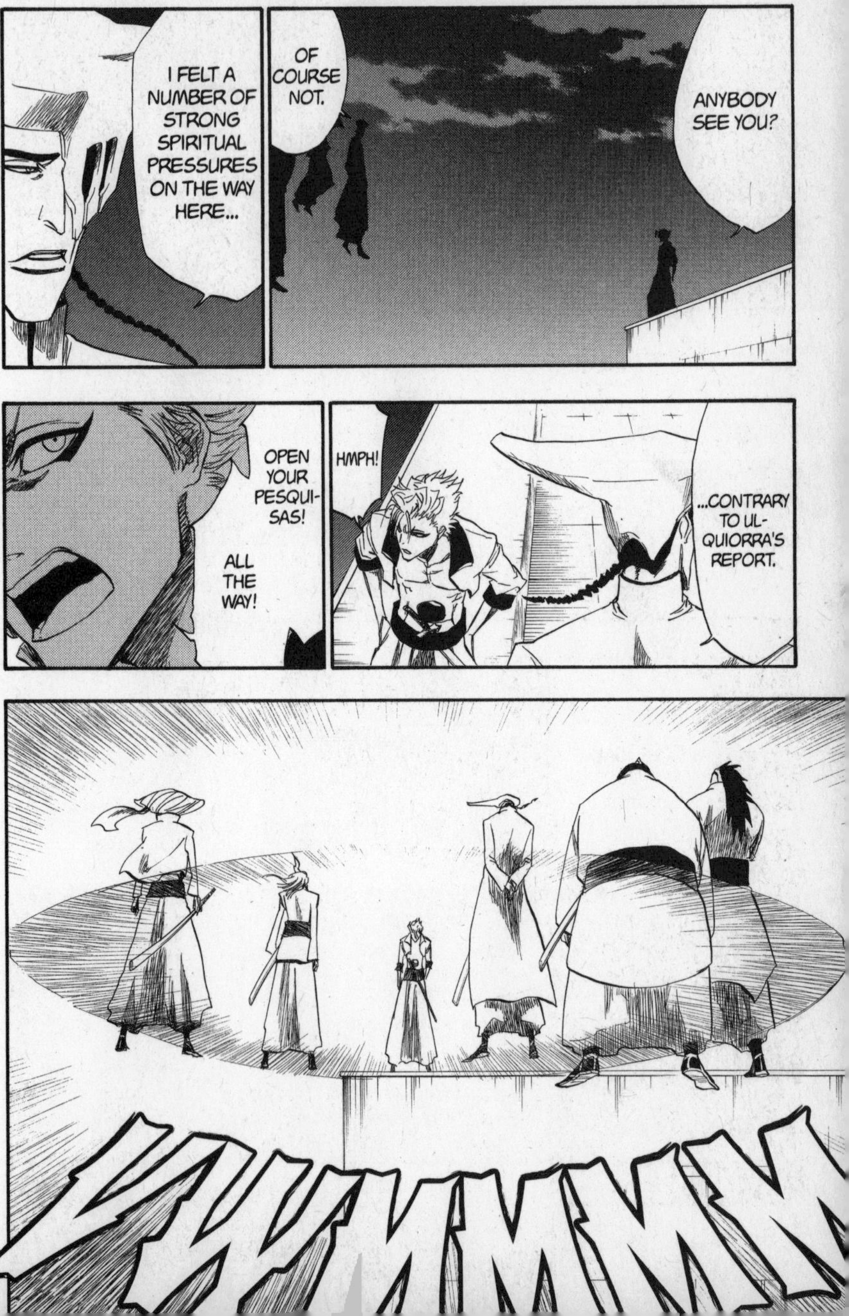
ANYBODY SEE YOU?
OF COURSE NOT.
I FELT A NUMBER OF STRONG SPIRITUAL PRESSURES ON THE WAY HERE...
...CONTRARY TO UL-QUIORRA'S REPORT.
HMPH!
OPEN YOUR PESQUI-SAS!
ALL THE WAY!

READ THIS WAY

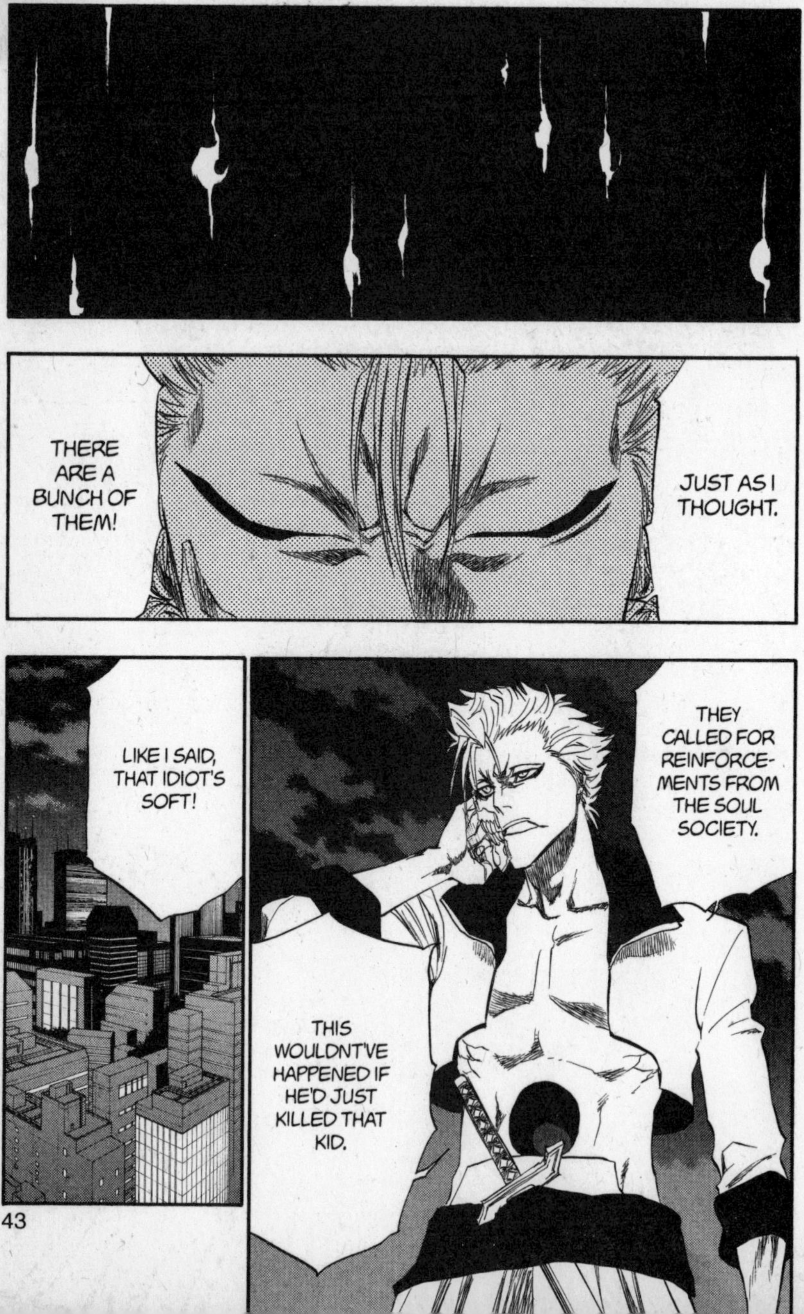
JUST AS I THOUGHT.
THERE ARE A BUNCH OF THEM!
THEY CALLED FOR REINFORCEMENTS FROM THE SOUL SOCIETY.
THIS WOULDNT'VE HAPPENED IF HE'D JUST KILLED THAT KID.
LIKE I SAID, THAT IDIOT'S SOFT!

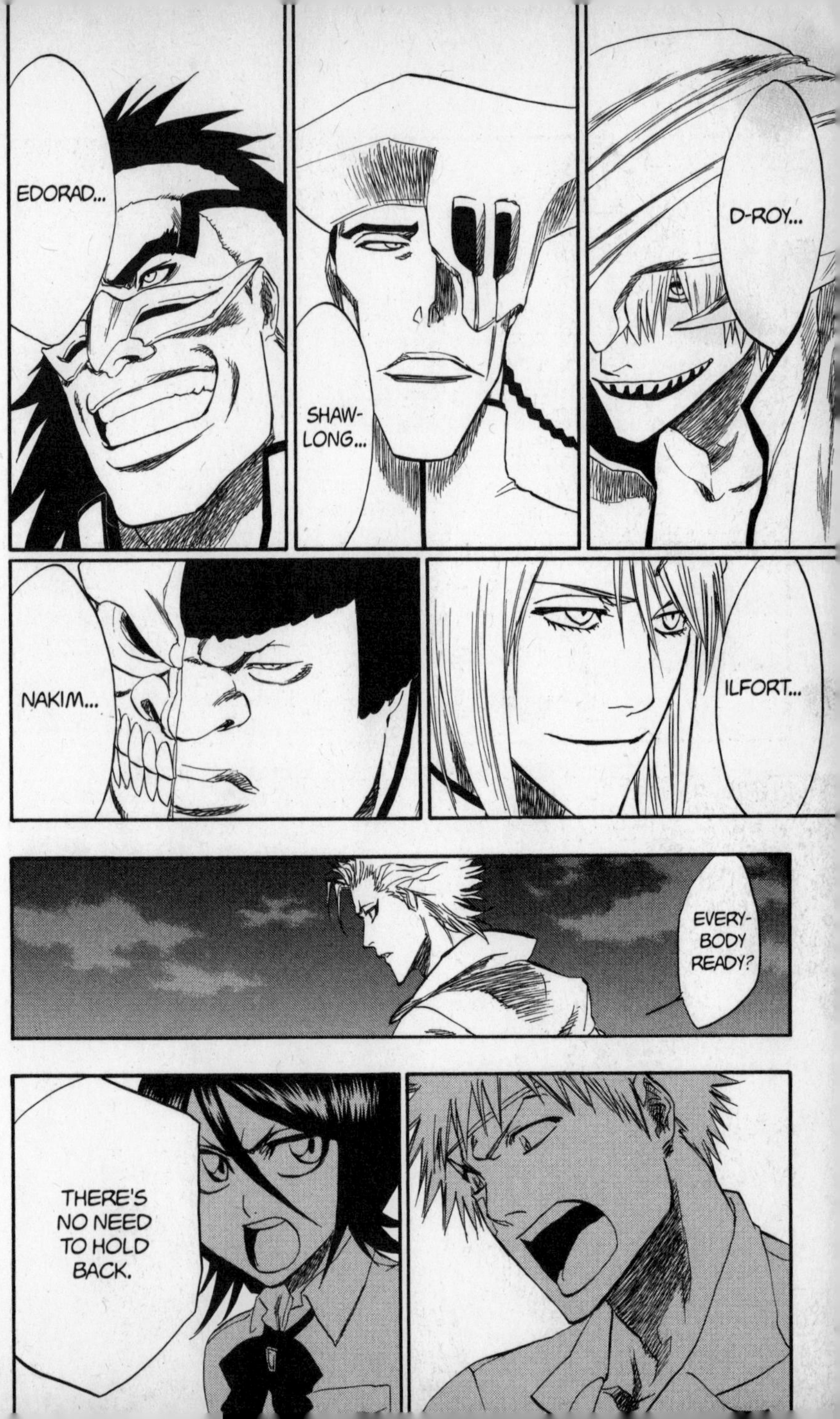
D-ROY...
SHAW-LONG...
EDORAD...
ILFORT...
NAKIM...
EVERY-BODY READY?
THERE'S NO NEED TO HOLD BACK.

READ THIS WAY

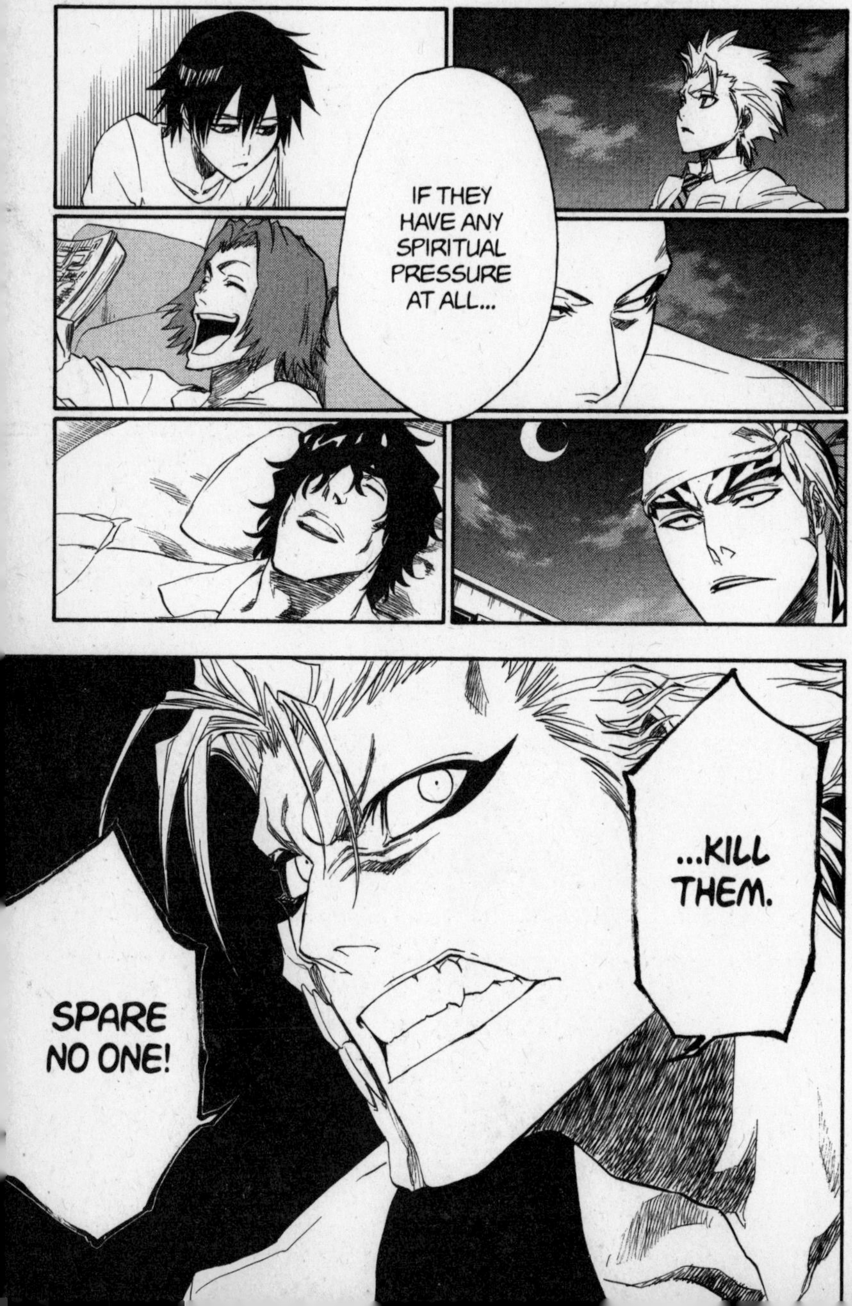
IF THEY HAVE ANY SPIRITUAL PRESSURE AT ALL...
...KILL THEM.
SPARE NO ONE!

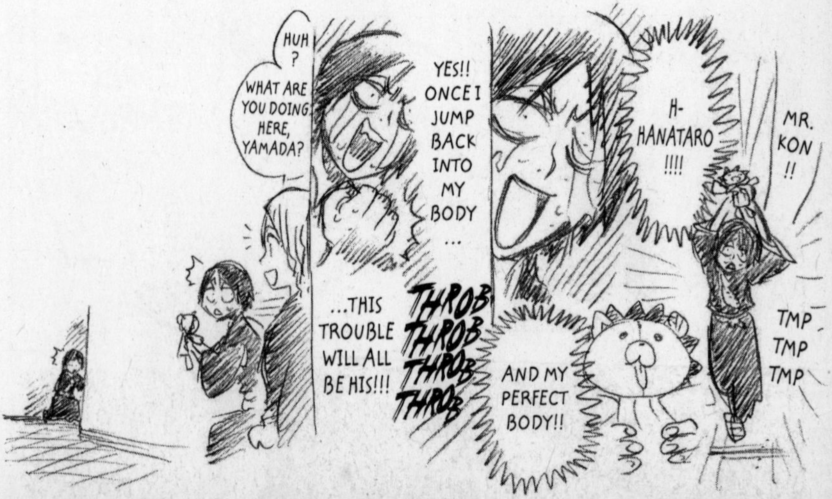
MR. KON !!
TMP TMP TMP
H-HANATARO !!!!
AND MY PERFECT BODY!!
YES!! ONCE I JUMP BACK INTO MY BODY ...
...THIS TROUBLE WILL ALL BE HIS!!!
THROB THROB THROB THROB
HUH ? WHAT ARE YOU DOING HERE, YAMADA?

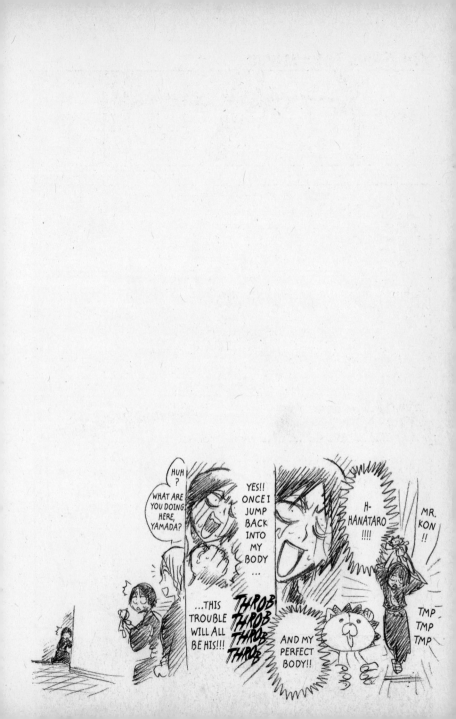

200. Night of Sledgehammer

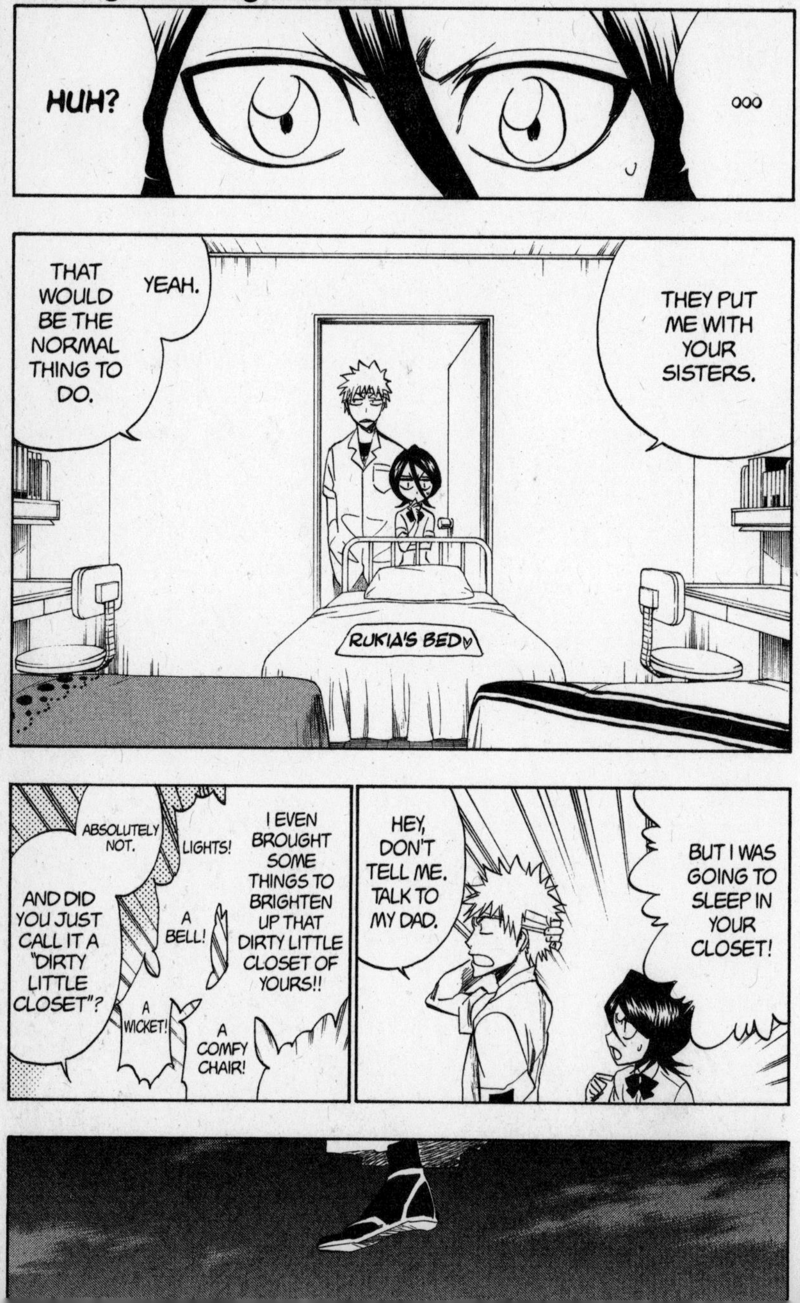

ooo
HUH?
THEY PUT ME WITH YOUR SISTERS.
YEAH.
THAT WOULD BE THE NORMAL THING TO DO.
RUKIA'S BED♡
BUT I WAS GOING TO SLEEP IN YOUR CLOSET!
HEY, DON'T TELL ME. TALK TO MY DAD.
I EVEN BROUGHT SOME THINGS TO BRIGHTEN UP THAT DIRTY LITTLE CLOSET OF YOURS!!
LIGHTS!
A BELL!
A WICKET!
A COMFY CHAIR!
ABSOLUTELY NOT.
AND DID YOU JUST CALL IT A "DIRTY LITTLE CLOSET"?

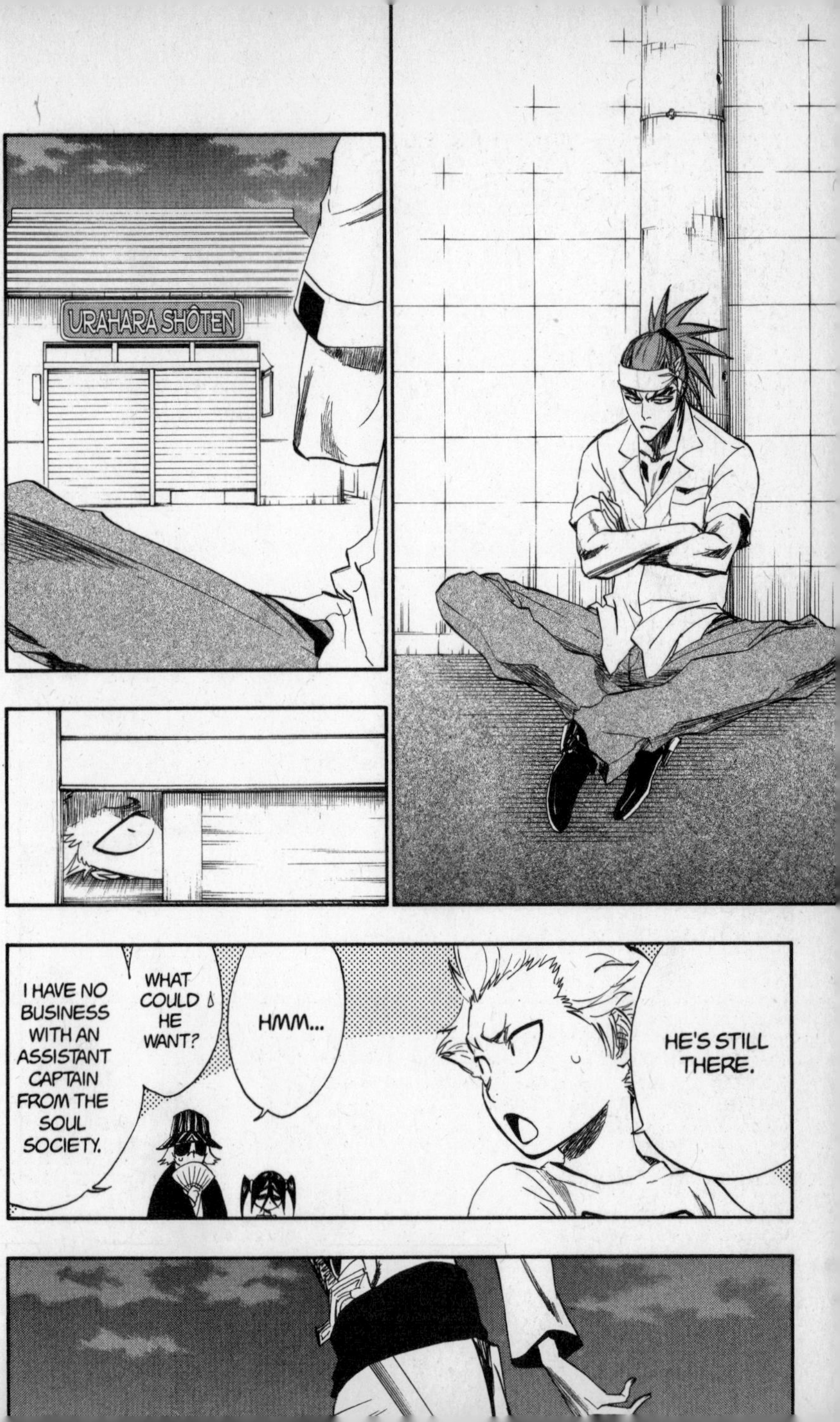
URAHARA SHÔTEN
HE'S STILL THERE.
HMM...
WHAT COULD HE WANT?
I HAVE NO BUSINESS WITH AN ASSISTANT CAPTAIN FROM THE SOUL SOCIETY.

READ THIS WAY

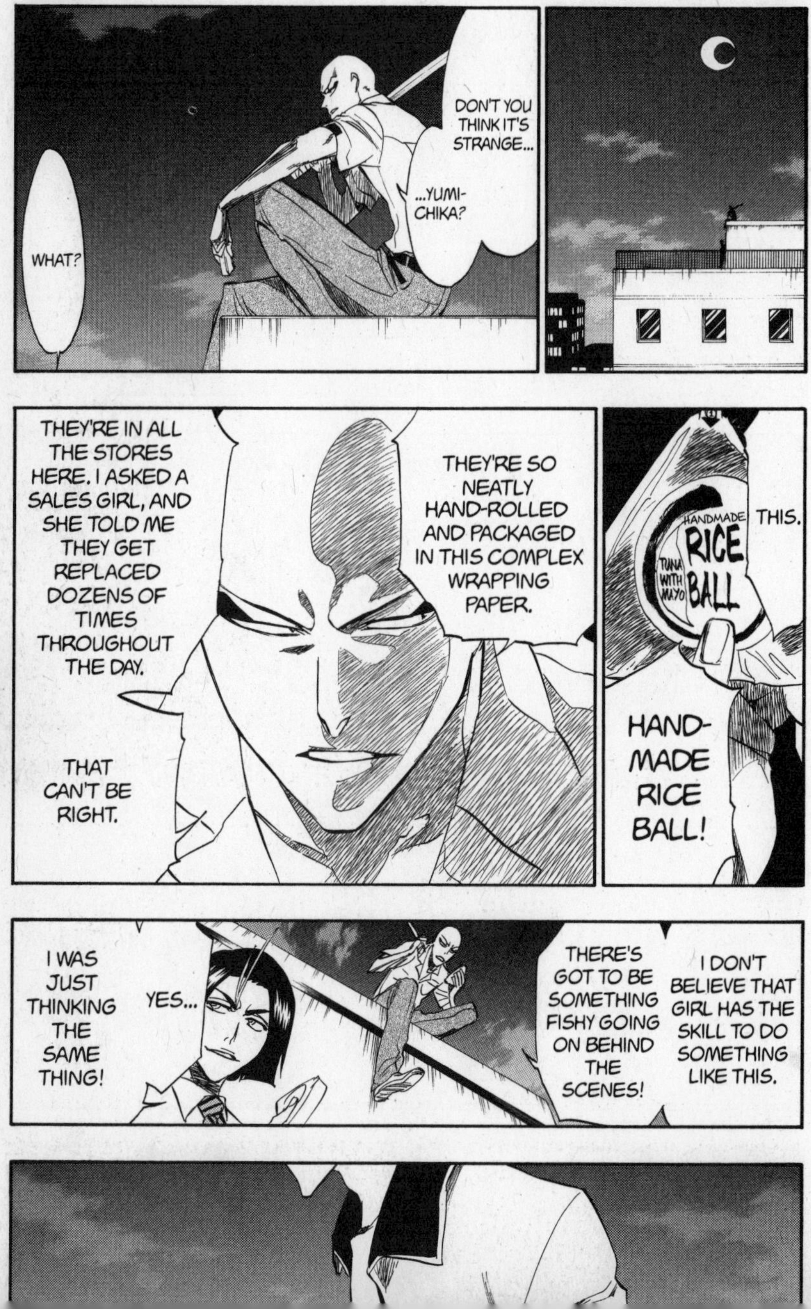
DON'T YOU THINK IT'S STRANGE...
...YUMI-CHIKA?
WHAT?
THIS.
HANDMADE RICE BALL TUNA WITH MAYO
HAND-MADE RICE BALL!
THEY'RE SO NEATLY HAND-ROLLED AND PACKAGED IN THIS COMPLEX WRAPPING PAPER.
THEY'RE IN ALL THE STORES HERE. I ASKED A SALES GIRL, AND SHE TOLD ME THEY GET REPLACED DOZENS OF TIMES THROUGHOUT THE DAY.
THAT CAN'T BE RIGHT.
I DON'T BELIEVE THAT GIRL HAS THE SKILL TO DO SOMETHING LIKE THIS.
THERE'S GOT TO BE SOMETHING FISHY GOING ON BEHIND THE SCENES!
YES...
I WAS JUST THINKING THE SAME THING!

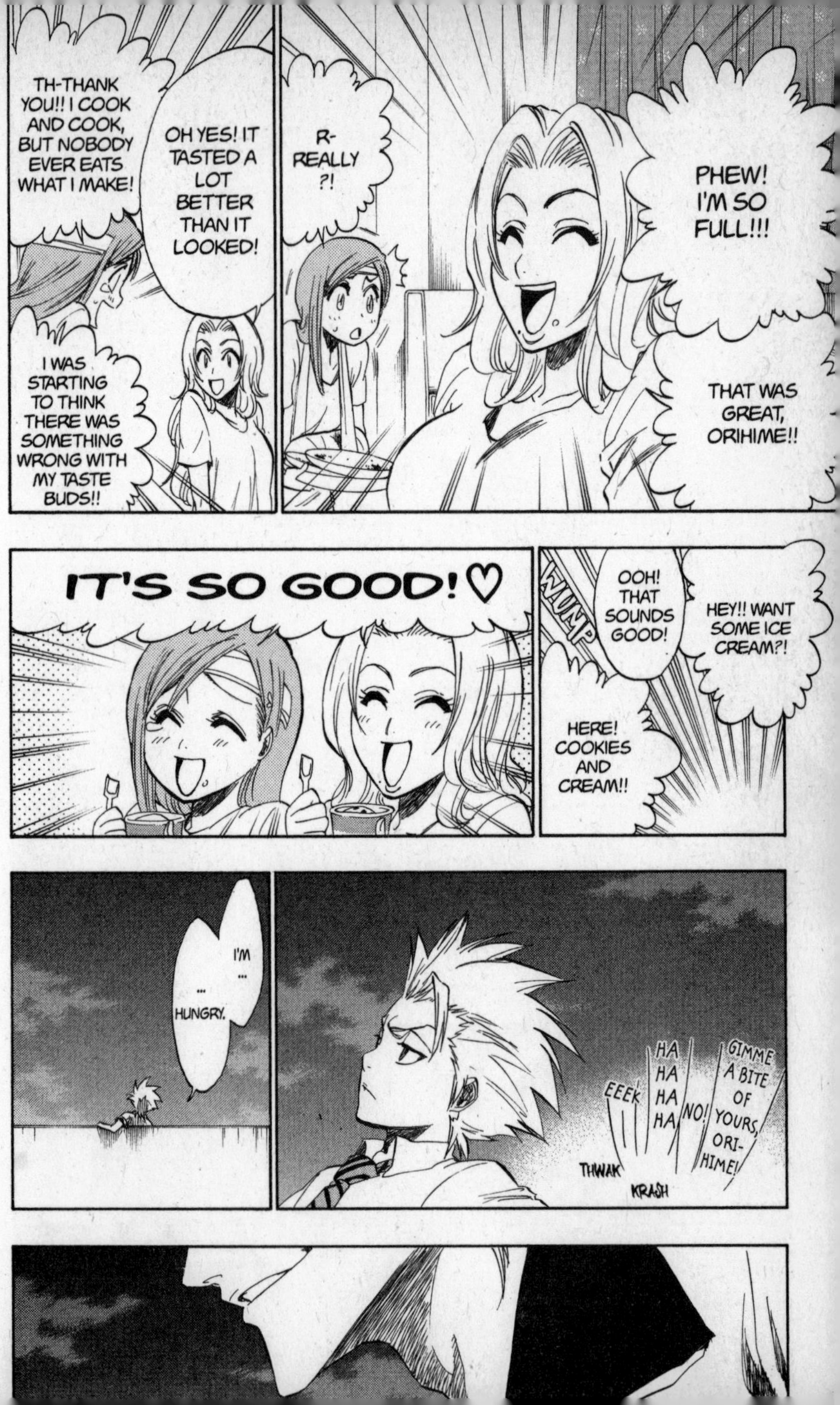
PHEW! I'M SO FULL!!!
THAT WAS GREAT, ORIHIME!!
R- REALLY ?!
OH YES! IT TASTED A LOT BETTER THAN IT LOOKED!
TH-THANK YOU!! I COOK AND COOK, BUT NOBODY EVER EATS WHAT I MAKE!
I WAS STARTING TO THINK THERE WAS SOMETHING WRONG WITH MY TASTE BUDS!!
HEY!! WANT SOME ICE CREAM?!
OOH! THAT SOUNDS GOOD!
WUMP
HERE! COOKIES AND CREAM!!
IT'S SO GOOD!♡
GIMME A BITE OF YOURS, ORIHIME!
NO!
HA HA HA HA
EEEK
THWAK
KRASH
I'M ...
... HUNGRY.

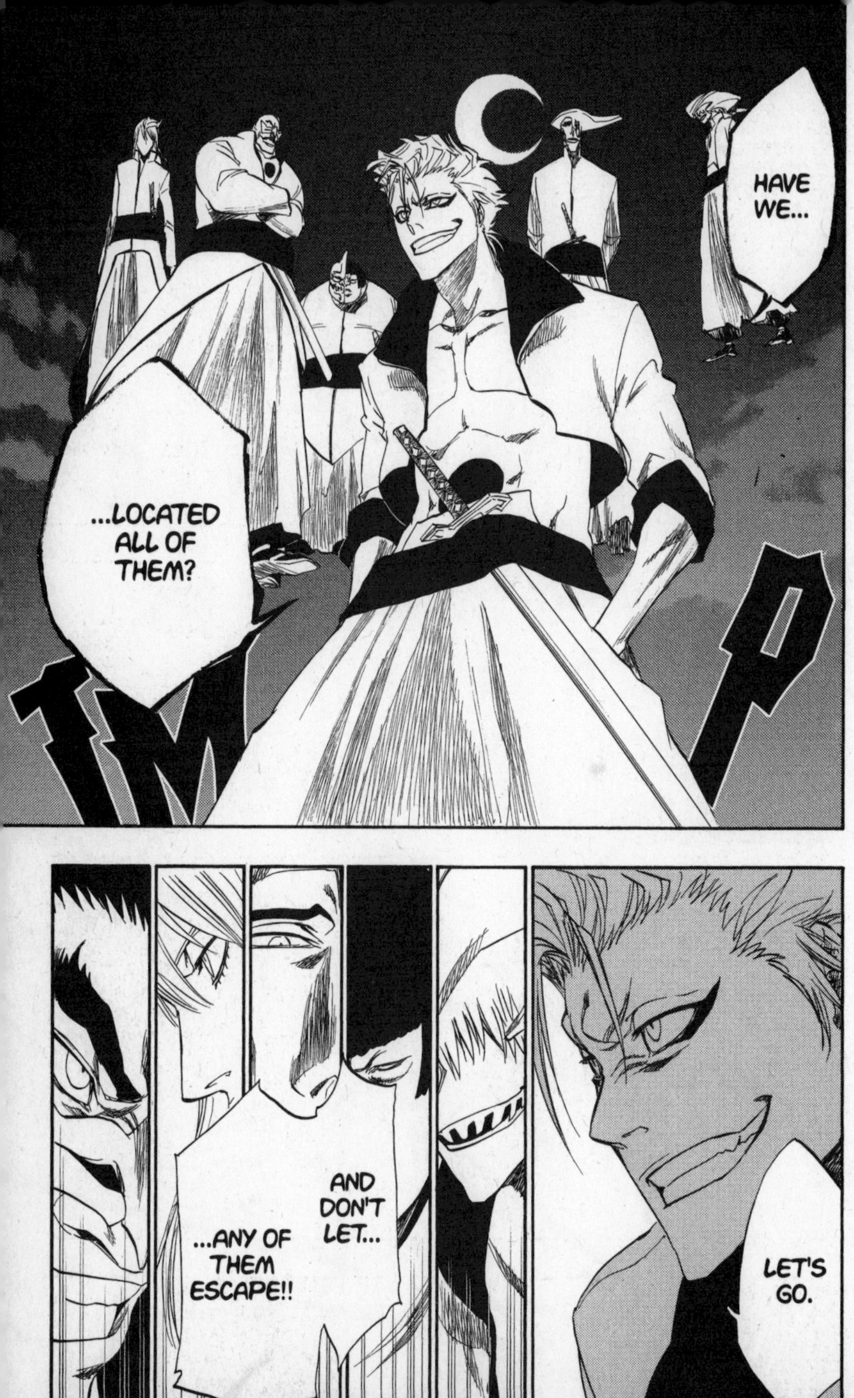
HAVE WE...
...LOCATED ALL OF THEM?
TMP
LET'S GO.
AND DON'T LET...
...ANY OF THEM ESCAPE!!

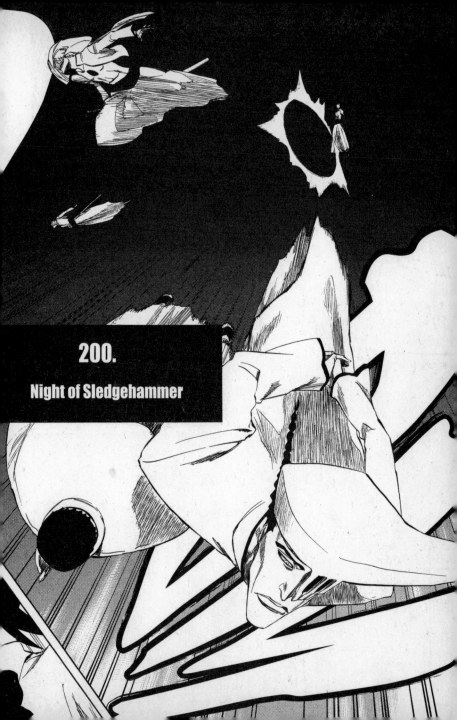

200.

Night of Sledgehammer

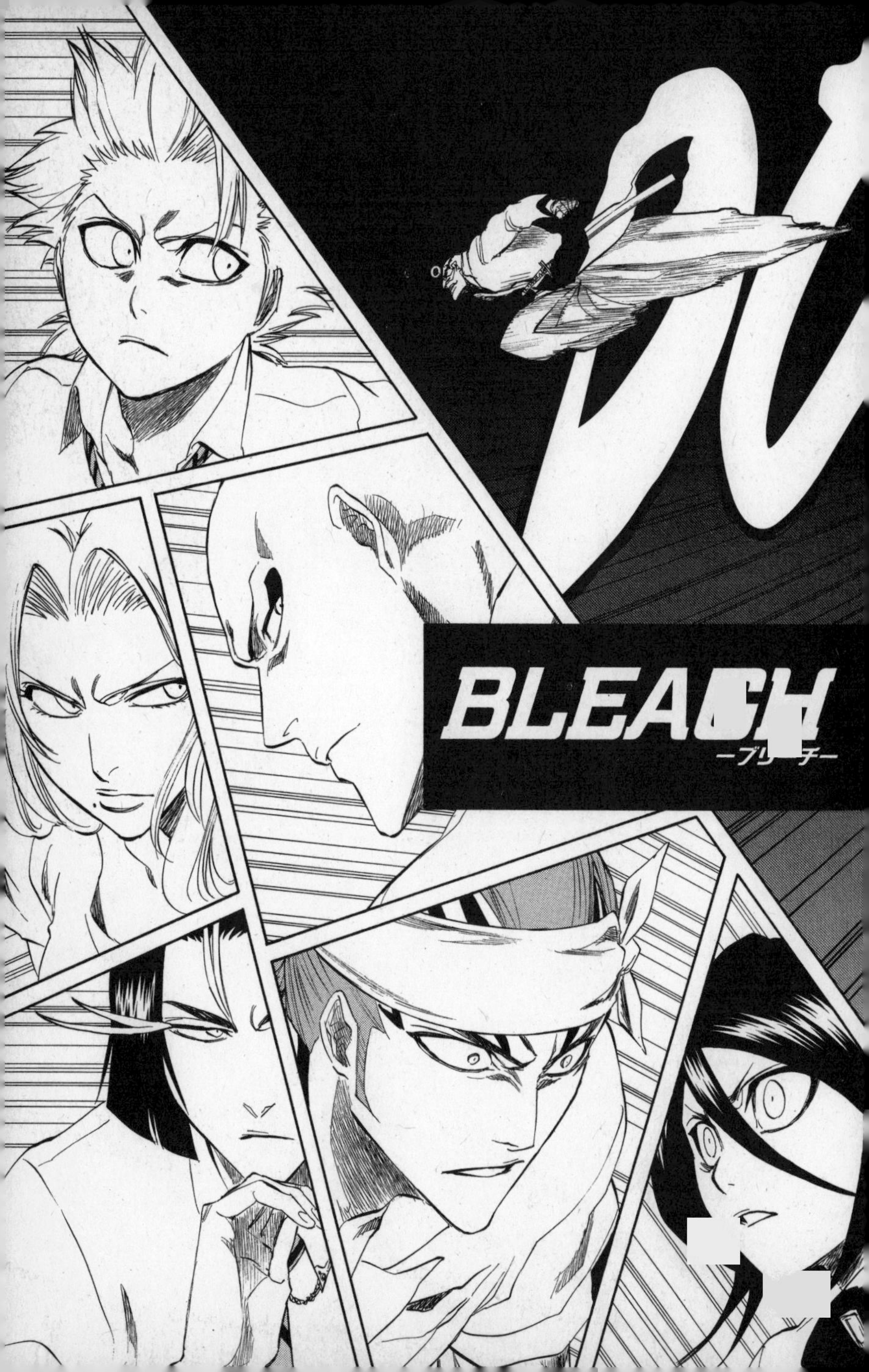
BLEACH
ブリーチ

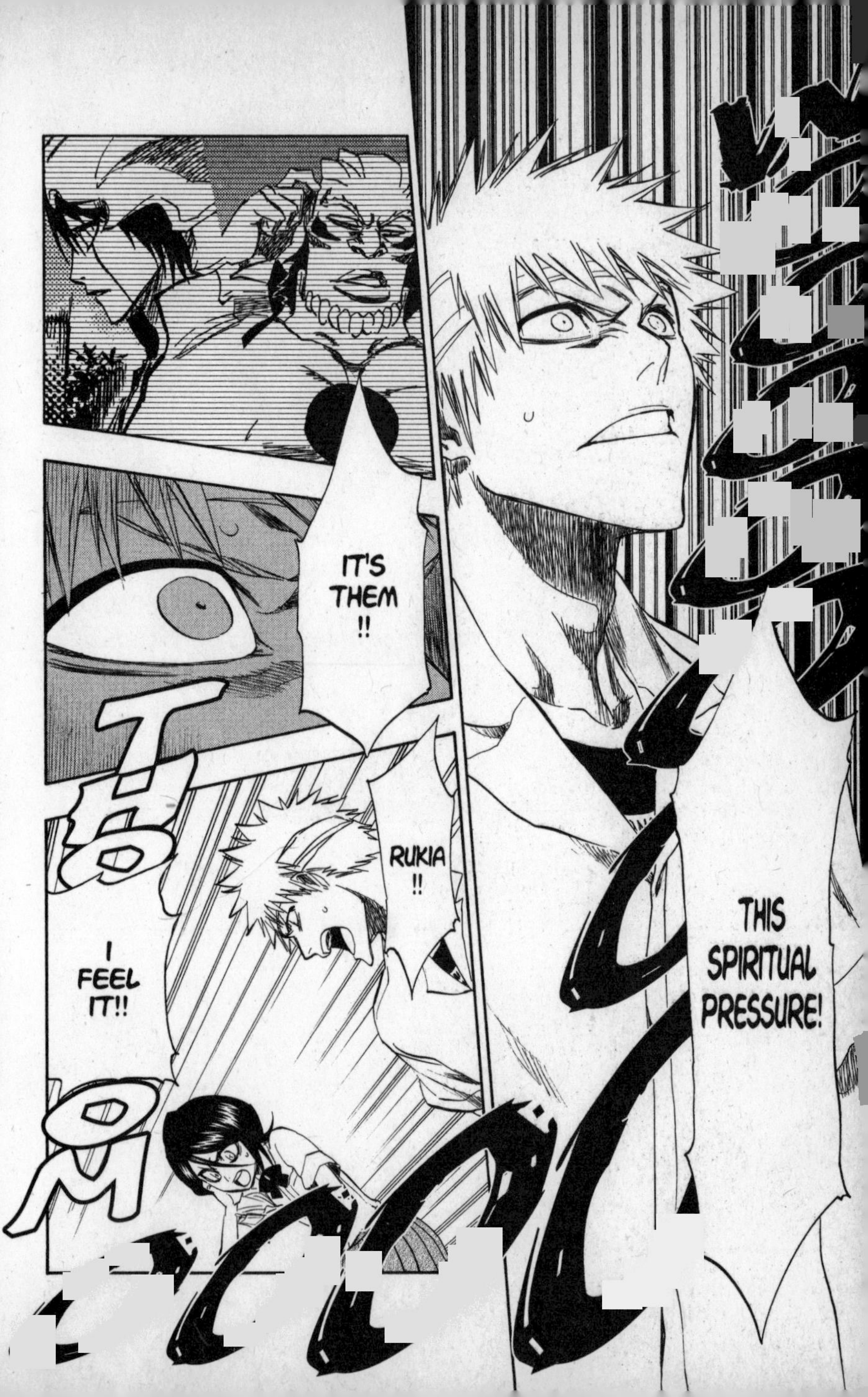
THIS SPIRITUAL PRESSURE!
IT'S THEM!!
RUKIA!!
I FEEL IT!!

READ THIS WAY

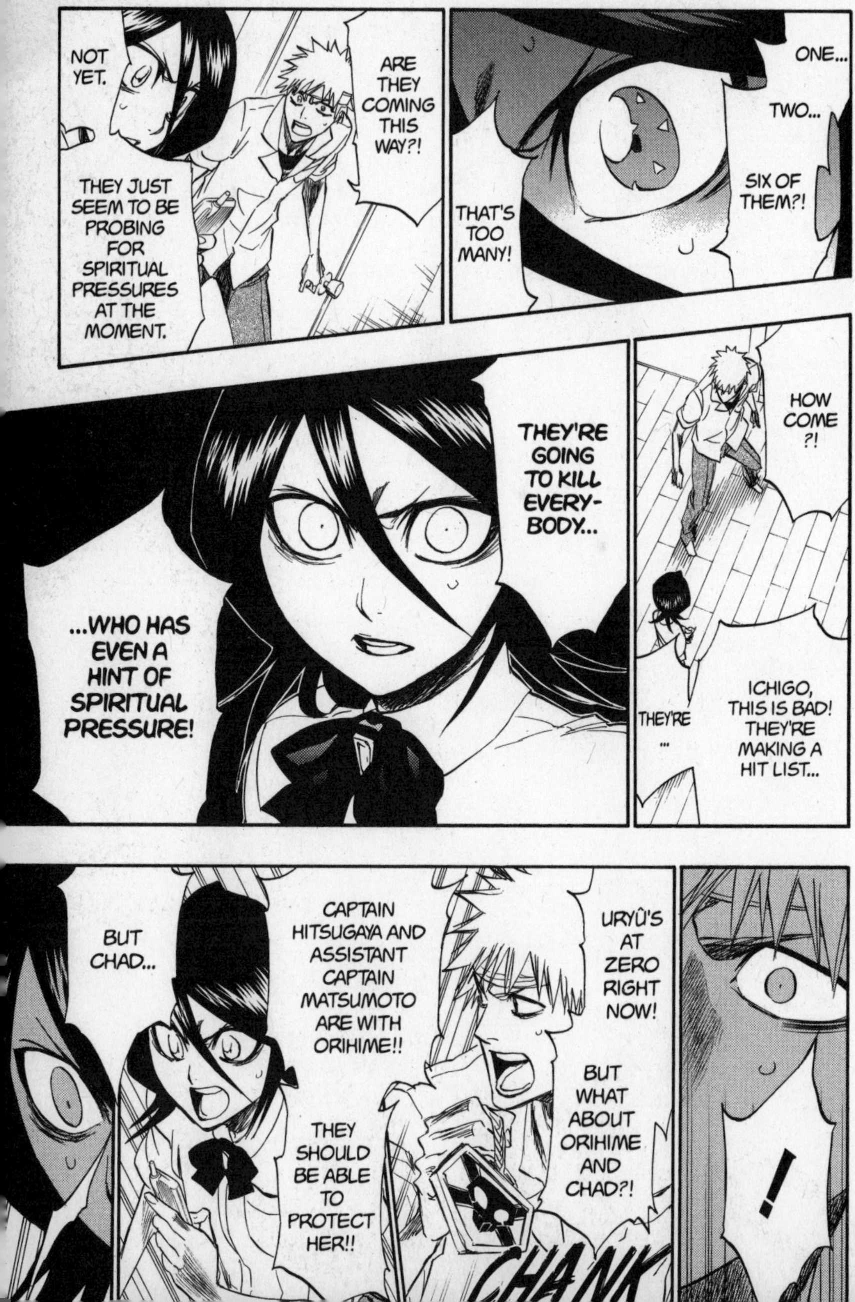

ONE...
TWO...
SIX OF THEM?!
THAT'S TOO MANY!
ARE THEY COMING THIS WAY?!
NOT YET.
THEY JUST SEEM TO BE PROBING FOR SPIRITUAL PRESSURES AT THE MOMENT.
HOW COME?!
ICHIGO, THIS IS BAD! THEY'RE MAKING A HIT LIST...
THEY'RE ...
THEY'RE GOING TO KILL EVERYBODY...
...WHO HAS EVEN A HINT OF SPIRITUAL PRESSURE!
!
URYÛ'S AT ZERO RIGHT NOW!
BUT WHAT ABOUT ORIHIME AND CHAD?!
CAPTAIN HITSUGAYA AND ASSISTANT CAPTAIN MATSUMOTO ARE WITH ORIHIME!!
THEY SHOULD BE ABLE TO PROTECT HER!!
BUT CHAD...
CHANK

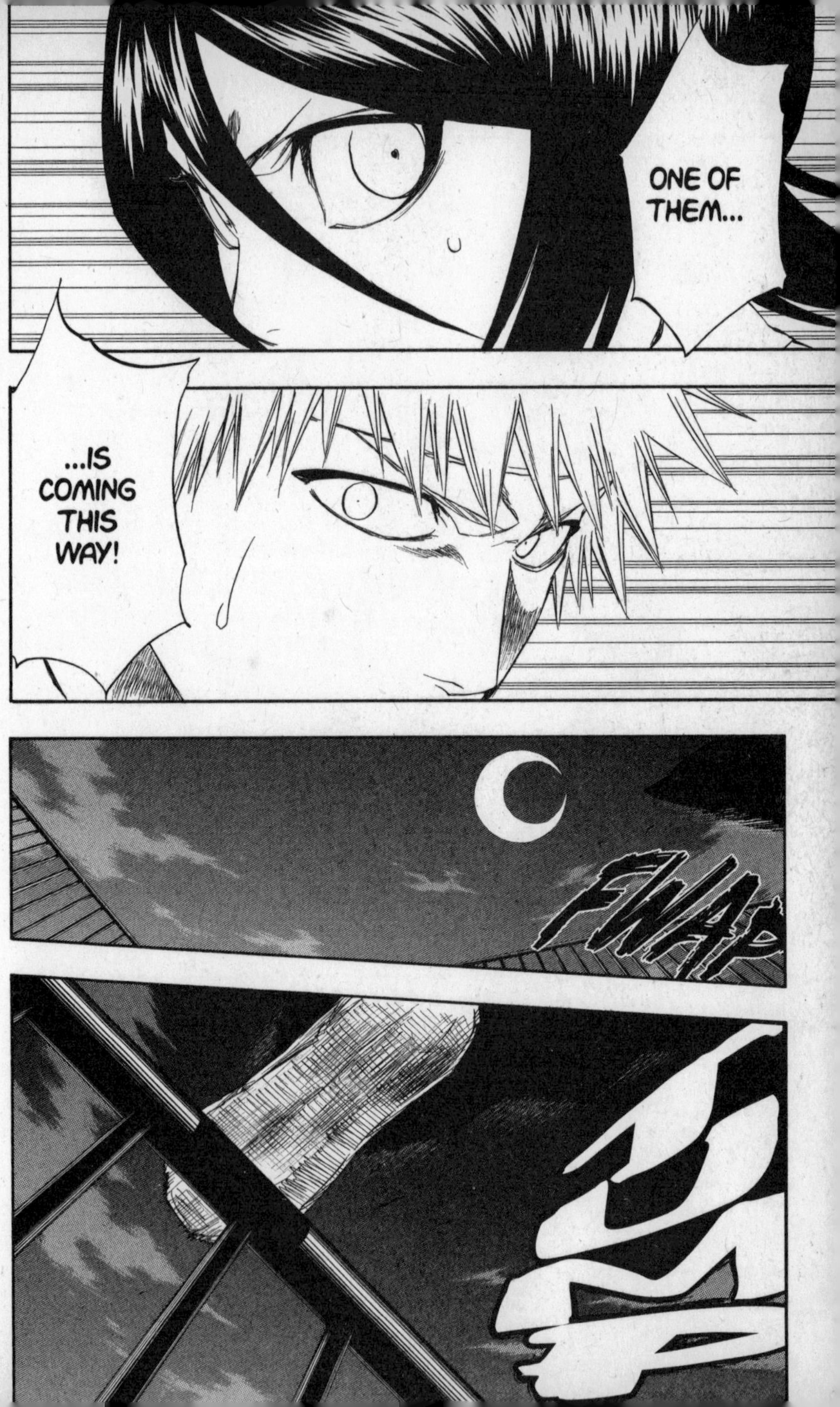
ONE OF THEM...
...IS COMING THIS WAY!
FWAP

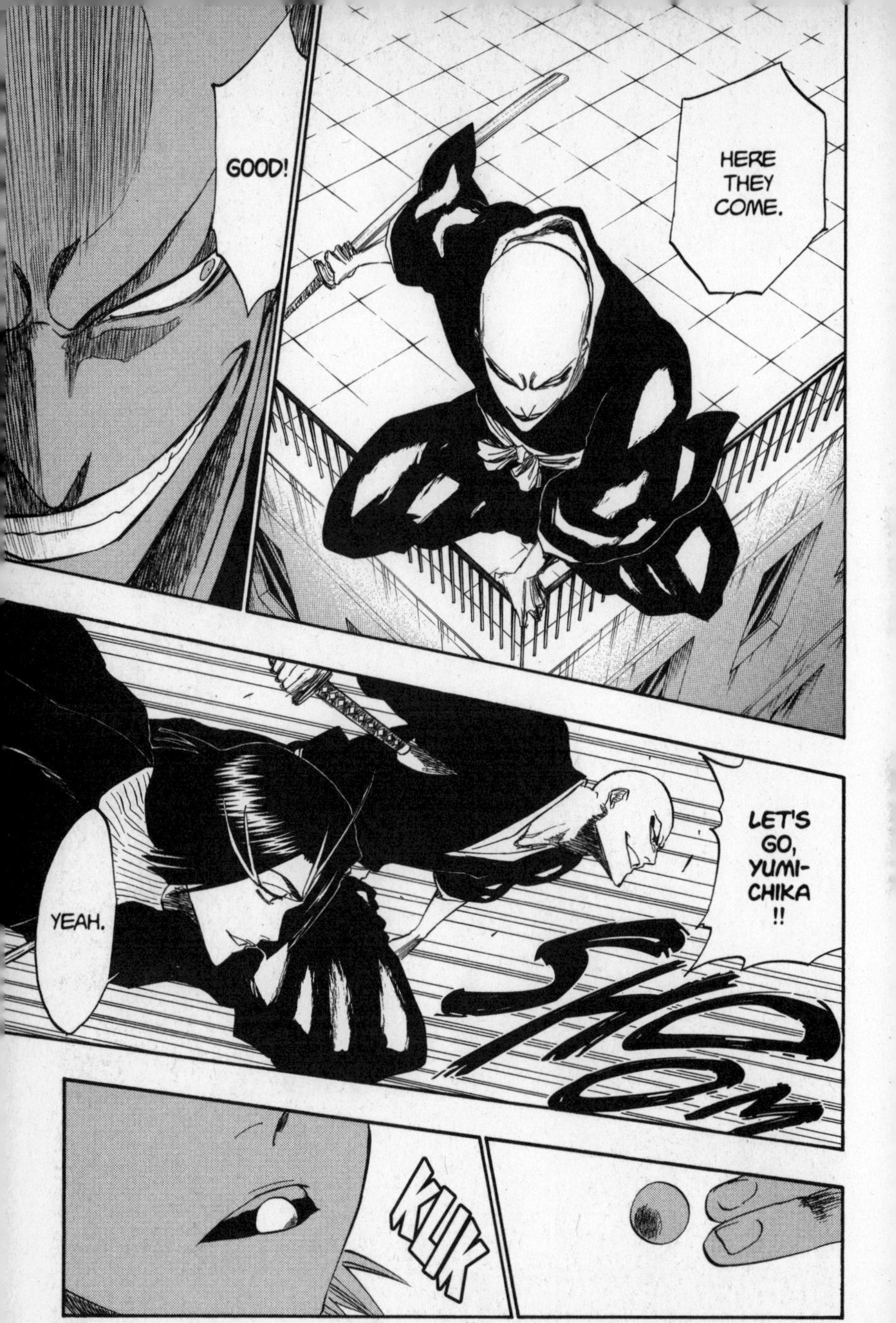
HERE THEY COME.
GOOD!
LET'S GO, YUMI-CHIKA!!
YEAH.
KLIK

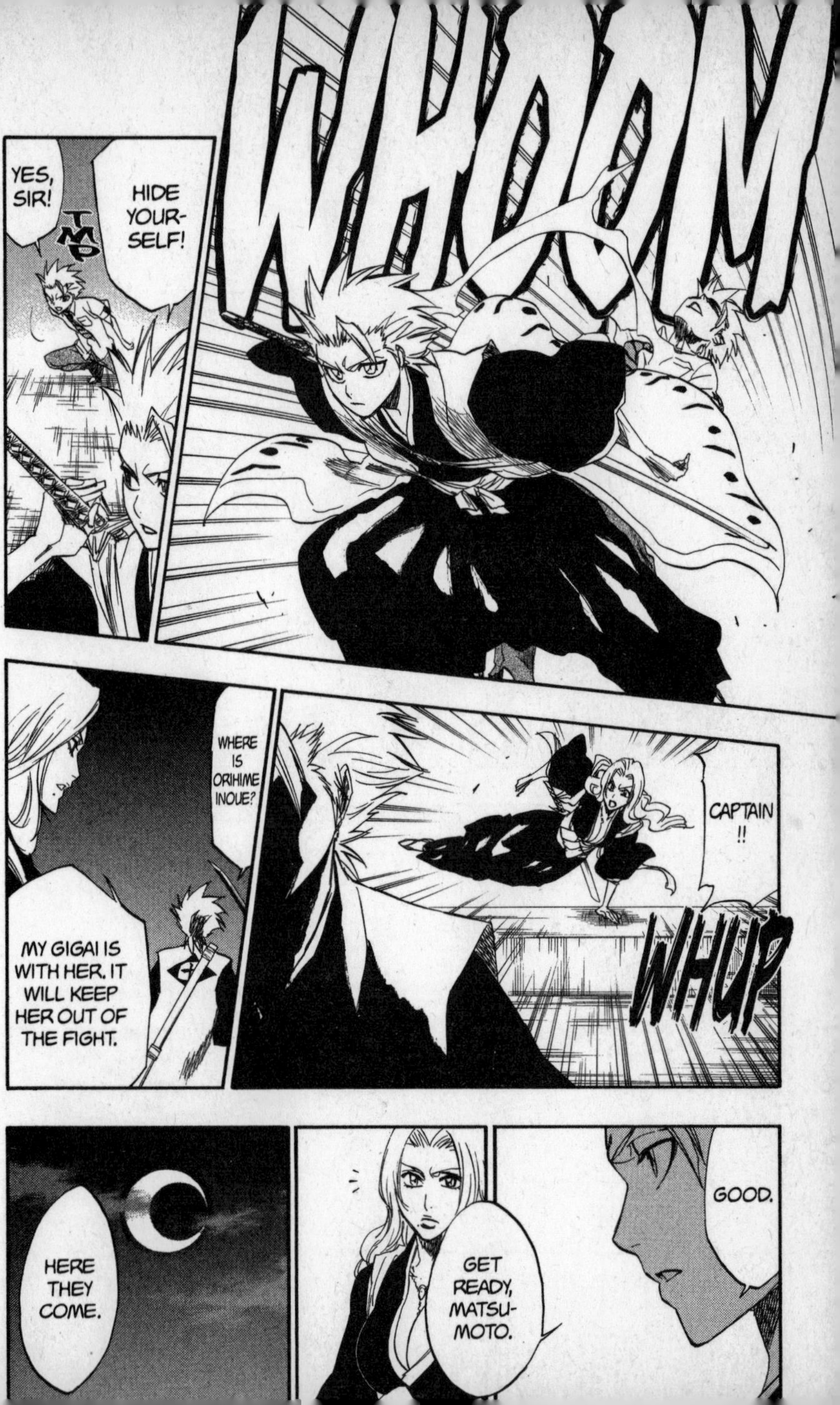
WHOOM
HIDE YOURSELF!
YES, SIR!
TMP
CAPTAIN!!
WHUP
WHERE IS ORIHIME INOUE?
MY GIGAI IS WITH HER. IT WILL KEEP HER OUT OF THE FIGHT.
GOOD.
GET READY, MATSUMOTO.
HERE THEY COME.

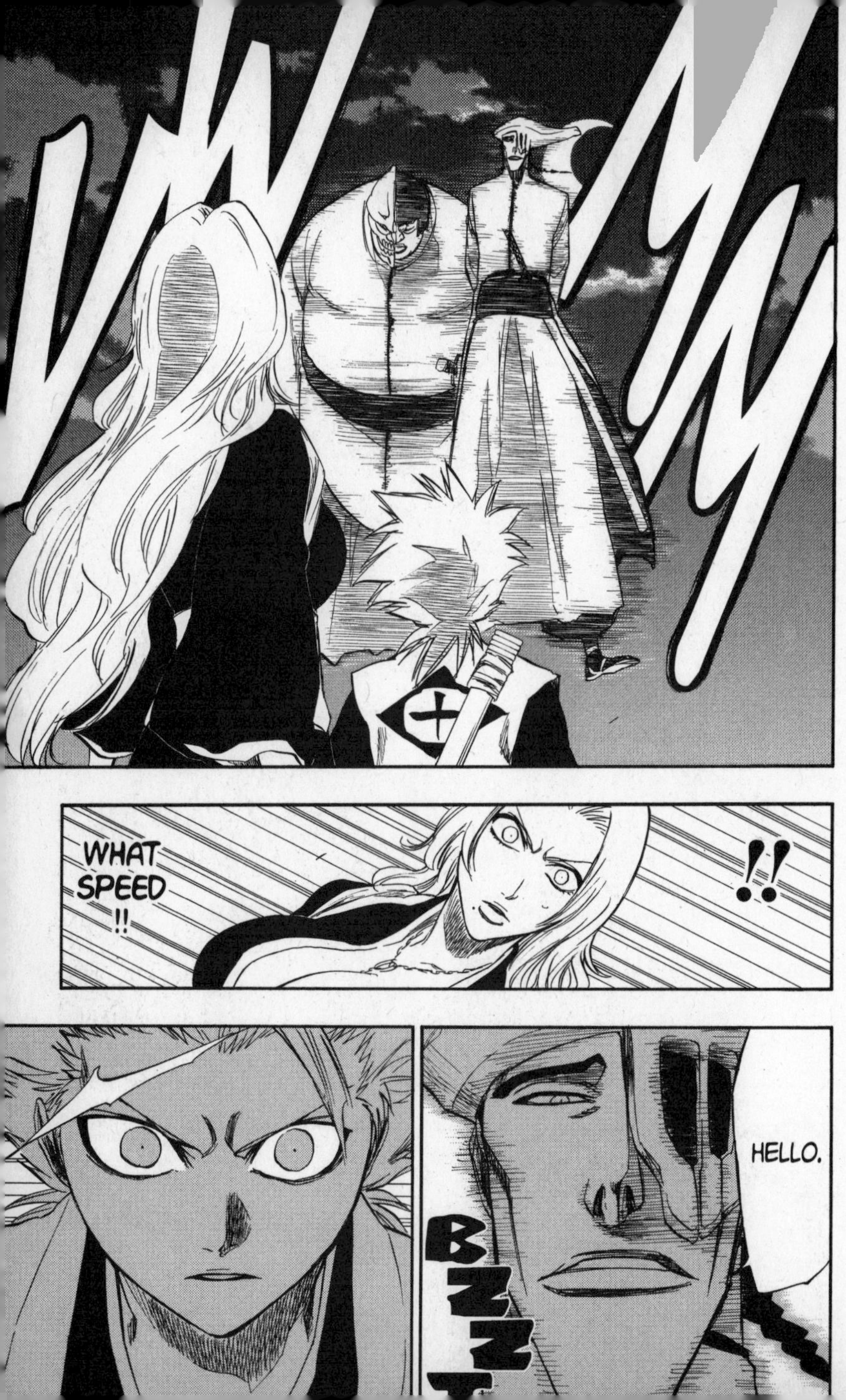
WHAT SPEED !!
!!
HELLO.
BZZ

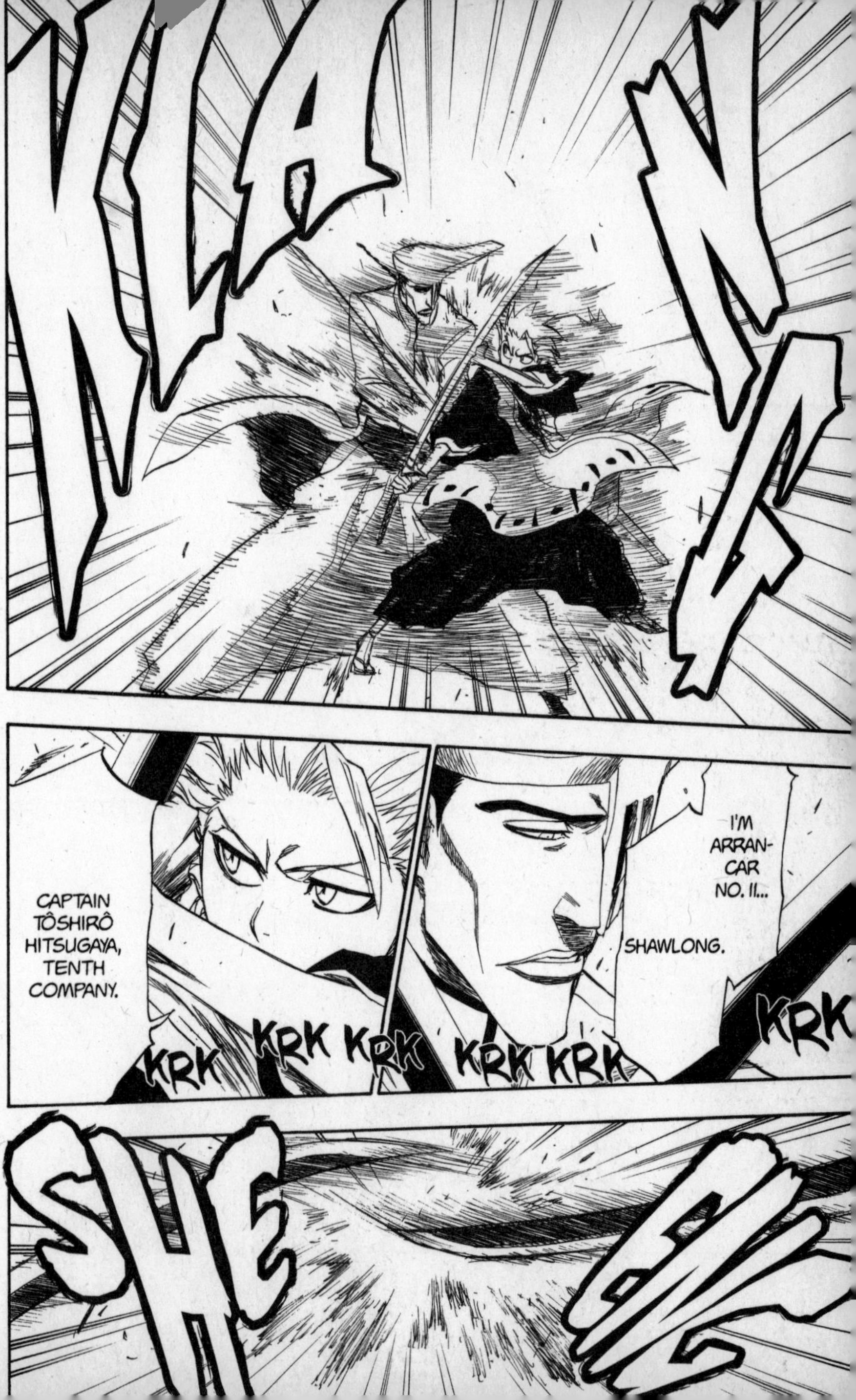
KLANG
I'M ARRANCAR NO. 11...
SHAWLONG.
CAPTAIN TÔSHIRÔ HITSUGAYA, TENTH COMPANY.
KRK KRK KRK KRK KRK KRK

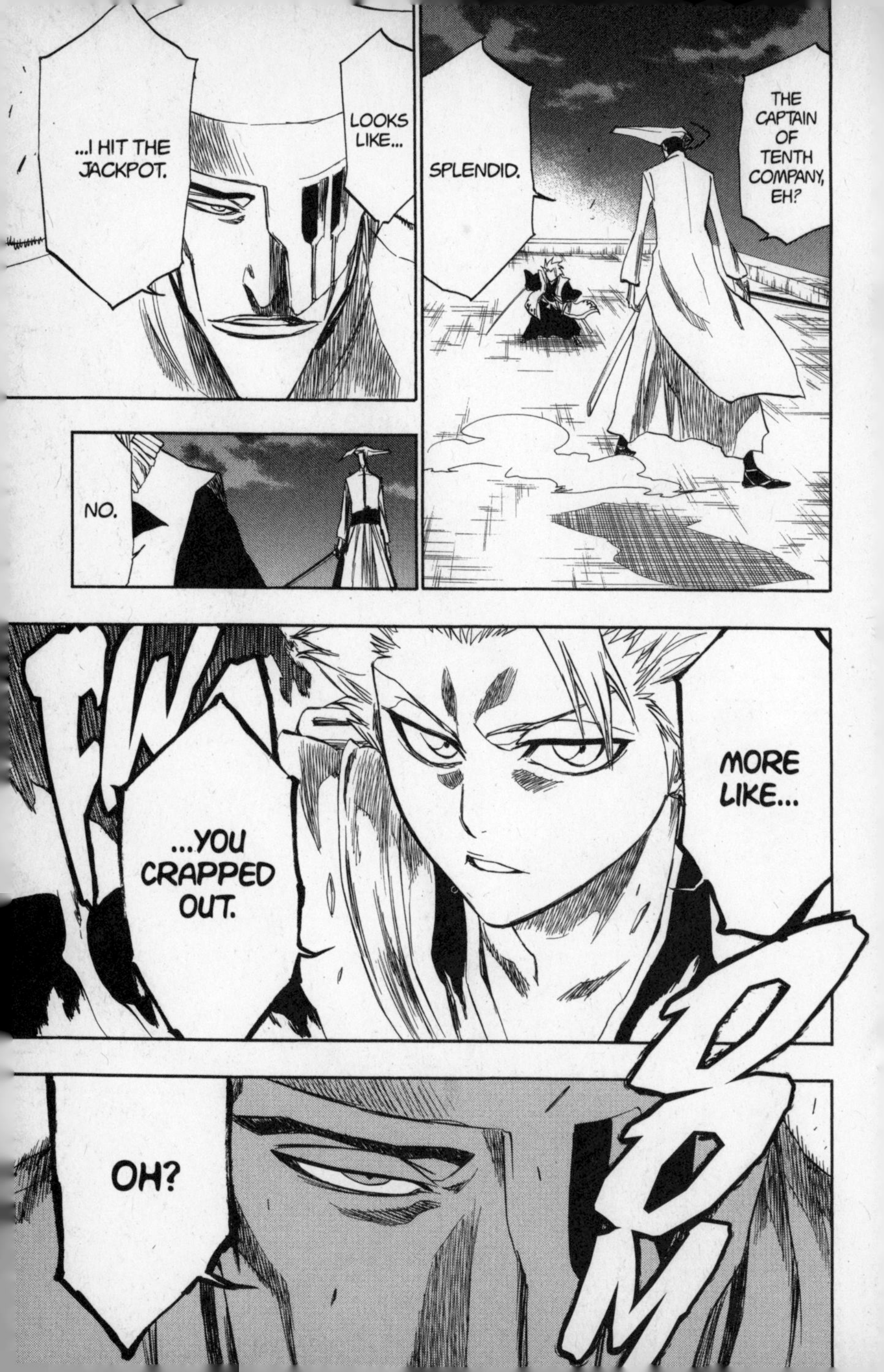
THE CAPTAIN OF TENTH COMPANY, EH?
SPLENDID.
LOOKS LIKE...
...I HIT THE JACKPOT.
NO.
MORE LIKE...
...YOU CRAPPED OUT.
OH?

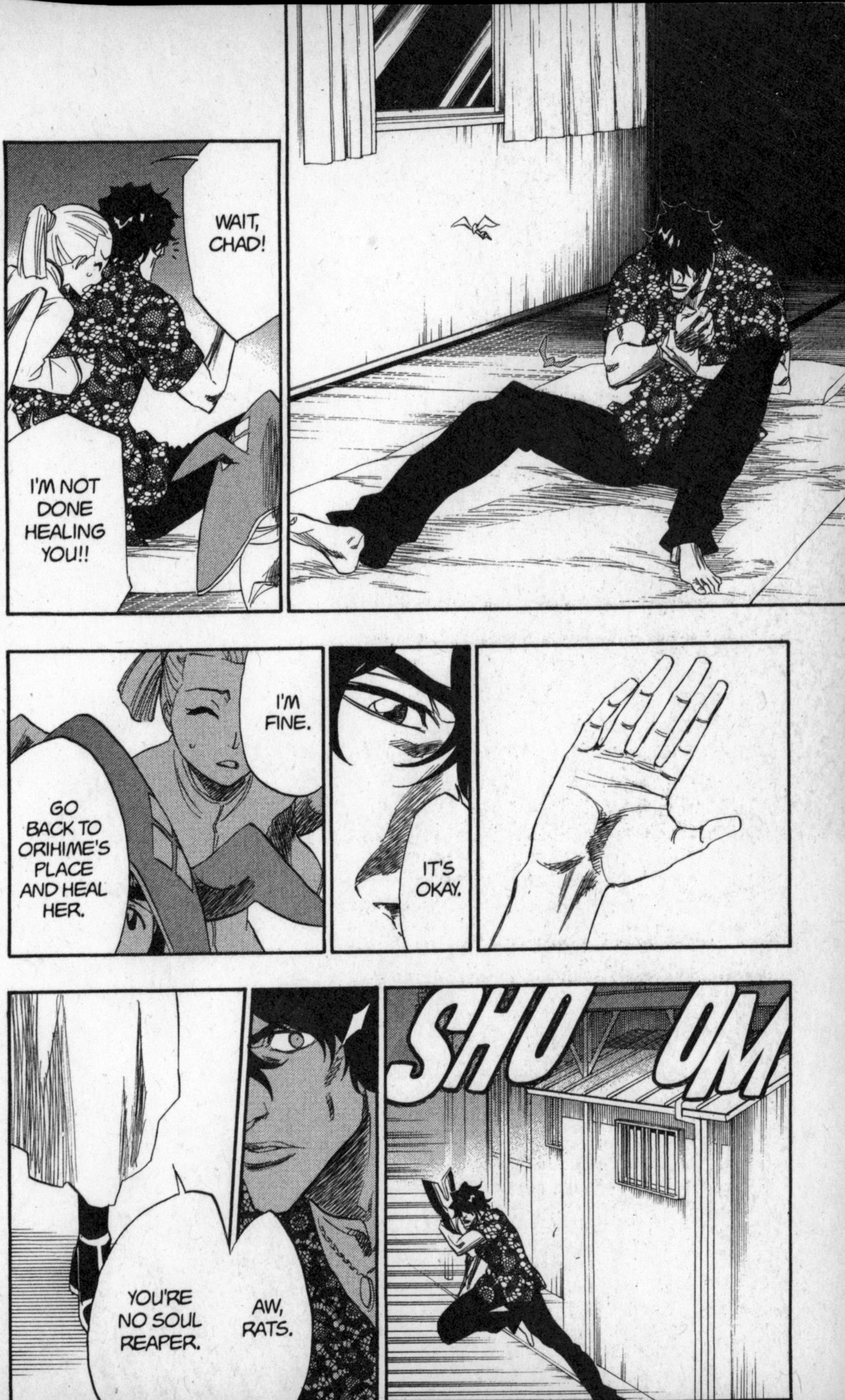
WAIT, CHAD!
I'M NOT DONE HEALING YOU!!
IT'S OKAY.
I'M FINE.
GO BACK TO ORIHIME'S PLACE AND HEAL HER.
SHOOM
AW, RATS.
YOU'RE NO SOUL REAPER.

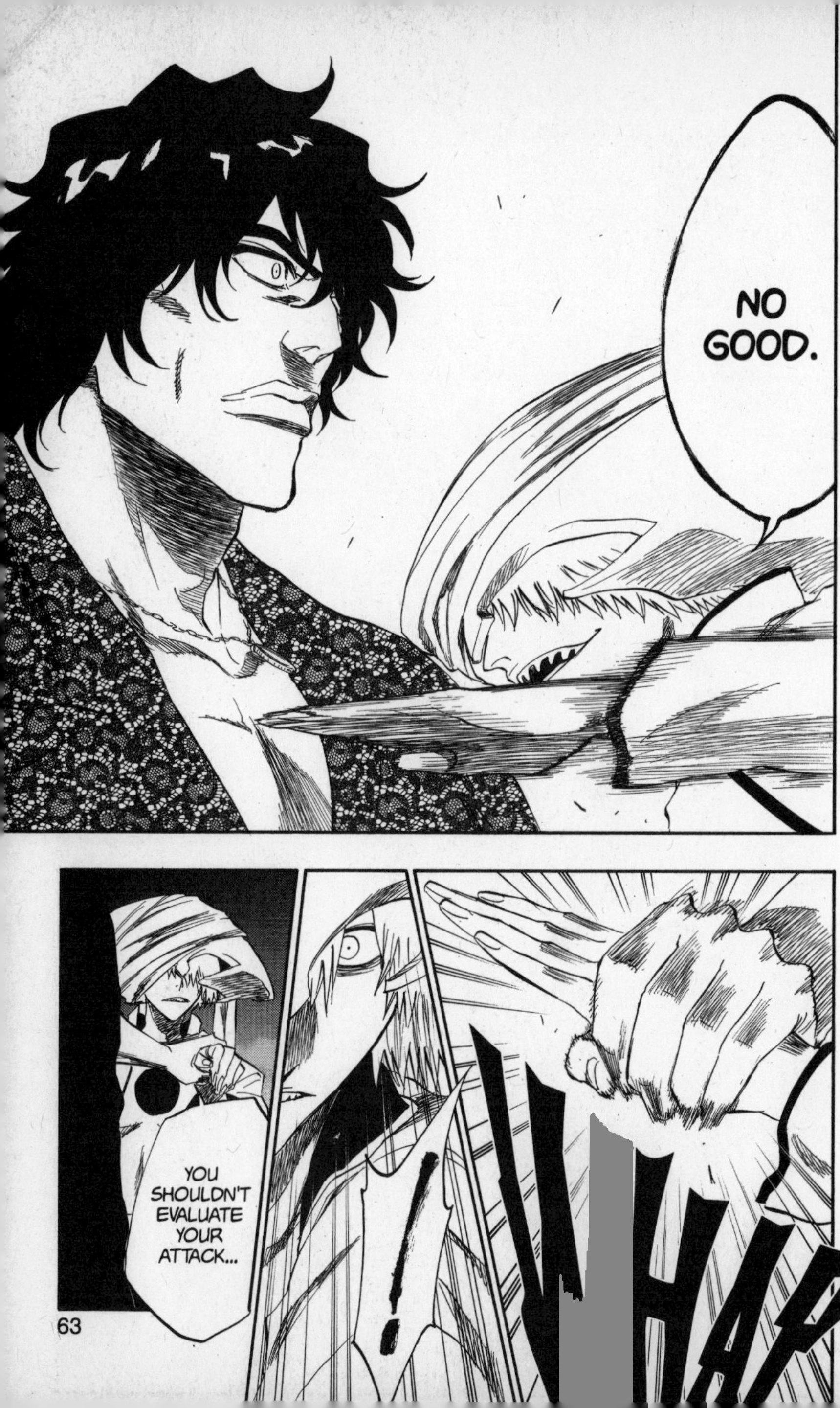
NO GOOD.
WHAP
YOU SHOULDN'T EVALUATE YOUR ATTACK...

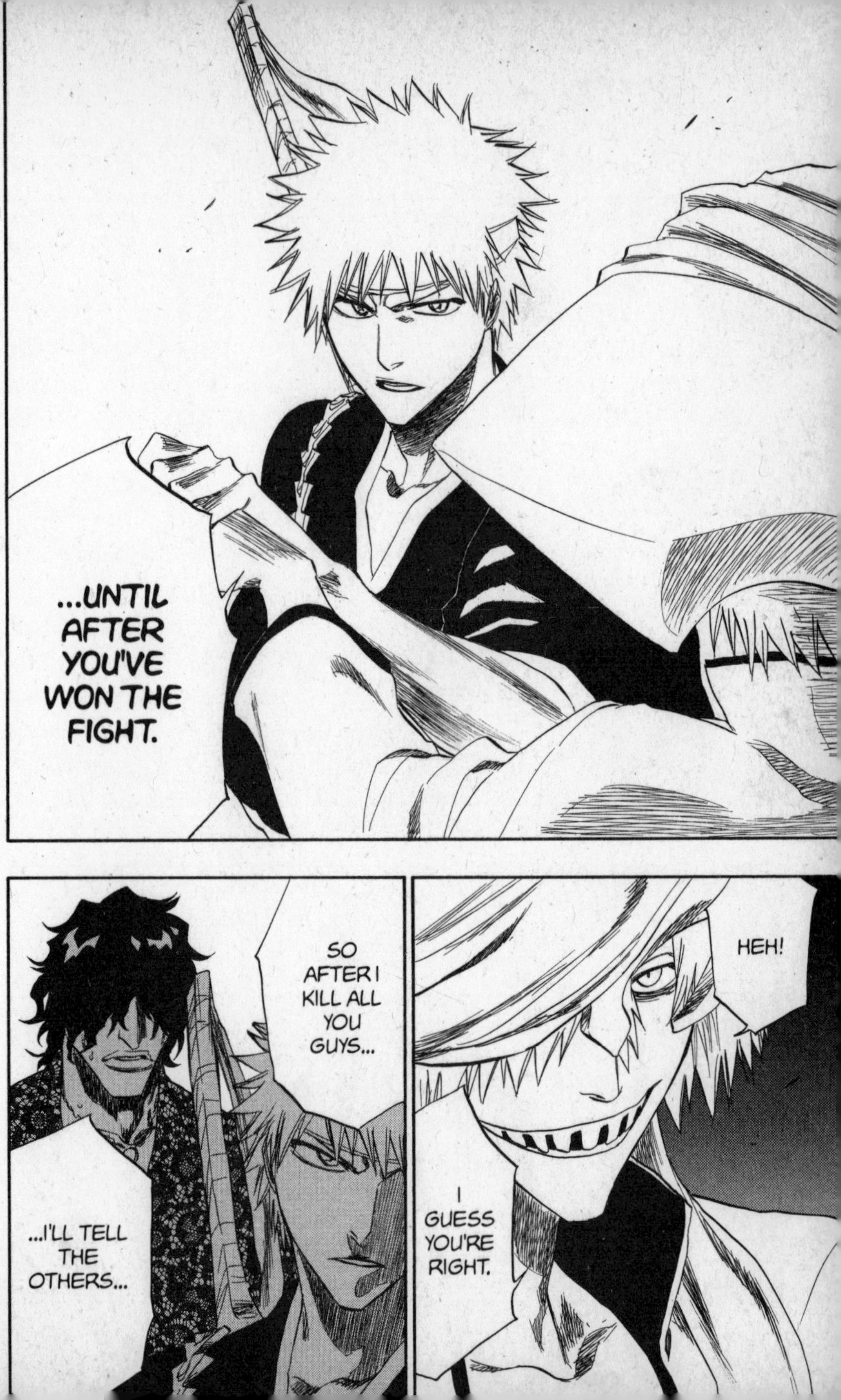
...UNTIL AFTER YOU'VE WON THE FIGHT.
HEH!
I GUESS YOU'RE RIGHT.
SO AFTER I KILL ALL YOU GUYS...
...I'LL TELL THE OTHERS...

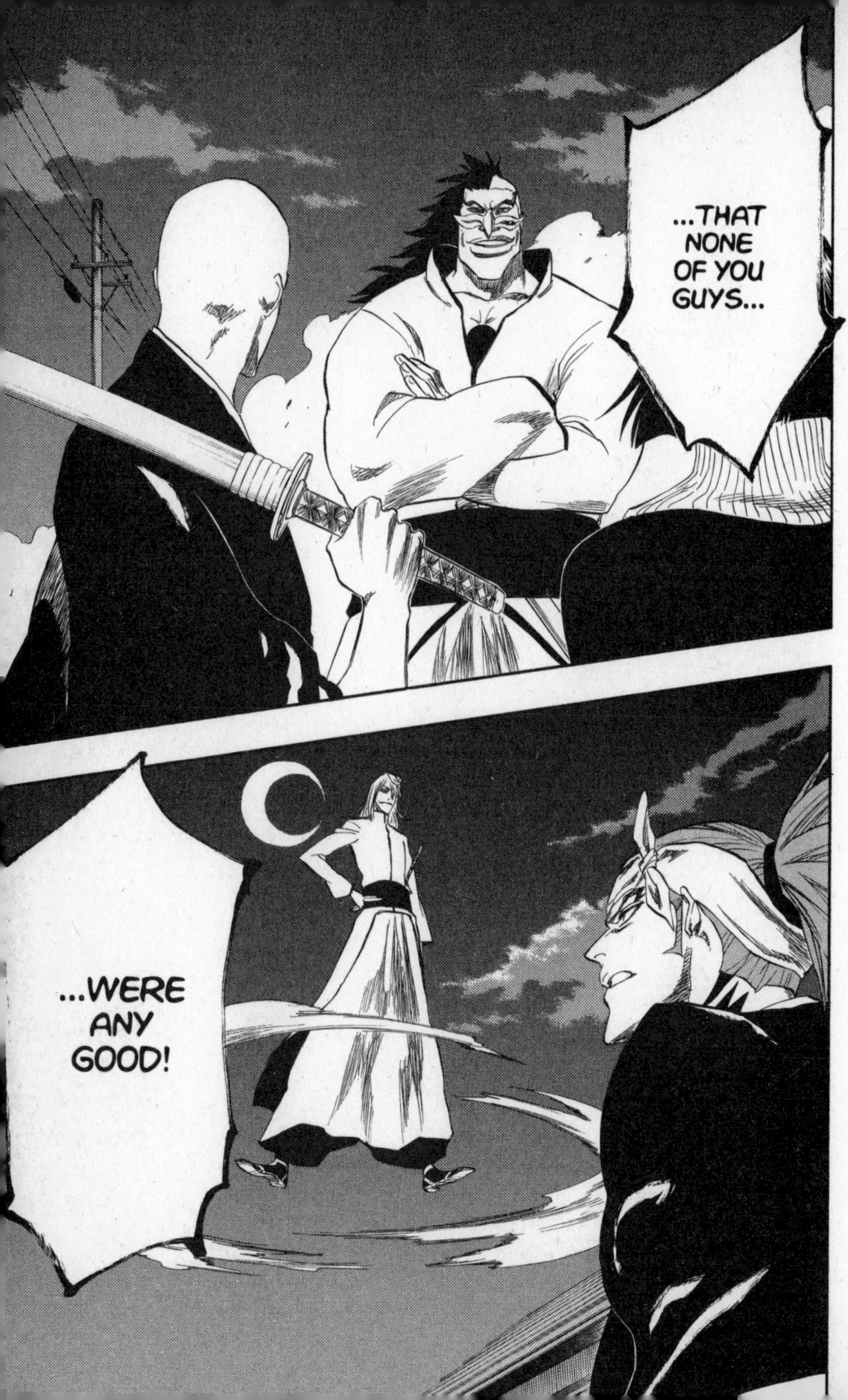
...THAT NONE OF YOU GUYS...
...WERE ANY GOOD!

EEEEK
FOURTH COMPANY GIRLS
AAAH!! A TEDDY BEAR?!
IT'S SO CUTE!
OOOOH
WHAT?!!
THEY LIKE ME?! DARN IT!! THAT'S NEVER HAPPENED TO ME BEFORE!! EVER!!
SWUFF

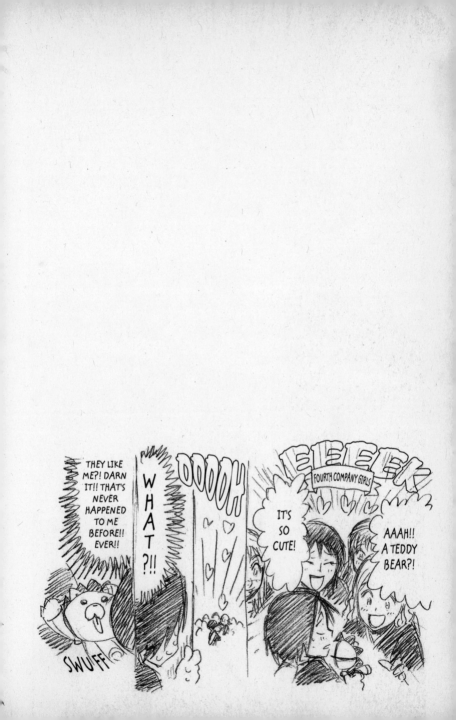

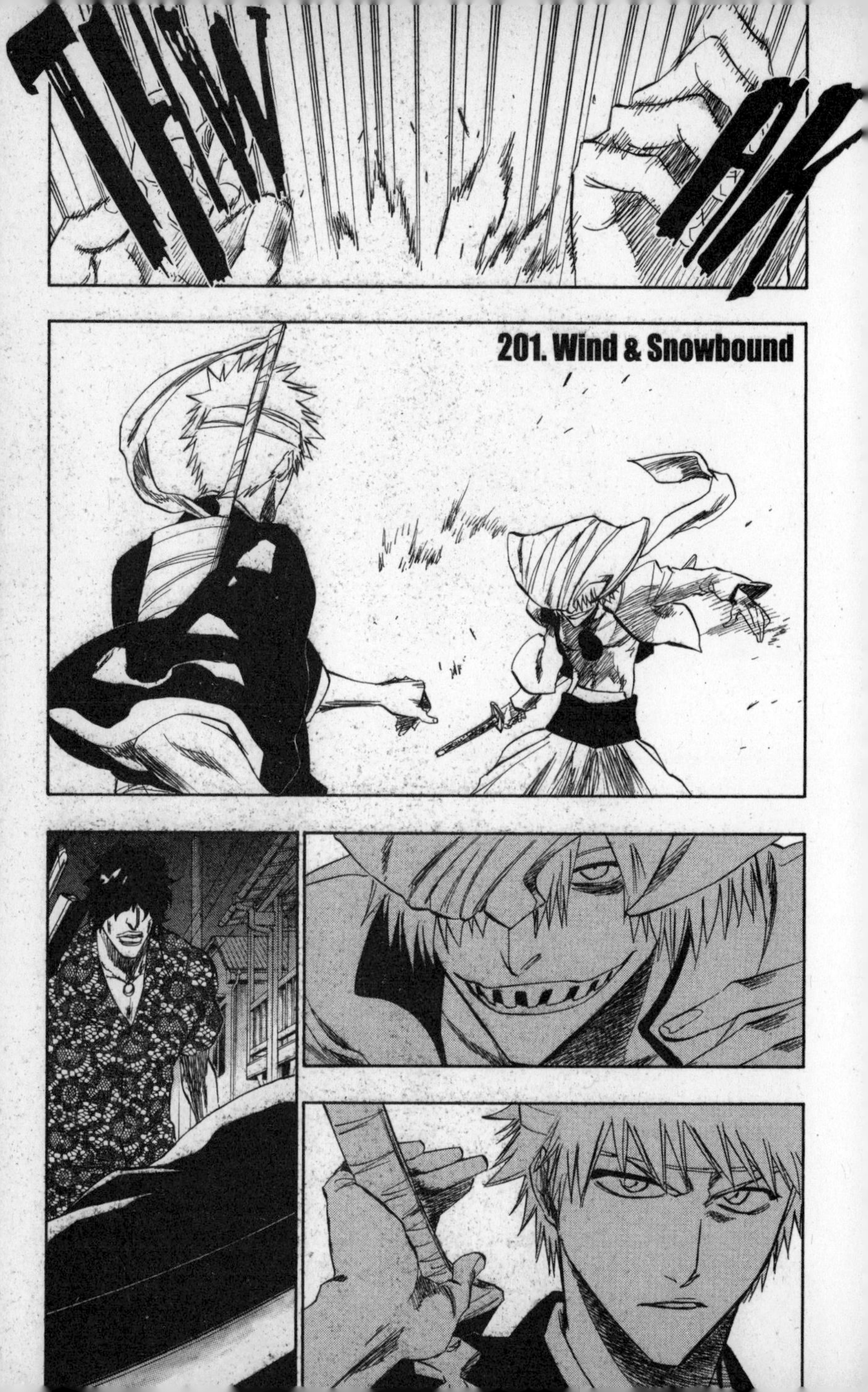
THWAK
201. Wind & Snowbound

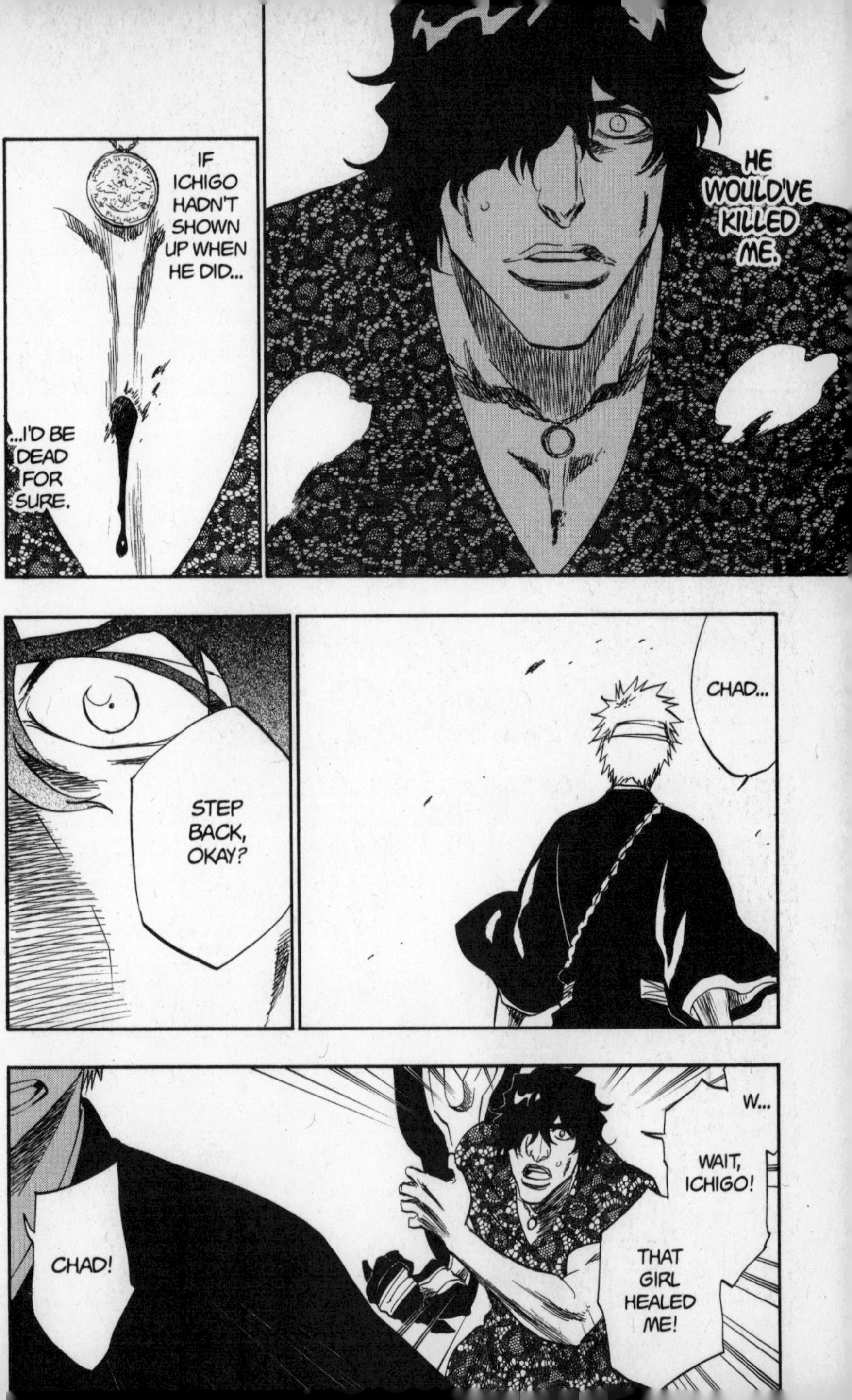
HE WOULD'VE KILLED ME.
IF ICHIGO HADN'T SHOWN UP WHEN HE DID...
...I'D BE DEAD FOR SURE.
CHAD...
STEP BACK, OKAY?
W...
WAIT, ICHIGO!
THAT GIRL HEALED ME!
CHAD!

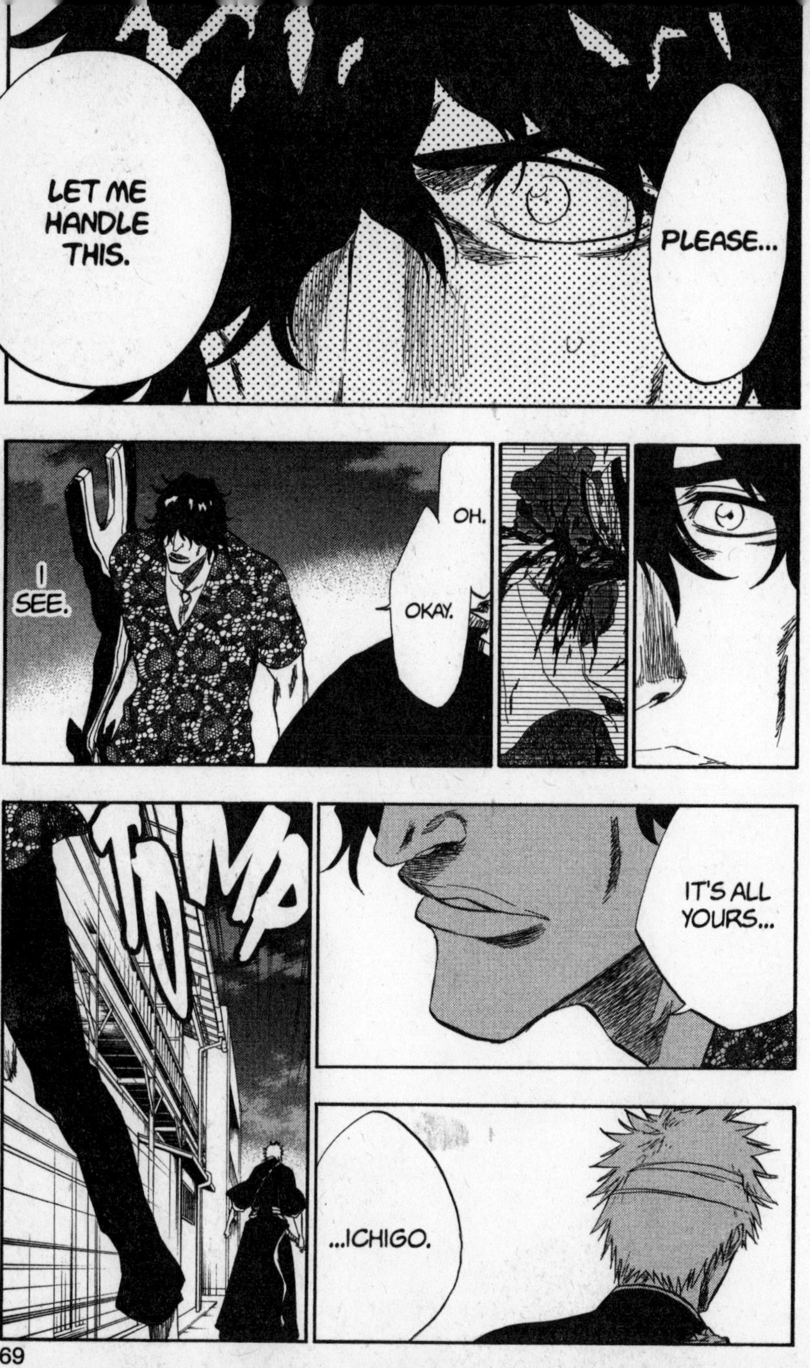
PLEASE...
LET ME HANDLE THIS.
OH.
OKAY.
I SEE.
IT'S ALL YOURS...
...ICHIGO.
TOMP

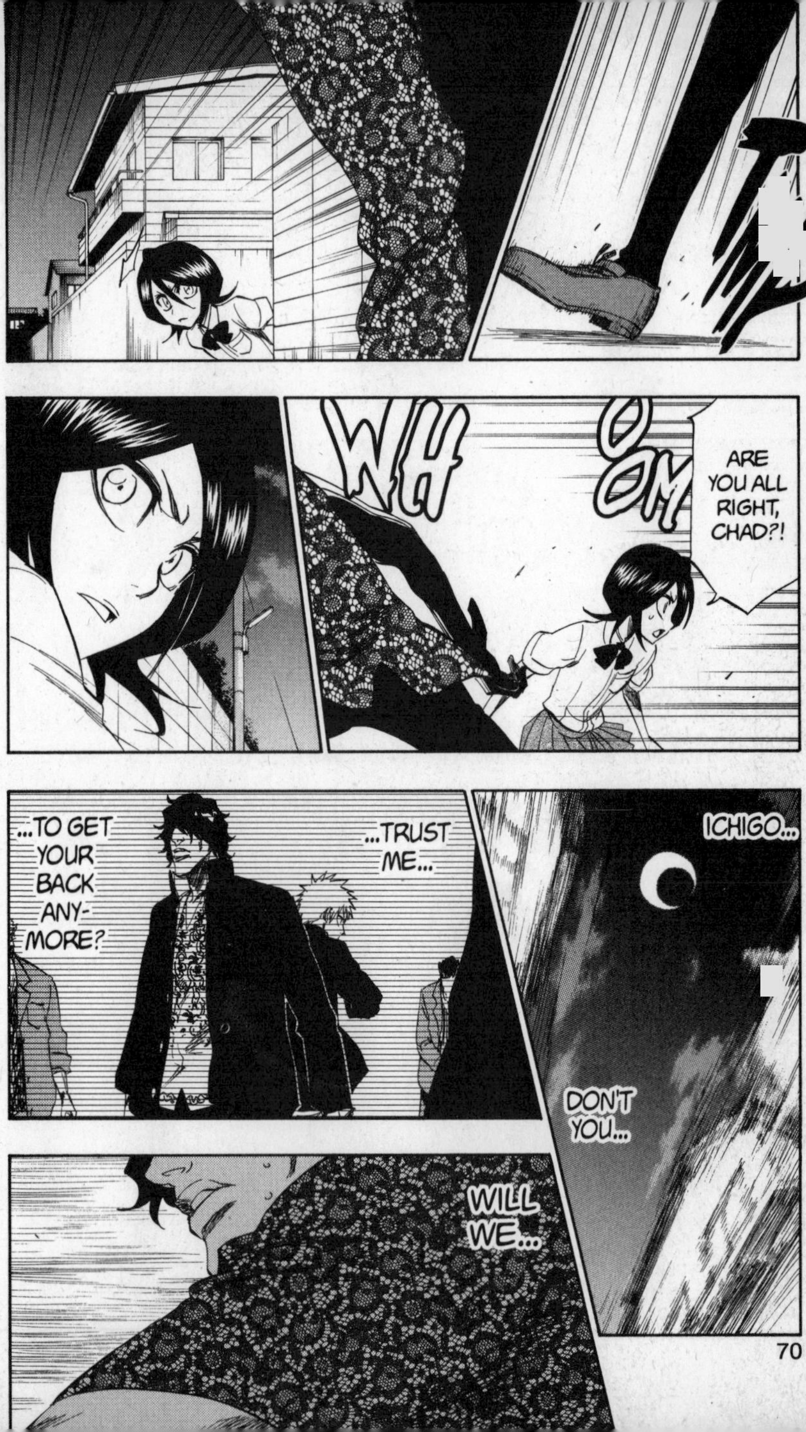
WHOOM
ARE YOU ALL RIGHT, CHAD?!
ICHIGO...
DON'T YOU...
...TRUST ME...
...TO GET YOUR BACK ANYMORE?
WILL WE...

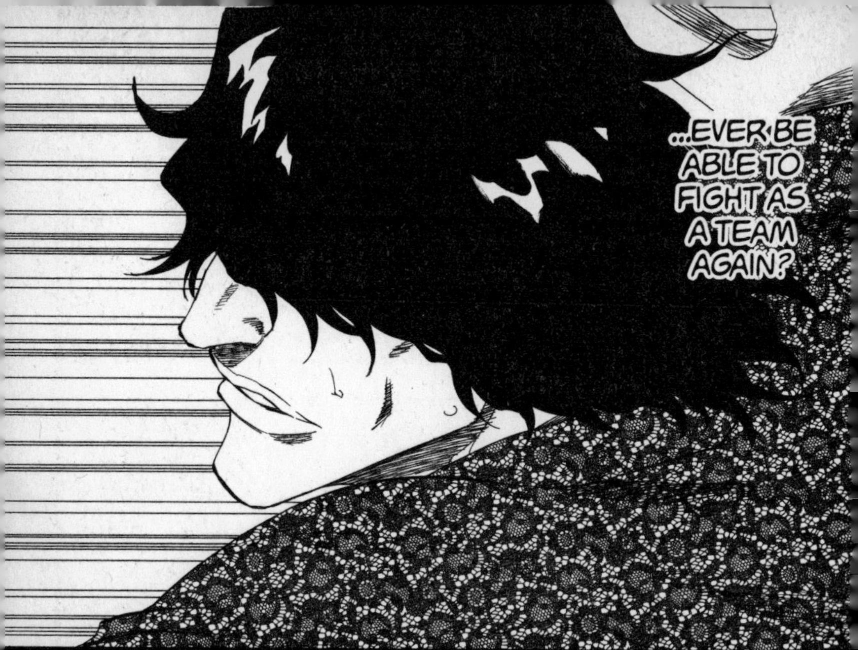
...EVER BE ABLE TO FIGHT AS A TEAM AGAIN?

BLEACH

201.

Wind & Snowbound

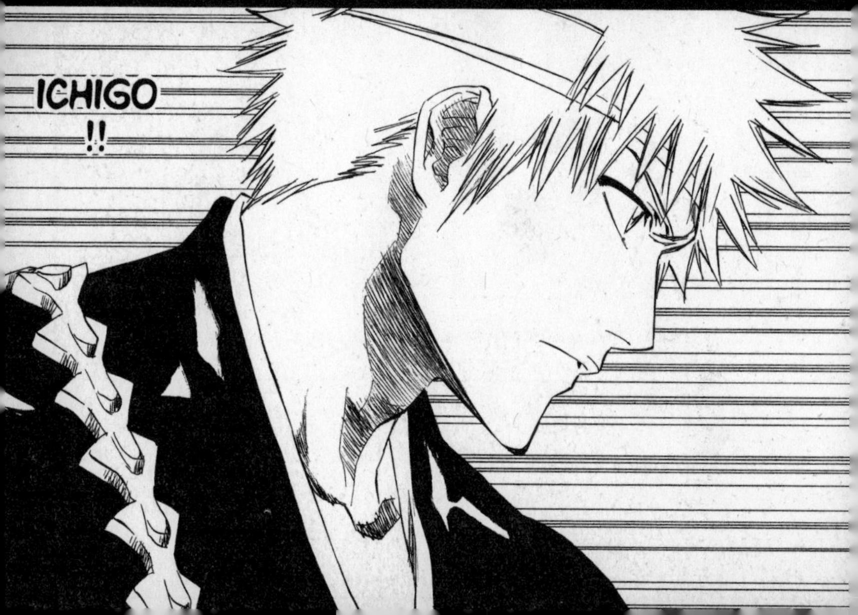
ICHIGO !!

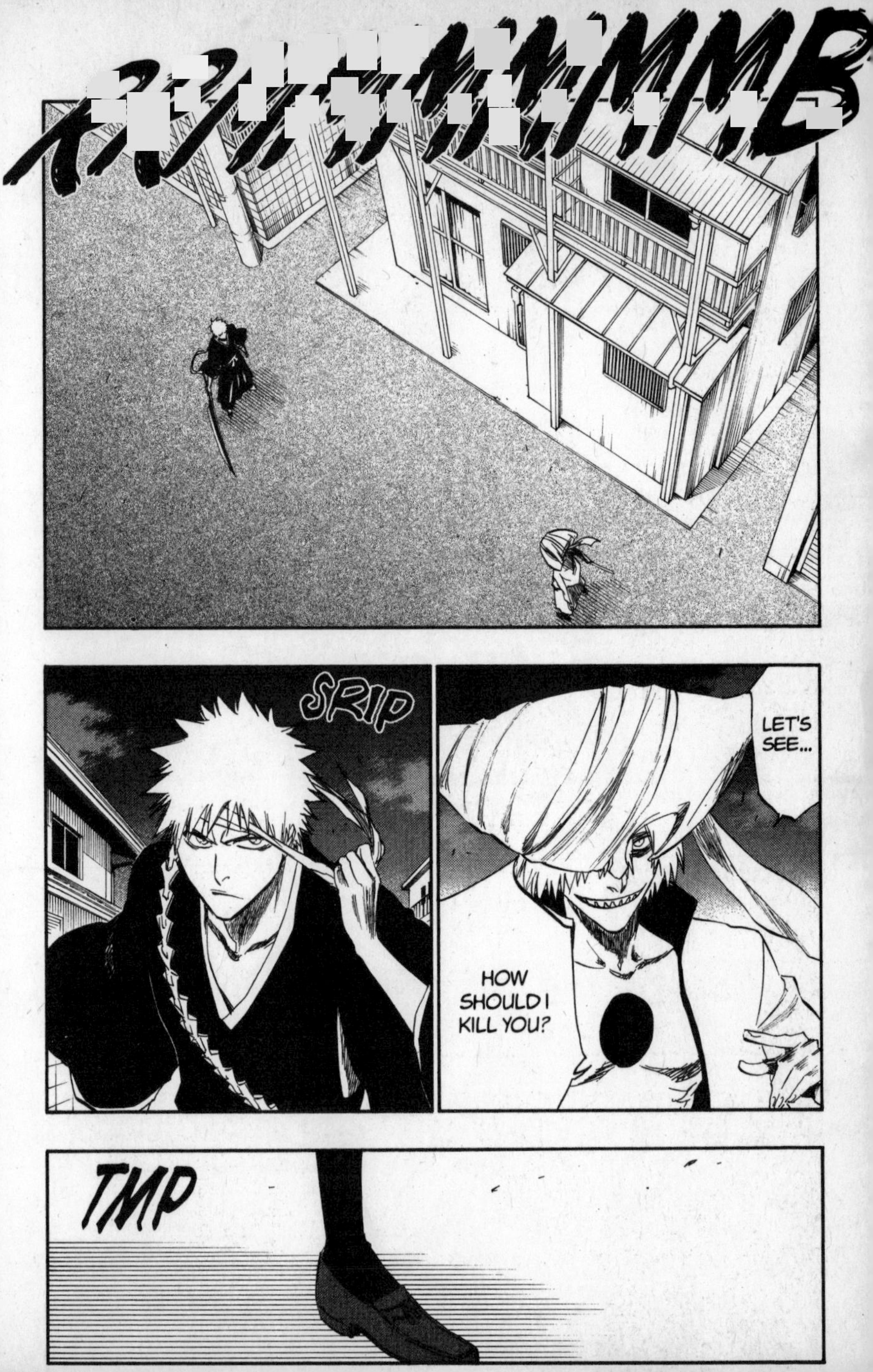
LET'S SEE...
HOW SHOULD I KILL YOU?
SRIP
TMP

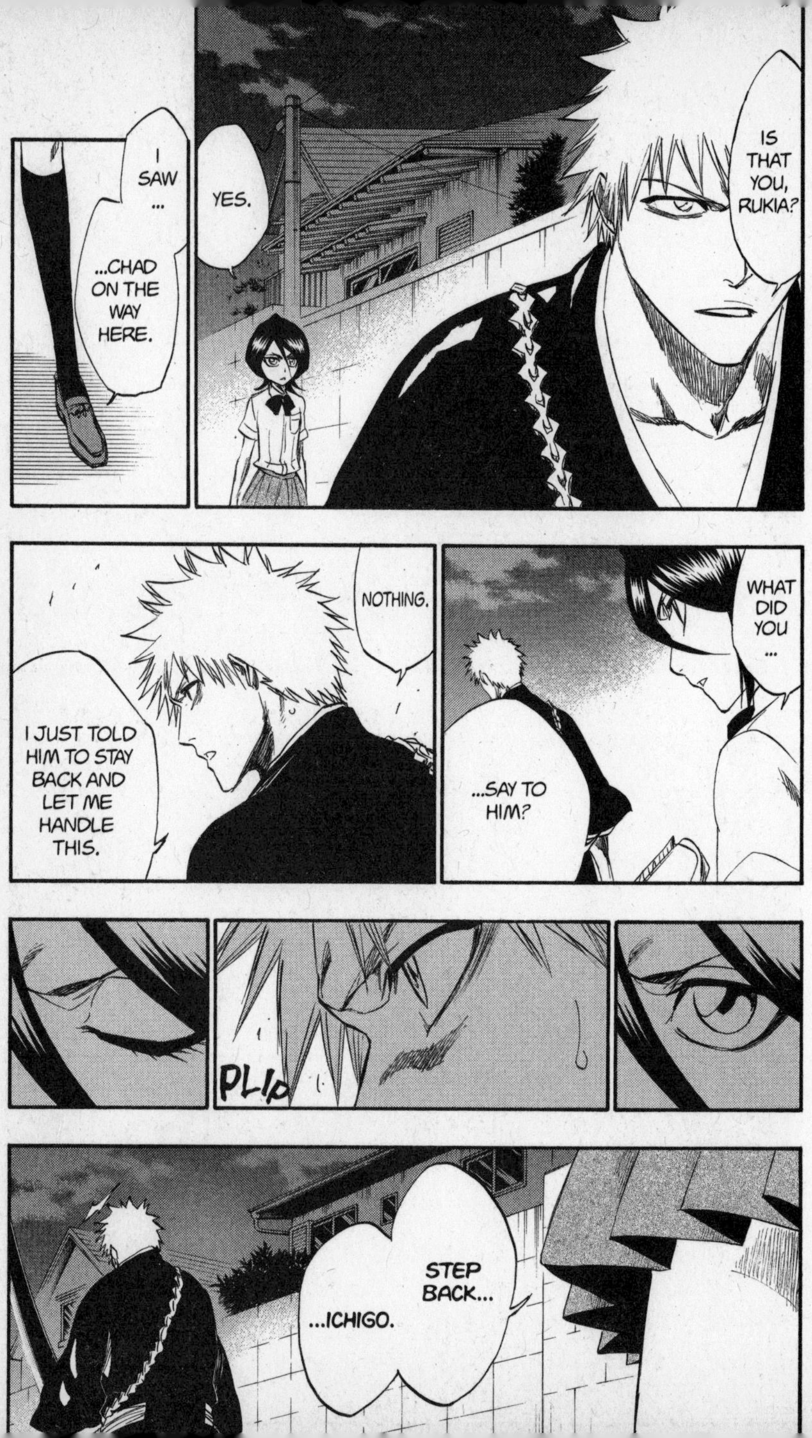
IS THAT YOU, RUKIA?
YES.
I SAW ...
...CHAD ON THE WAY HERE.
WHAT DID YOU ...
...SAY TO HIM?
NOTHING.
I JUST TOLD HIM TO STAY BACK AND LET ME HANDLE THIS.
PLIP
STEP BACK...
...ICHIGO.

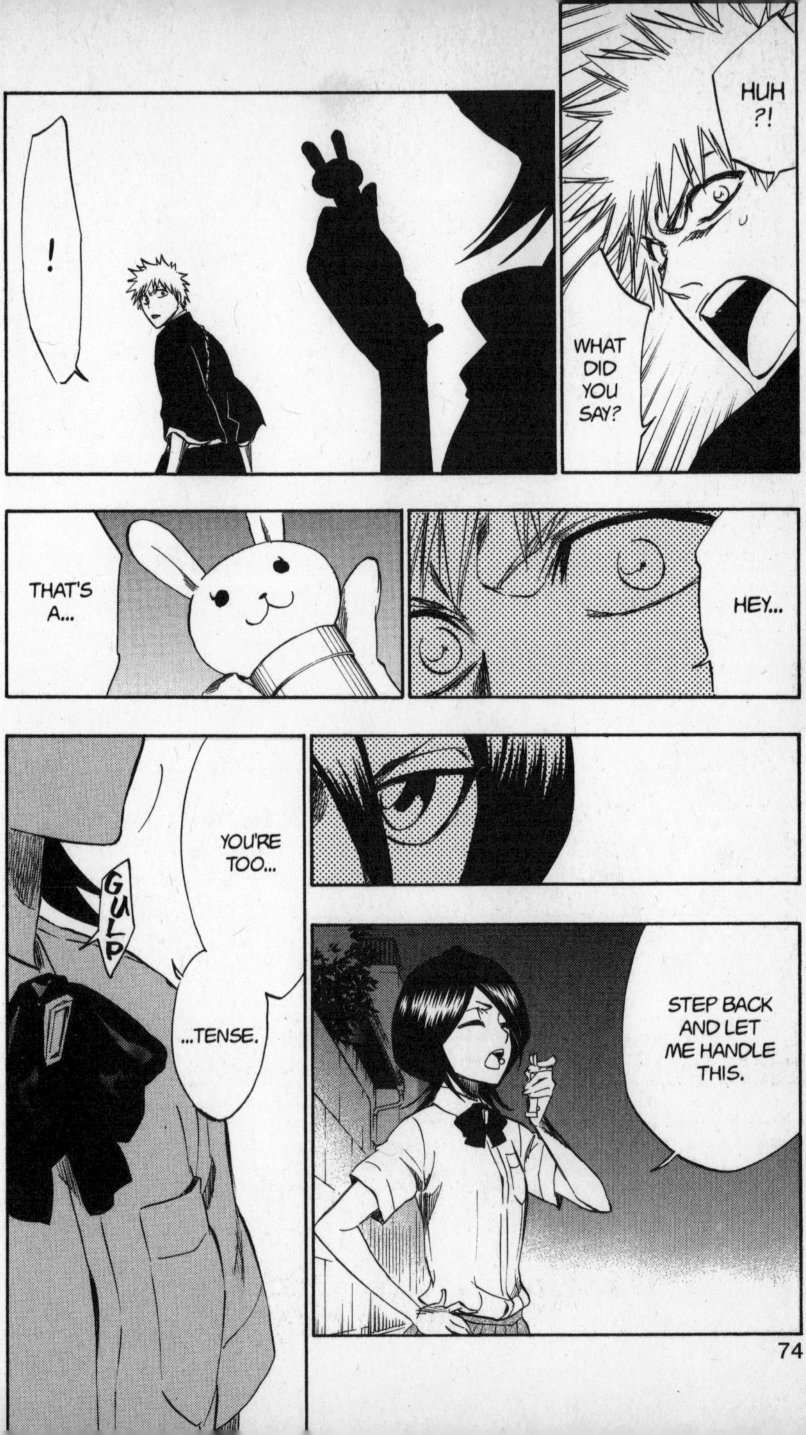
HUH ?!
WHAT DID YOU SAY?
!
HEY...
THAT'S A...
STEP BACK AND LET ME HANDLE THIS.
YOU'RE TOO...
GULP
...TENSE.

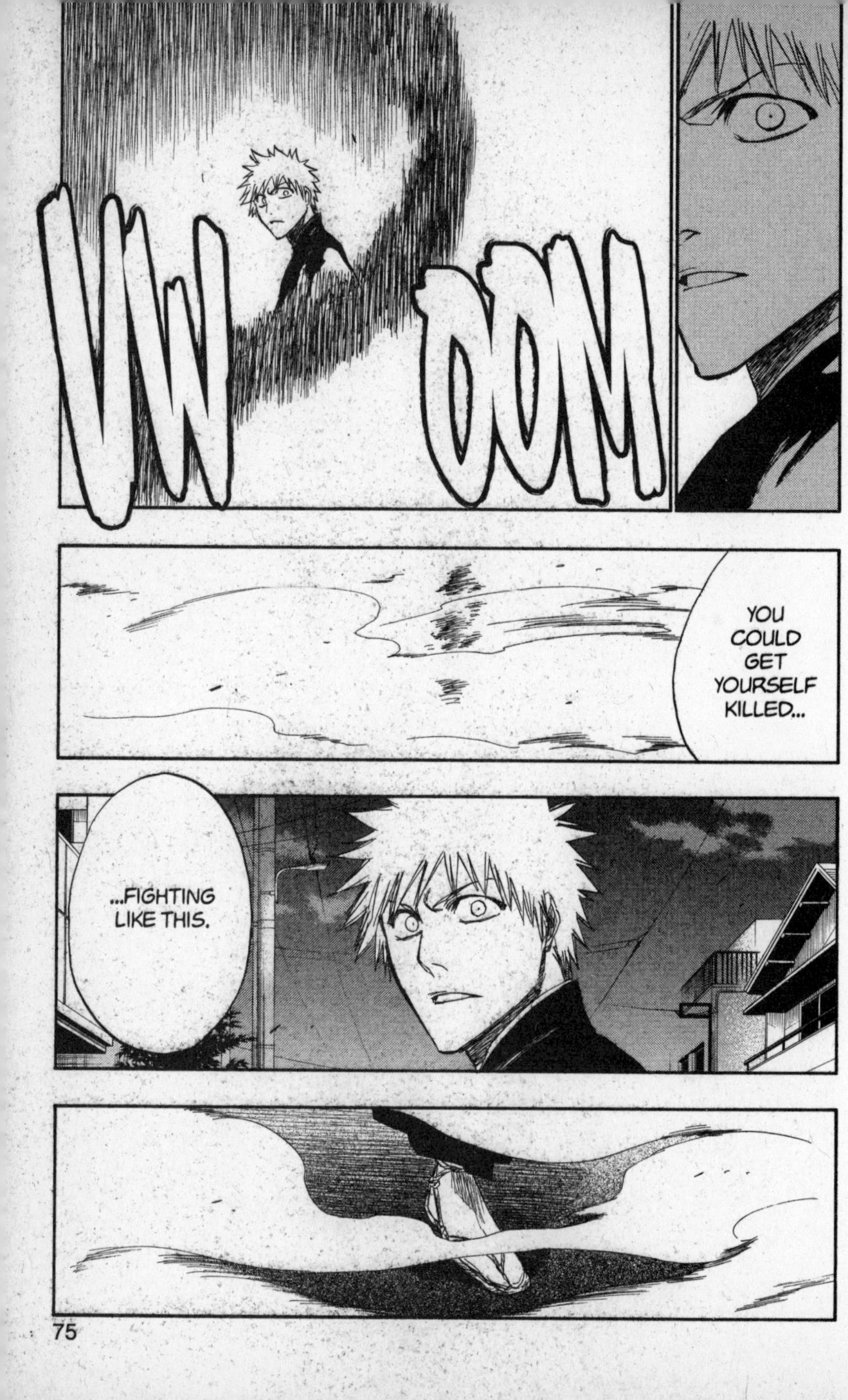
VWOOM
YOU COULD GET YOURSELF KILLED...
...FIGHTING LIKE THIS.

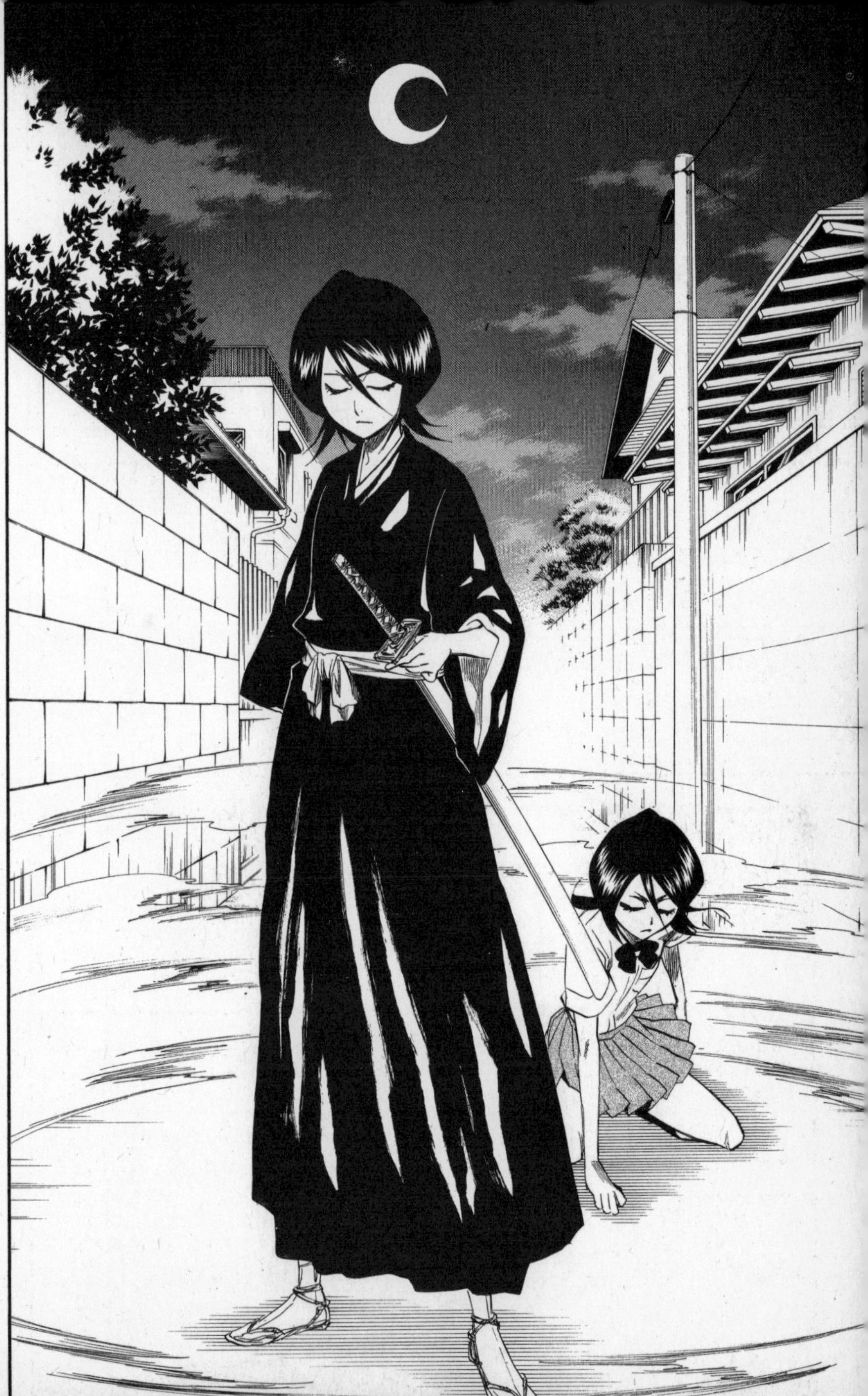

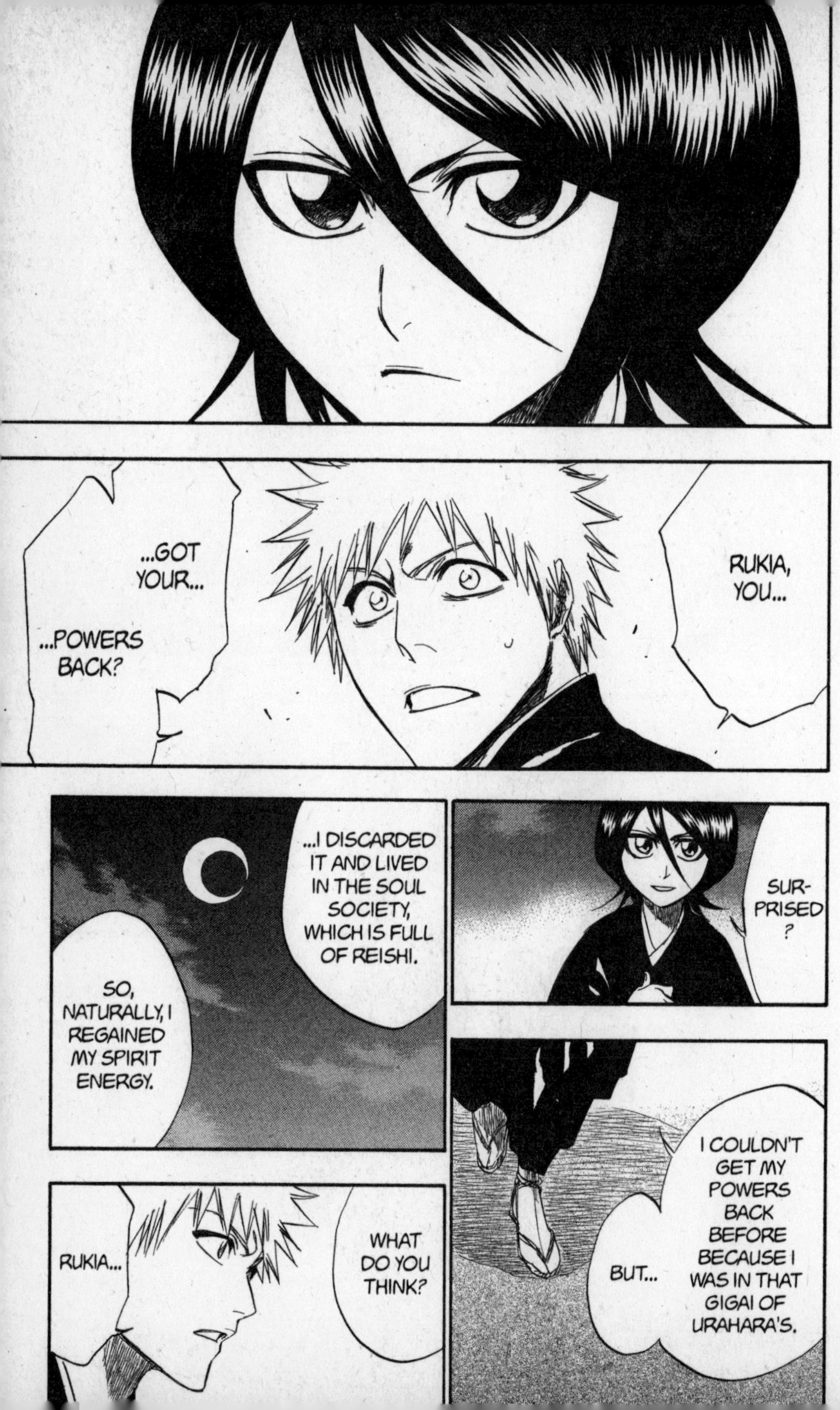
RUKIA, YOU...
...GOT YOUR...
...POWERS BACK?
SUR-PRISED?
I COULDN'T GET MY POWERS BACK BEFORE BECAUSE I WAS IN THAT GIGAI OF URAHARA'S.
BUT...
...I DISCARDED IT AND LIVED IN THE SOUL SOCIETY, WHICH IS FULL OF REISHI.
SO, NATURALLY, I REGAINED MY SPIRIT ENERGY.
WHAT DO YOU THINK?
RUKIA...

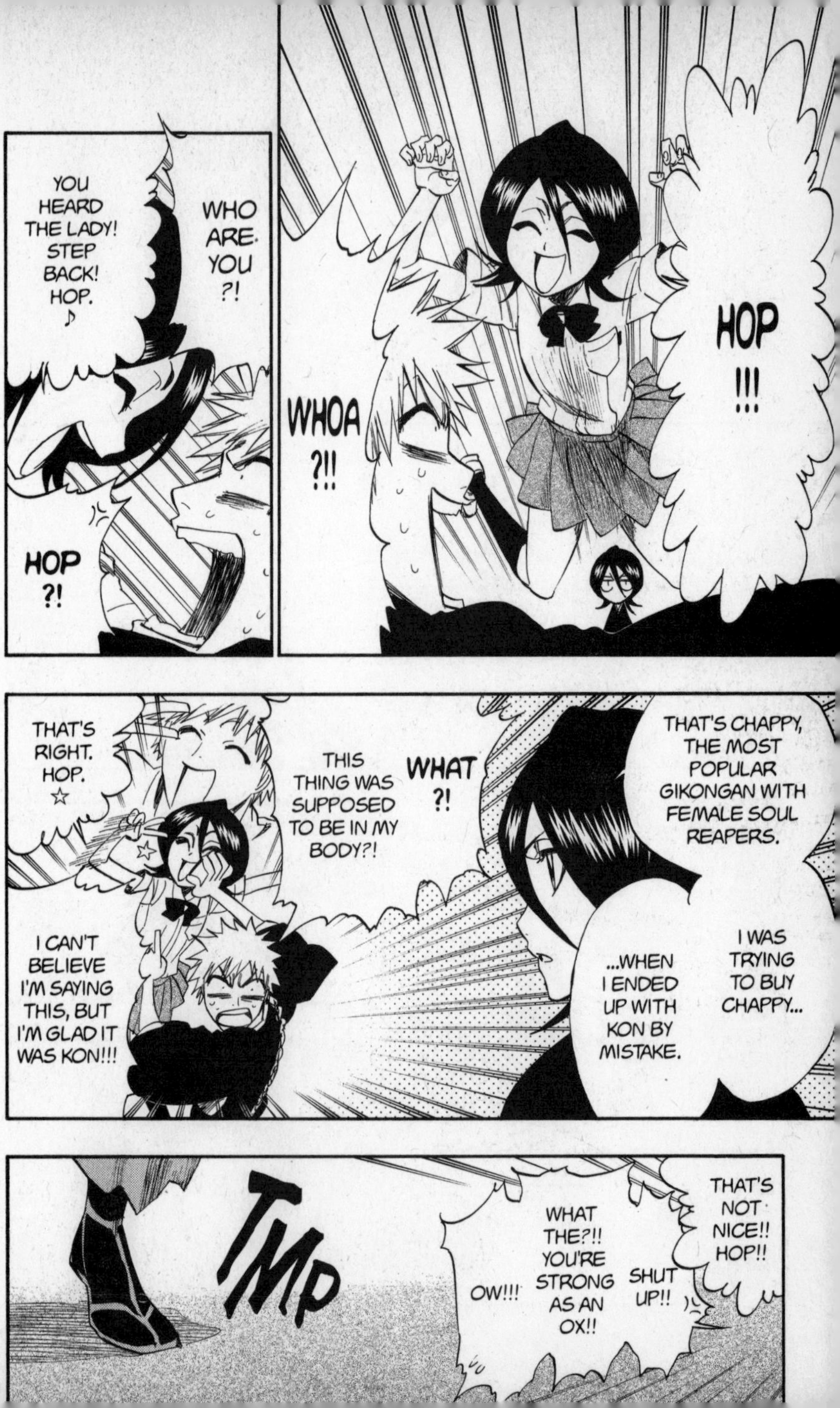
HOP !!!
WHOA ?!!
WHO ARE YOU ?!
YOU HEARD THE LADY! STEP BACK! HOP. ♪
HOP ?!
THAT'S CHAPPY, THE MOST POPULAR GIKONGAN WITH FEMALE SOUL REAPERS.
I WAS TRYING TO BUY CHAPPY...
...WHEN I ENDED UP WITH KON BY MISTAKE.
WHAT ?!
THIS THING WAS SUPPOSED TO BE IN MY BODY?!
THAT'S RIGHT. HOP. ☆
I CAN'T BELIEVE I'M SAYING THIS, BUT I'M GLAD IT WAS KON!!!
THAT'S NOT NICE!! HOP!!
SHUT UP!!
WHAT THE?!! YOU'RE STRONG AS AN OX!!
OW!!!
TMP

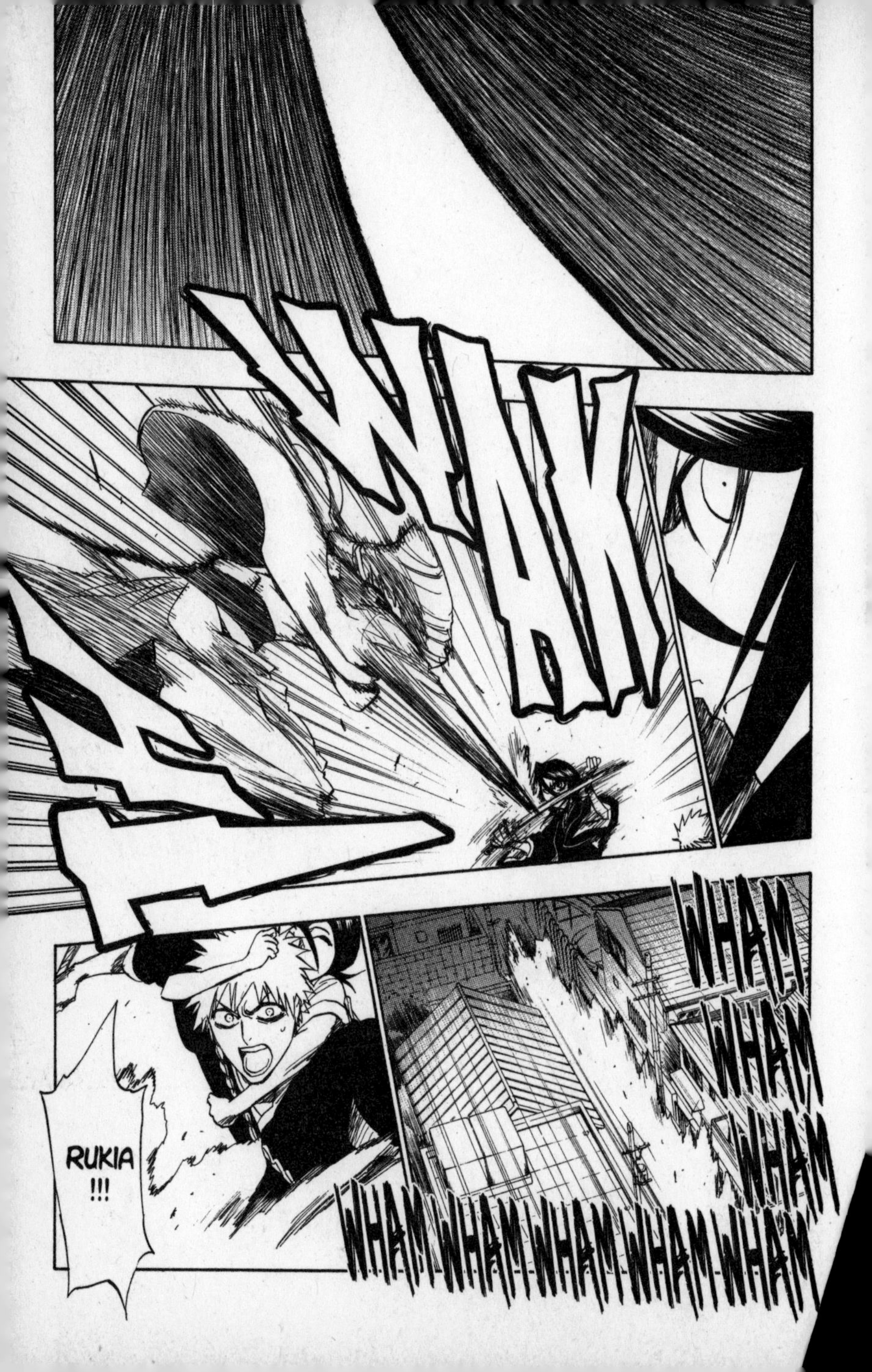
WHAK
WHAM WHAM WHAM WHAM
WHAM WHAM WHAM WHAM WHAM
RUKIA !!!

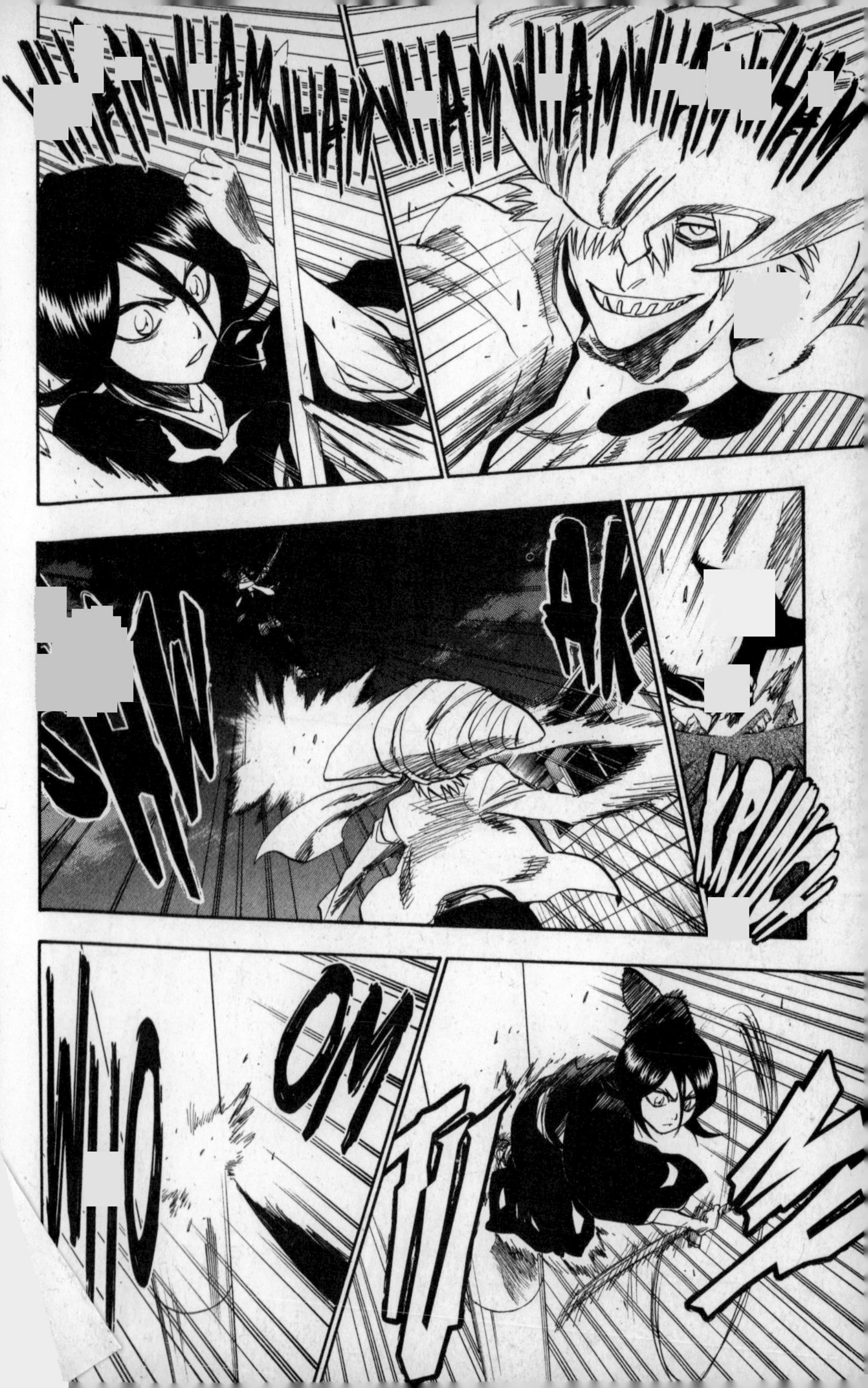
WHAM WHAM WHAM WHAM WHAM WHAM

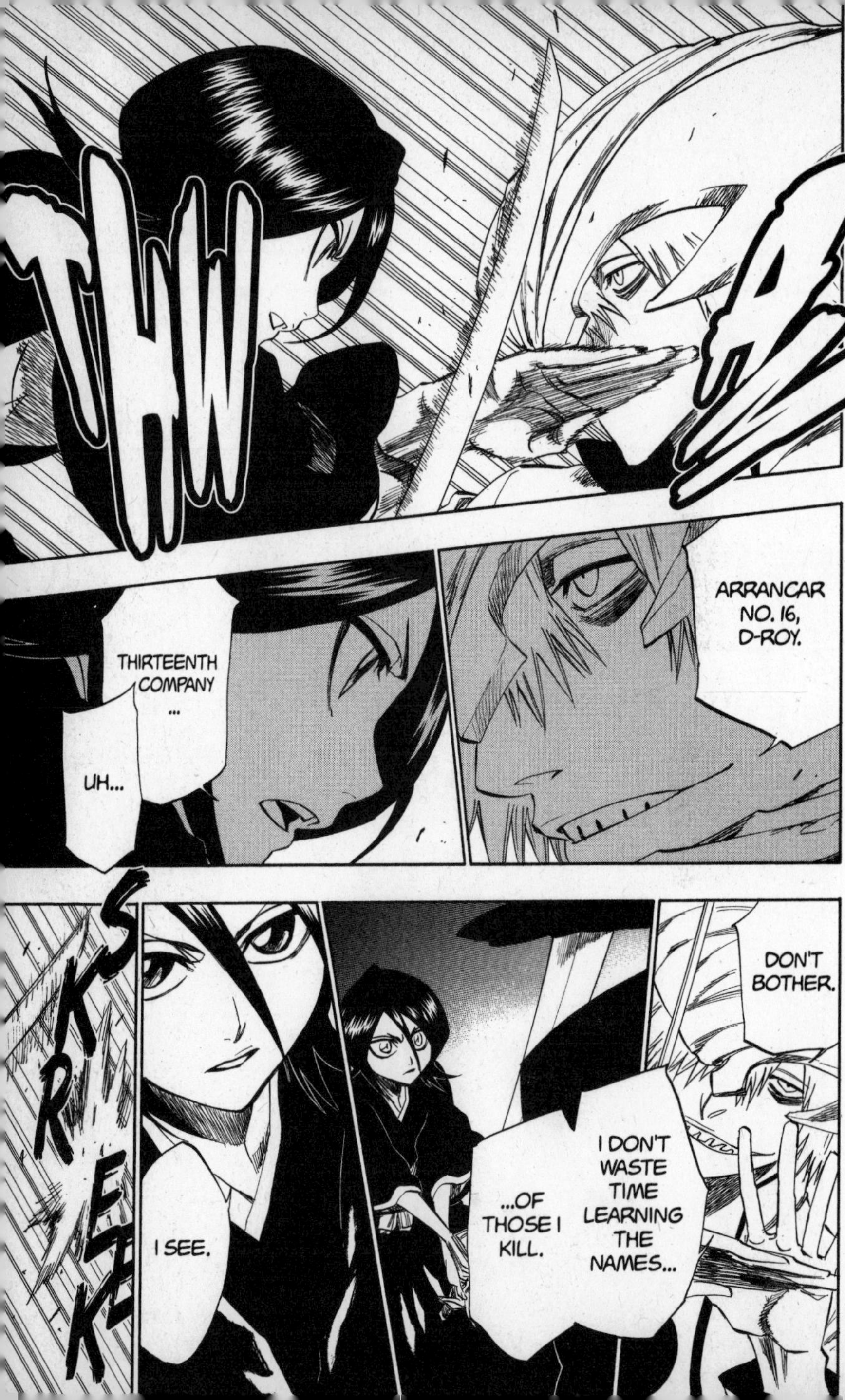
THW
ARRANCAR NO. 16, D-ROY.
THIRTEENTH COMPANY ...
UH...
DON'T BOTHER.
I DON'T WASTE TIME LEARNING THE NAMES...
...OF THOSE I KILL.
I SEE.
SKREEK

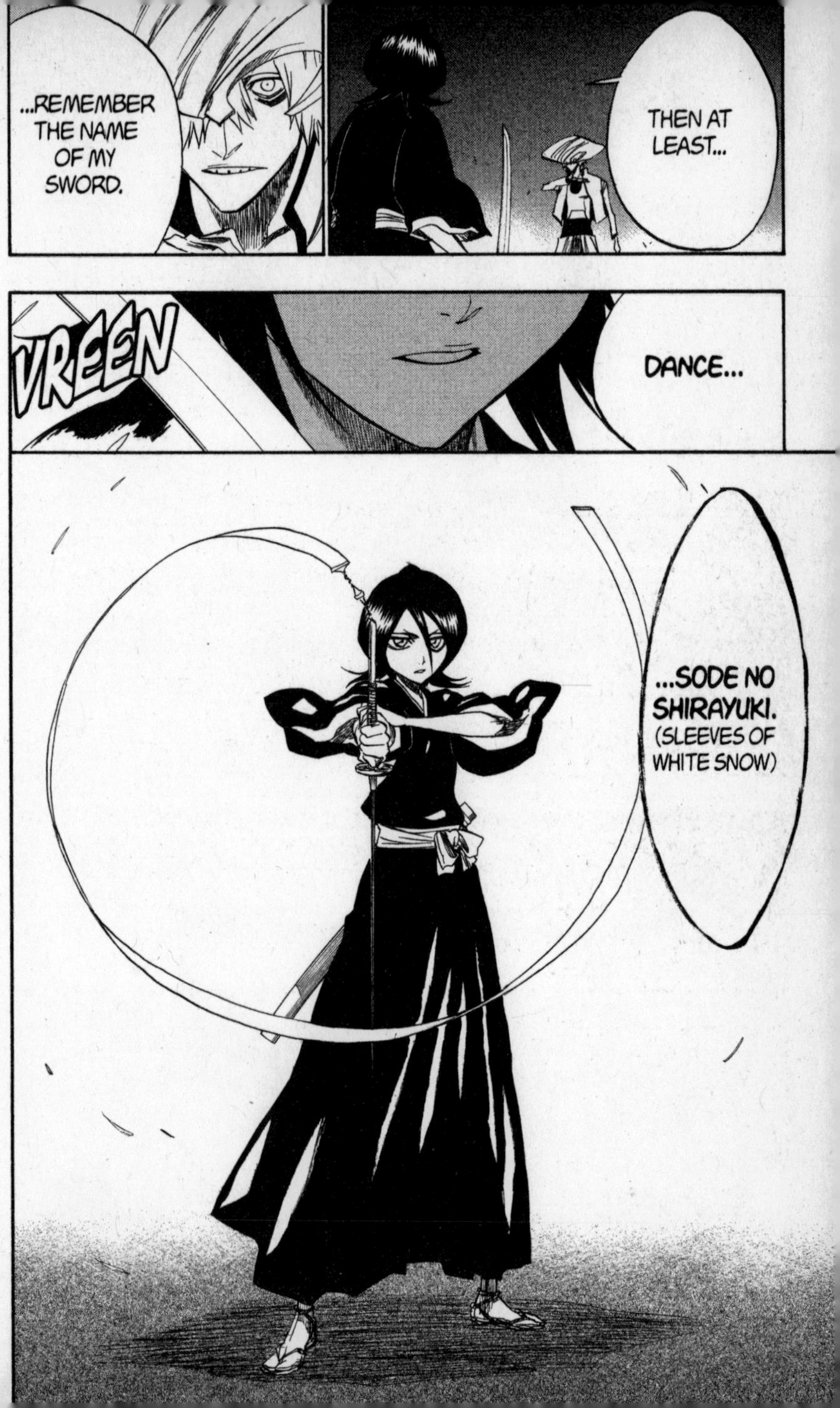
THEN AT LEAST...
...REMEMBER THE NAME OF MY SWORD.
DANCE...
VREEN
...SODE NO SHIRAYUKI.
(SLEEVES OF WHITE SNOW)

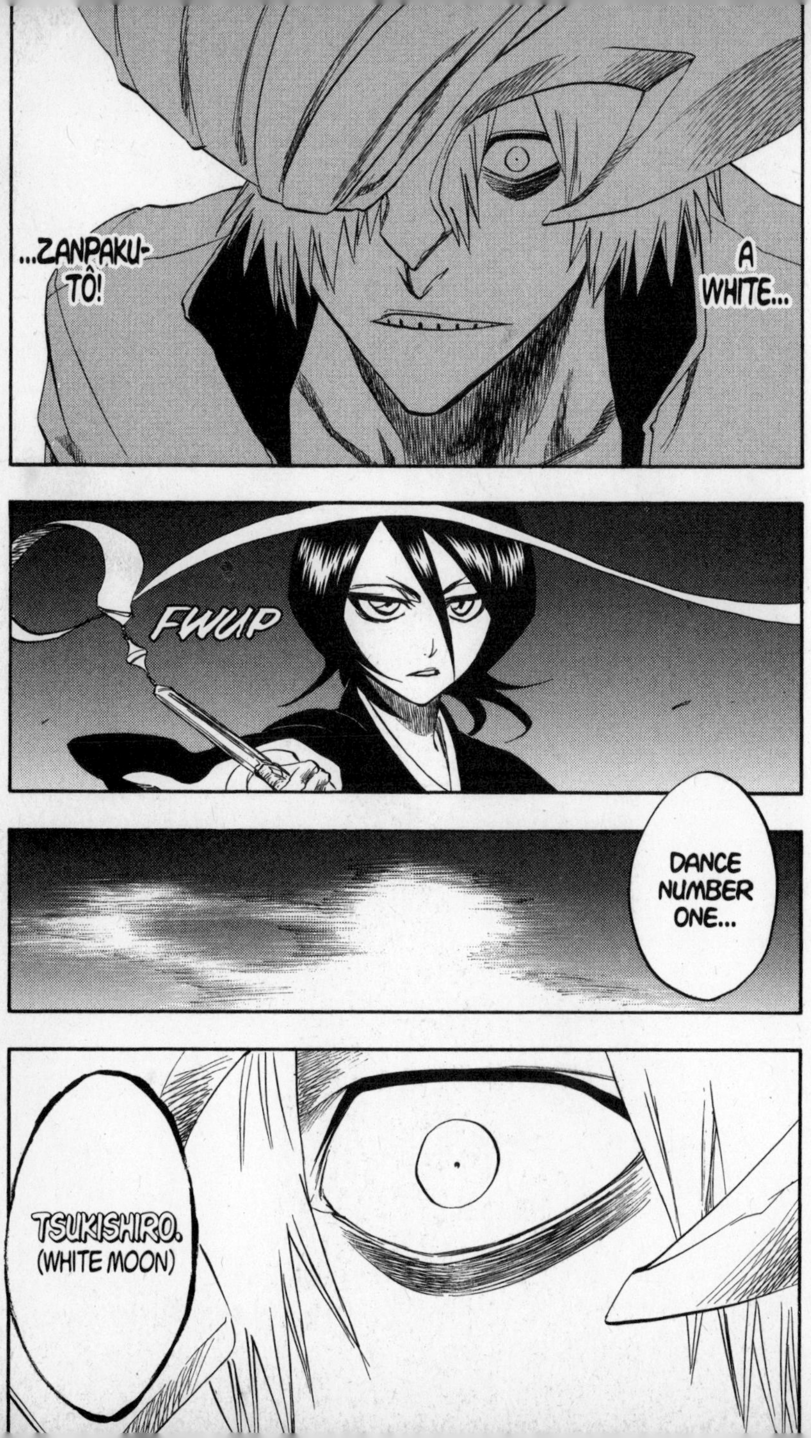
A WHITE...
...ZANPAKU-TÔ!
FWUP
DANCE NUMBER ONE...
TSUKISHIRO. (WHITE MOON)

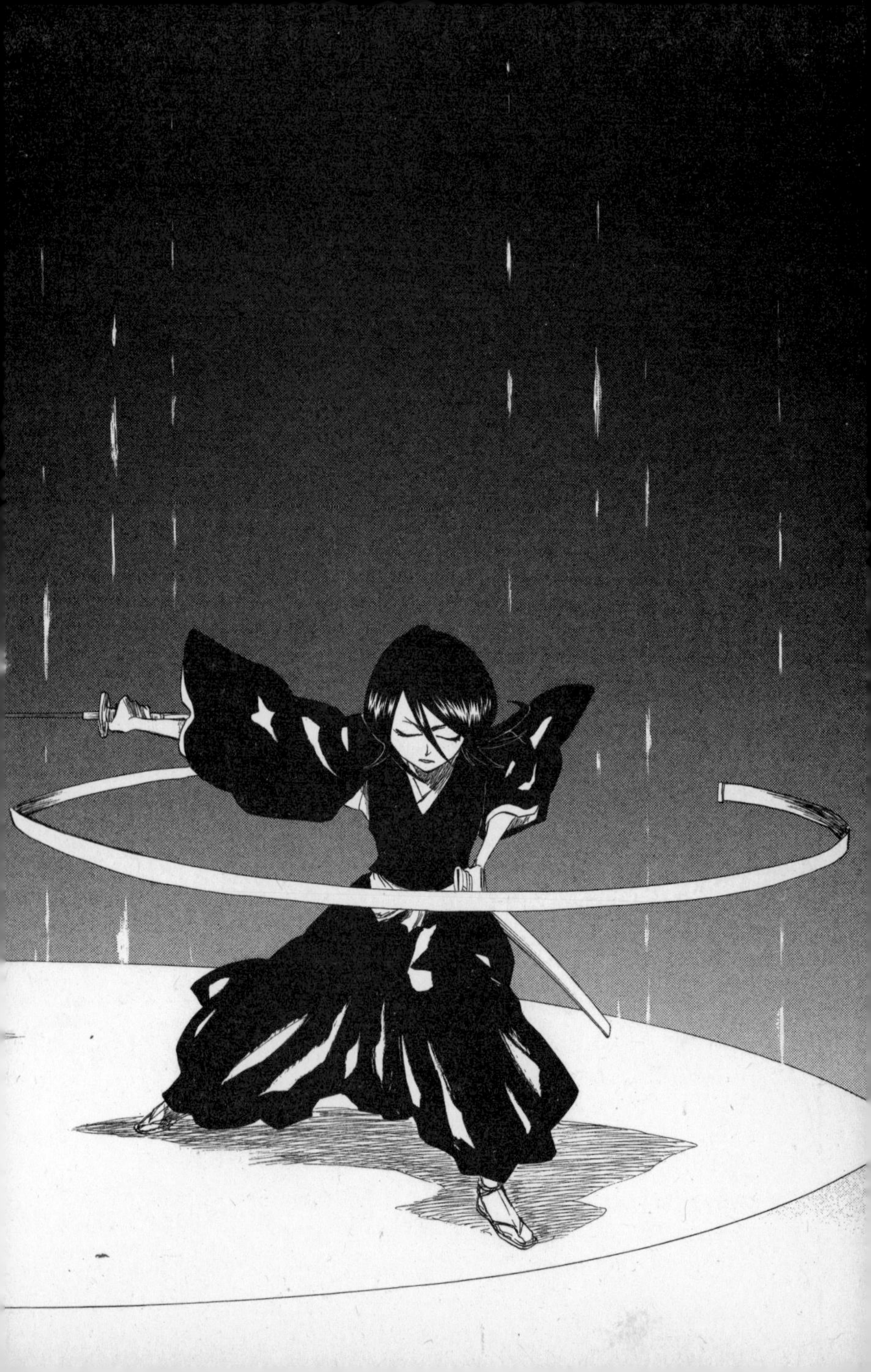

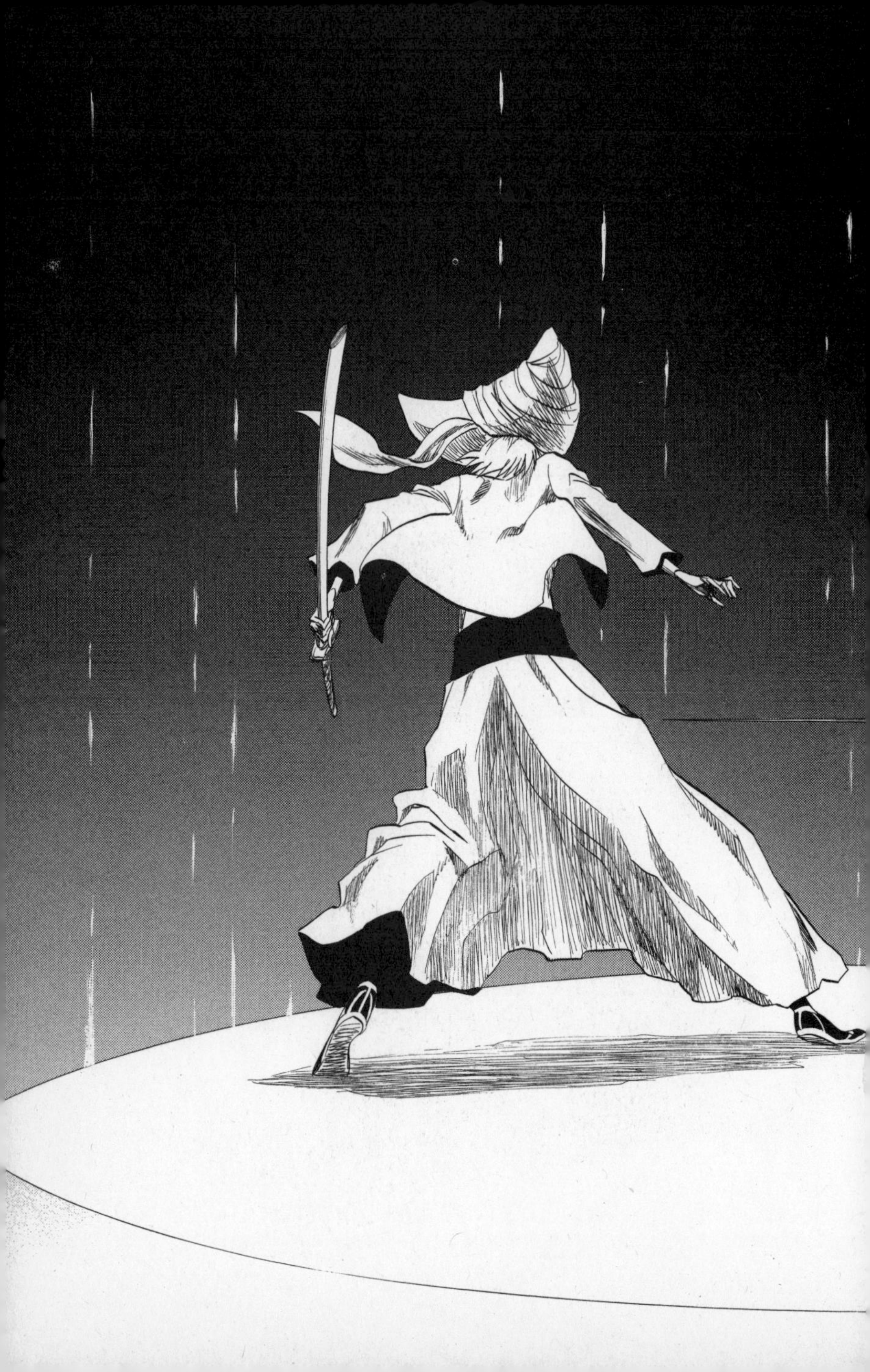

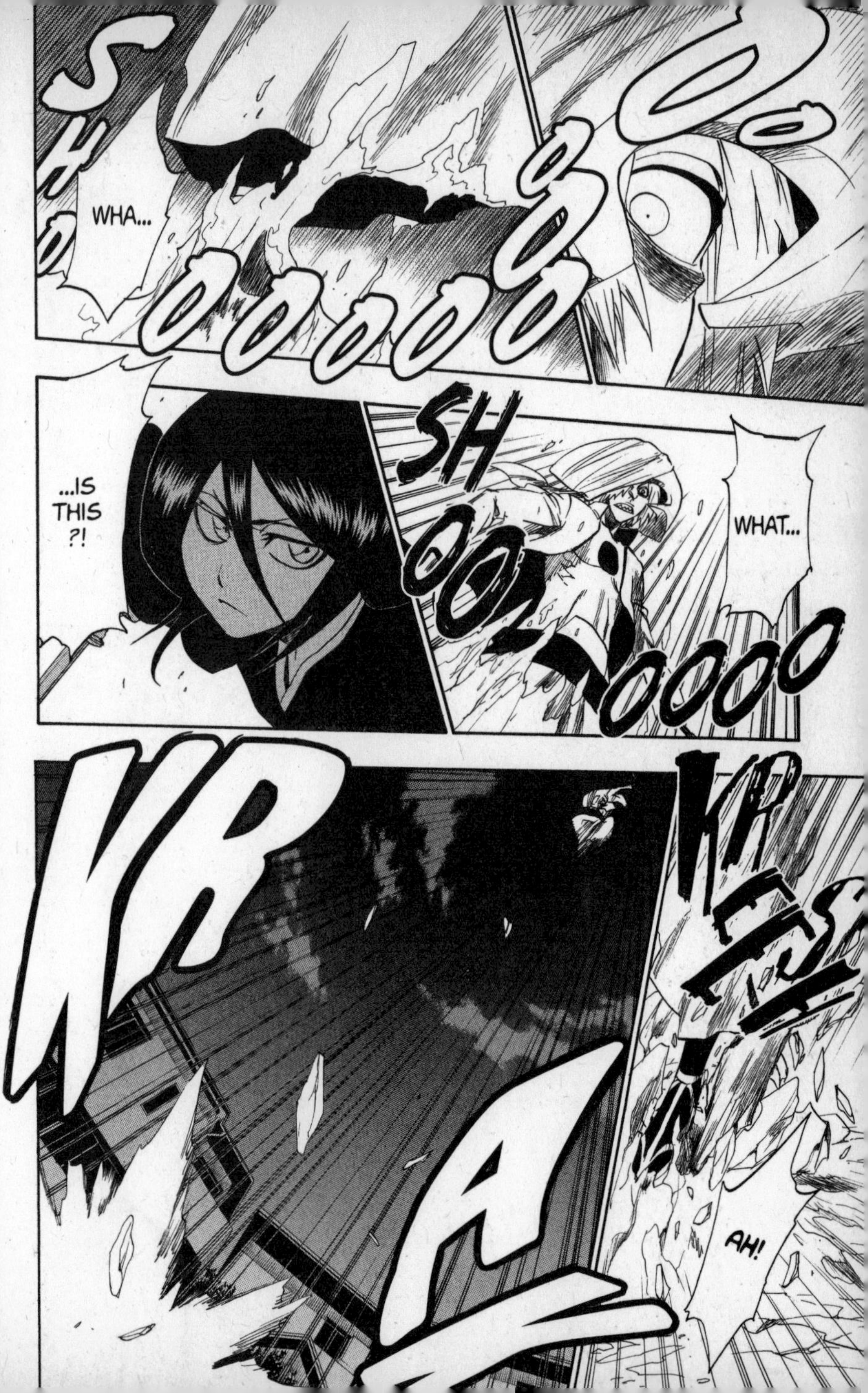
WHA...
WHAT...
...IS THIS ?!
AH!

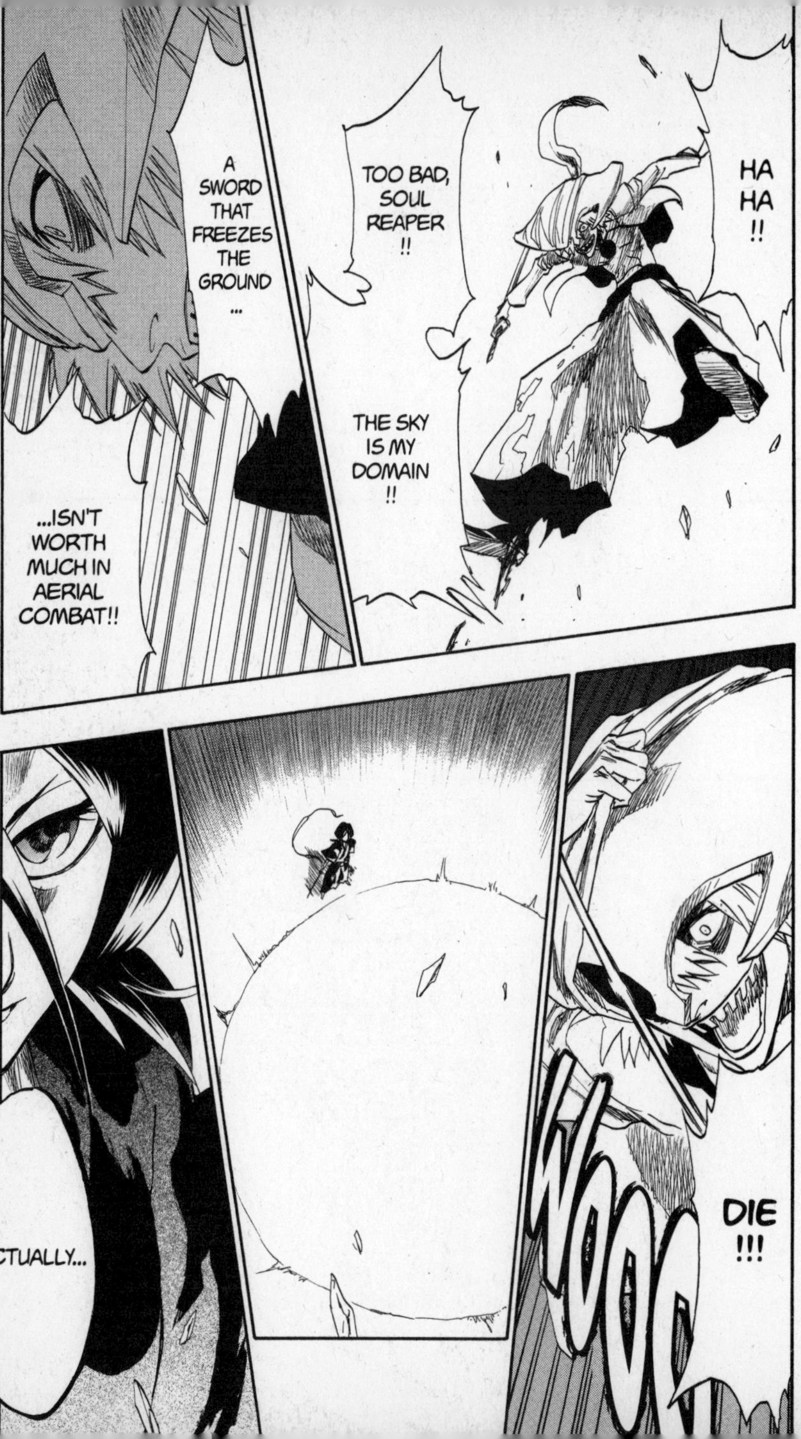
HA HA!!
TOO BAD, SOUL REAPER!!
THE SKY IS MY DOMAIN!!
A SWORD THAT FREEZES THE GROUND...
...ISN'T WORTH MUCH IN AERIAL COMBAT!!
DIE!!!
WOOO
ACTUALLY...

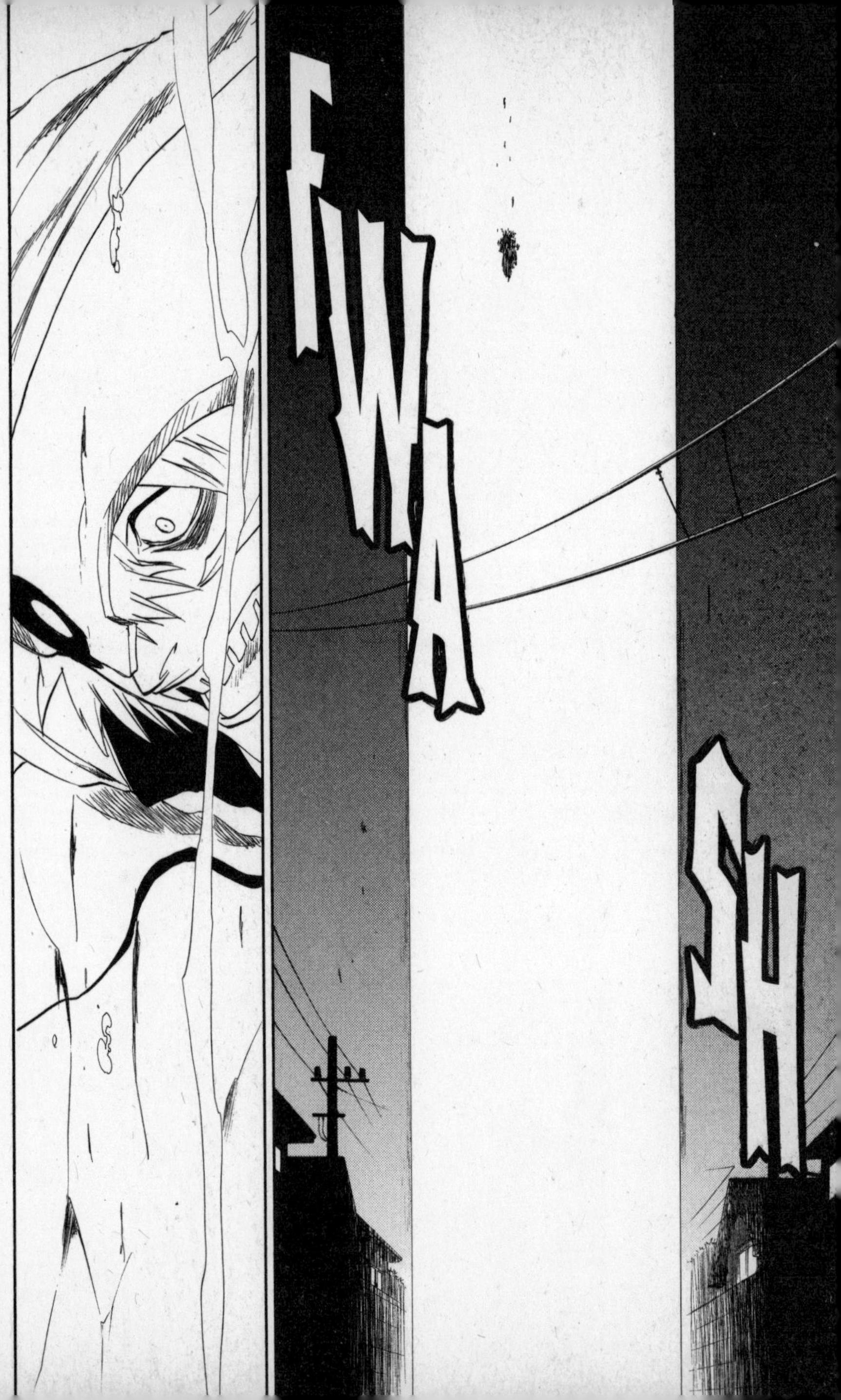
FWA
SH

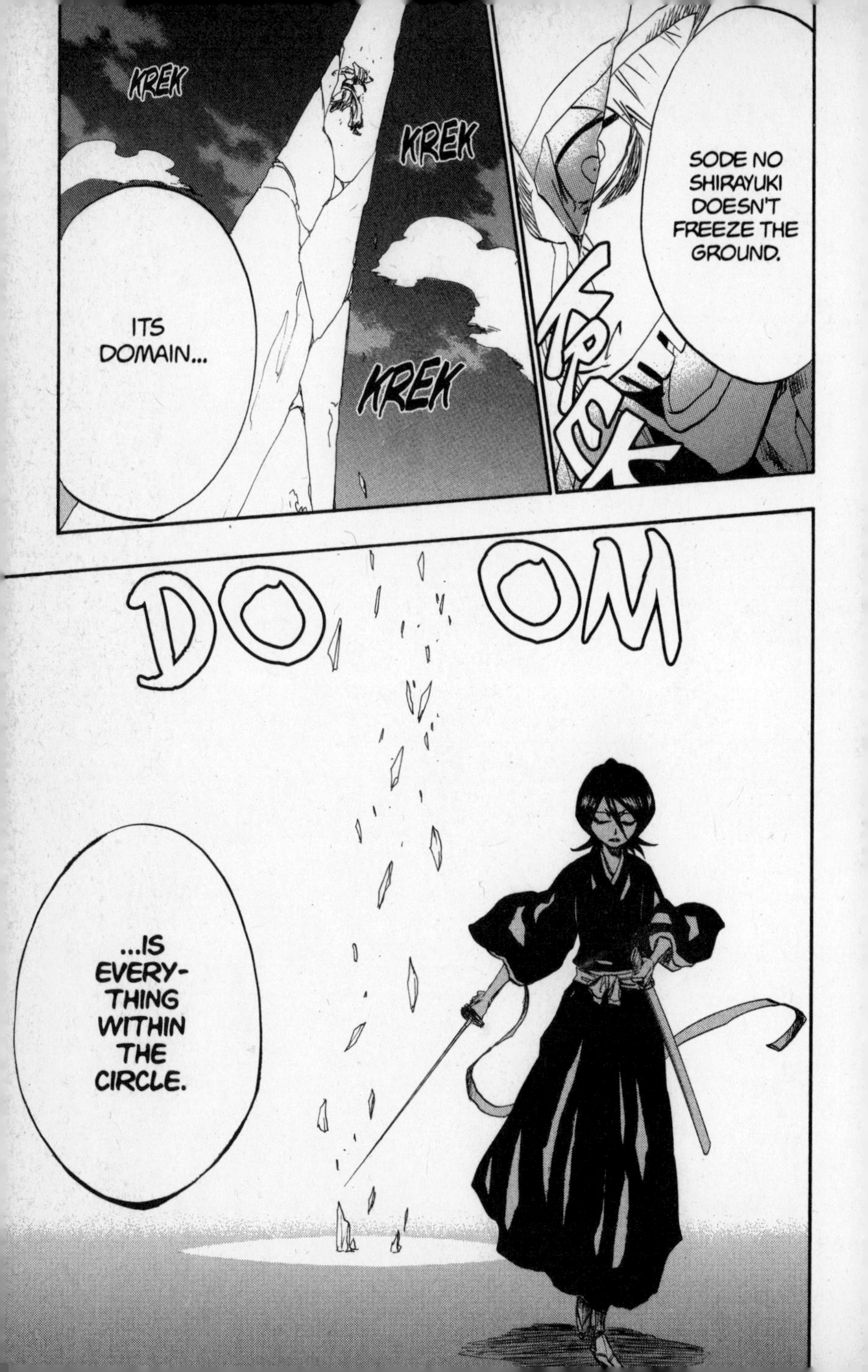
SODE NO SHIRAYUKI DOESN'T FREEZE THE GROUND.
KREK
KREK
KREK
ITS DOMAIN...
DO OM
...IS EVERY-THING WITHIN THE CIRCLE.

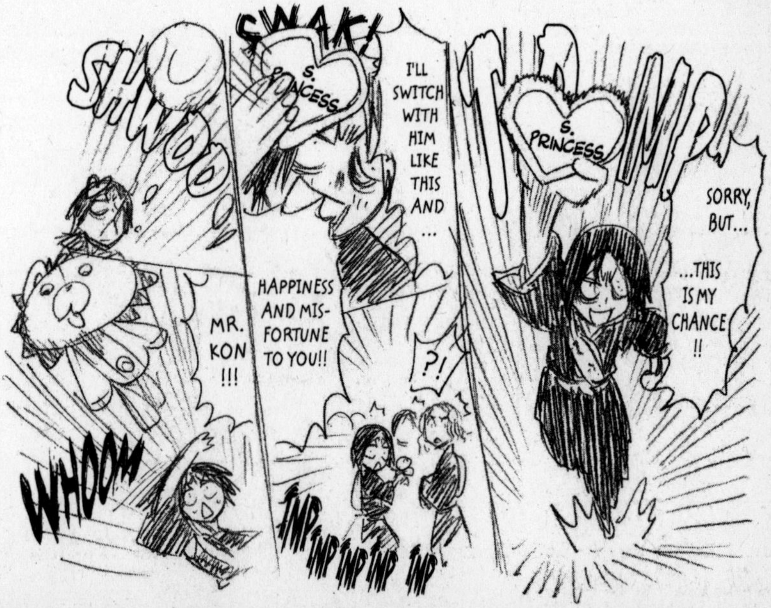
TOMP!
S. PRINCESS
SORRY, BUT...
...THIS IS MY CHANCE!!
SWAK!
S. PRINCESS
I'LL SWITCH WITH HIM LIKE THIS AND...
HAPPINESS AND MIS-FORTUNE TO YOU!!
?!
TMP TMP TMP TMP TMP
SHWOO!!
MR. KON!!!
WHOOM

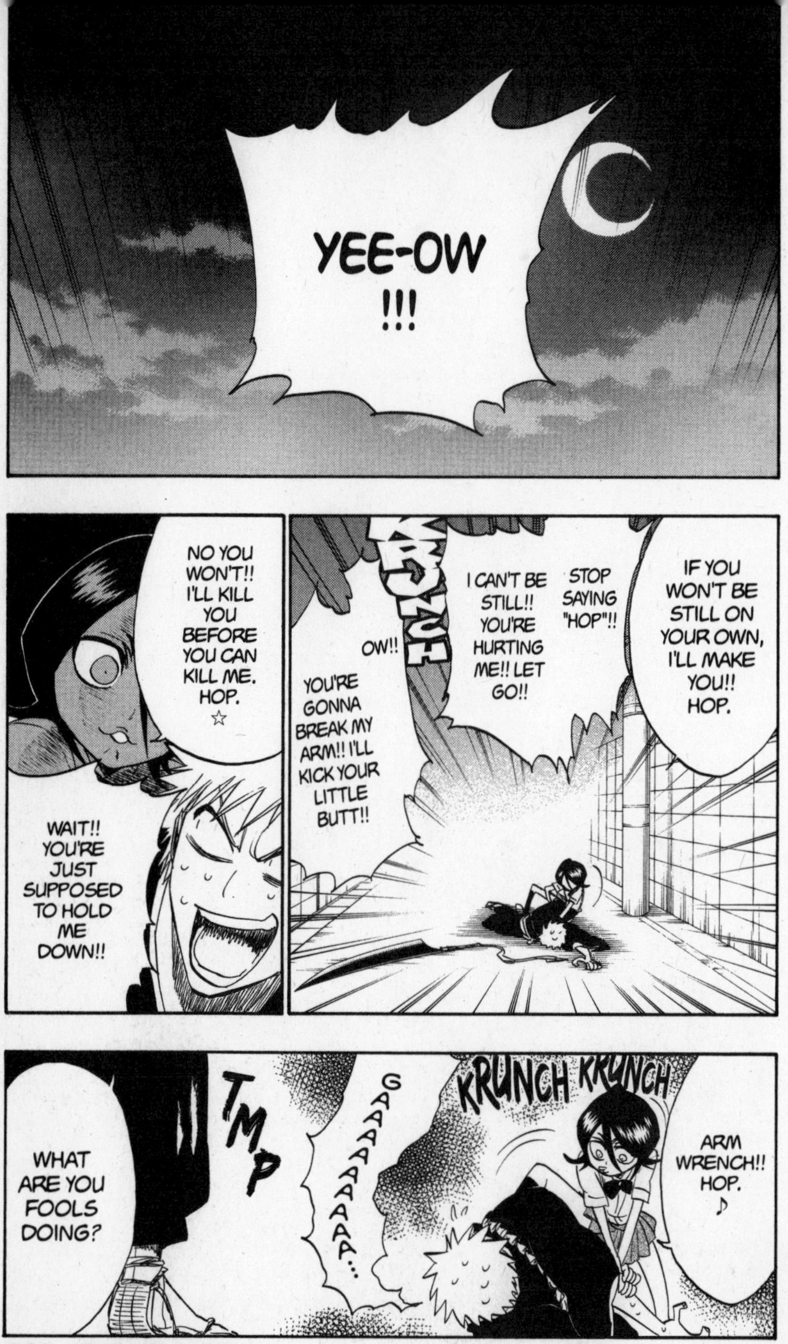
YEE-OW !!!
IF YOU WON'T BE STILL ON YOUR OWN, I'LL MAKE YOU!! HOP.
STOP SAYING "HOP"!!
I CAN'T BE STILL!! YOU'RE HURTING ME!! LET GO!!
KRUNCH
OW!!
YOU'RE GONNA BREAK MY ARM!! I'LL KICK YOUR LITTLE BUTT!!
NO YOU WON'T!! I'LL KILL YOU BEFORE YOU CAN KILL ME. HOP. ☆
WAIT!! YOU'RE JUST SUPPOSED TO HOLD ME DOWN!!
KRUNCH KRUNCH
ARM WRENCH!! HOP. ♪
GAAAAAAAAAA...
TMP
WHAT ARE YOU FOOLS DOING?

202. ¡Mala Suerte!

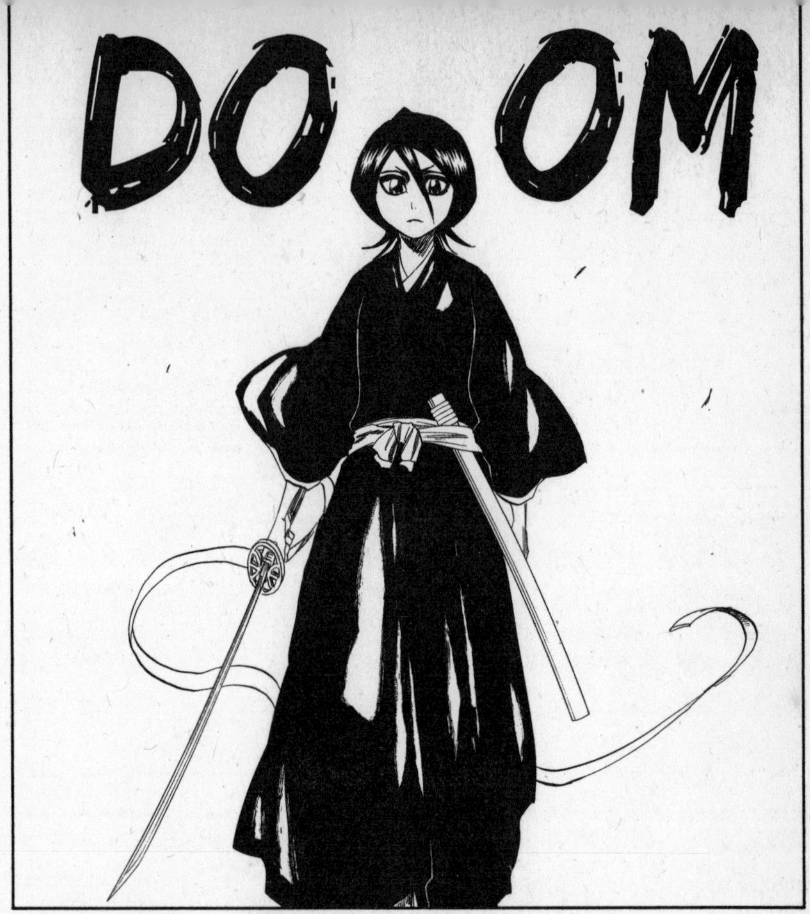
DO OM
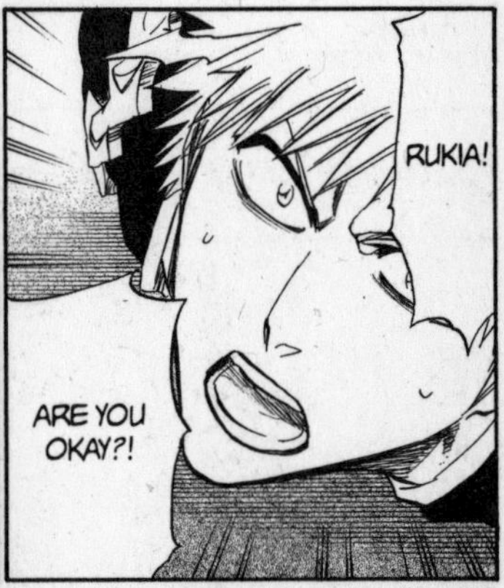
RUKIA!
ARE YOU OKAY?!
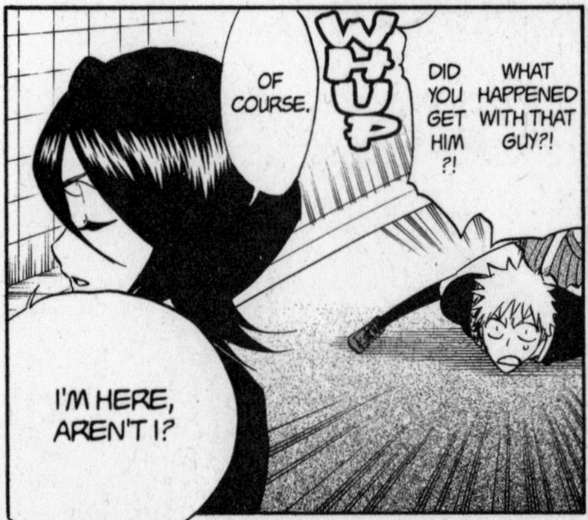
WHAT HAPPENED WITH THAT GUY?!
DID YOU GET HIM ?!
WHUP
OF COURSE.
I'M HERE, AREN'T I?

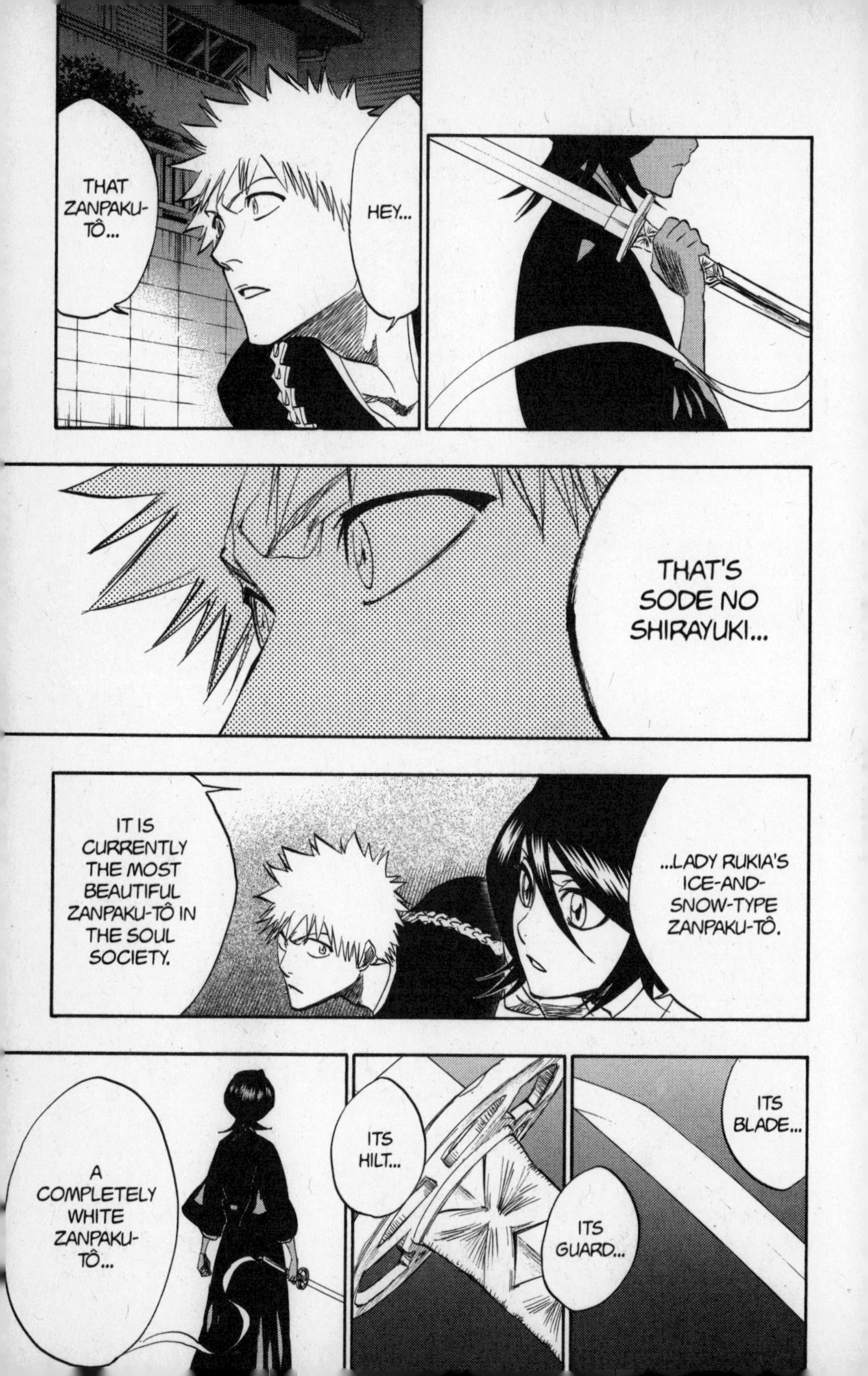
HEY...
THAT ZANPAKU-TÔ...
THAT'S SODE NO SHIRAYUKI...
...LADY RUKIA'S ICE-AND-SNOW-TYPE ZANPAKU-TÔ.
IT IS CURRENTLY THE MOST BEAUTIFUL ZANPAKU-TÔ IN THE SOUL SOCIETY.
ITS BLADE...
ITS HILT...
ITS GUARD...
A COMPLETELY WHITE ZANPAKU-TÔ...

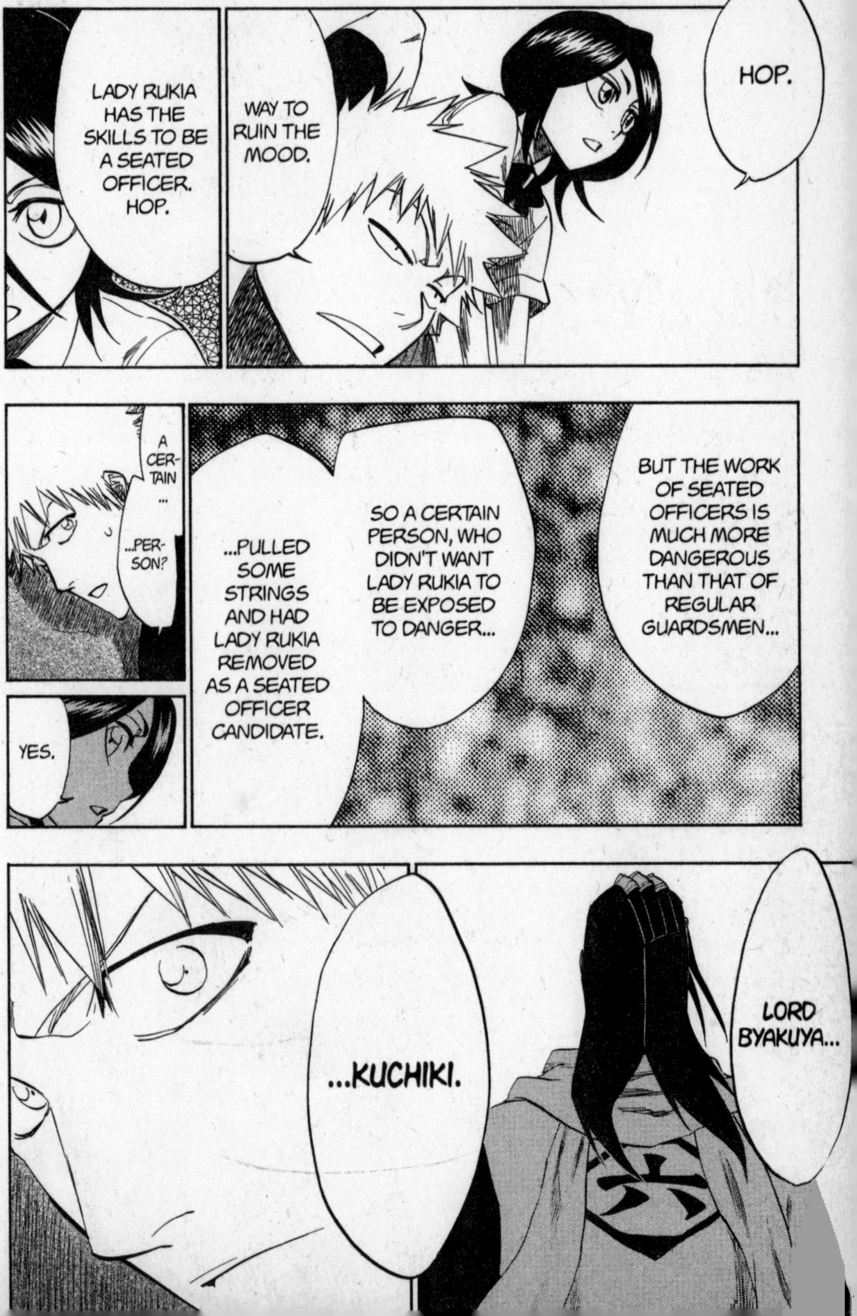
HOP.
WAY TO RUIN THE MOOD.
LADY RUKIA HAS THE SKILLS TO BE A SEATED OFFICER. HOP.
BUT THE WORK OF SEATED OFFICERS IS MUCH MORE DANGEROUS THAN THAT OF REGULAR GUARDSMEN...
SO A CERTAIN PERSON, WHO DIDN'T WANT LADY RUKIA TO BE EXPOSED TO DANGER...
...PULLED SOME STRINGS AND HAD LADY RUKIA REMOVED AS A SEATED OFFICER CANDIDATE.
A CERTAIN...
...PERSON?
YES.
LORD BYAKUYA...
...KUCHIKI.

READ THIS WAY

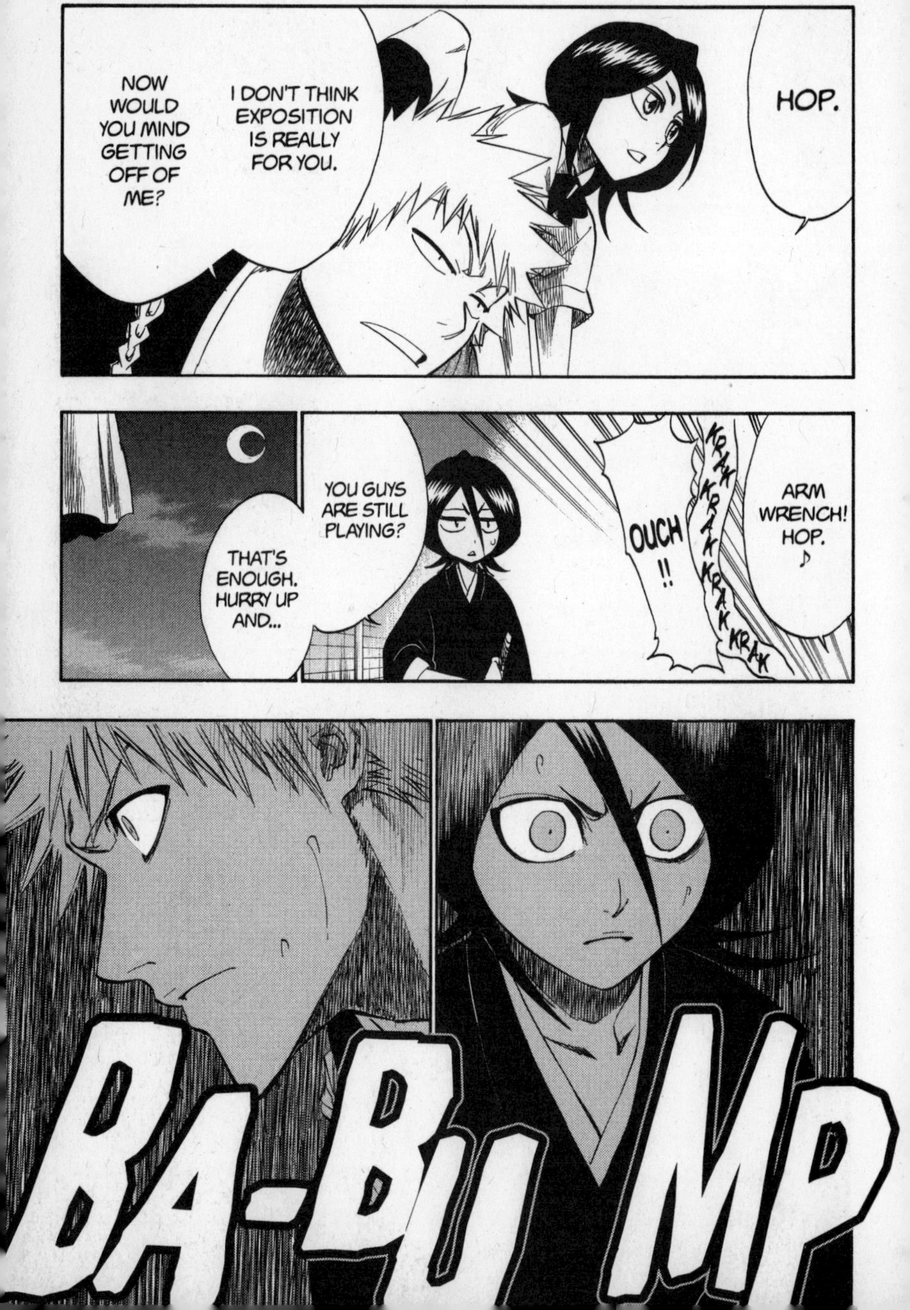
HOP.
I DON'T THINK EXPOSITION IS REALLY FOR YOU.
NOW WOULD YOU MIND GETTING OFF OF ME?
ARM WRENCH! HOP. ♪
KRAK KRAK KRAK KRAK KRAK KRAK
OUCH!!
YOU GUYS ARE STILL PLAYING?
THAT'S ENOUGH. HURRY UP AND...
BA-BUMP

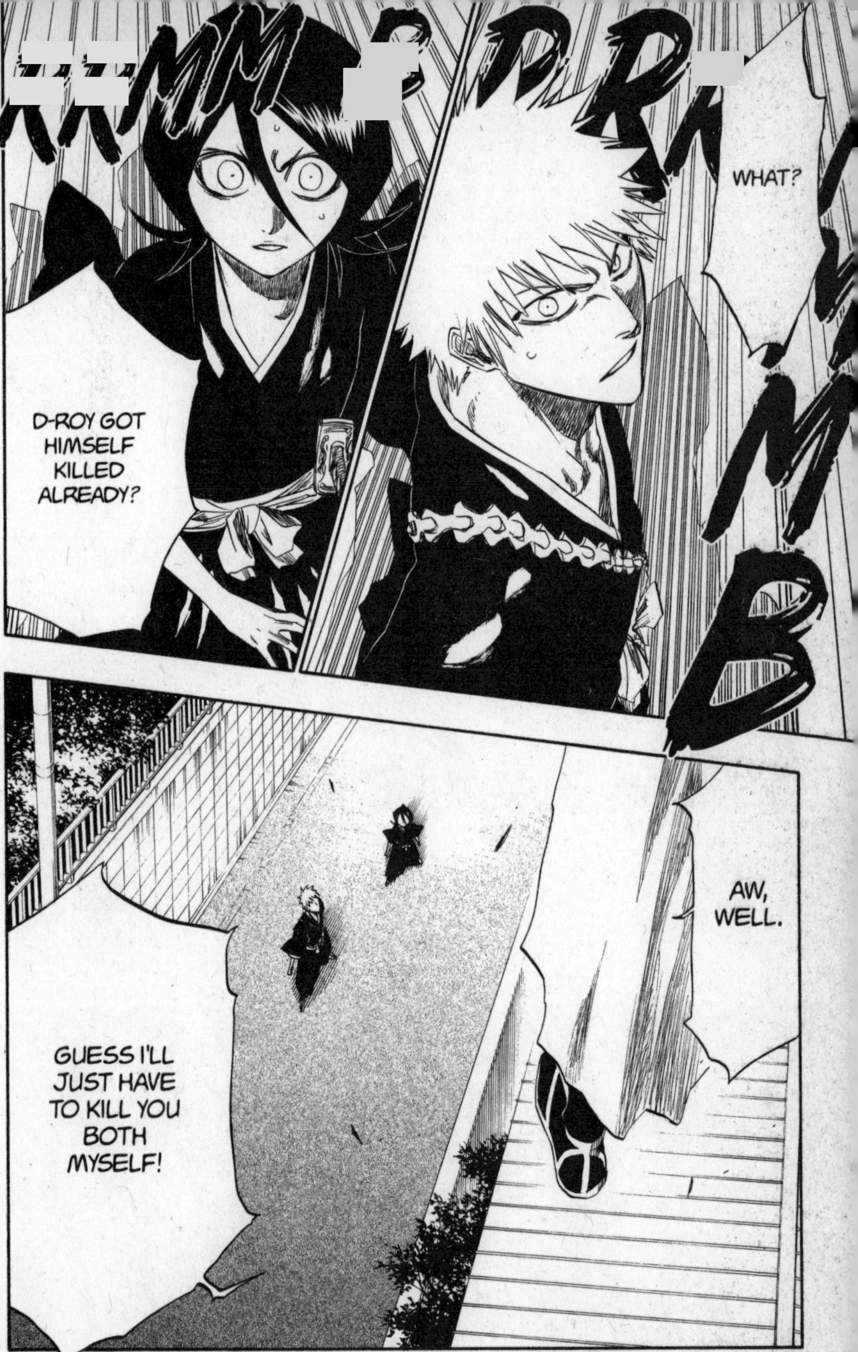
WHAT?
D-ROY GOT HIMSELF KILLED ALREADY?
AW, WELL.
GUESS I'LL JUST HAVE TO KILL YOU BOTH MYSELF!

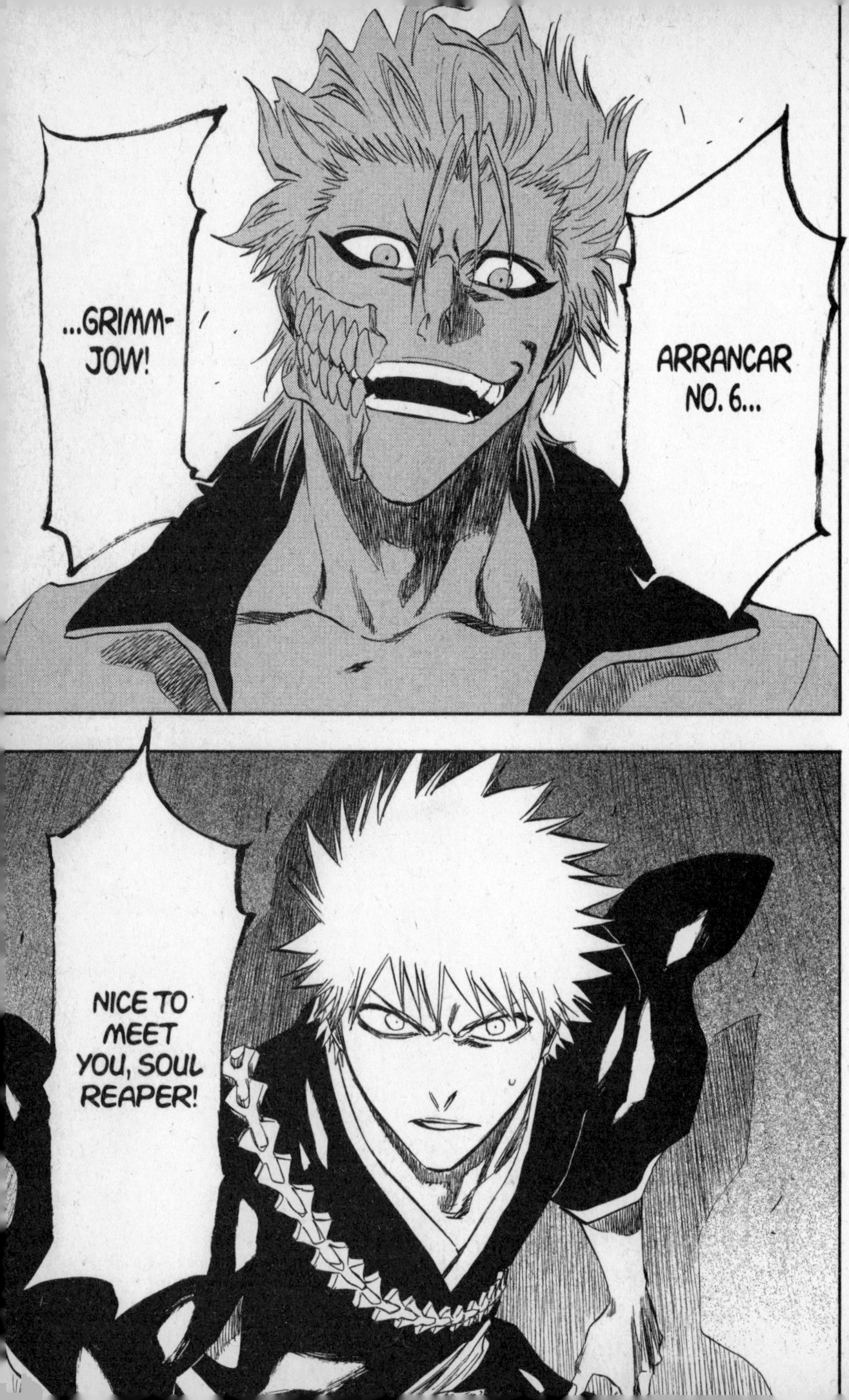
ARRANCAR NO. 6...
...GRIMM-JOW!
NICE TO MEET YOU, SOUL REAPER!

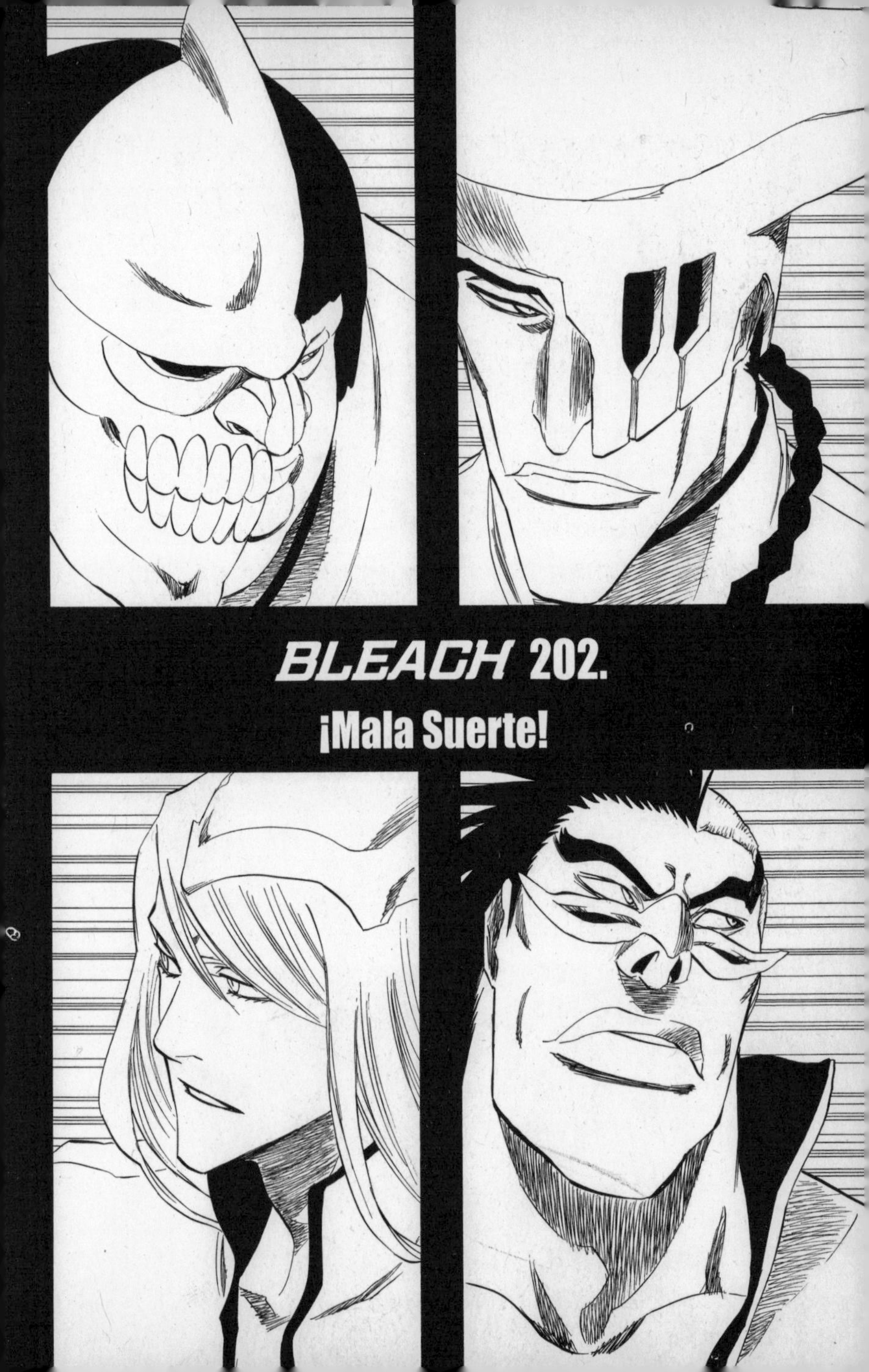
BLEACH 202.
¡Mala Suerte!

READ THIS WAY

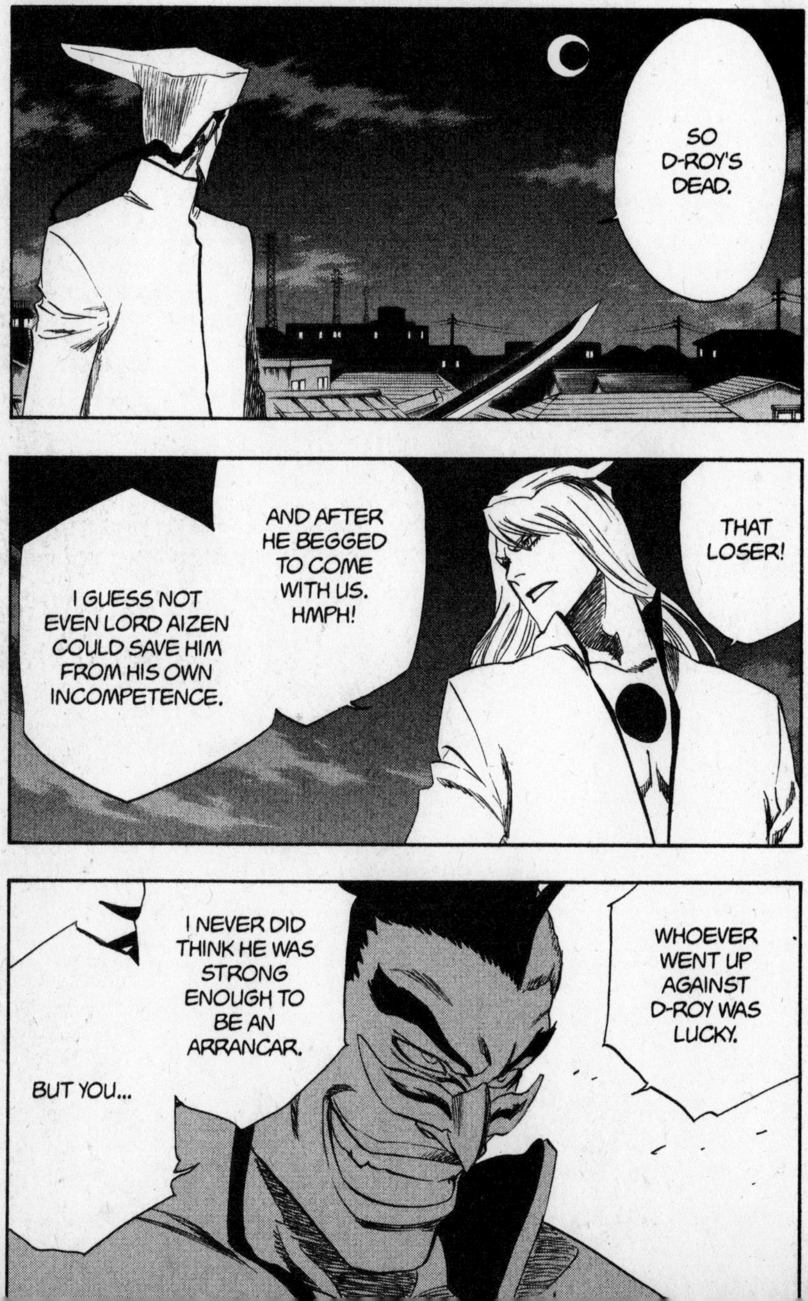
SO D-ROY'S DEAD.
THAT LOSER!
AND AFTER HE BEGGED TO COME WITH US. HMPH!
I GUESS NOT EVEN LORD AIZEN COULD SAVE HIM FROM HIS OWN INCOMPETENCE.
WHOEVER WENT UP AGAINST D-ROY WAS LUCKY.
I NEVER DID THINK HE WAS STRONG ENOUGH TO BE AN ARRANCAR.
BUT YOU...

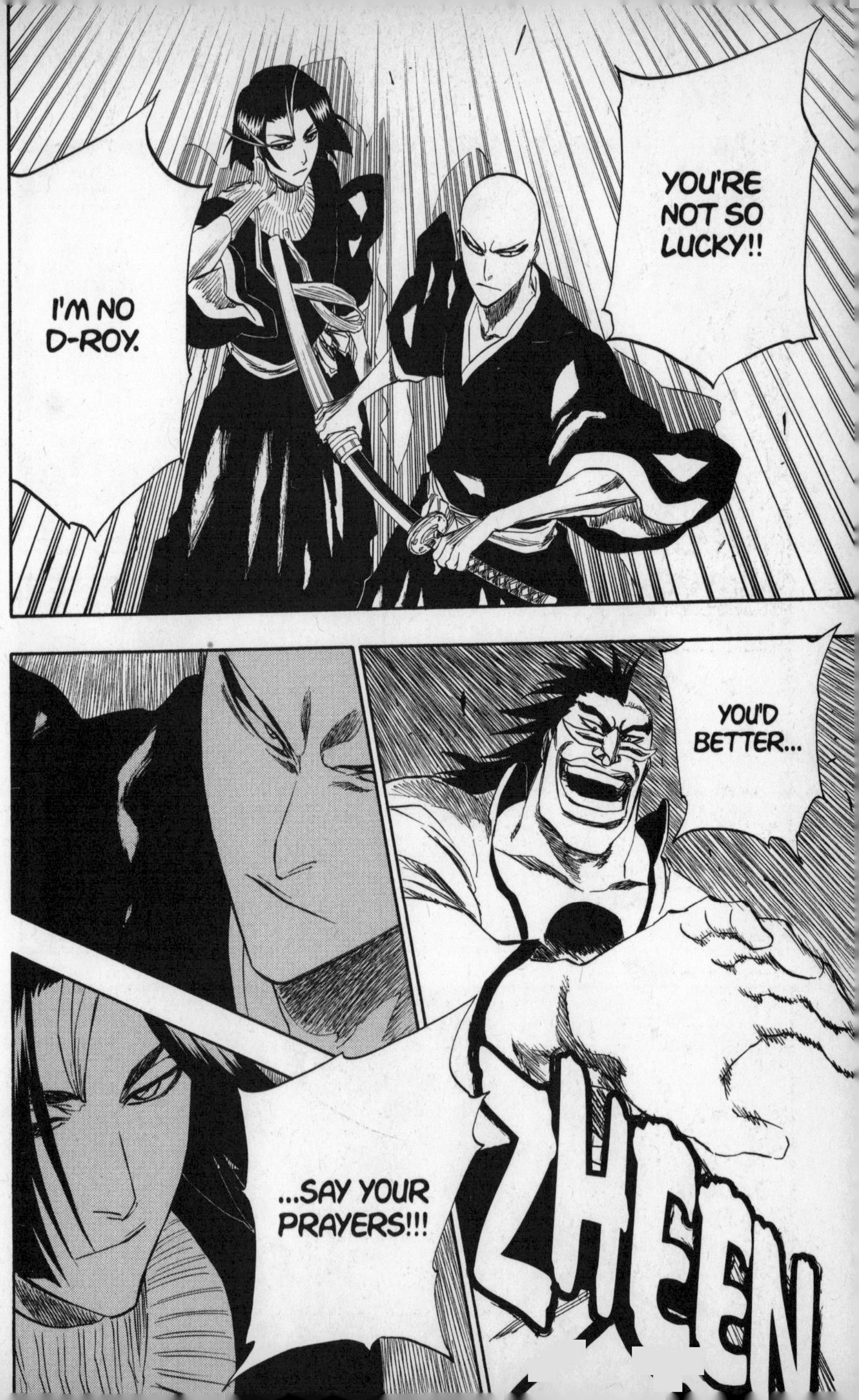
YOU'RE NOT SO LUCKY!!
I'M NO D-ROY.
YOU'D BETTER...
...SAY YOUR PRAYERS!!!

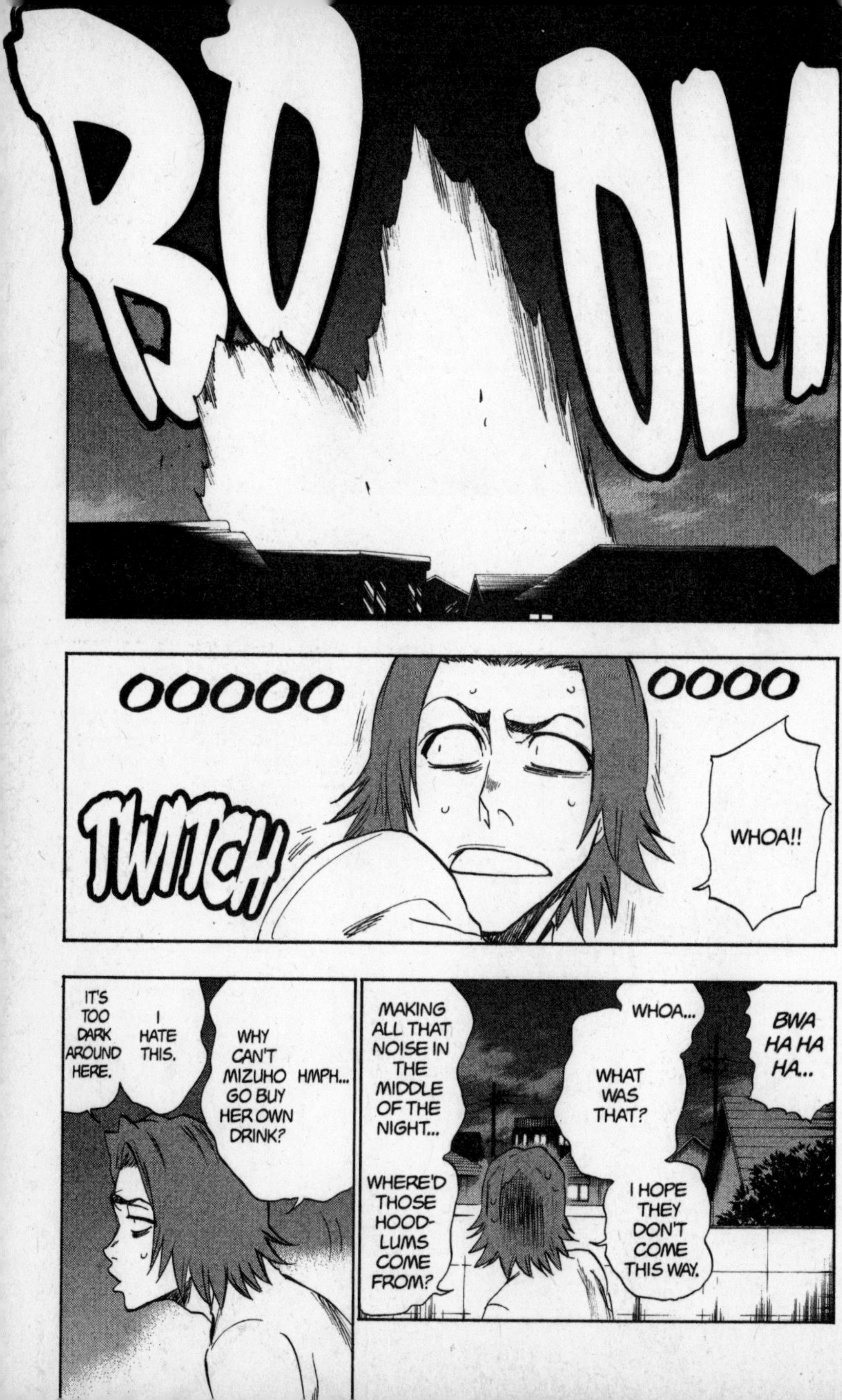
BOOM
OOOOO OOOO
WHOA!!
TWITCH
BWA HA HA HA...
WHOA...
WHAT WAS THAT?
MAKING ALL THAT NOISE IN THE MIDDLE OF THE NIGHT...
I HOPE THEY DON'T COME THIS WAY.
WHERE'D THOSE HOODLUMS COME FROM?
HMPH...
WHY CAN'T MIZUHO GO BUY HER OWN DRINK?
I HATE THIS.
IT'S TOO DARK AROUND HERE.

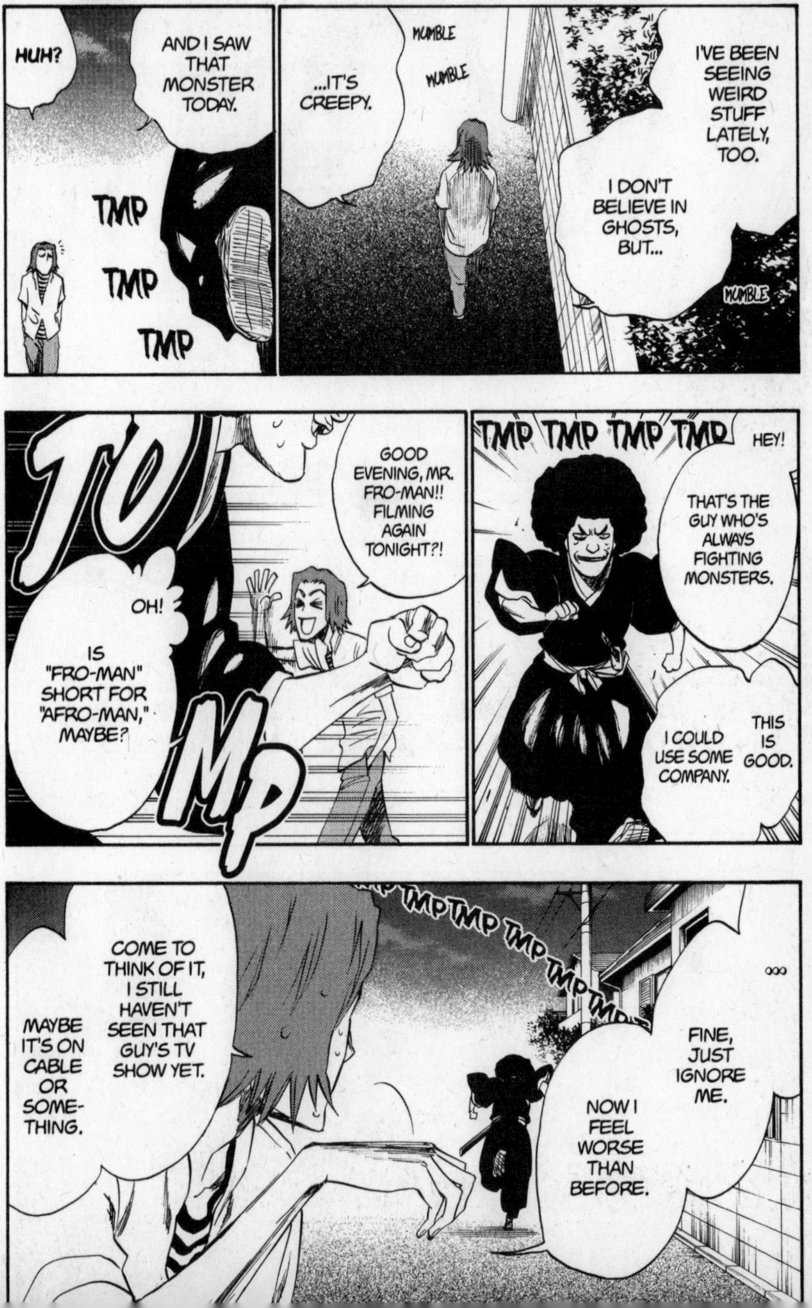
I'VE BEEN SEEING WEIRD STUFF LATELY, TOO.
I DON'T BELIEVE IN GHOSTS, BUT...
MUMBLE
MUMBLE
MUMBLE
...IT'S CREEPY.
AND I SAW THAT MONSTER TODAY.
HUH?
TMP
TMP
TMP
TMP TMP TMP TMP
HEY!
THAT'S THE GUY WHO'S ALWAYS FIGHTING MONSTERS.
THIS IS GOOD.
I COULD USE SOME COMPANY.
GOOD EVENING, MR. FRO-MAN!! FILMING AGAIN TONIGHT?!
TOMP
OH!
IS "FRO-MAN" SHORT FOR "AFRO-MAN," MAYBE?
...
FINE, JUST IGNORE ME.
NOW I FEEL WORSE THAN BEFORE.
TMP TMP TMP TMP TMP
COME TO THINK OF IT, I STILL HAVEN'T SEEN THAT GUY'S TV SHOW YET.
MAYBE IT'S ON CABLE OR SOME-THING.

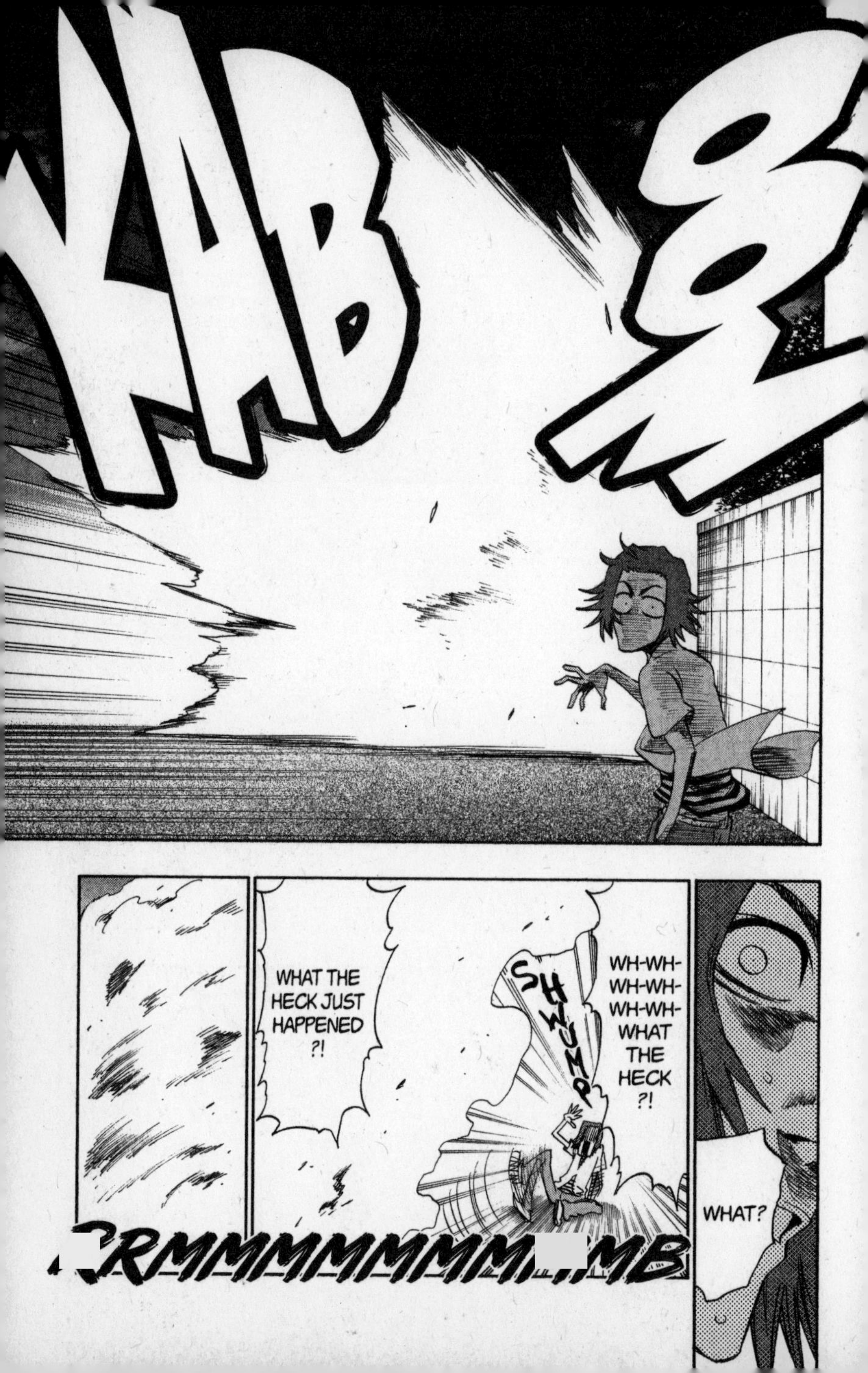
KABOOM
WHAT?
WH-WH-WH-WH-WH-WH-WHAT THE HECK?!
SHWUMP
WHAT THE HECK JUST HAPPENED?!
RMMMMMMMM
MB

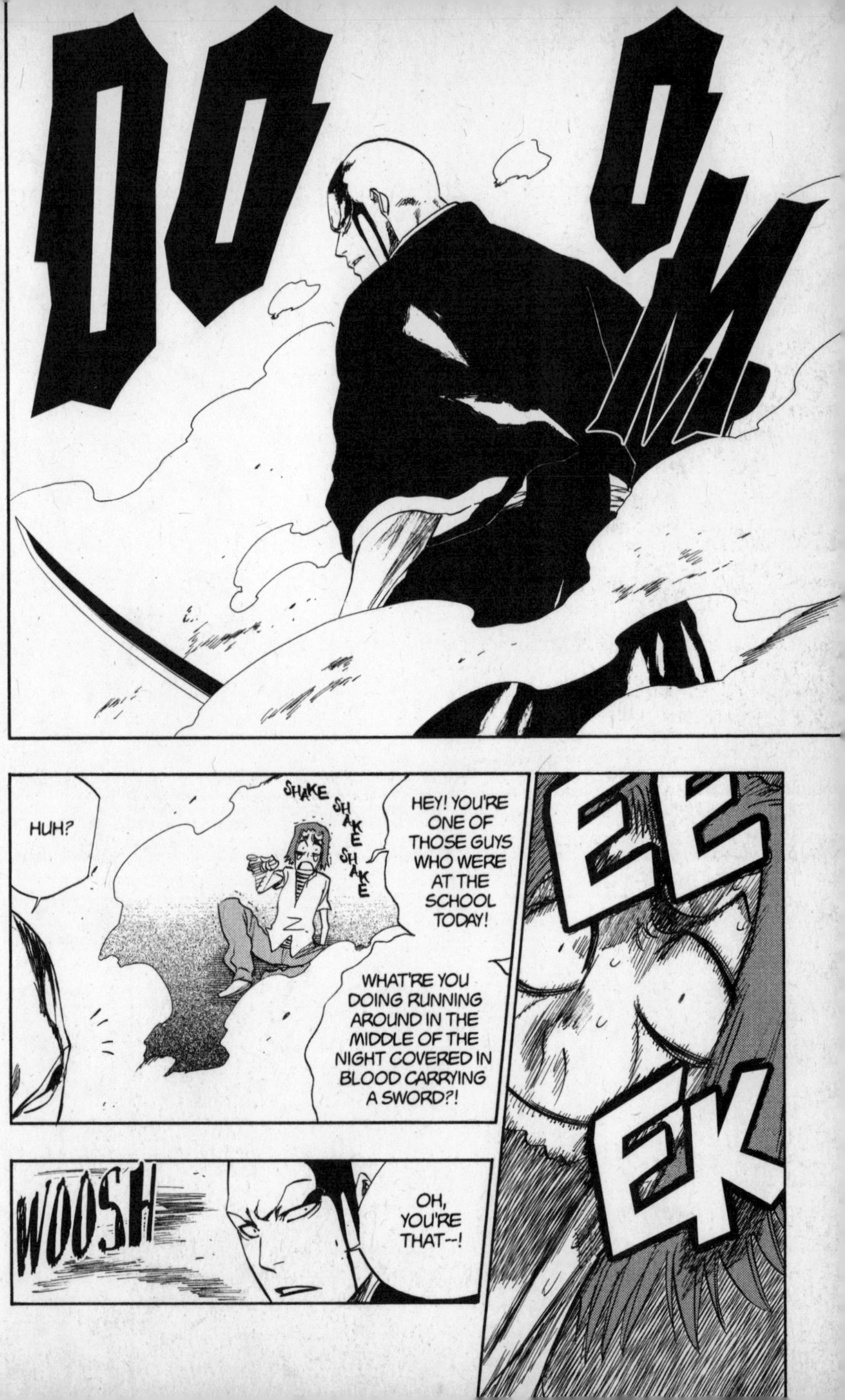
DOOOM
EEEK
SHAKE SHAKE SHAKE
HEY! YOU'RE ONE OF THOSE GUYS WHO WERE AT THE SCHOOL TODAY!
WHAT'RE YOU DOING RUNNING AROUND IN THE MIDDLE OF THE NIGHT COVERED IN BLOOD CARRYING A SWORD?!
HUH?
OH, YOU'RE THAT--!
WOOSH

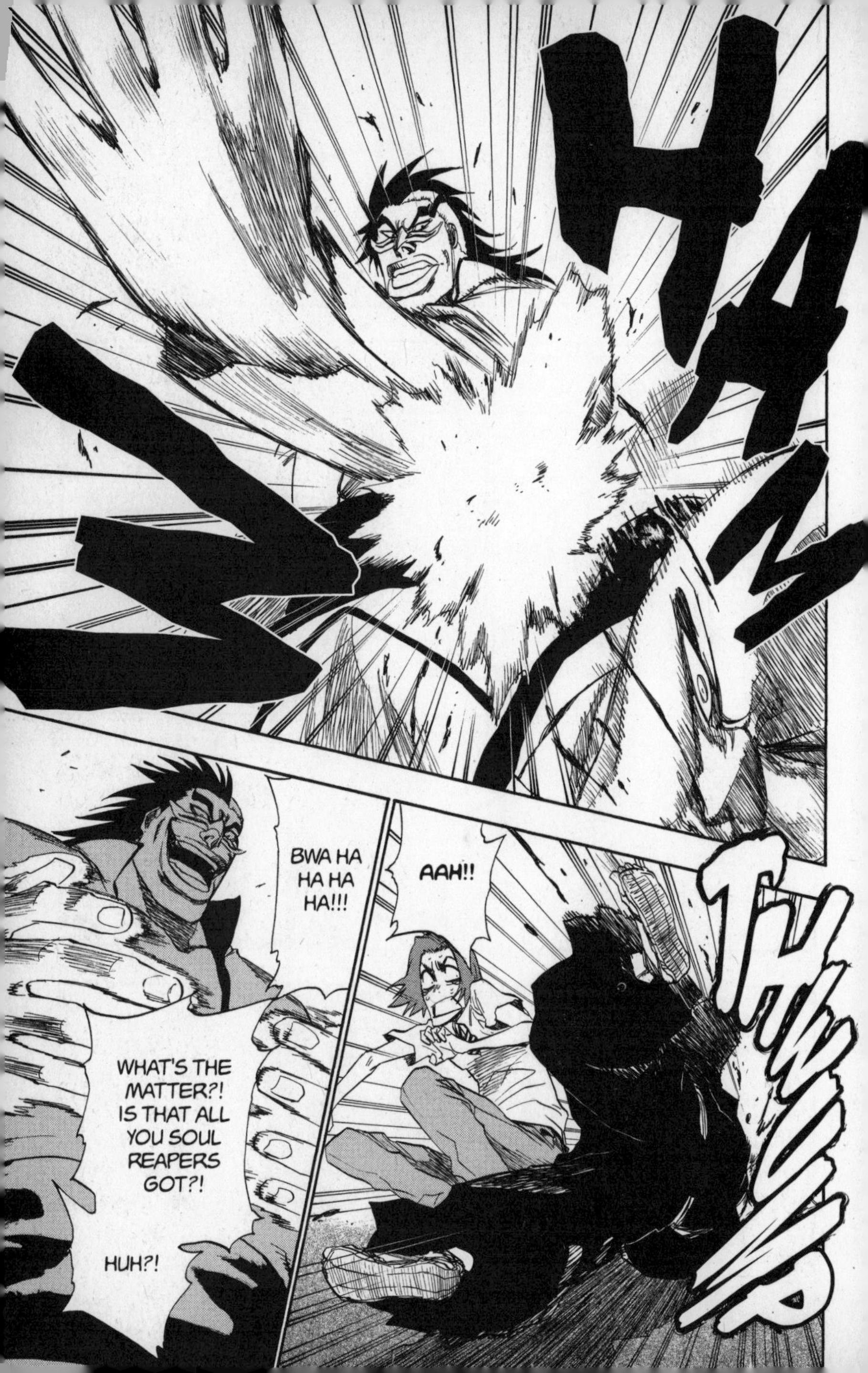
WHAM
AAH!!
BWA HA HA HA HA!!!
THWUMP
WHAT'S THE MATTER?! IS THAT ALL YOU SOUL REAPERS GOT?!
HUH?!

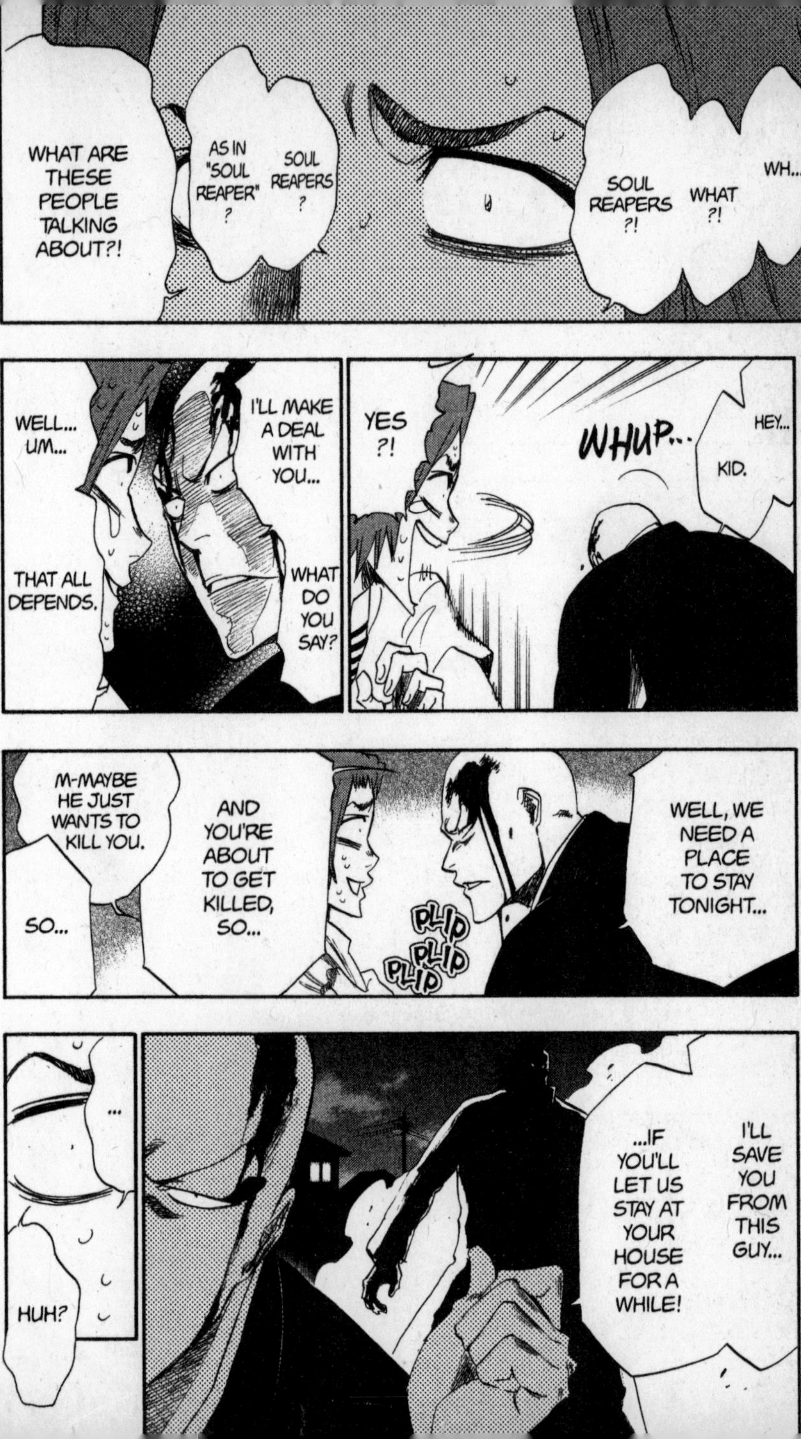
WH...
WHAT ?!
SOUL REAPERS ?!
SOUL REAPERS ?
AS IN "SOUL REAPER" ?
WHAT ARE THESE PEOPLE TALKING ABOUT?!
HEY... KID.
WHUP...
YES ?!
I'LL MAKE A DEAL WITH YOU...
WELL... UM...
WHAT DO YOU SAY?
THAT ALL DEPENDS.
WELL, WE NEED A PLACE TO STAY TONIGHT...
PLIP PLIP PLIP
AND YOU'RE ABOUT TO GET KILLED, SO...
M-MAYBE HE JUST WANTS TO KILL YOU.
SO...
I'LL SAVE YOU FROM THIS GUY...
...IF YOU'LL LET US STAY AT YOUR HOUSE FOR A WHILE!
...
HUH?

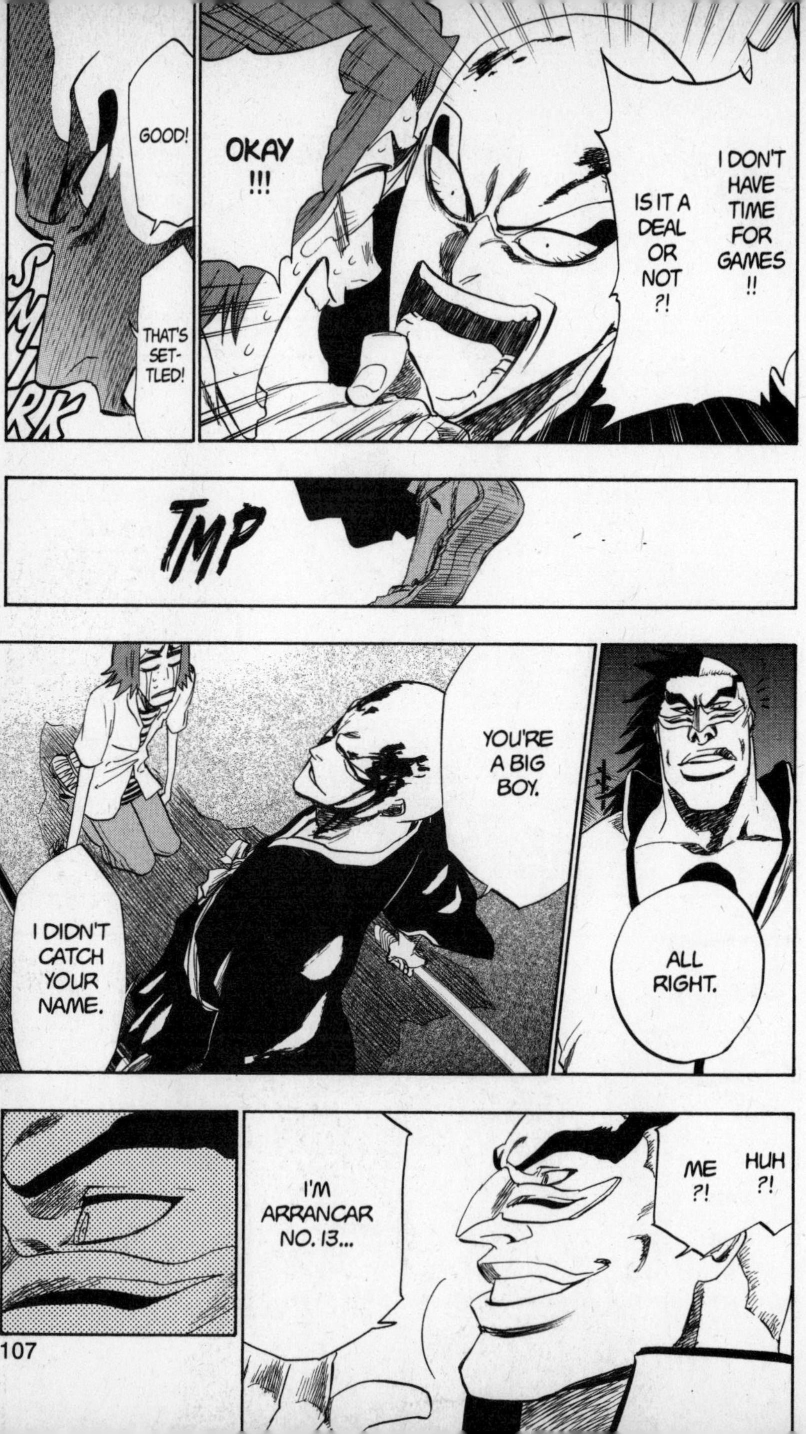
I DON'T HAVE TIME FOR GAMES!!
IS IT A DEAL OR NOT?!
OKAY!!!
GOOD!
SMIRK
THAT'S SET-TLED!
TMP
ALL RIGHT.
YOU'RE A BIG BOY.
I DIDN'T CATCH YOUR NAME.
HUH?!
ME?!
I'M ARRANCAR NO. 13...

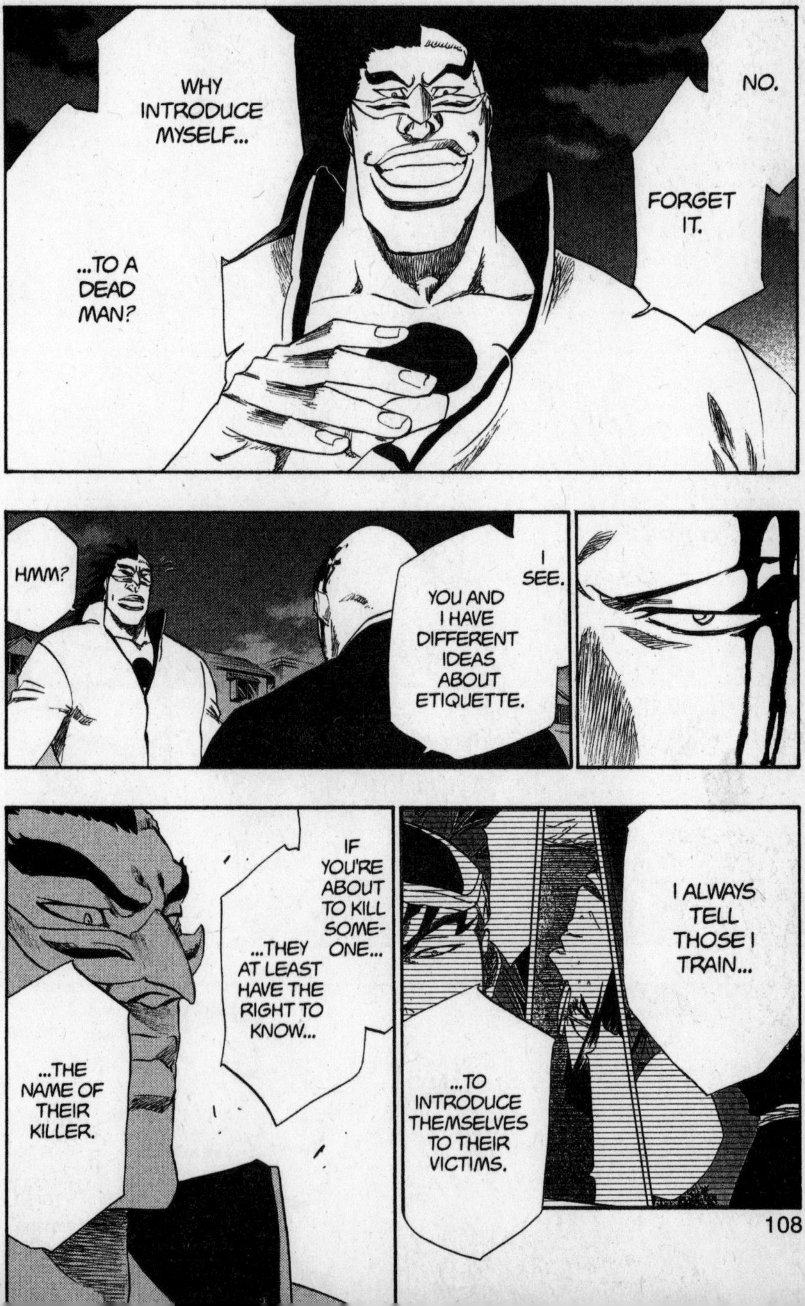
NO.
FORGET IT.
WHY INTRODUCE MYSELF...
...TO A DEAD MAN?
I SEE.
YOU AND I HAVE DIFFERENT IDEAS ABOUT ETIQUETTE.
HMM?
I ALWAYS TELL THOSE I TRAIN...
...TO INTRODUCE THEMSELVES TO THEIR VICTIMS.
IF YOU'RE ABOUT TO KILL SOME-ONE...
...THEY AT LEAST HAVE THE RIGHT TO KNOW...
...THE NAME OF THEIR KILLER.

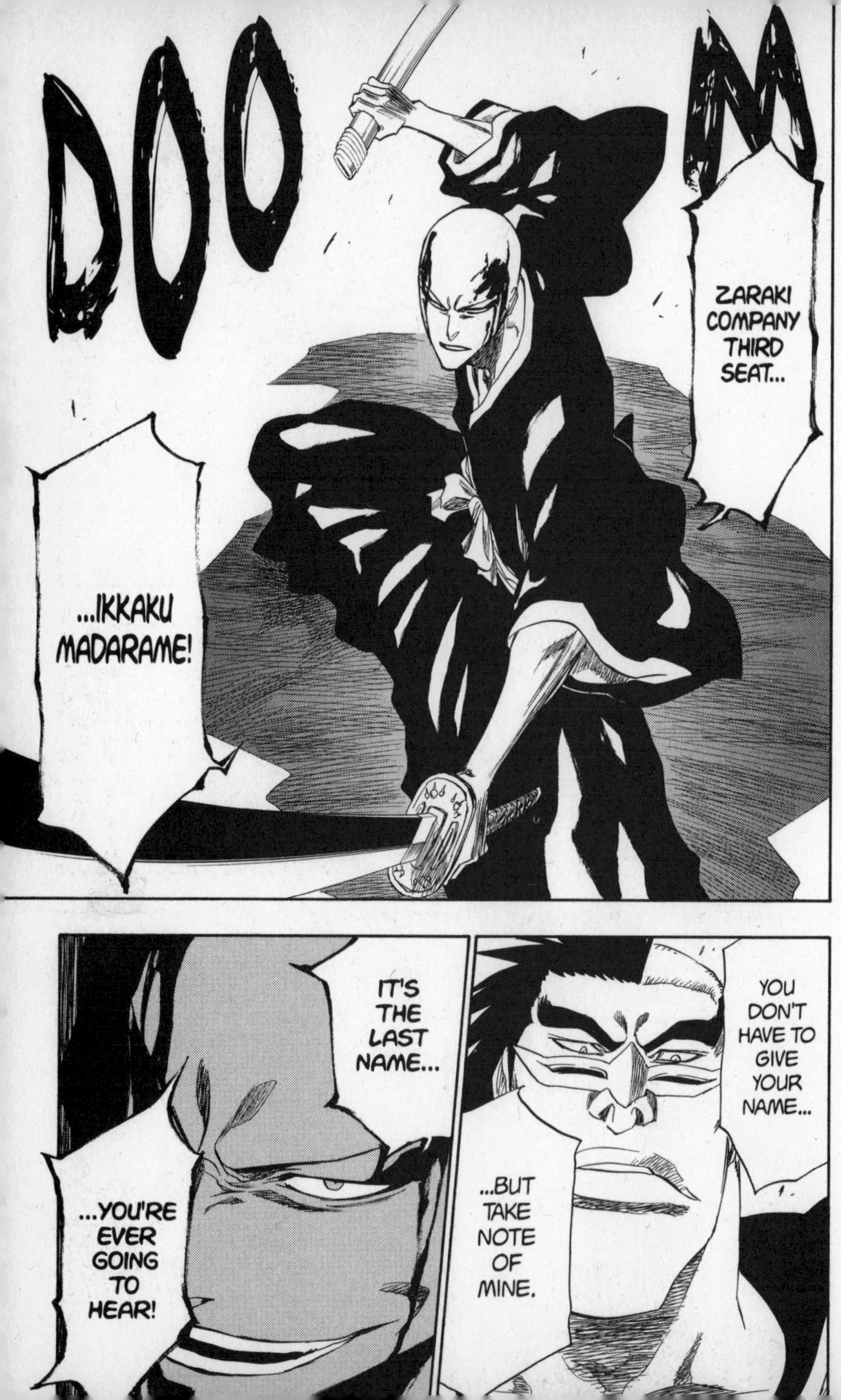
DOOOM
ZARAKI COMPANY THIRD SEAT...
...IKKAKU MADARAME!
YOU DON'T HAVE TO GIVE YOUR NAME...
...BUT TAKE NOTE OF MINE.
IT'S THE LAST NAME...
...YOU'RE EVER GOING TO HEAR!

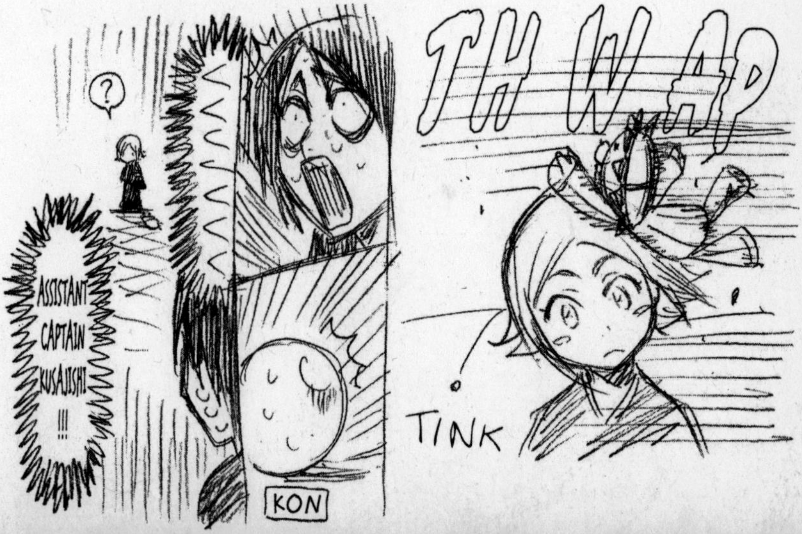
THWAP
TINK
KON
?
ASSISTANT CAPTAIN KUSAJISHI !!!

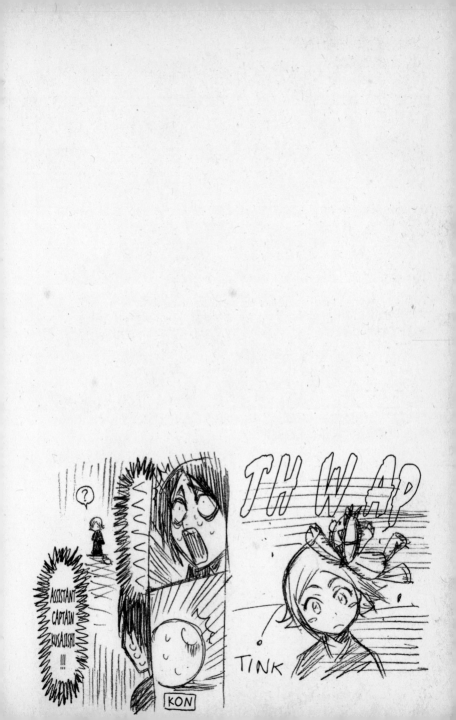

203. ¡Mala Suerte! 2
[El Monstruo]

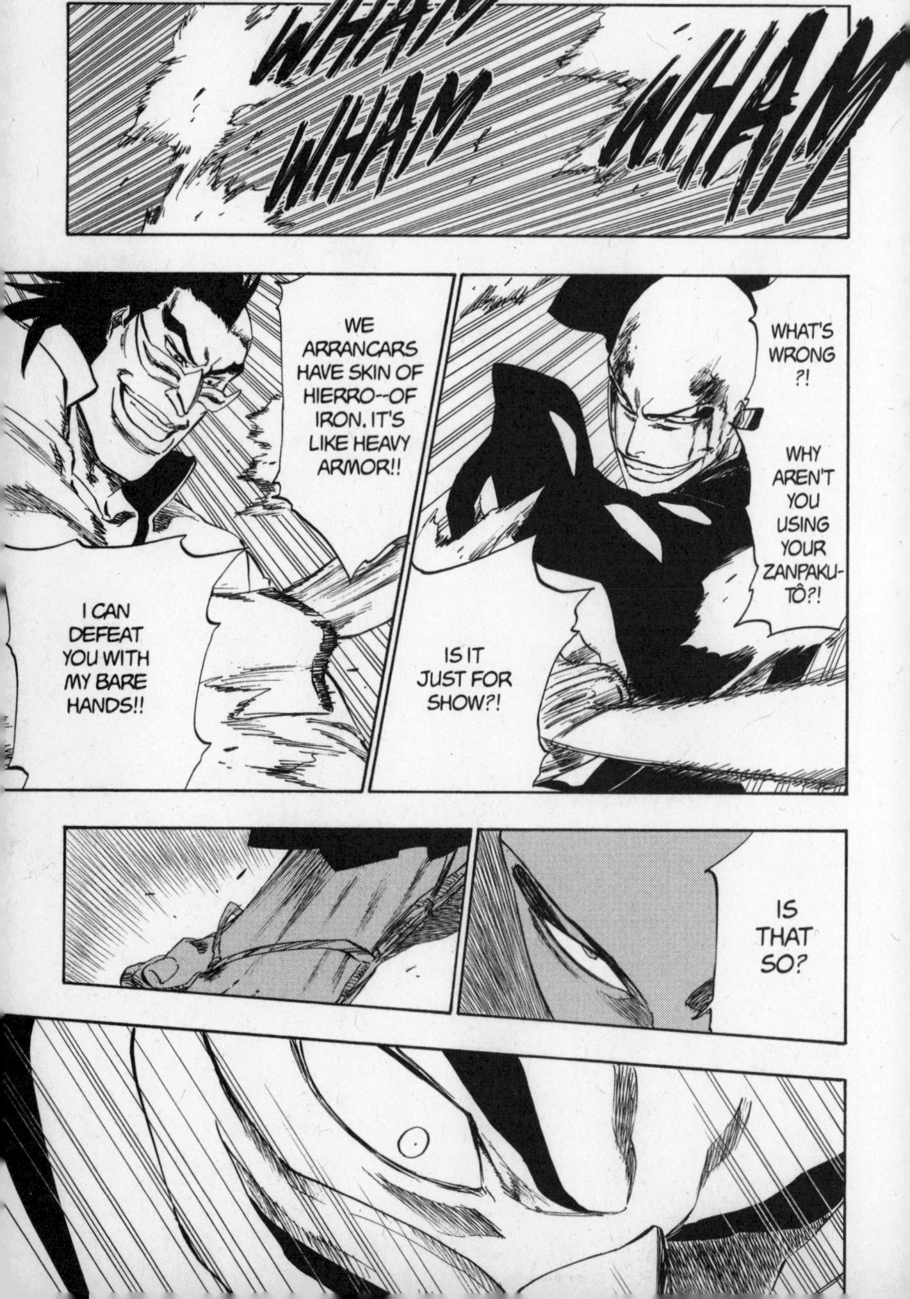
WHAM
WHAM
WHAM
WHAM
WHAT'S WRONG?!
WHY AREN'T YOU USING YOUR ZANPAKU-TÔ?!
IS IT JUST FOR SHOW?!
WE ARRANCARS HAVE SKIN OF HIERRO--OF IRON. IT'S LIKE HEAVY ARMOR!!
I CAN DEFEAT YOU WITH MY BARE HANDS!!
IS THAT SO?

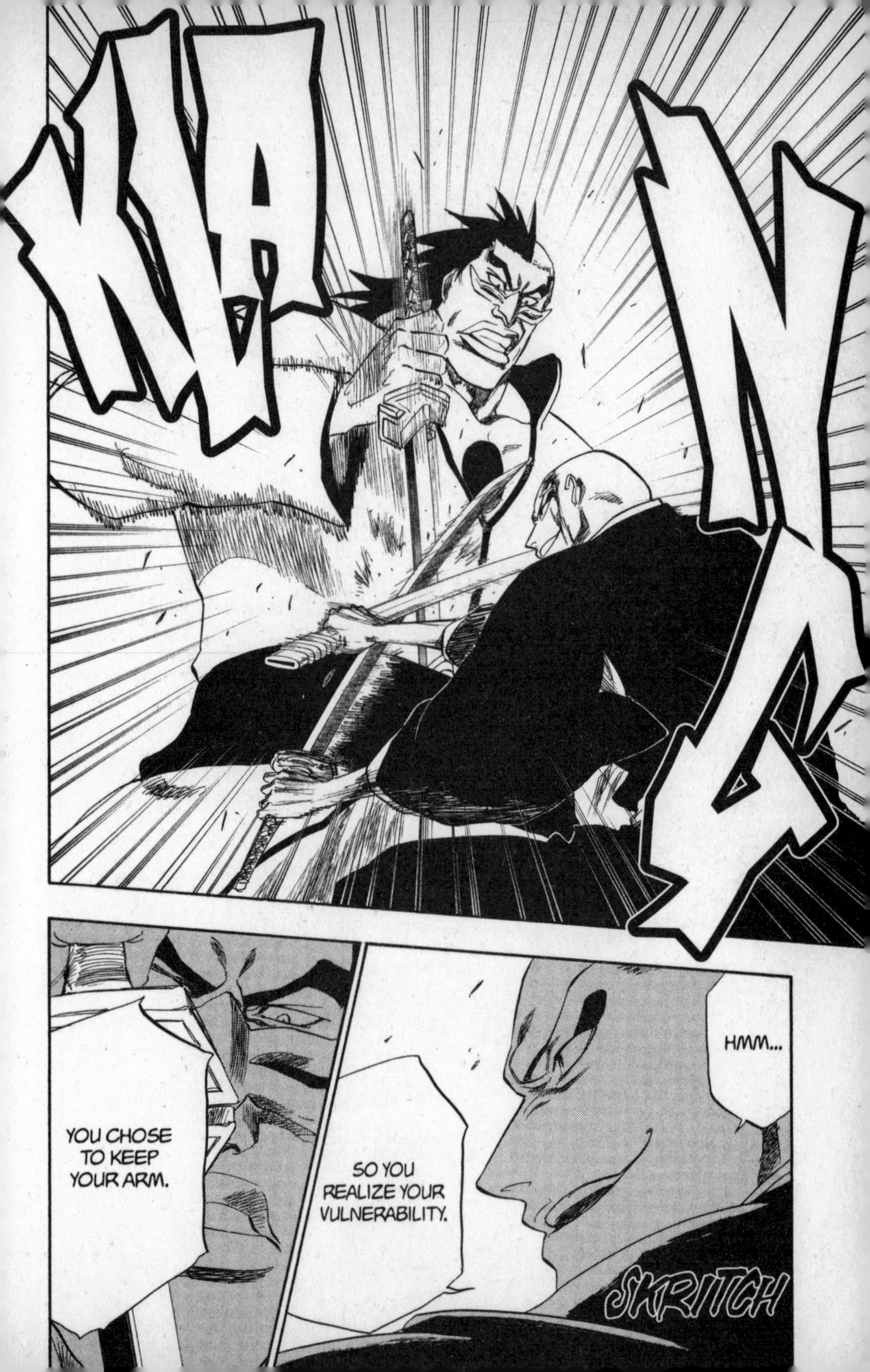
HMM...
SO YOU REALIZE YOUR VULNERABILITY.
SKRITCH
YOU CHOSE TO KEEP YOUR ARM.

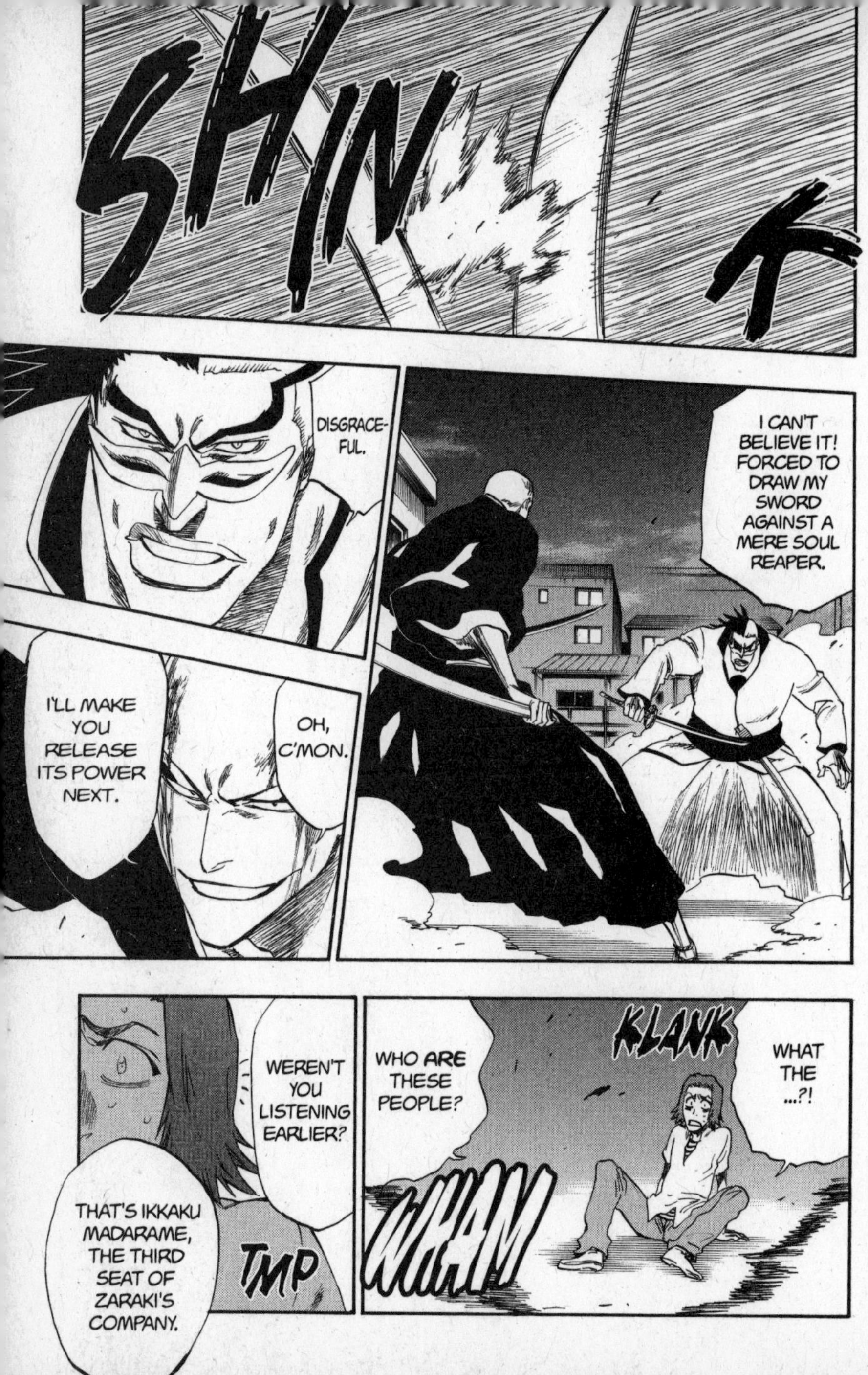
SHIN
I CAN'T BELIEVE IT! FORCED TO DRAW MY SWORD AGAINST A MERE SOUL REAPER.
DISGRACE-FUL.
OH, C'MON.
I'LL MAKE YOU RELEASE ITS POWER NEXT.
KLANK
WHAT THE ...?!
WHO ARE THESE PEOPLE?
WHAM
WEREN'T YOU LISTENING EARLIER?
THAT'S IKKAKU MADARAME, THE THIRD SEAT OF ZARAKI'S COMPANY.
TMP

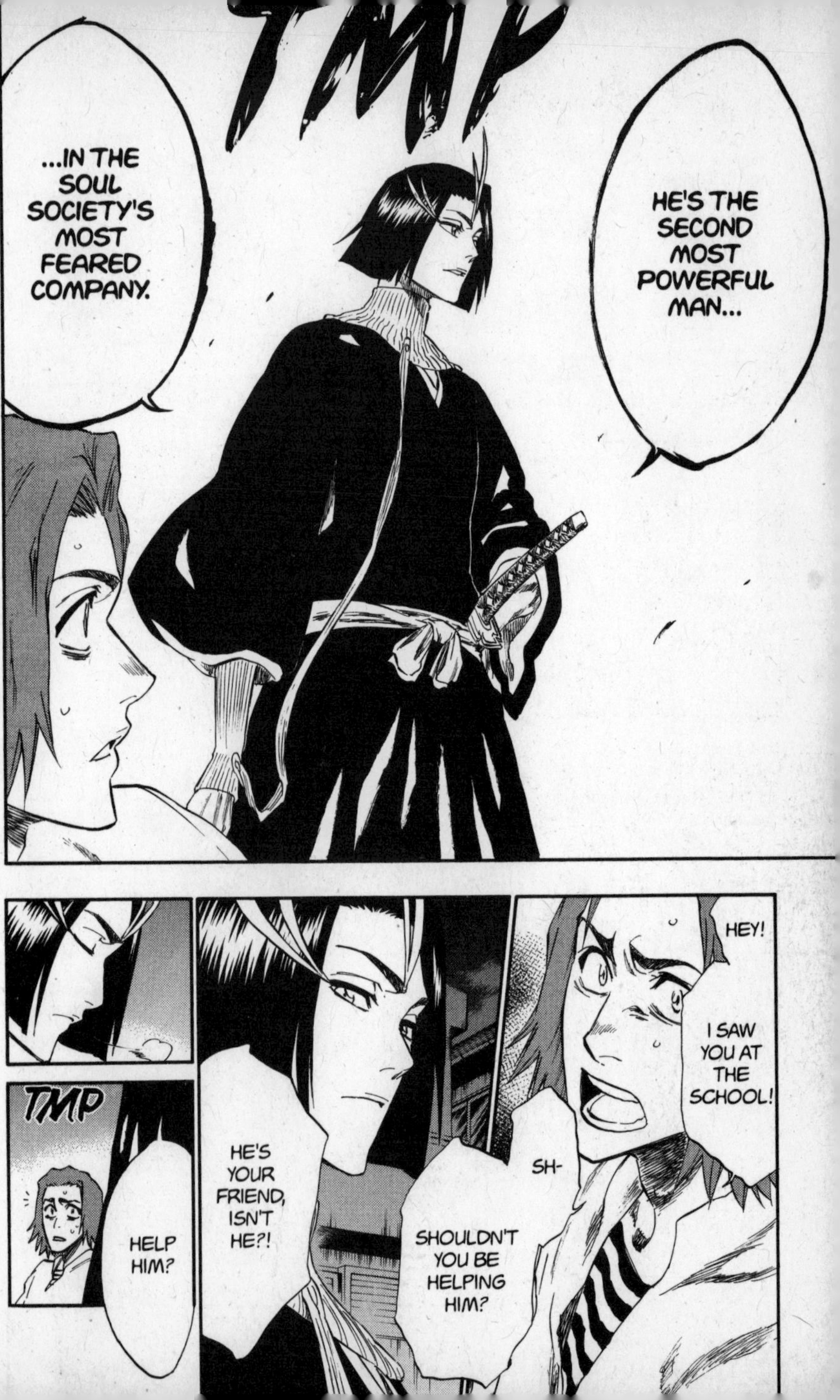
TMP
HE'S THE SECOND MOST POWERFUL MAN...
...IN THE SOUL SOCIETY'S MOST FEARED COMPANY.
HEY!
I SAW YOU AT THE SCHOOL!
SH-
SHOULDN'T YOU BE HELPING HIM?
HE'S YOUR FRIEND, ISN'T HE?!
TMP
HELP HIM?

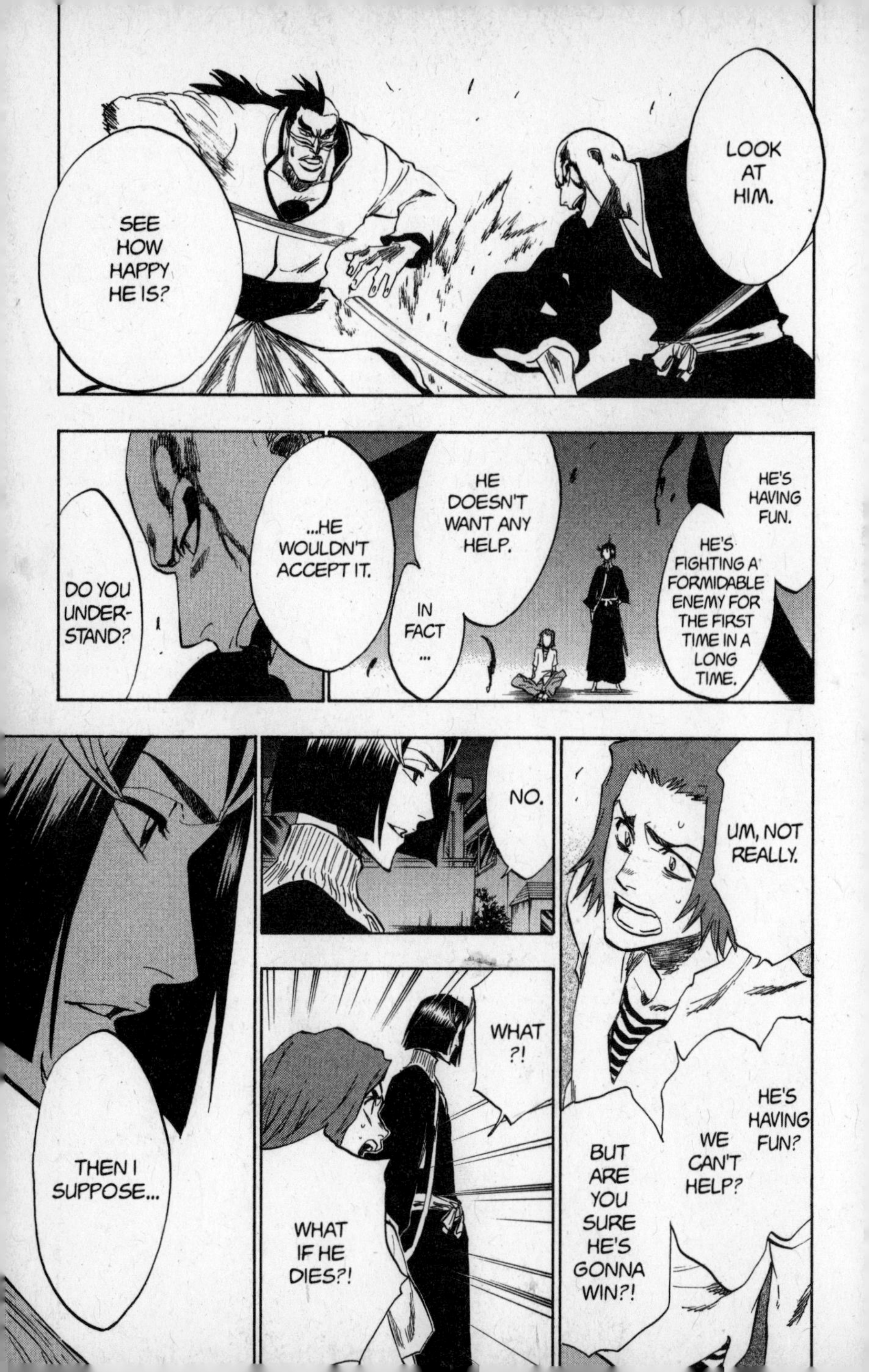
LOOK AT HIM.
SEE HOW HAPPY HE IS?
HE'S HAVING FUN.
HE'S FIGHTING A FORMIDABLE ENEMY FOR THE FIRST TIME IN A LONG TIME.
HE DOESN'T WANT ANY HELP.
IN FACT...
...HE WOULDN'T ACCEPT IT.
DO YOU UNDER-STAND?
UM, NOT REALLY.
HE'S HAVING FUN?
WE CAN'T HELP?
BUT ARE YOU SURE HE'S GONNA WIN?!
NO.
WHAT?!
WHAT IF HE DIES?!
THEN I SUPPOSE...

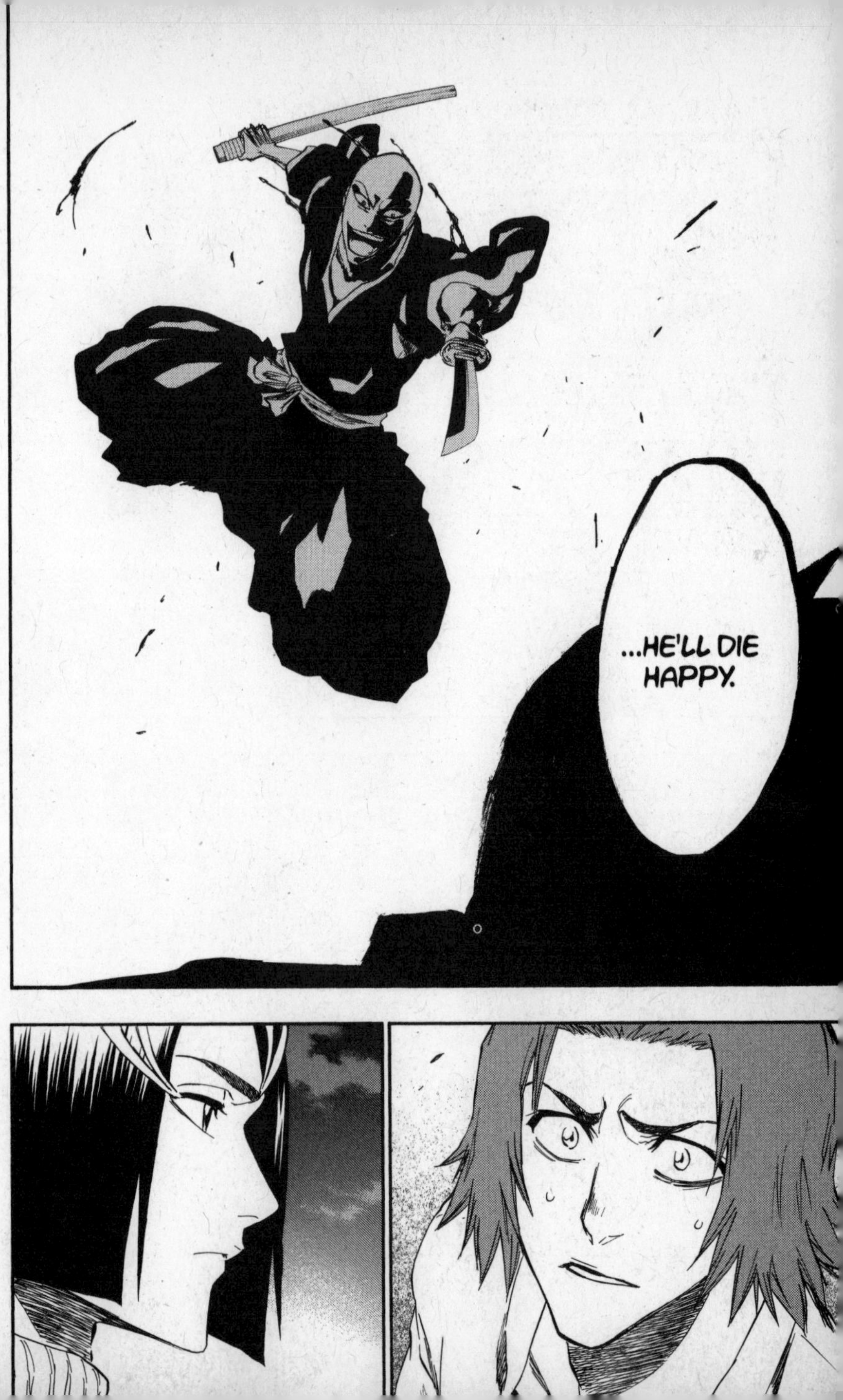
...HE'LL DIE HAPPY.

Bleach 203. ¡Mala Suerte! 2 [El Monstruo]

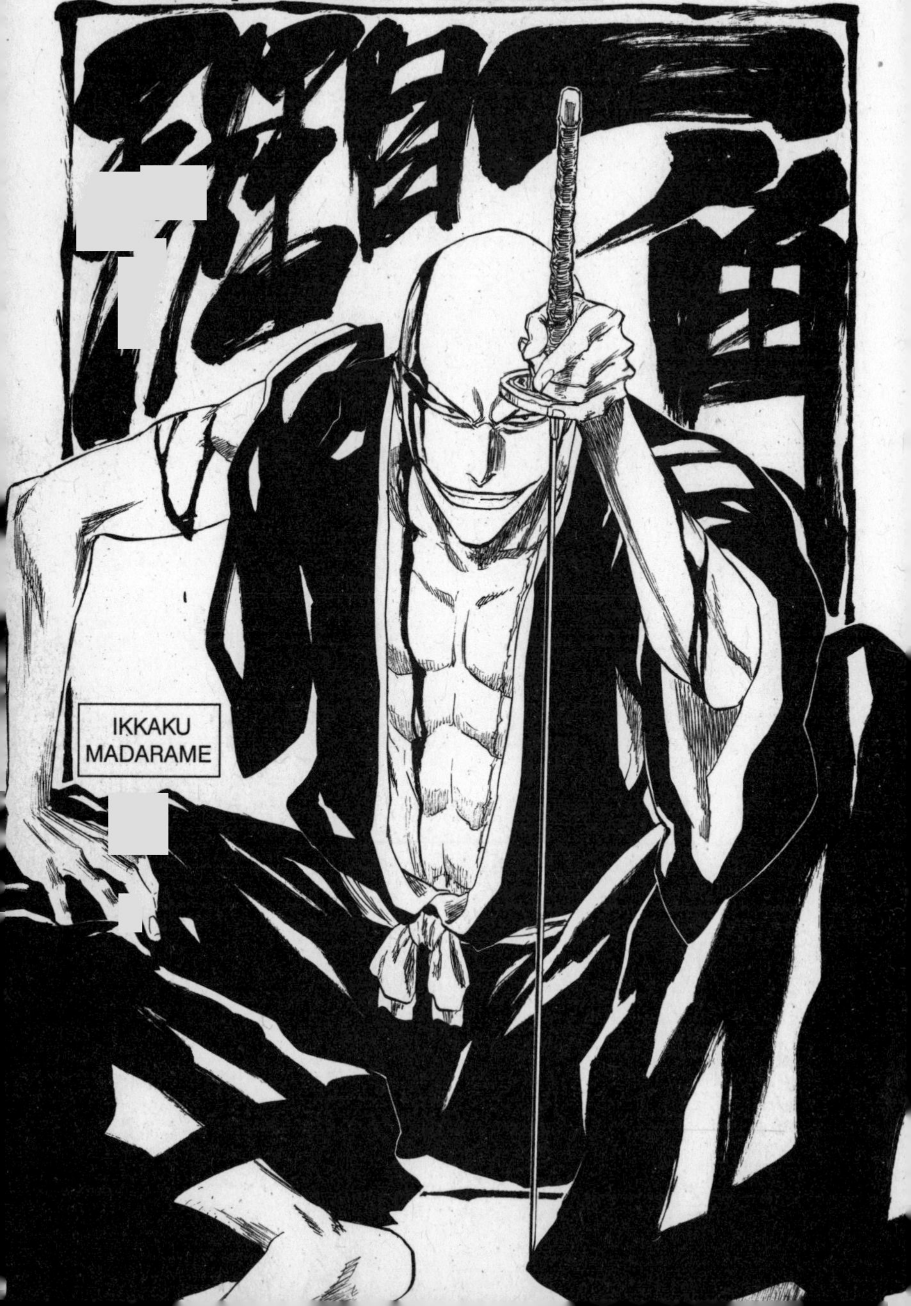
IKKAKU
MADARAME

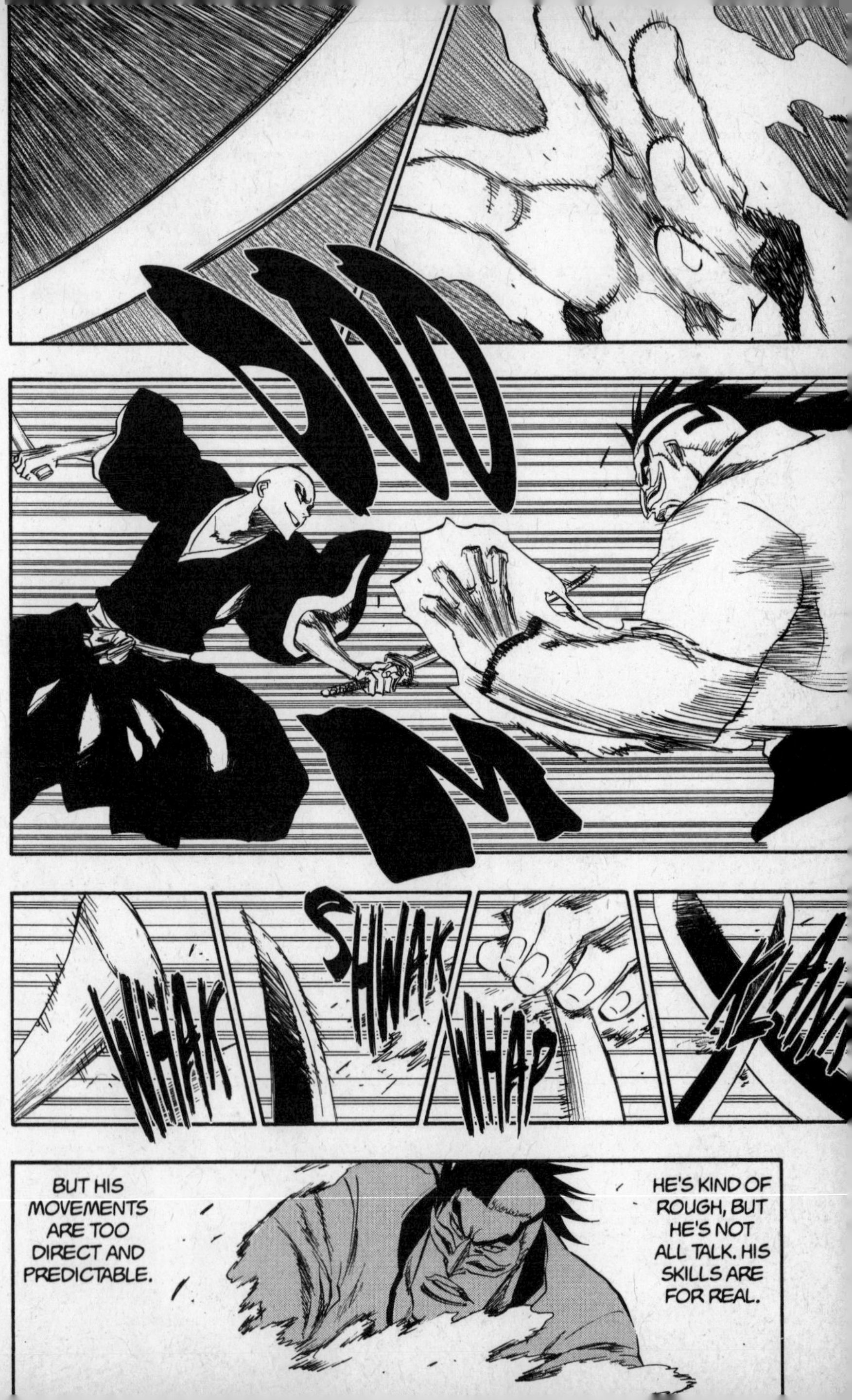
DOOM
KLAN
WHAP
SHWAK
WHAK
HE'S KIND OF ROUGH, BUT HE'S NOT ALL TALK. HIS SKILLS ARE FOR REAL.
BUT HIS MOVEMENTS ARE TOO DIRECT AND PREDICTABLE.

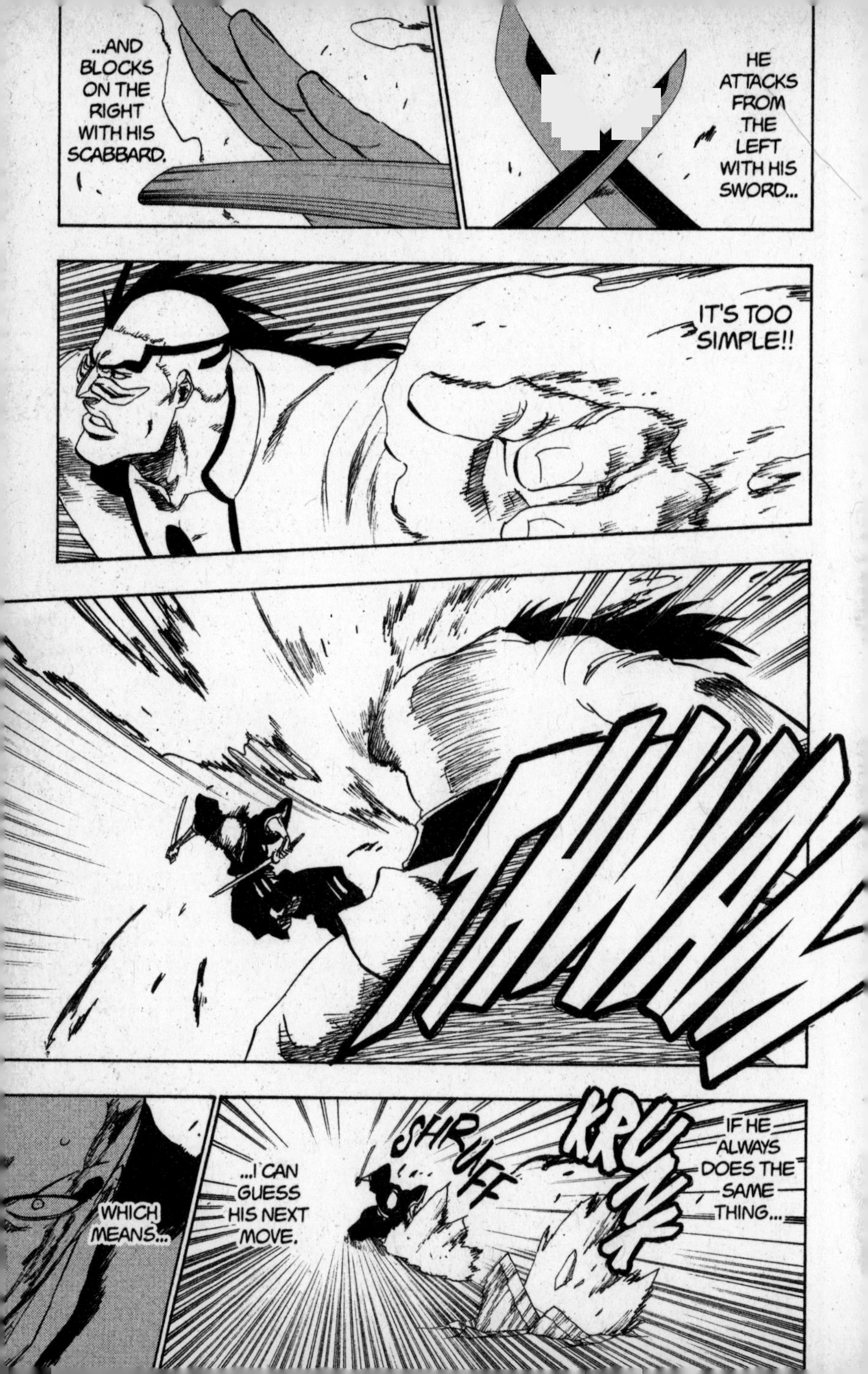
HE ATTACKS FROM THE LEFT WITH HIS SWORD...
...AND BLOCKS ON THE RIGHT WITH HIS SCABBARD.
IT'S TOO SIMPLE!!
IF HE ALWAYS DOES THE SAME THING...
KRUNK
SHRUFF
...I CAN GUESS HIS NEXT MOVE.
WHICH MEANS...

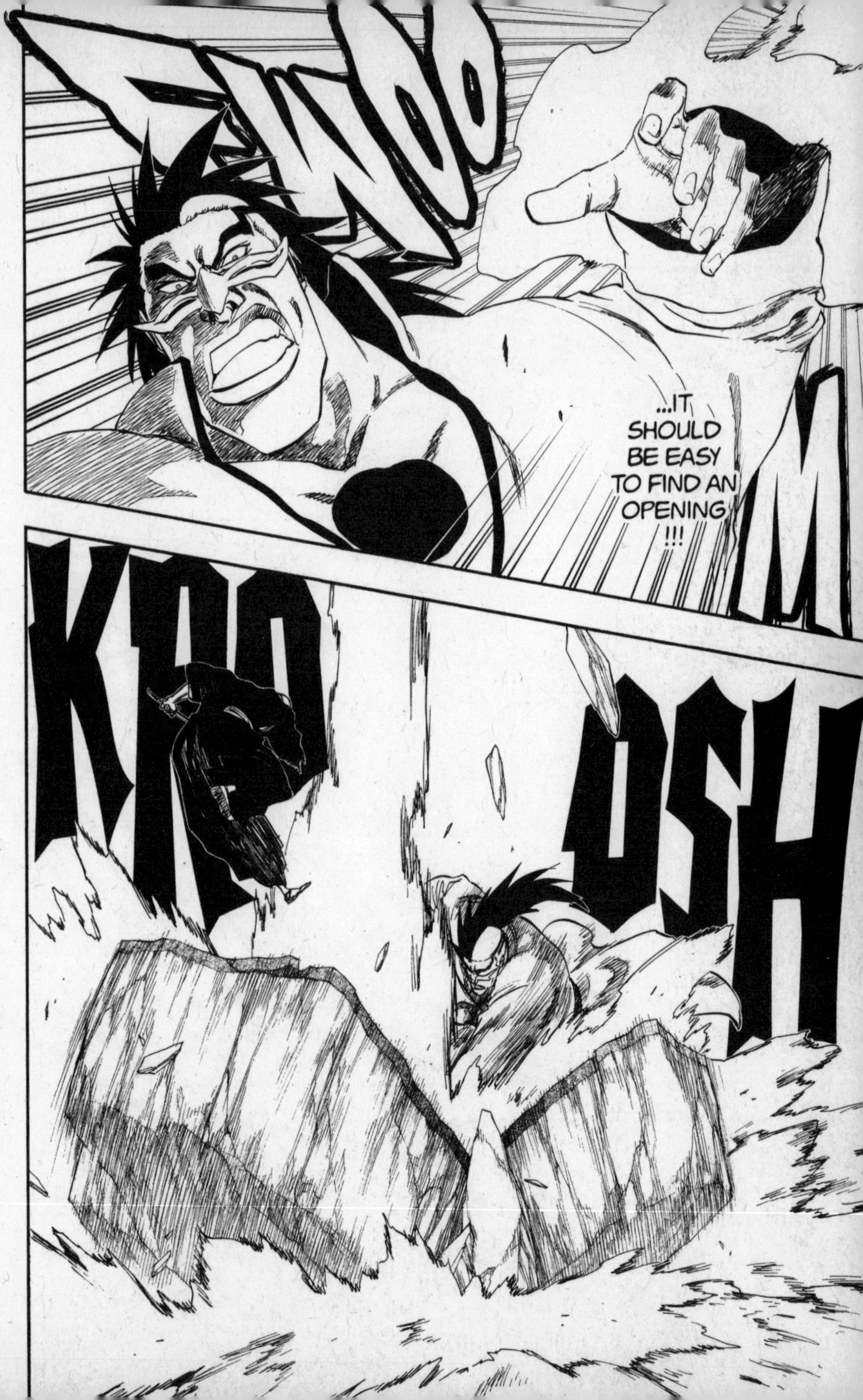
...IT SHOULD BE EASY TO FIND AN OPENING !!!

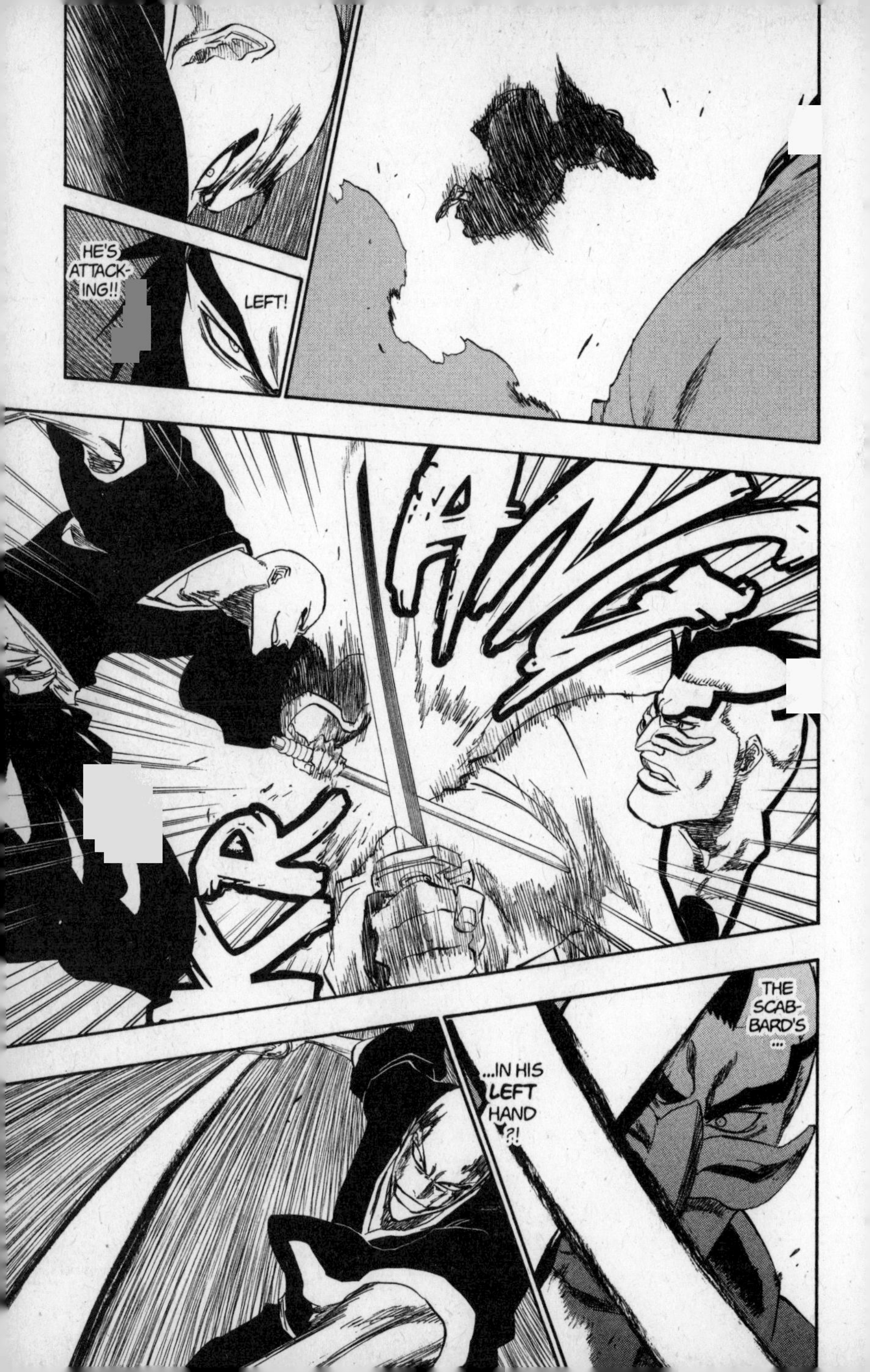
HE'S ATTACK-ING!!
LEFT!
THE SCAB-BARD'S...
...IN HIS LEFT HAND?!

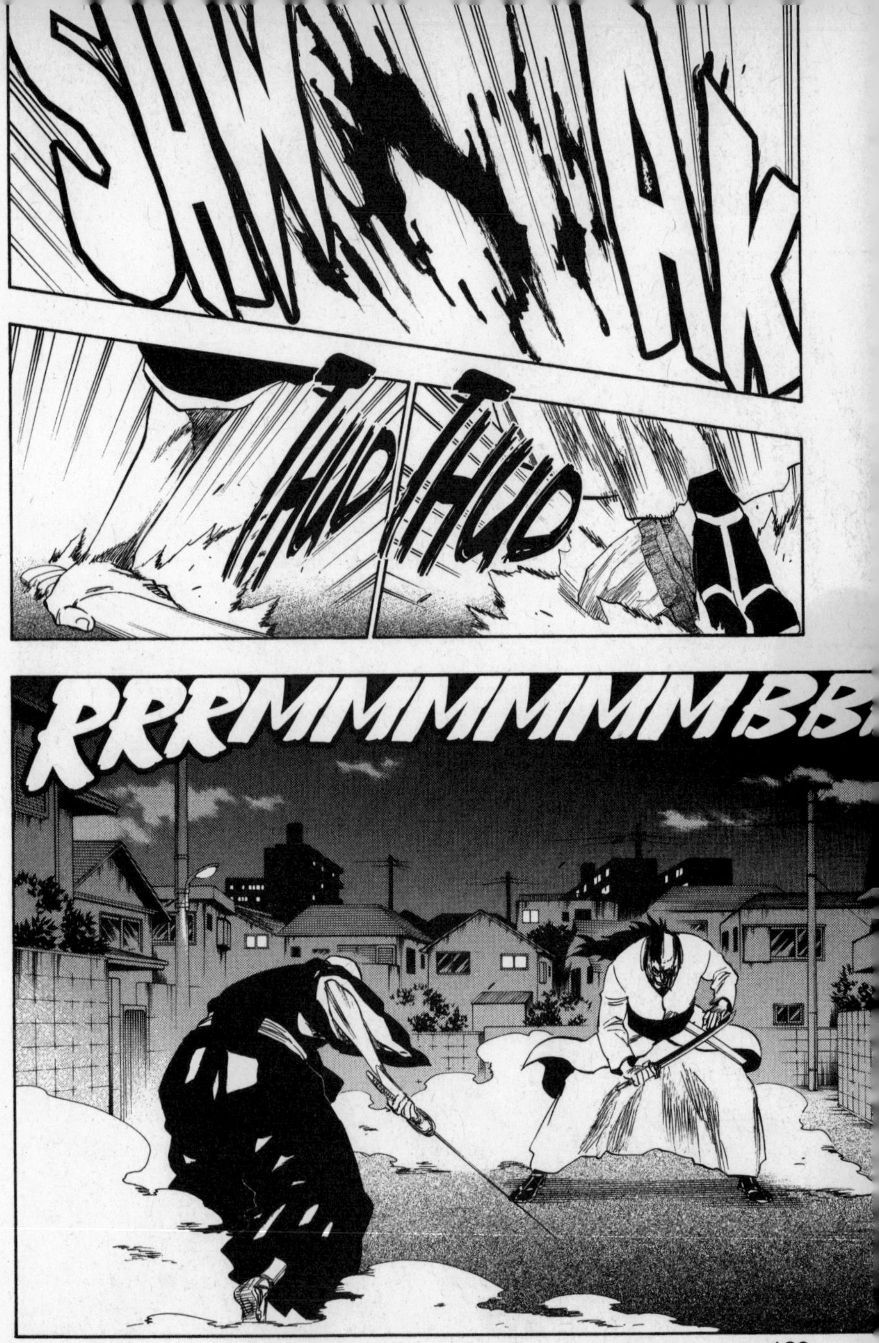
THUD
THUD
RRRMMMMMMMMMBB

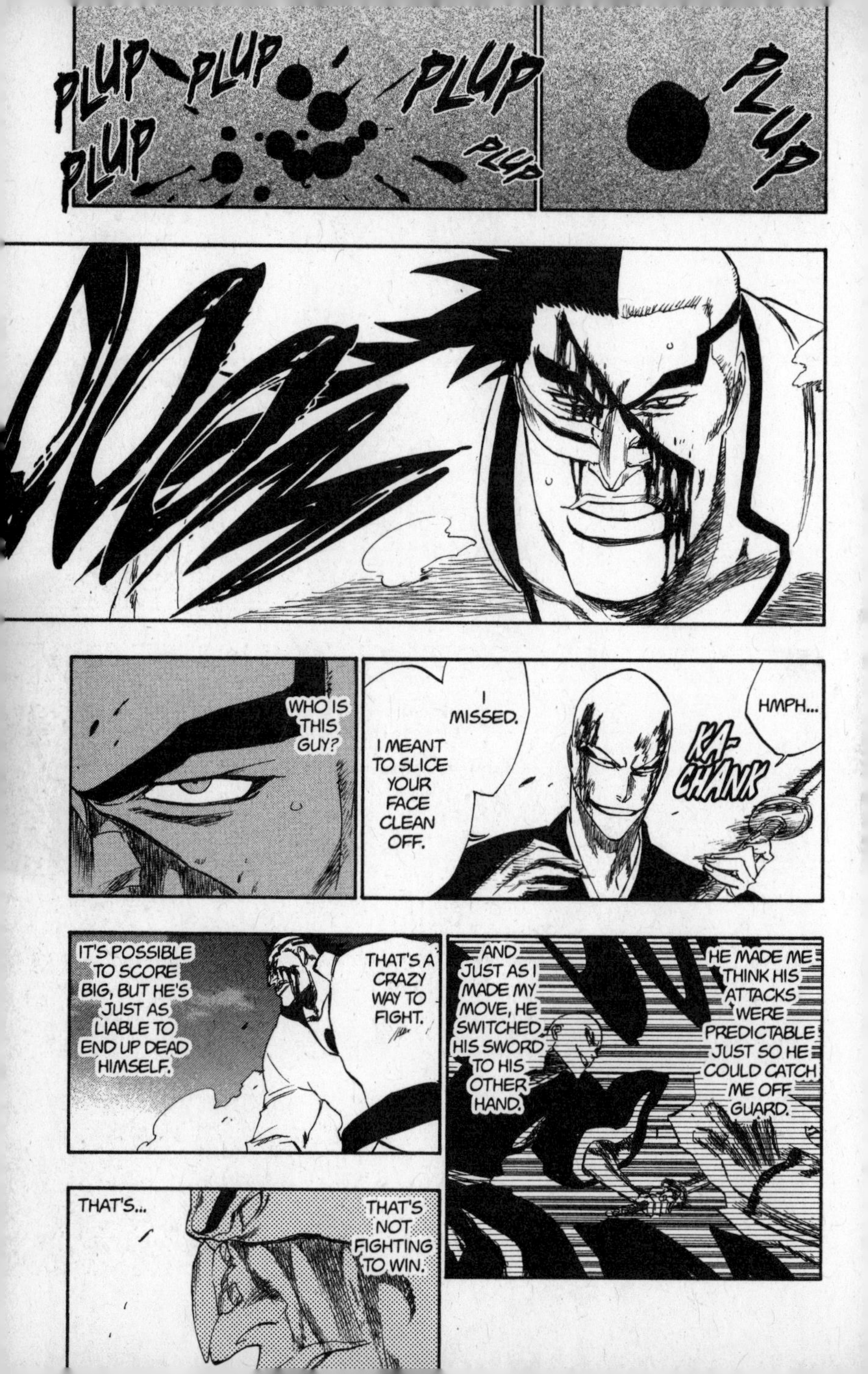
PLUP
PLUP
PLUP
PLUP
PLUP
PLUP
HMPH...
KA-CHANK
I MISSED.
I MEANT TO SLICE YOUR FACE CLEAN OFF.
WHO IS THIS GUY?
HE MADE ME THINK HIS ATTACKS WERE PREDICTABLE JUST SO HE COULD CATCH ME OFF GUARD.
AND JUST AS I MADE MY MOVE, HE SWITCHED HIS SWORD TO HIS OTHER HAND.
THAT'S A CRAZY WAY TO FIGHT.
IT'S POSSIBLE TO SCORE BIG, BUT HE'S JUST AS LIABLE TO END UP DEAD HIMSELF.
THAT'S NOT FIGHTING TO WIN.
THAT'S...

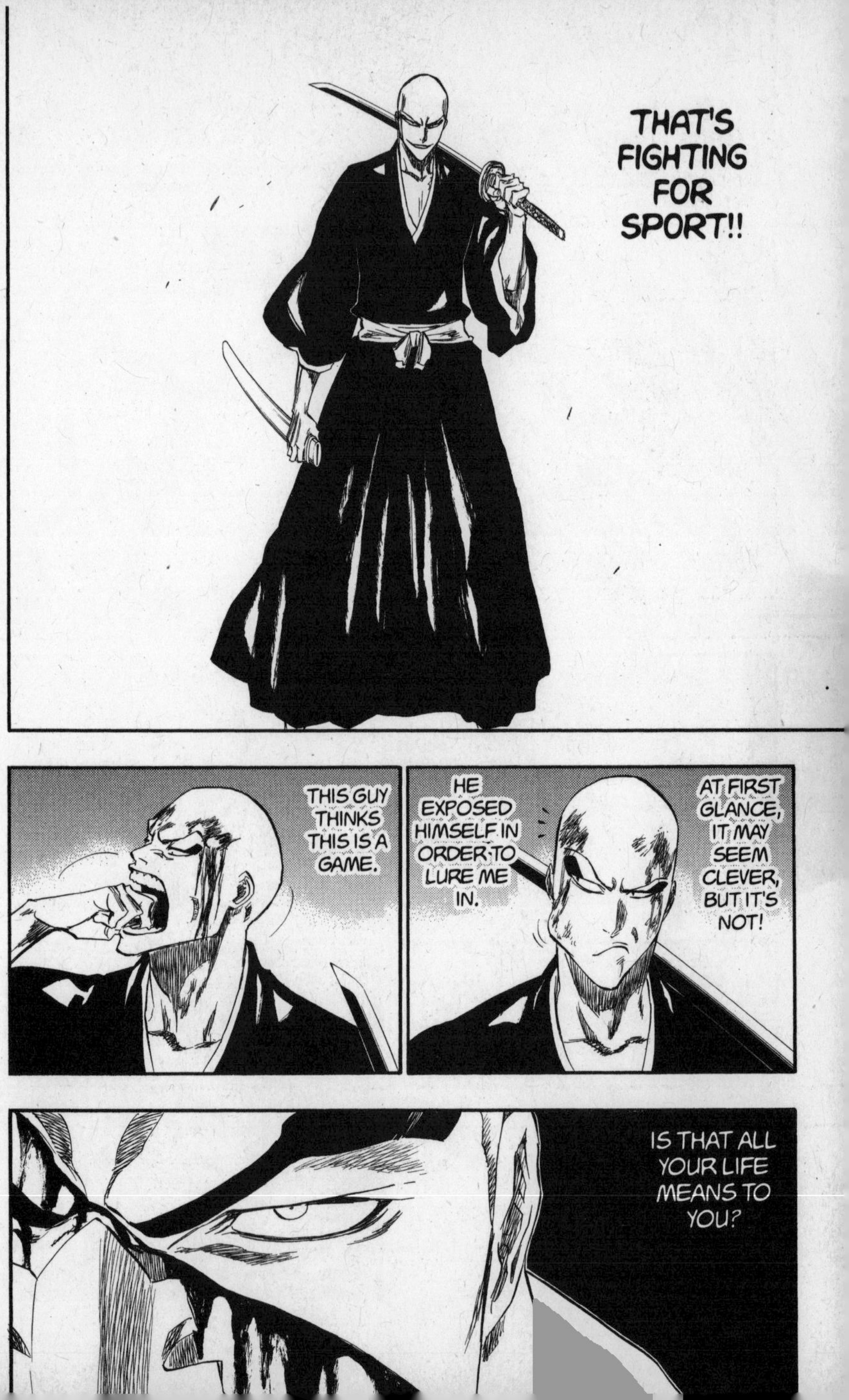
THAT'S FIGHTING FOR SPORT!!
AT FIRST GLANCE, IT MAY SEEM CLEVER, BUT IT'S NOT!
HE EXPOSED HIMSELF IN ORDER TO LURE ME IN.
THIS GUY THINKS THIS IS A GAME.
IS THAT ALL YOUR LIFE MEANS TO YOU?

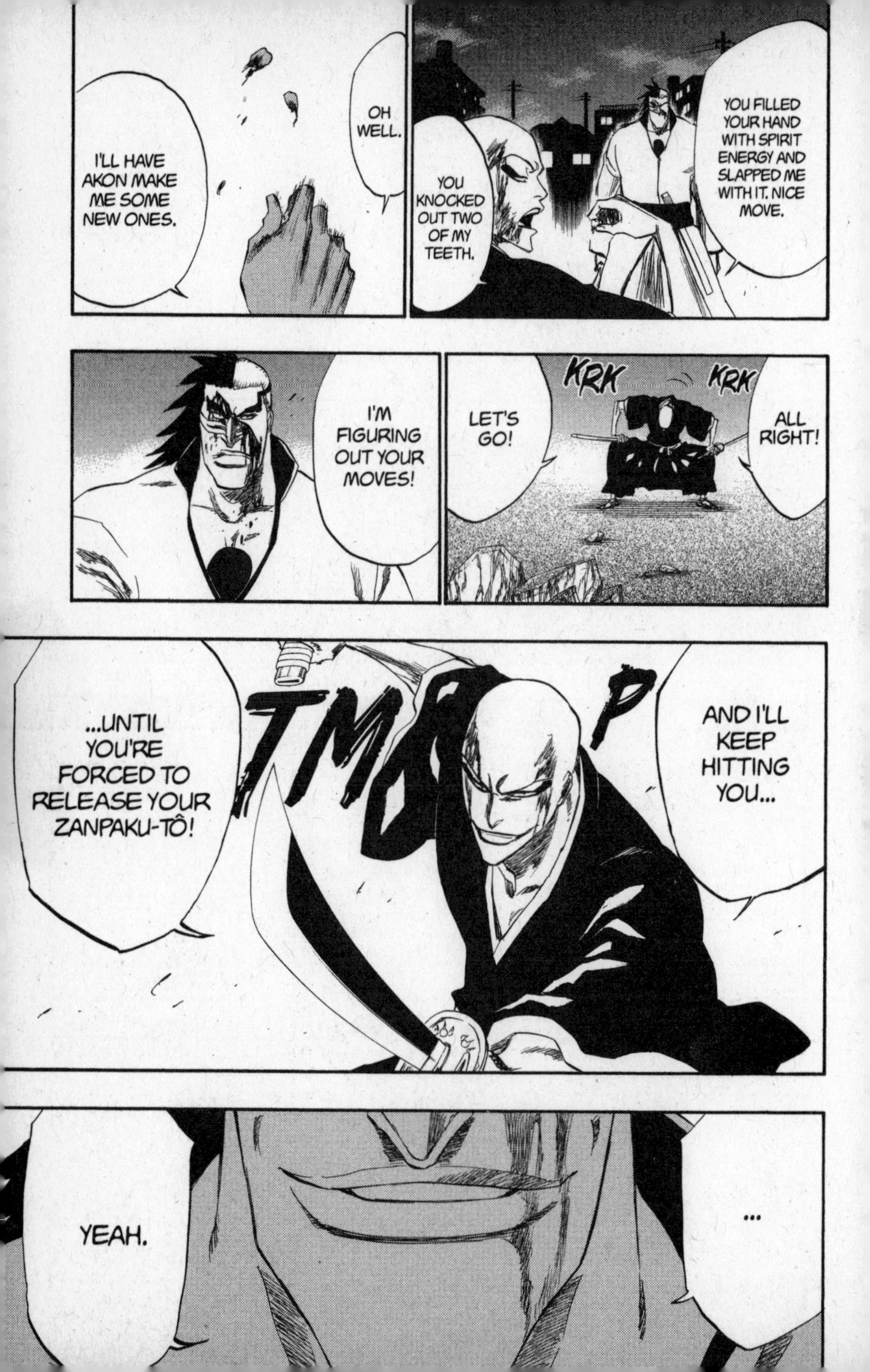
YOU FILLED YOUR HAND WITH SPIRIT ENERGY AND SLAPPED ME WITH IT. NICE MOVE.
YOU KNOCKED OUT TWO OF MY TEETH.
OH WELL.
I'LL HAVE AKON MAKE ME SOME NEW ONES.
KRK
KRK
ALL RIGHT!
LET'S GO!
I'M FIGURING OUT YOUR MOVES!
AND I'LL KEEP HITTING YOU...
TMP
...UNTIL YOU'RE FORCED TO RELEASE YOUR ZANPAKU-TÔ!
...
YEAH.

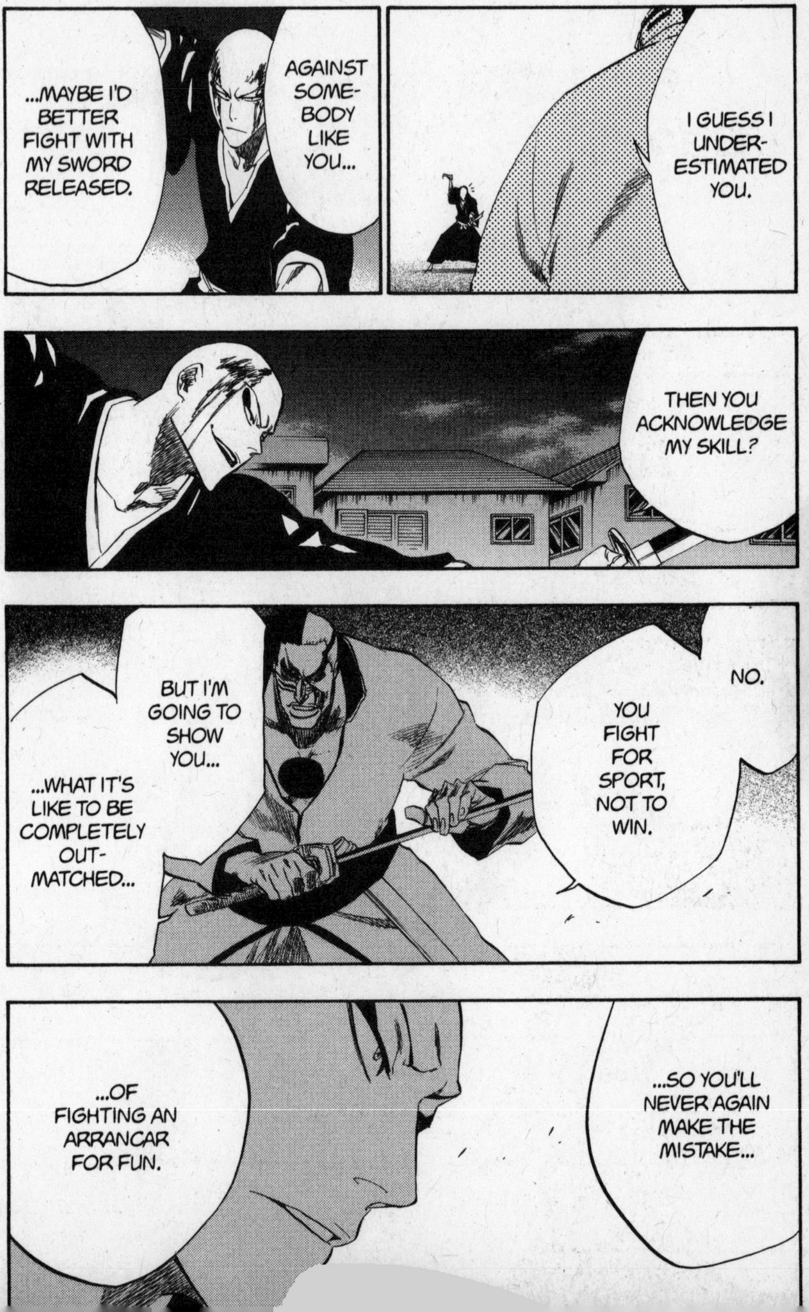
I GUESS I UNDER-ESTIMATED YOU.
AGAINST SOME-BODY LIKE YOU...
...MAYBE I'D BETTER FIGHT WITH MY SWORD RELEASED.
THEN YOU ACKNOWLEDGE MY SKILL?
NO.
YOU FIGHT FOR SPORT, NOT TO WIN.
BUT I'M GOING TO SHOW YOU...
...WHAT IT'S LIKE TO BE COMPLETELY OUT-MATCHED...
...SO YOU'LL NEVER AGAIN MAKE THE MISTAKE...
...OF FIGHTING AN ARRANCAR FOR FUN.

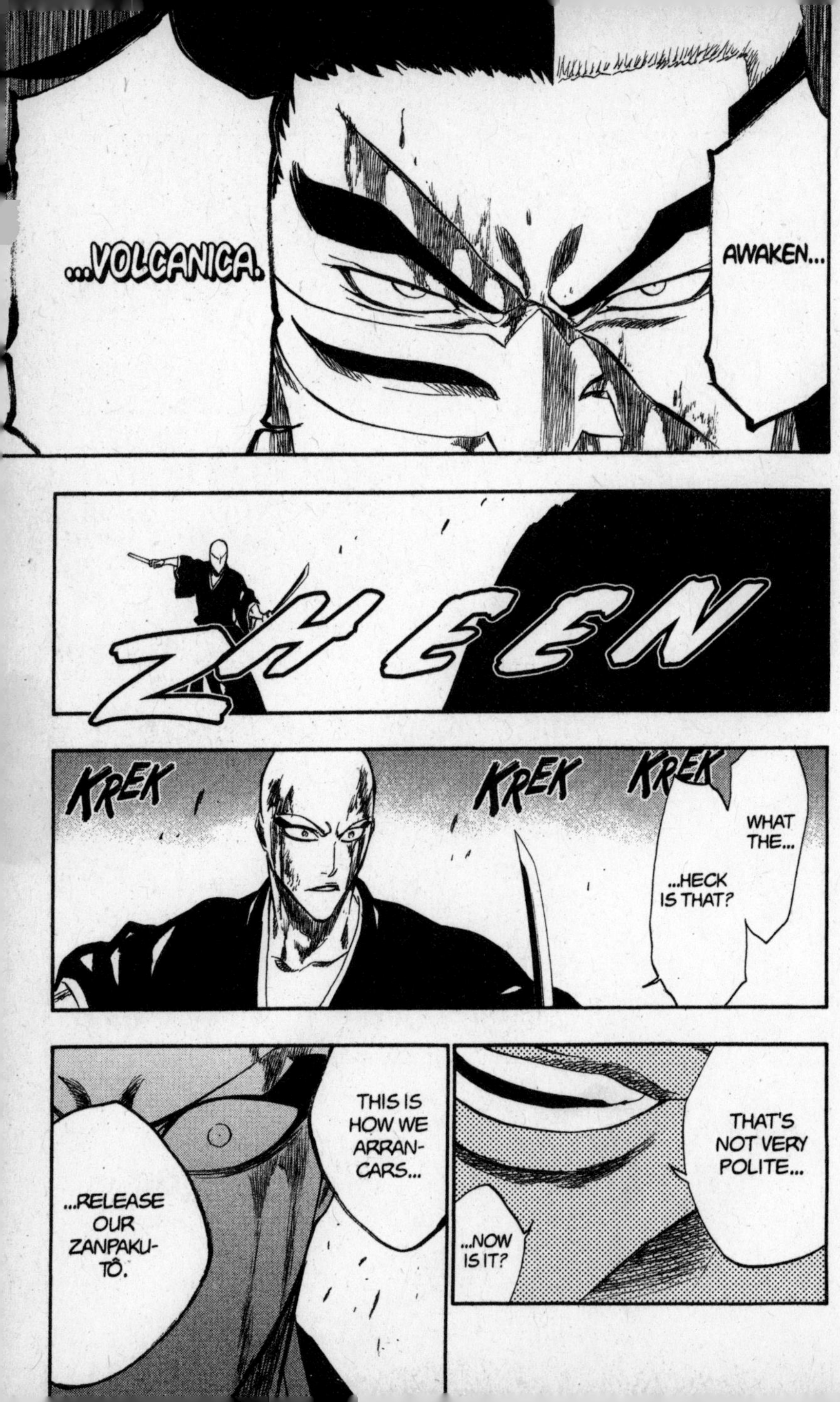
AWAKEN...
...VOLCANICA.
ZHEEN
KREK KREK KREK
WHAT THE...
...HECK IS THAT?
THAT'S NOT VERY POLITE...
...NOW IS IT?
THIS IS HOW WE ARRAN-CARS...
...RELEASE OUR ZANPAKU-TÔ.

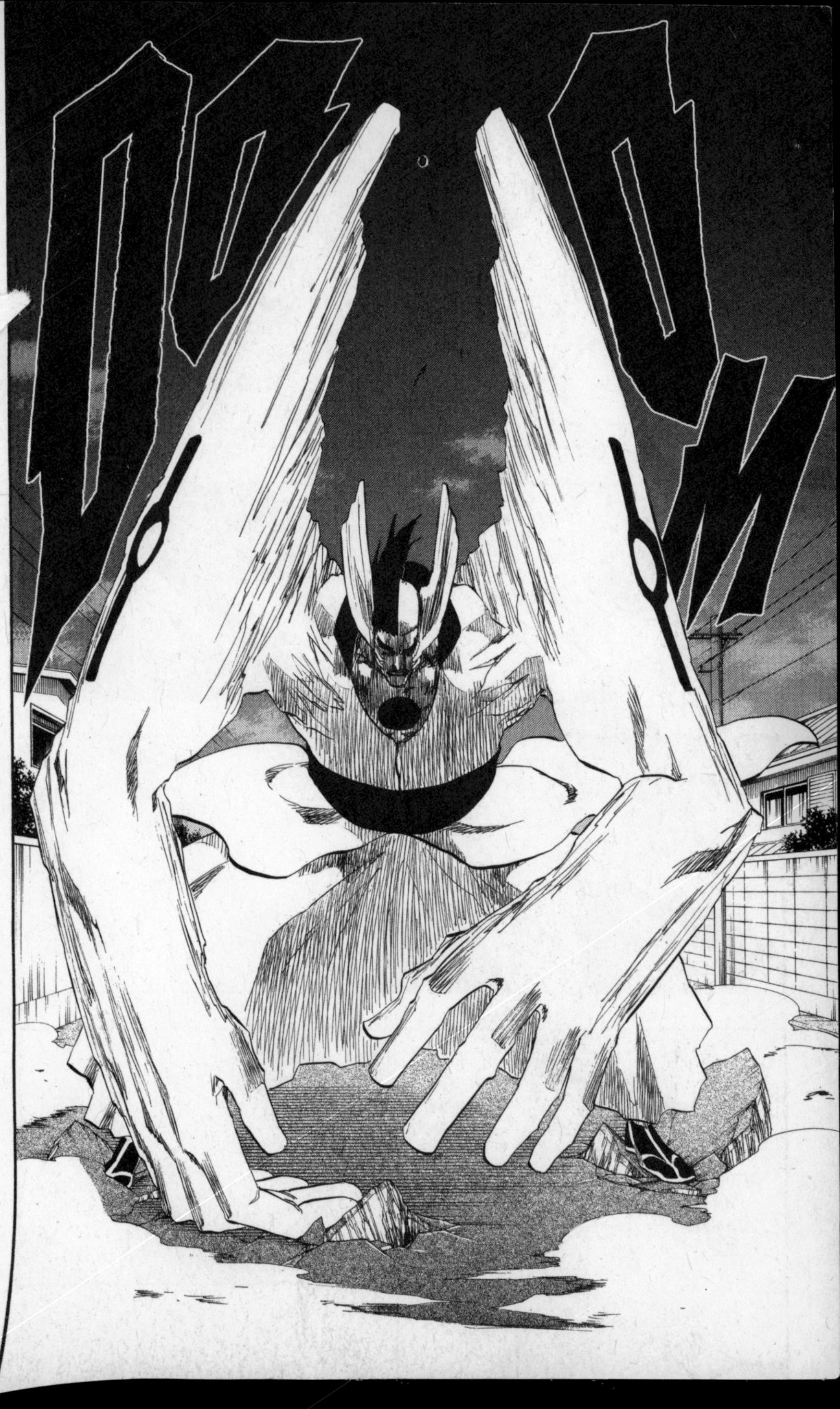
DOOM

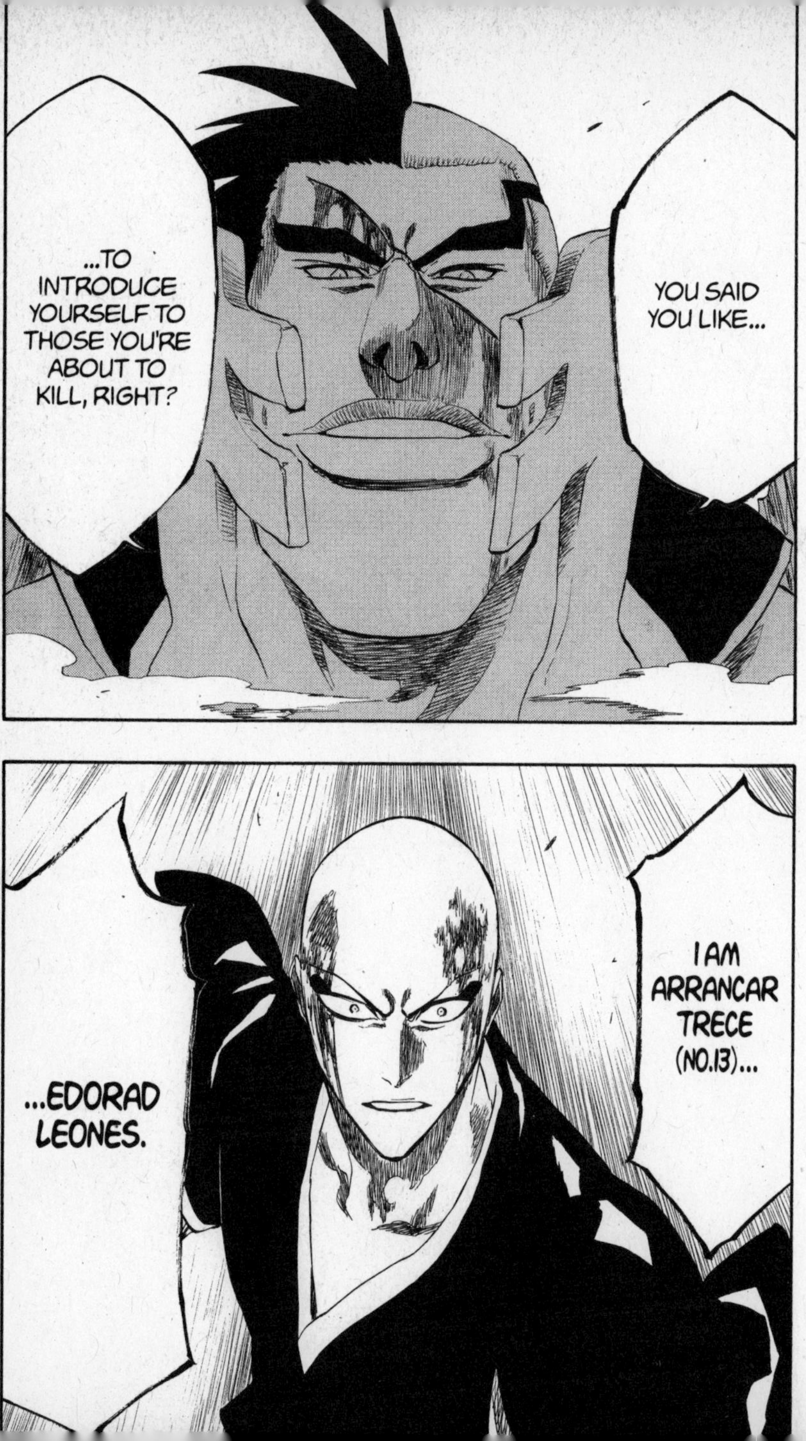
YOU SAID YOU LIKE...
...TO INTRODUCE YOURSELF TO THOSE YOU'RE ABOUT TO KILL, RIGHT?
I AM ARRANCAR TRECE (NO.13)...
...EDORAD LEONES.

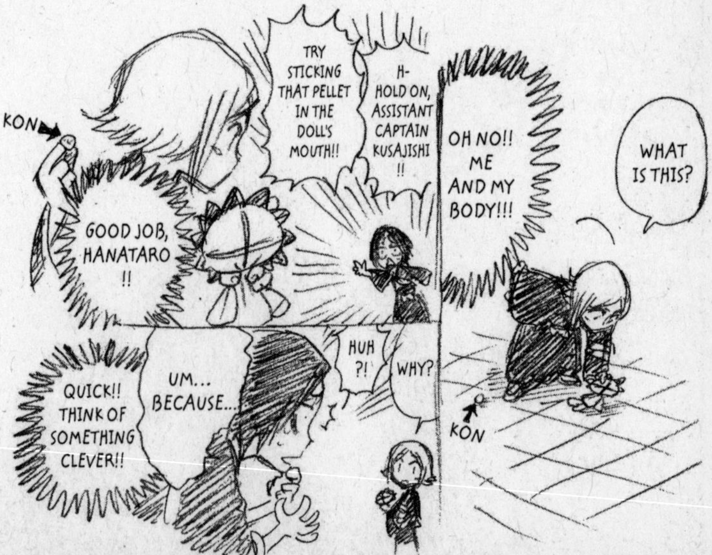
WHAT IS THIS?
OH NO!! ME AND MY BODY!!!
KON
H- HOLD ON, ASSISTANT CAPTAIN KUSAJISHI !!
TRY STICKING THAT PELLET IN THE DOLL'S MOUTH!!
KON
GOOD JOB, HANATARO !!
WHY?
HUH ?!
UM... BECAUSE...
QUICK!! THINK OF SOMETHING CLEVER!!

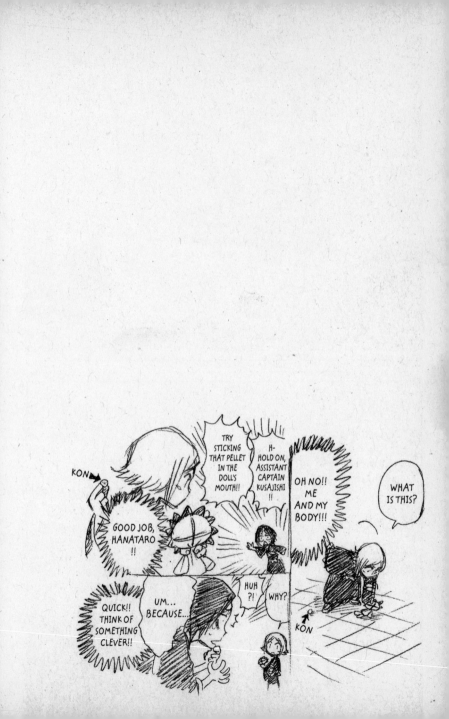

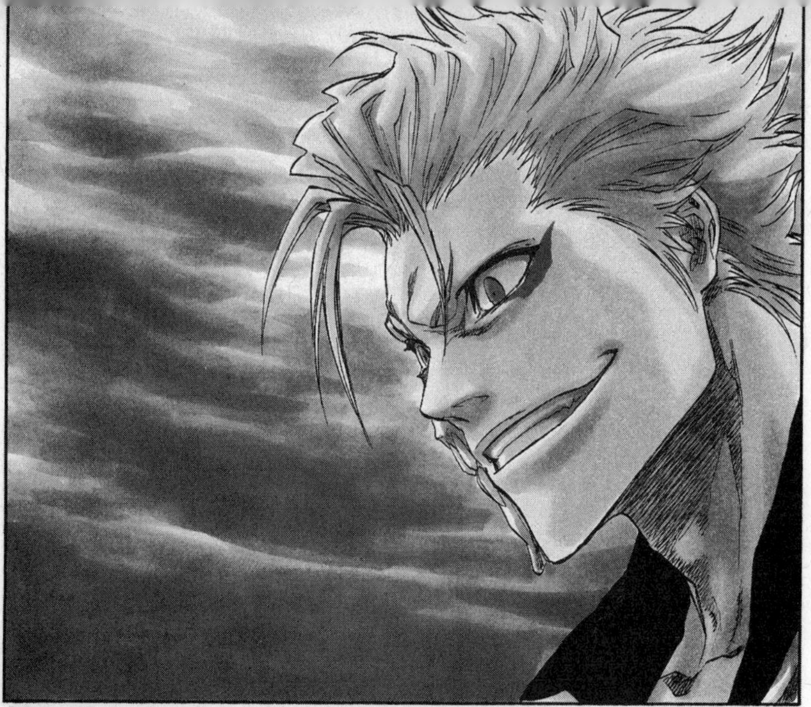

204. ¡Mala Suerte! 3 [Monstruo Sangrienta]

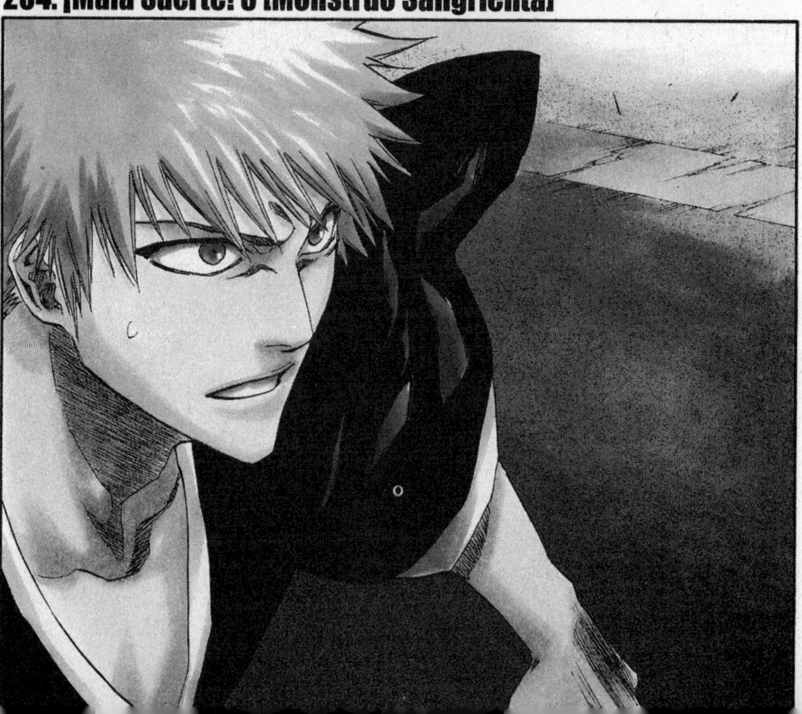

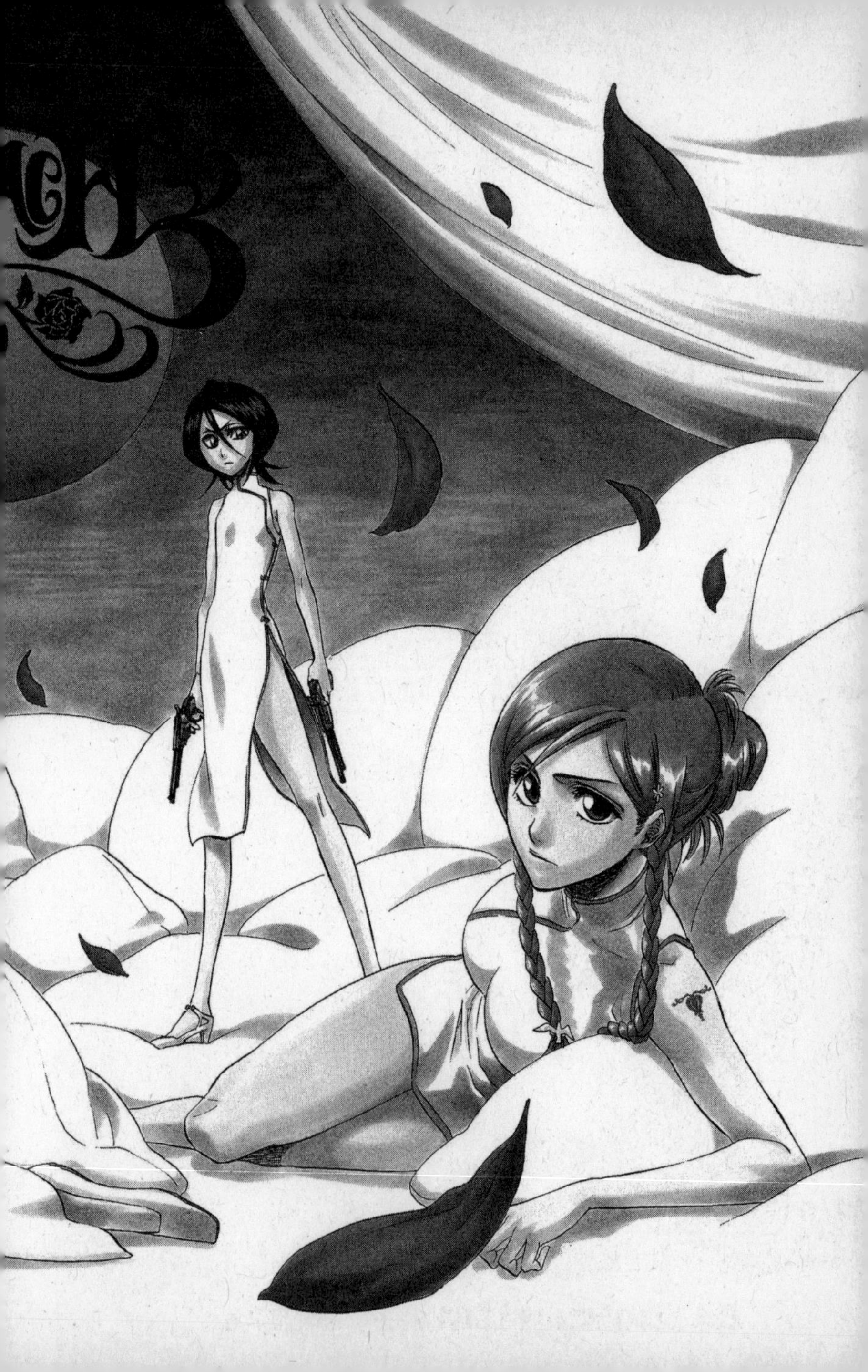

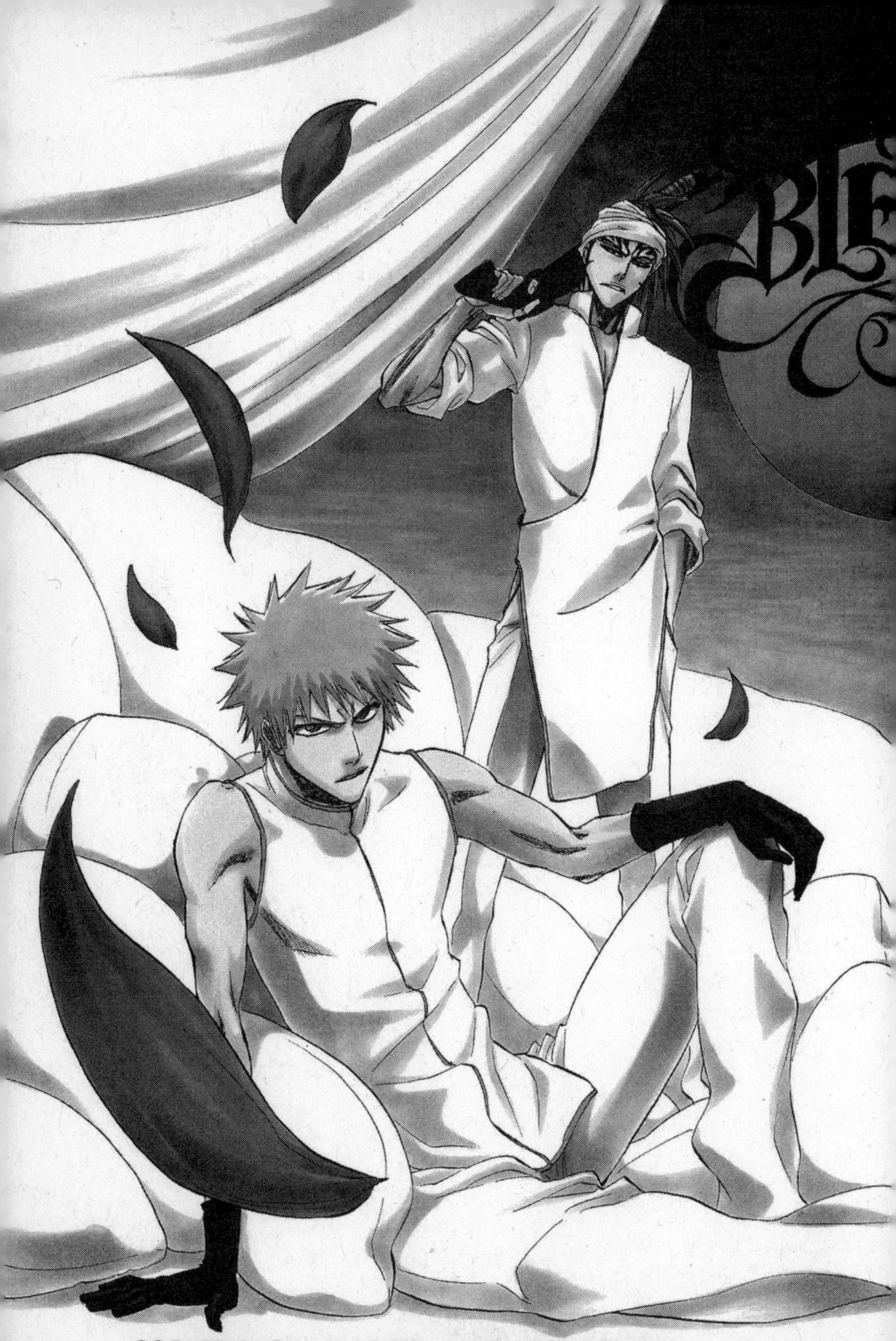

204. ¡Mala Suerte! 3 [Monstruo Sangrienta]

BLEACH
ブリーチ

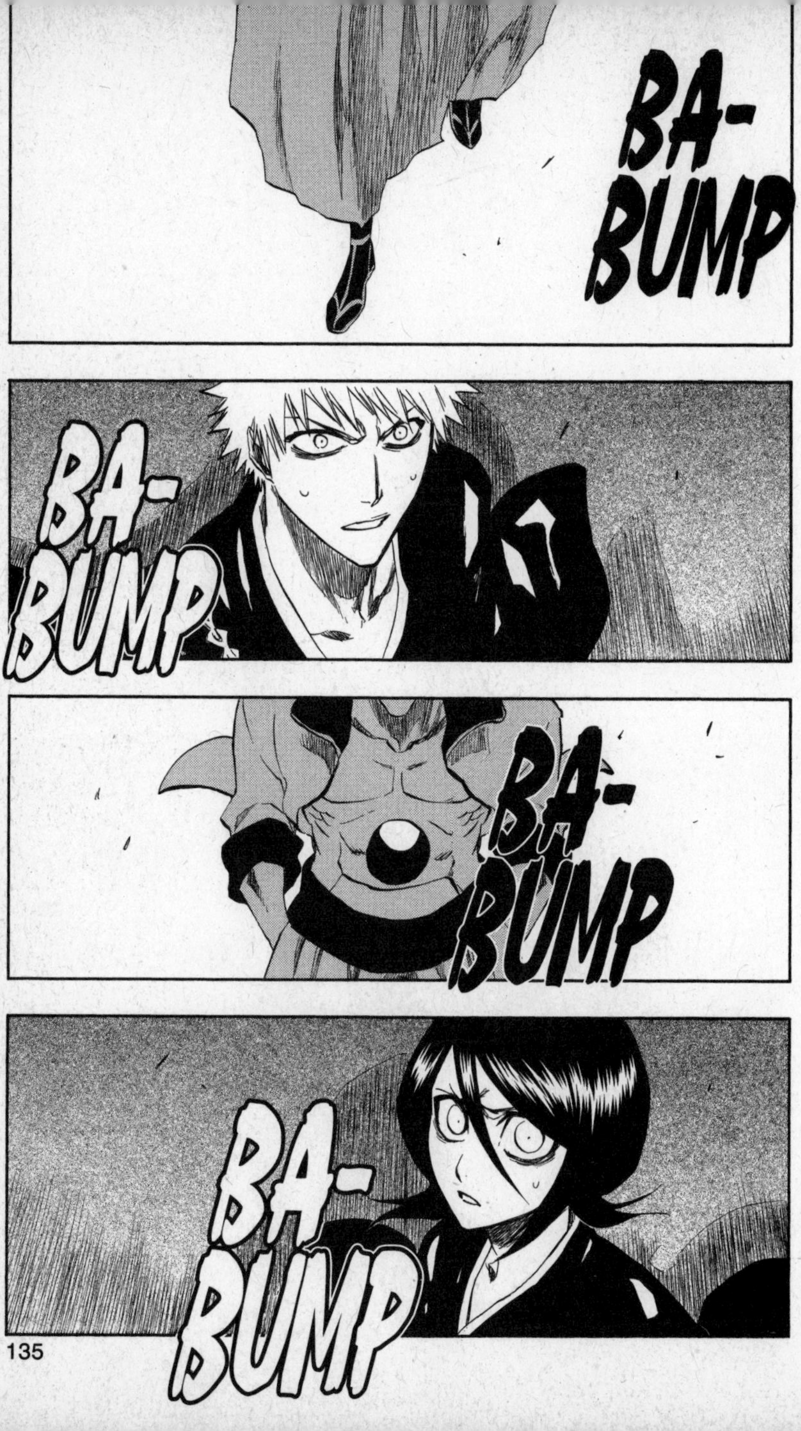
BA-
BUMP
BA-
BUMP
BA-
BUMP
BA-
BUMP

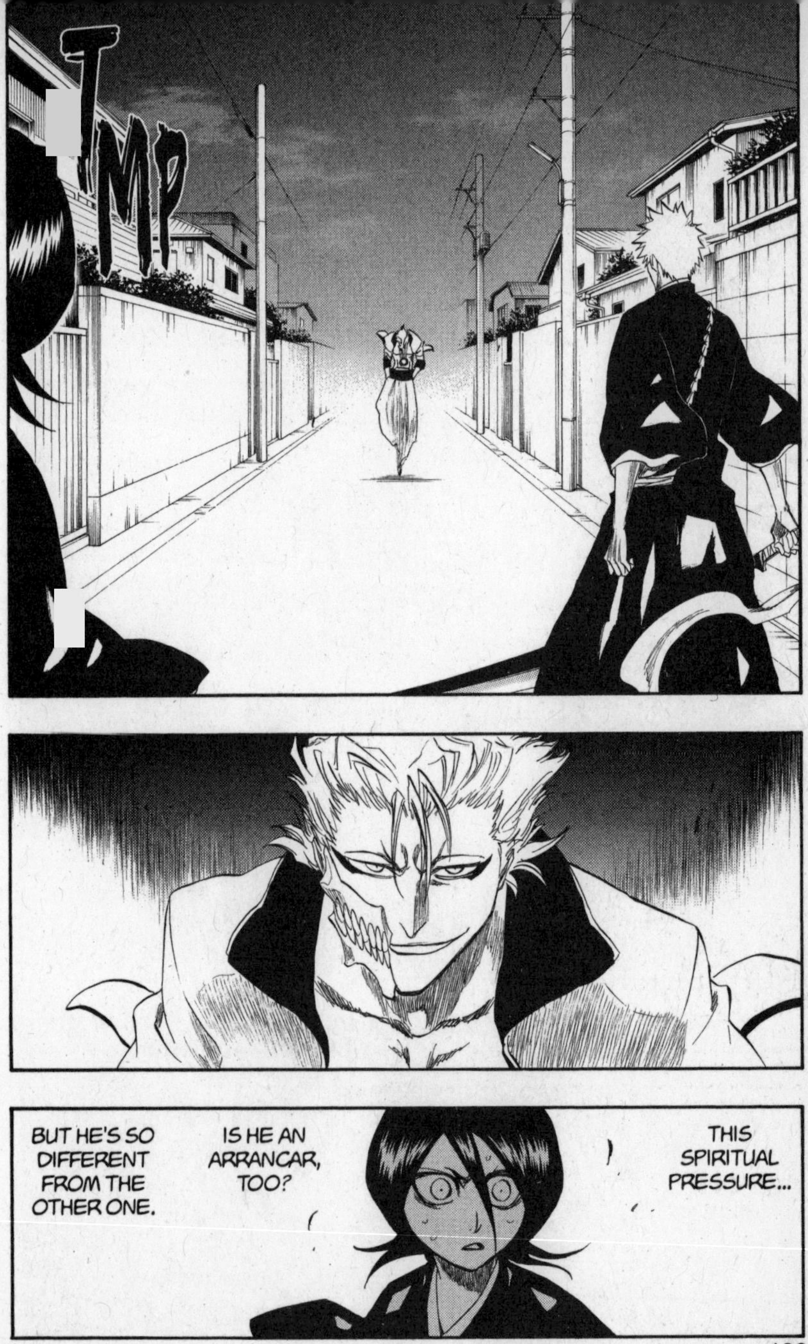
THIS SPIRITUAL PRESSURE...
IS HE AN ARRANCAR, TOO?
BUT HE'S SO DIFFERENT FROM THE OTHER ONE.

READ THIS WAY

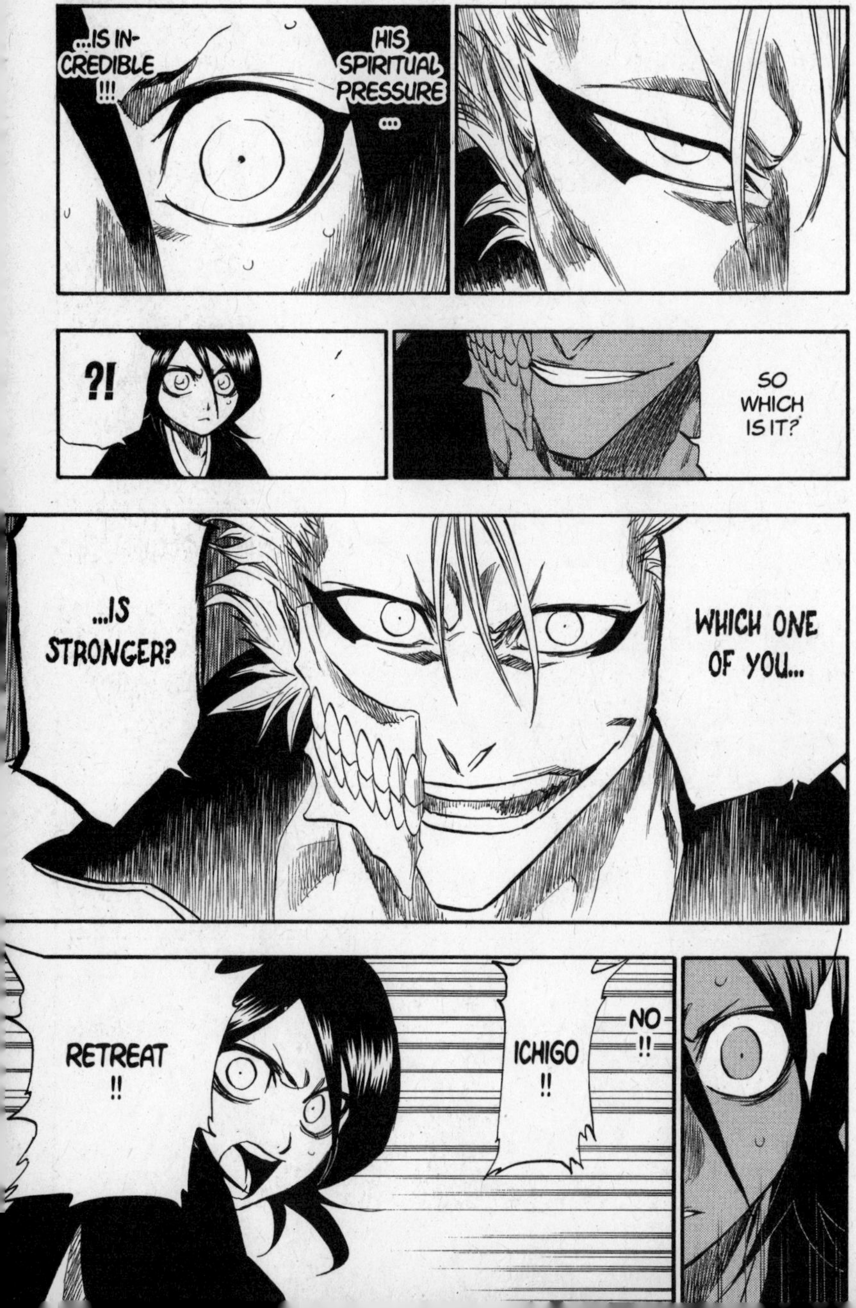
HIS SPIRITUAL PRESSURE ...
...IS IN-CREDIBLE !!!
SO WHICH IS IT?
?!
WHICH ONE OF YOU...
...IS STRONGER?
NO !!
ICHIGO !!
RETREAT !!

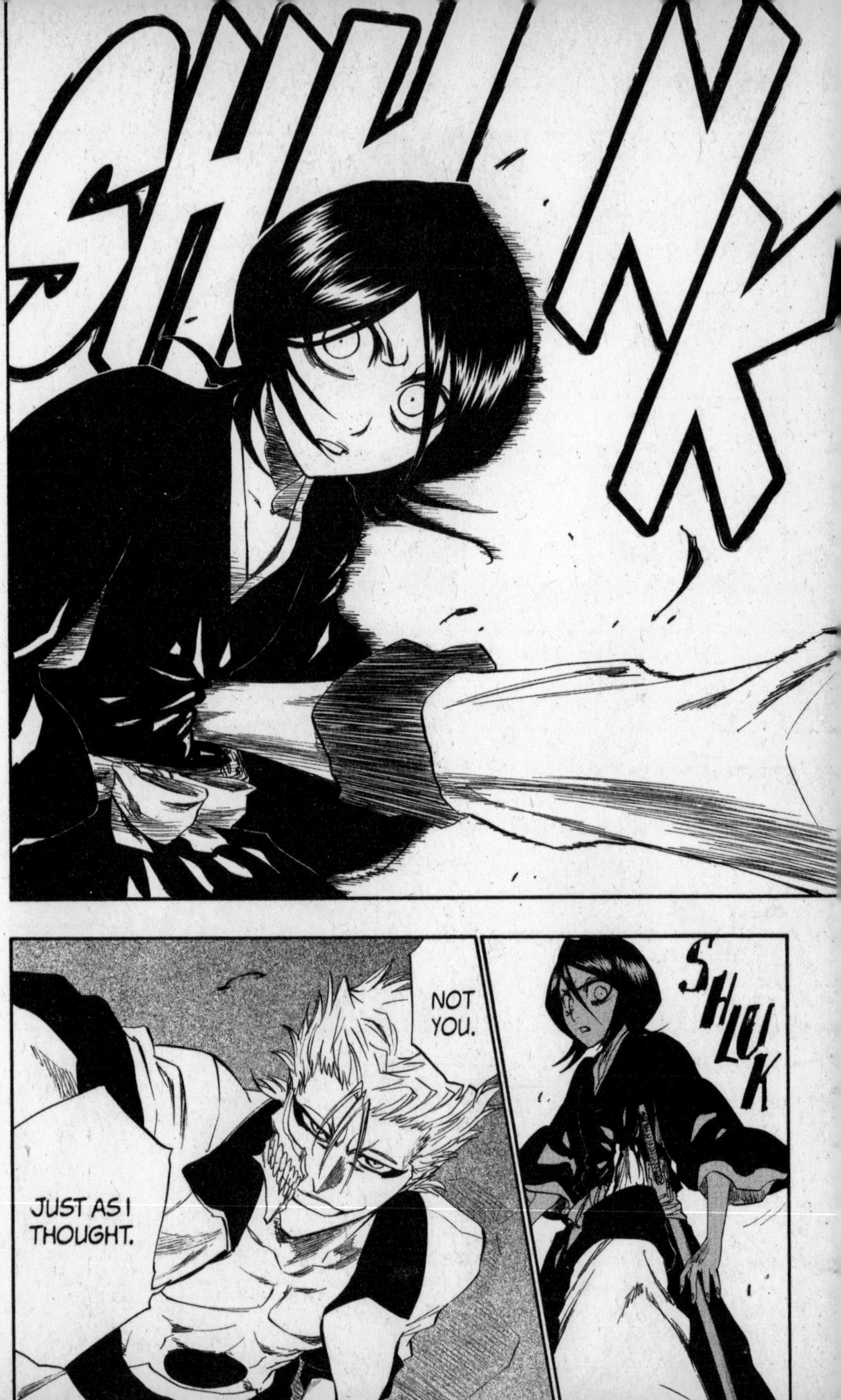
SHLINK
SHLUK
NOT YOU.
JUST AS I THOUGHT.

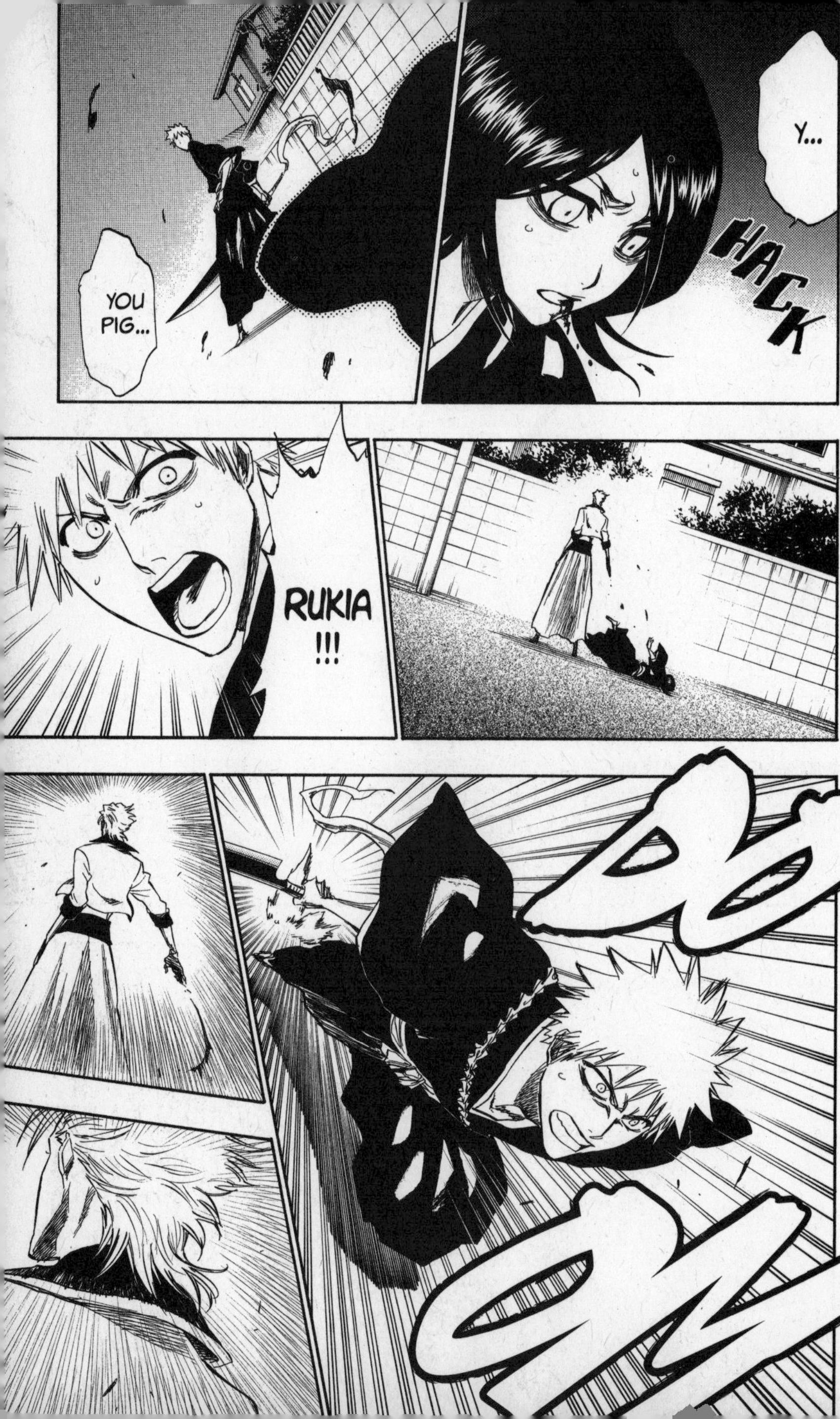
Y...
HACK
YOU PIG...
RUKIA !!!

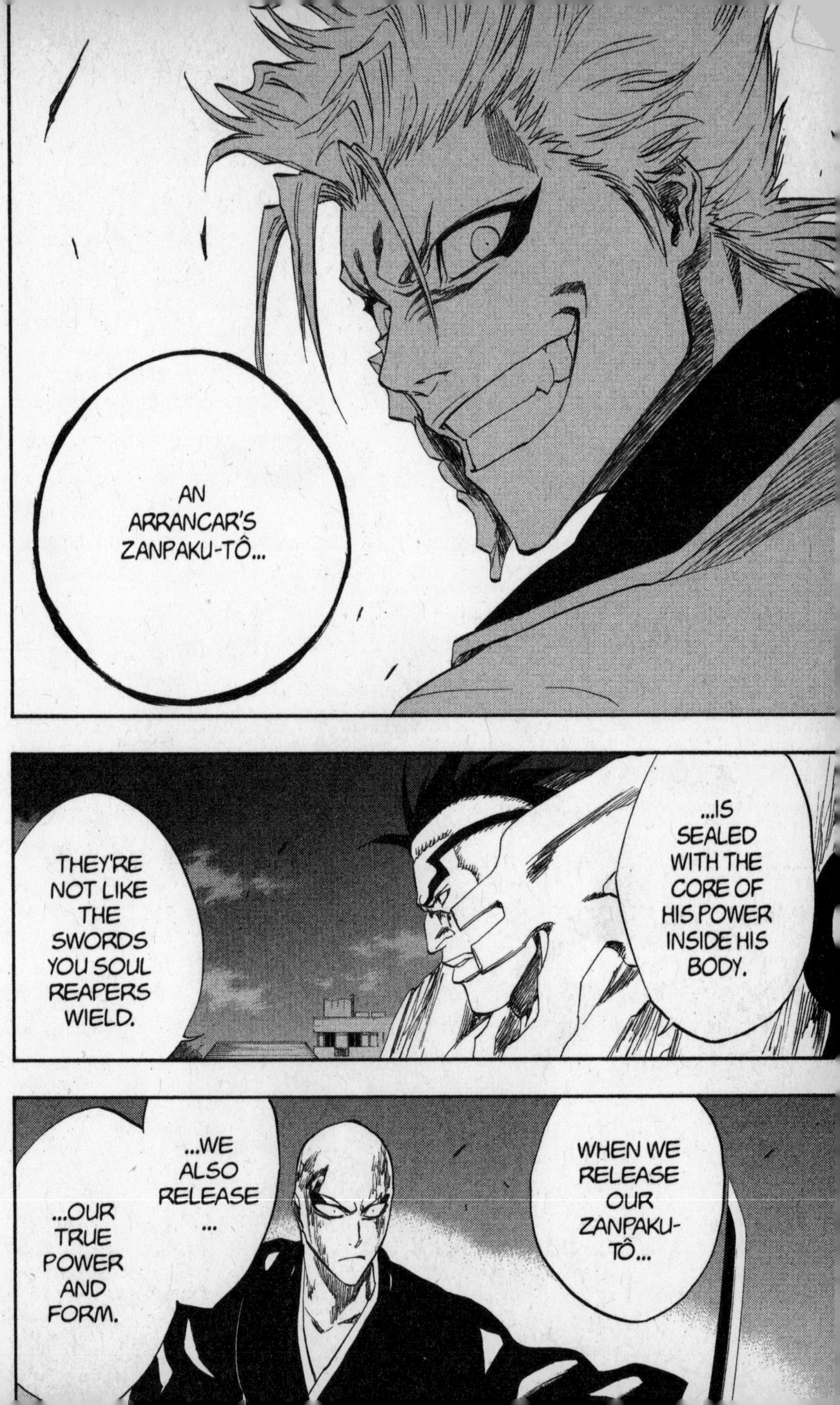
AN ARRANCAR'S ZANPAKU-TÔ...
...IS SEALED WITH THE CORE OF HIS POWER INSIDE HIS BODY.
THEY'RE NOT LIKE THE SWORDS YOU SOUL REAPERS WIELD.
WHEN WE RELEASE OUR ZANPAKU-TÔ...
...WE ALSO RELEASE...
...OUR TRUE POWER AND FORM.

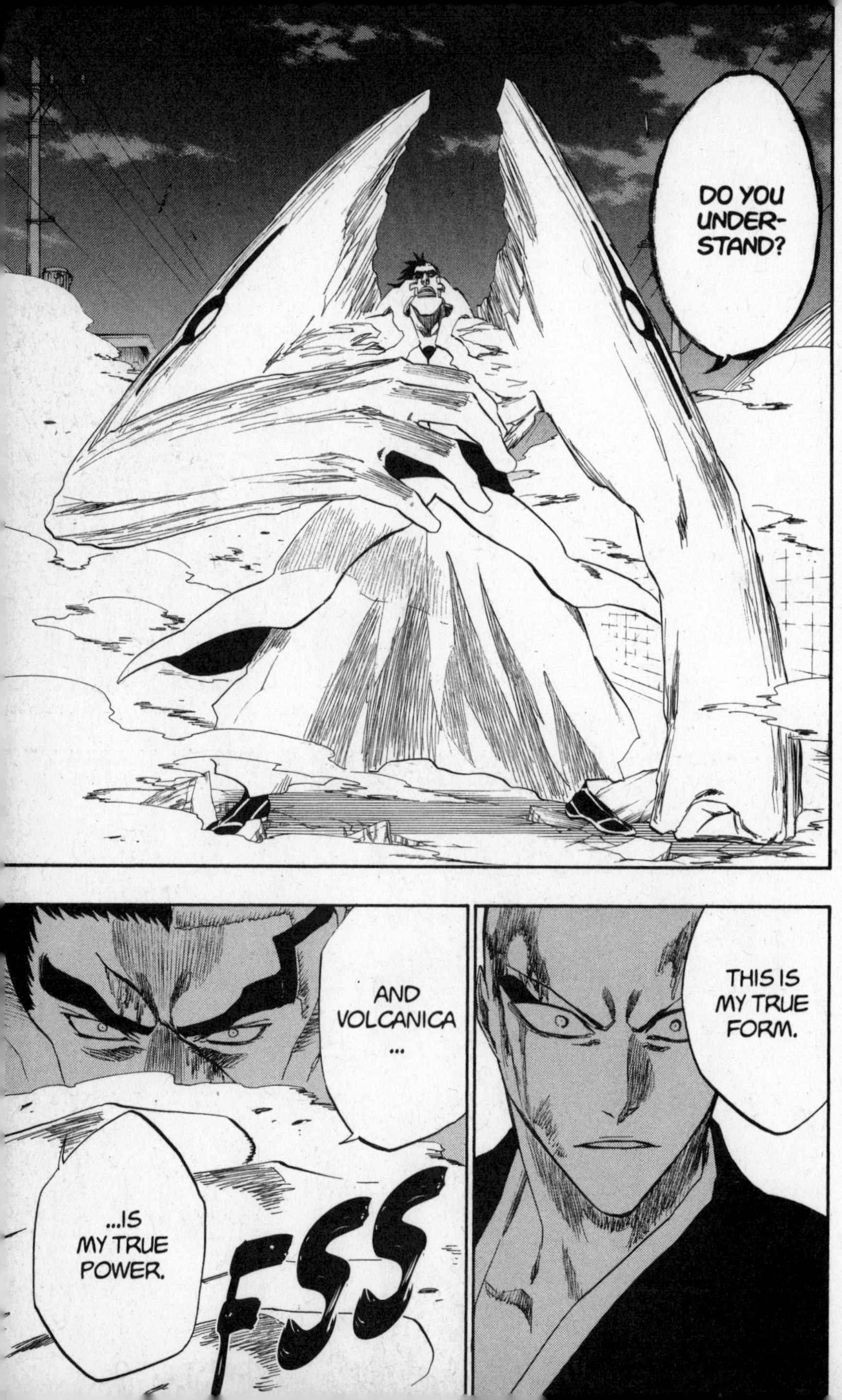
DO YOU UNDER-STAND?
THIS IS MY TRUE FORM.
AND VOLCANICA ...
...IS MY TRUE POWER.
FSS

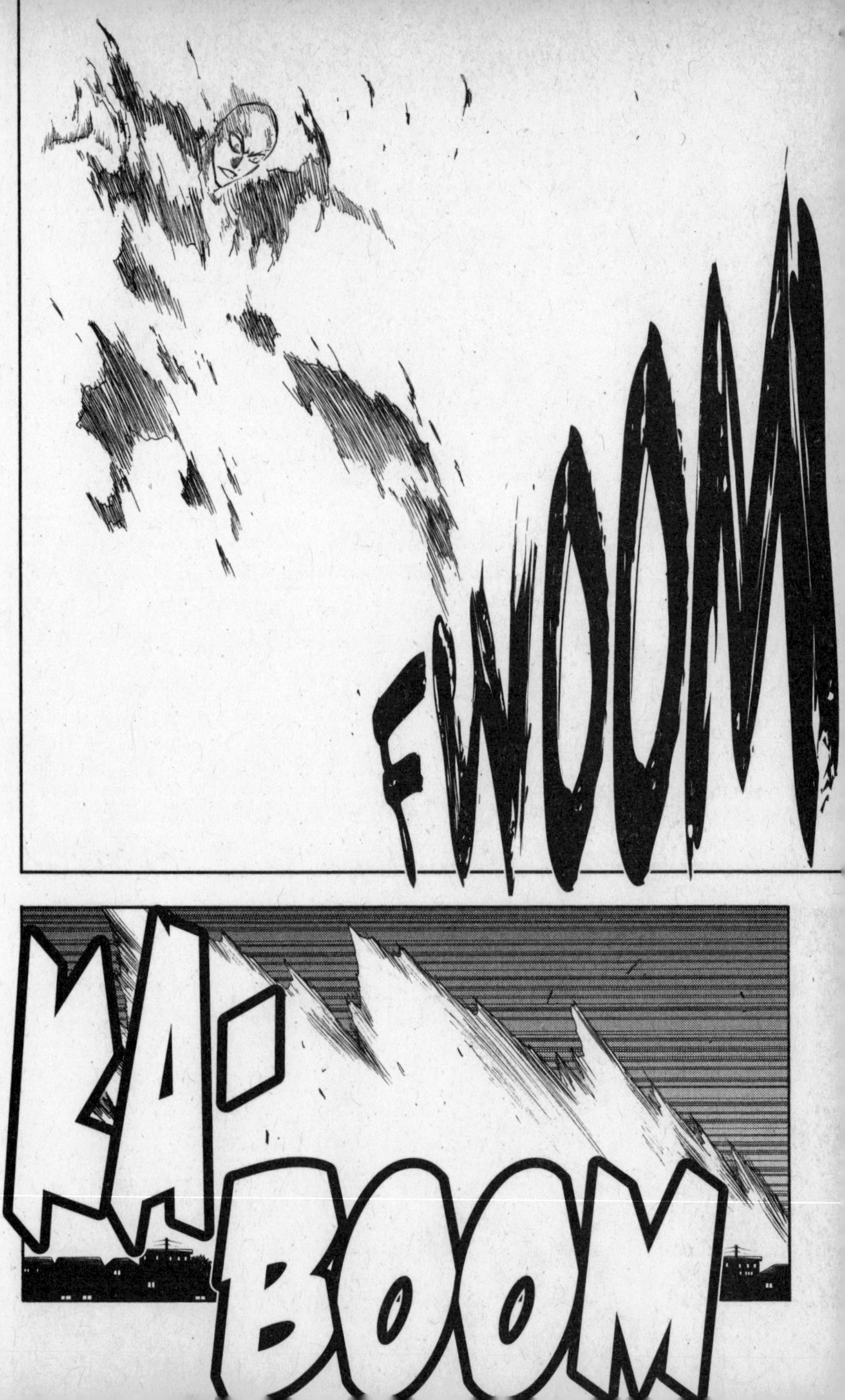
FWOOM
KA-
BOOM

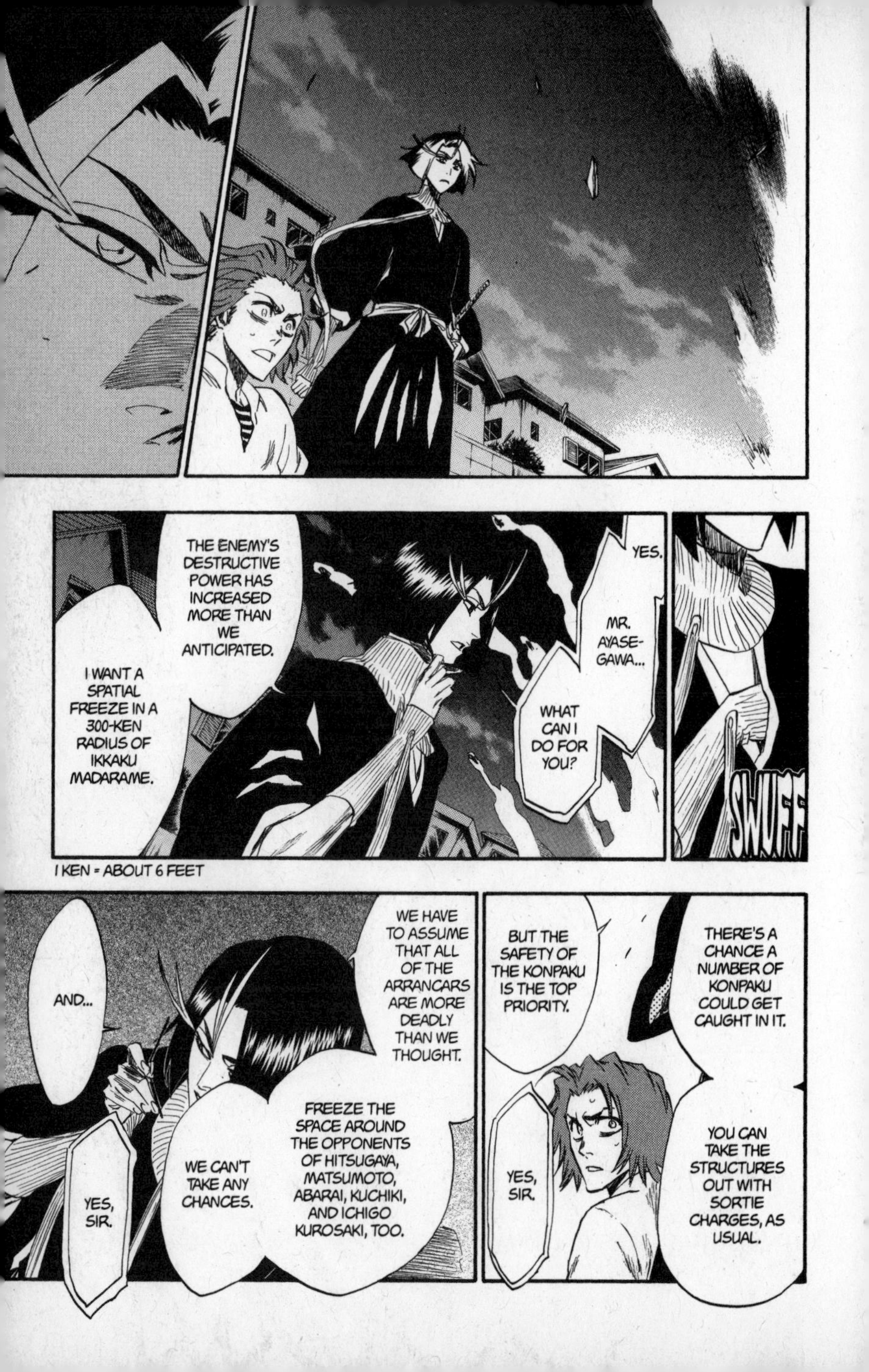
SWUFF
YES.
MR. AYASE-GAWA...
WHAT CAN I DO FOR YOU?
THE ENEMY'S DESTRUCTIVE POWER HAS INCREASED MORE THAN WE ANTICIPATED.
I WANT A SPATIAL FREEZE IN A 300-KEN RADIUS OF IKKAKU MADARAME.
THERE'S A CHANCE A NUMBER OF KONPAKU COULD GET CAUGHT IN IT.
BUT THE SAFETY OF THE KONPAKU IS THE TOP PRIORITY.
YOU CAN TAKE THE STRUCTURES OUT WITH SORTIE CHARGES, AS USUAL.
YES, SIR.
WE HAVE TO ASSUME THAT ALL OF THE ARRANCARS ARE MORE DEADLY THAN WE THOUGHT.
AND...
FREEZE THE SPACE AROUND THE OPPONENTS OF HITSUGAYA, MATSUMOTO, ABARAI, KUCHIKI, AND ICHIGO KUROSAKI, TOO.
WE CAN'T TAKE ANY CHANCES.
YES, SIR.

1 KEN = ABOUT 6 FEET

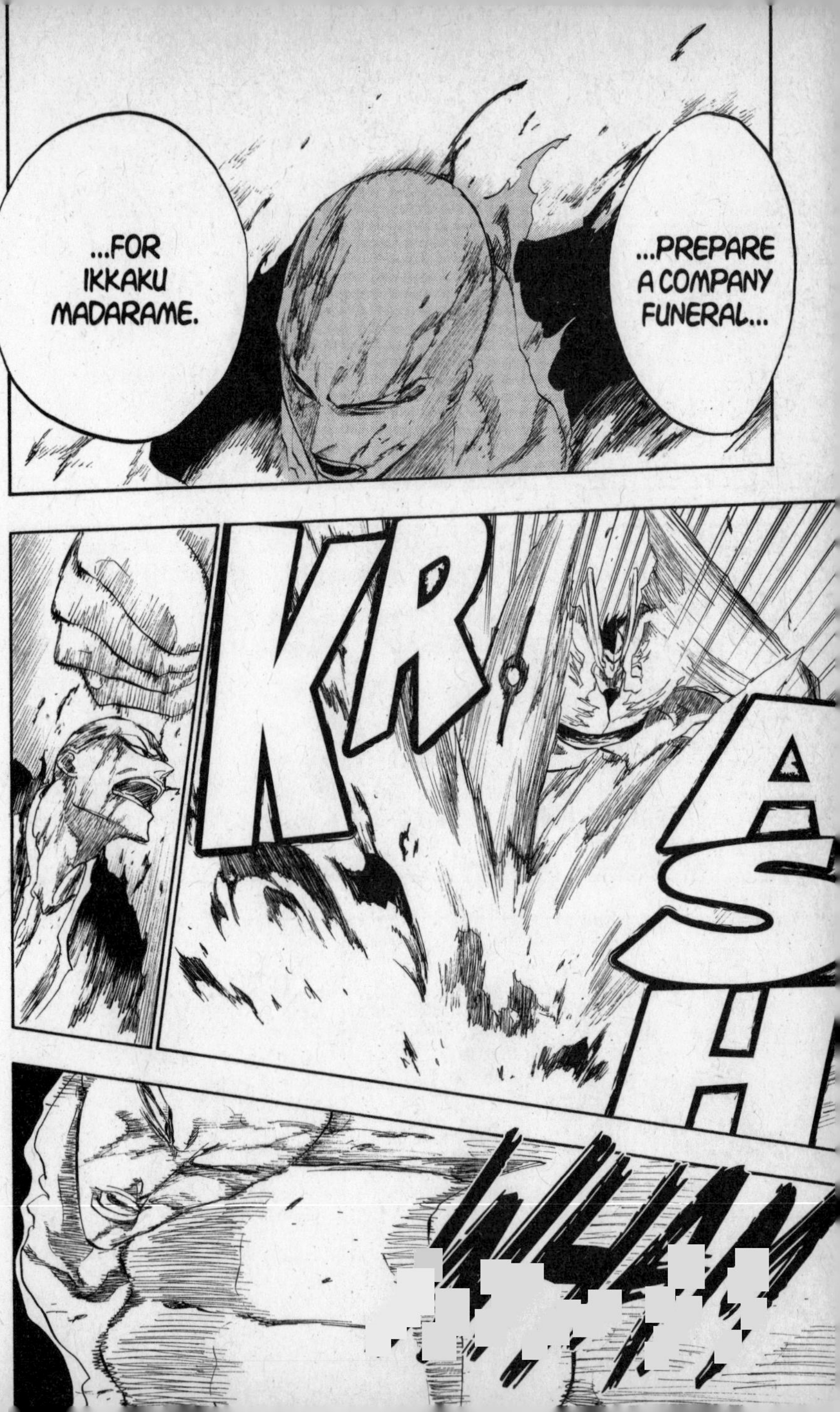
...PREPARE A COMPANY FUNERAL...
...FOR IKKAKU MADARAME.
KRASH

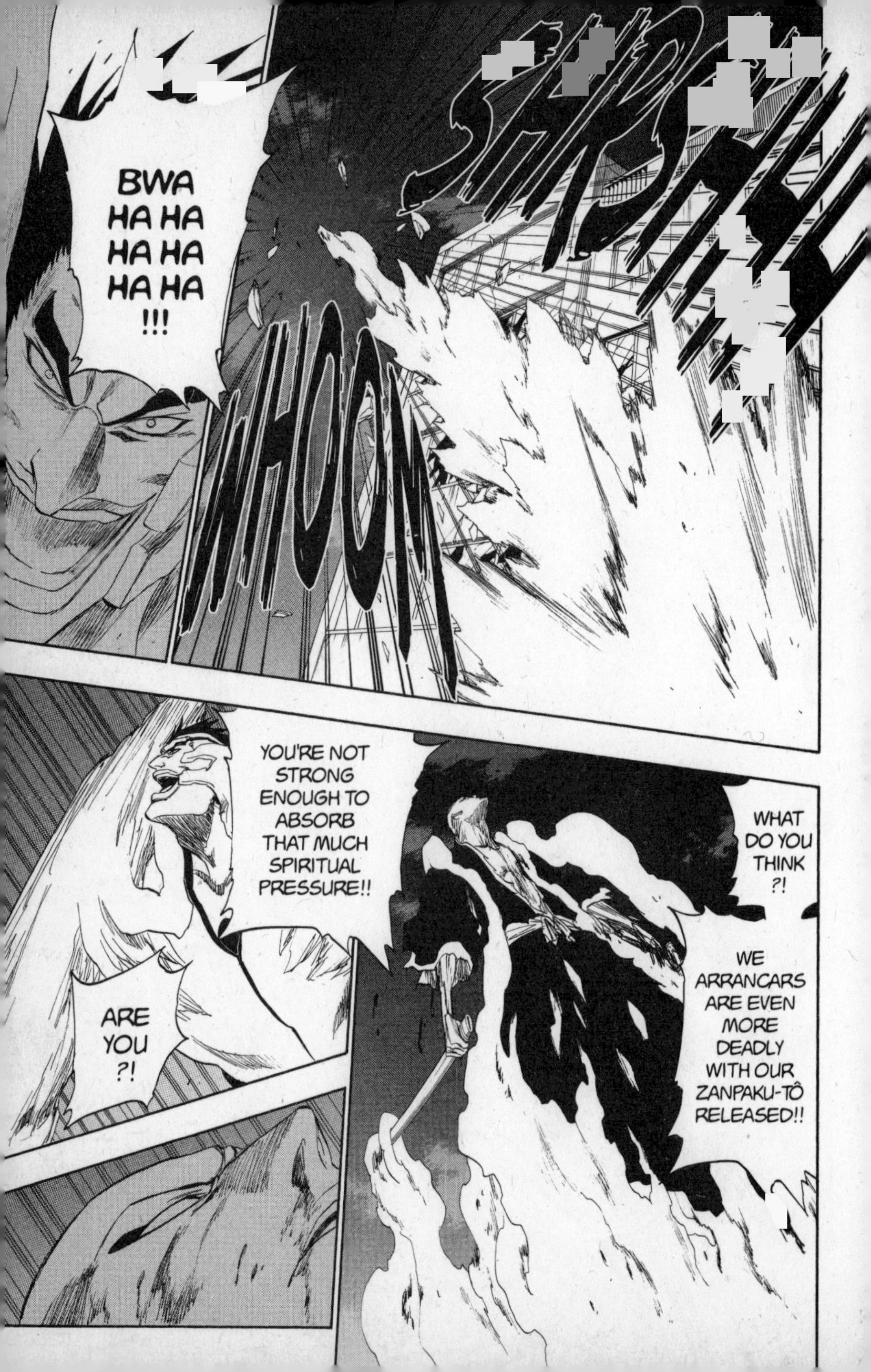
WHOOM
BWA HA HA HA HA HA HA !!!
YOU'RE NOT STRONG ENOUGH TO ABSORB THAT MUCH SPIRITUAL PRESSURE!!
ARE YOU ?!
WHAT DO YOU THINK ?!
WE ARRANCARS ARE EVEN MORE DEADLY WITH OUR ZANPAKU-TÔ RELEASED!!

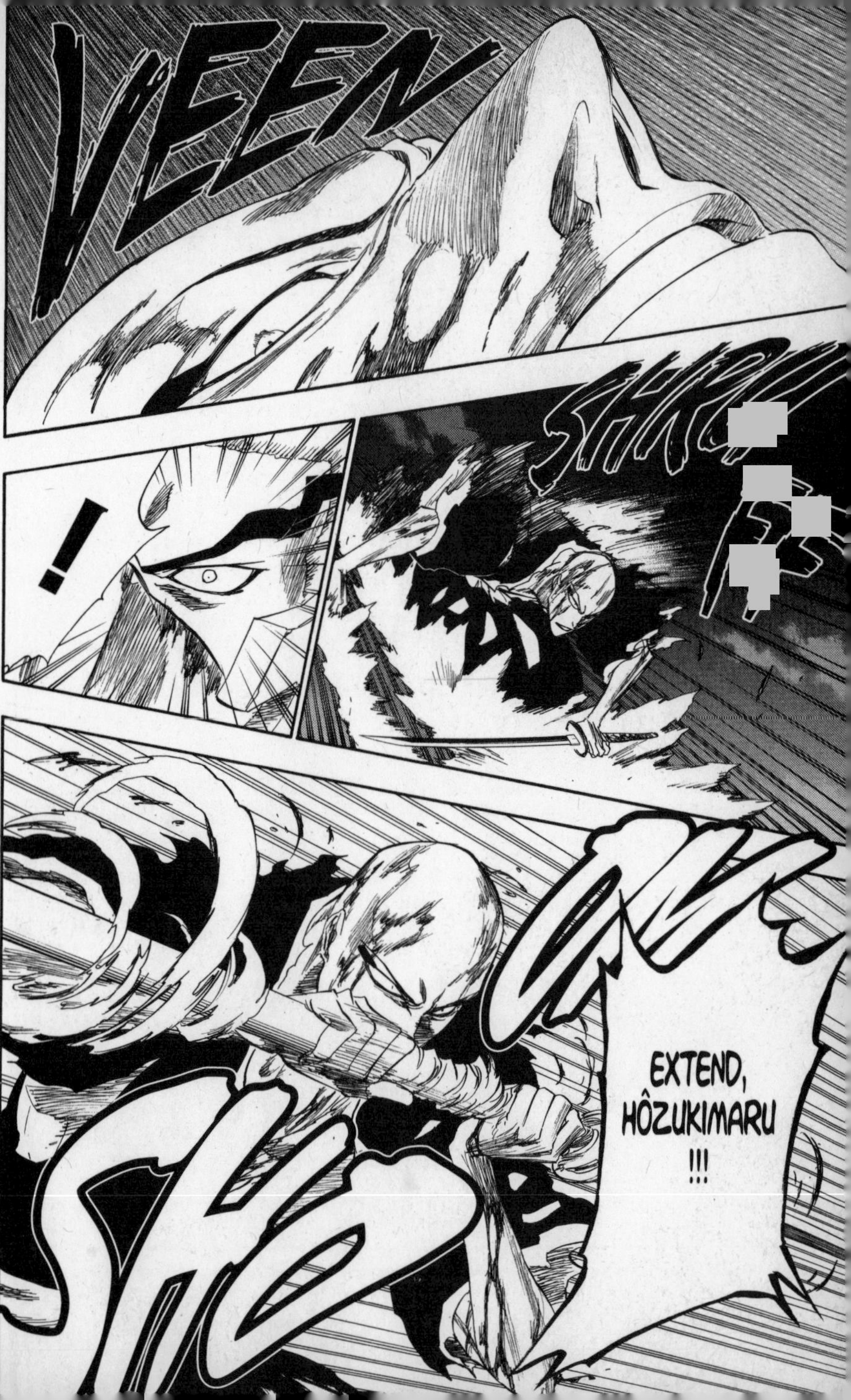
VEEN
!
EXTEND, HÔZUKIMARU !!!

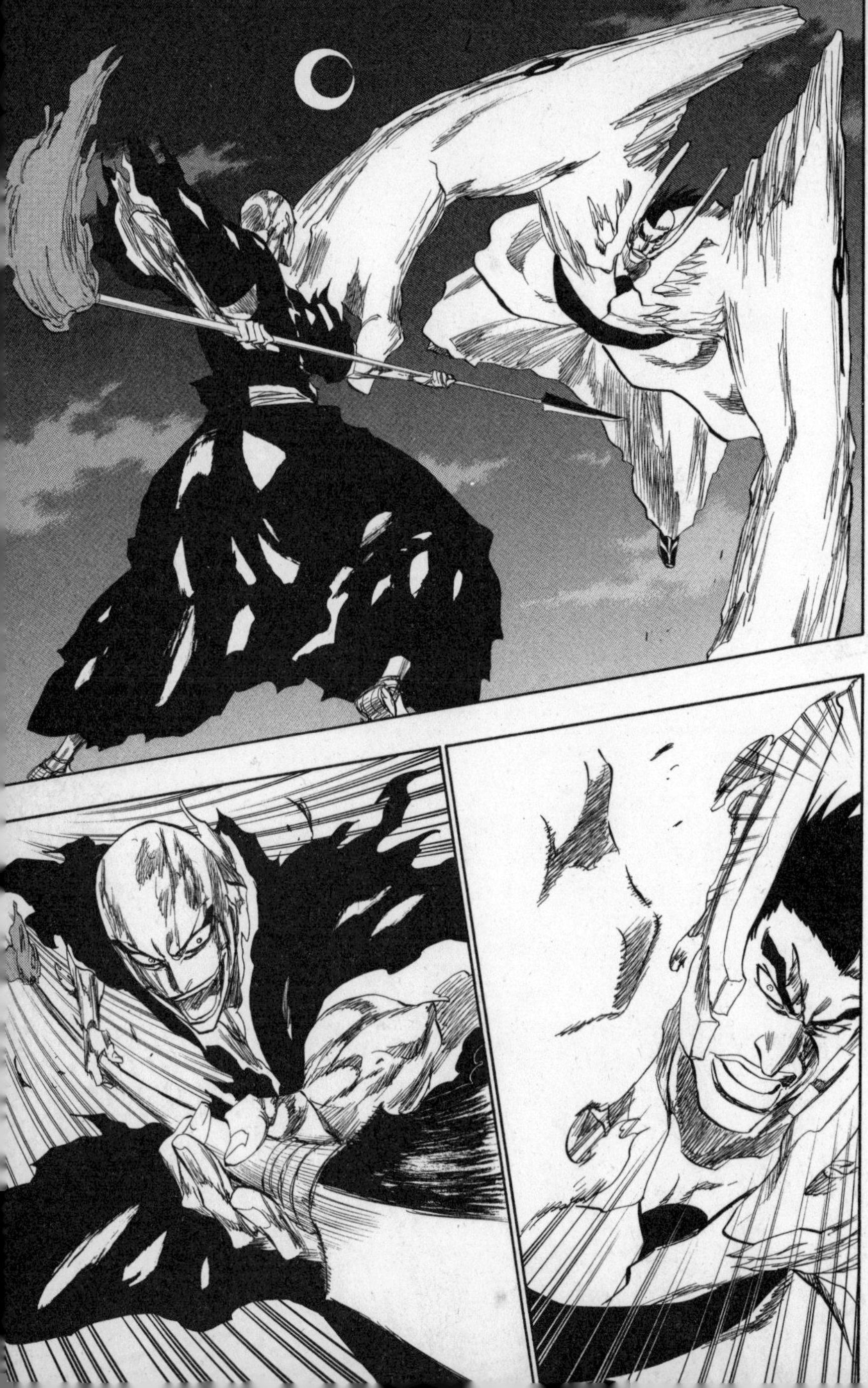

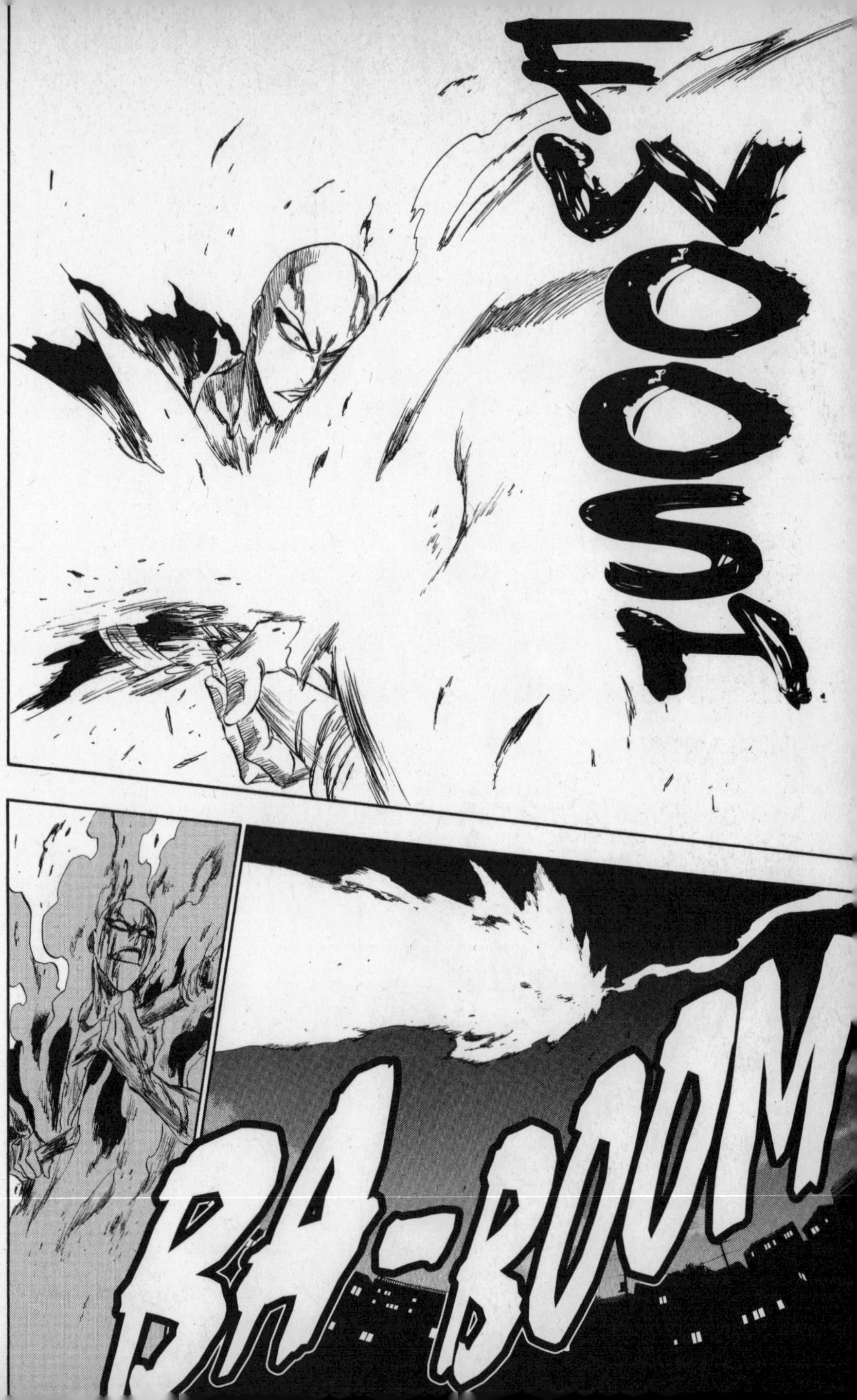
BA-BOOM

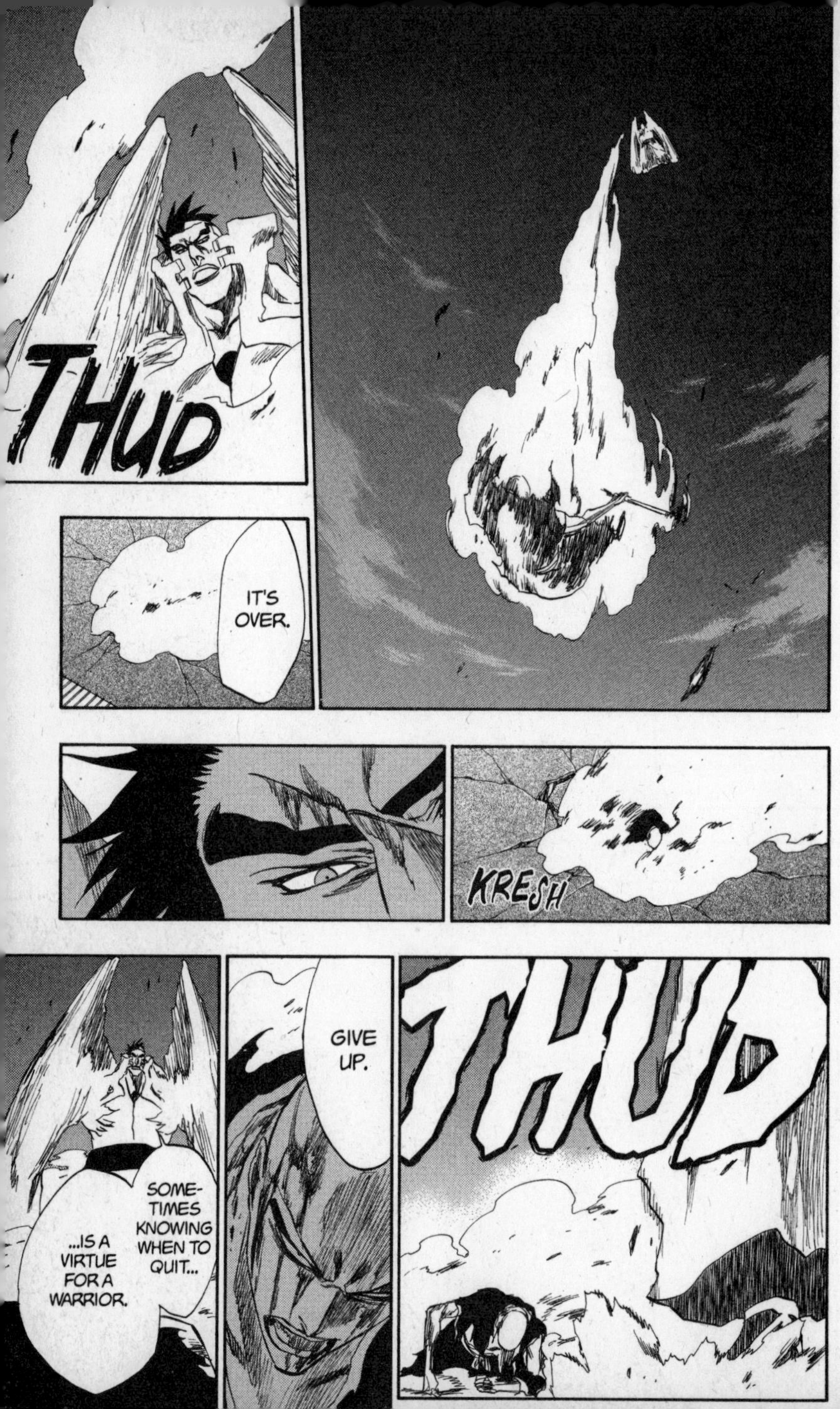
THUD
IT'S OVER.
KRESH
THUD
GIVE UP.
SOME-TIMES KNOWING WHEN TO QUIT...
...IS A VIRTUE FOR A WARRIOR.

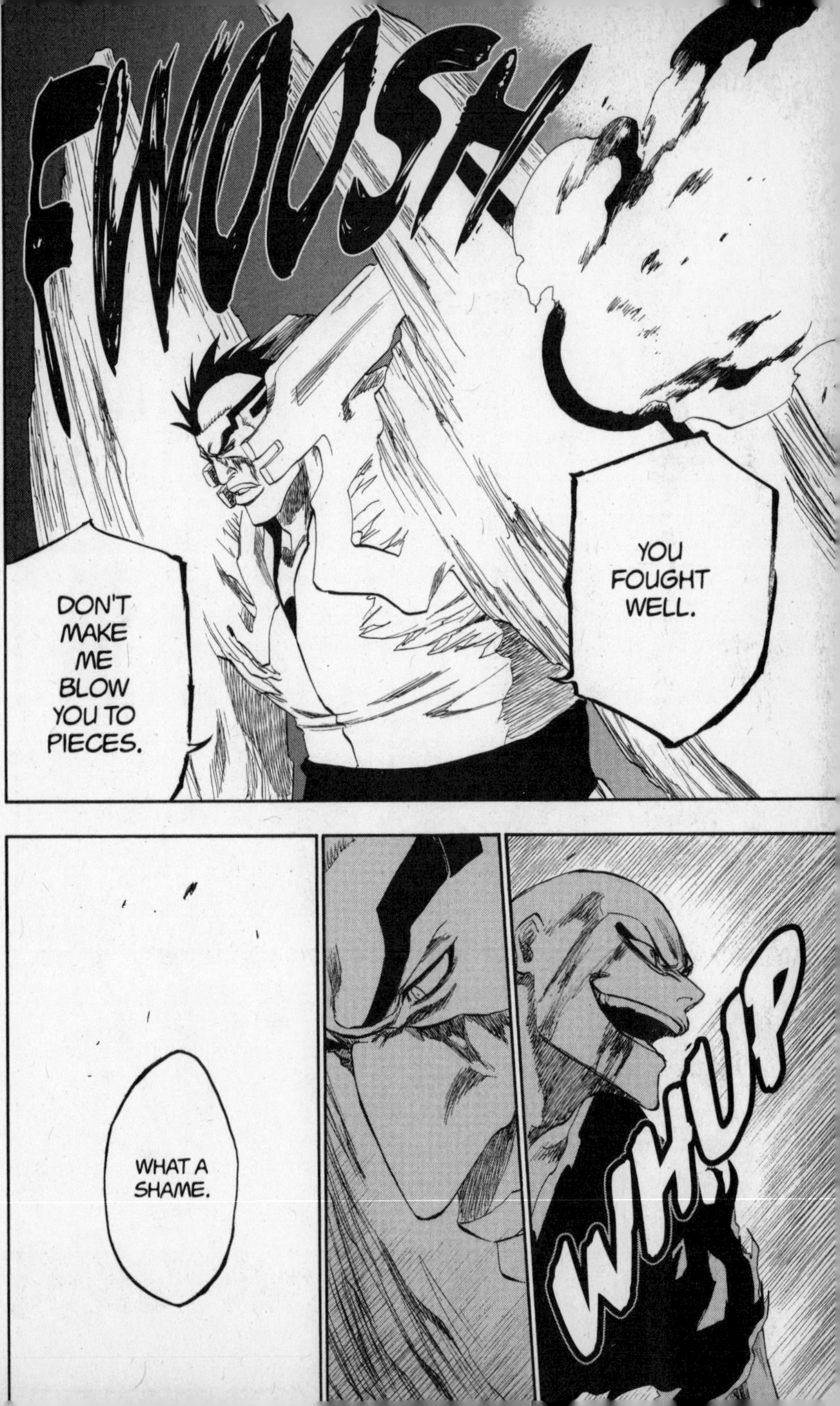
FWOOSH
YOU FOUGHT WELL.
DON'T MAKE ME BLOW YOU TO PIECES.
WHUP
WHAT A SHAME.

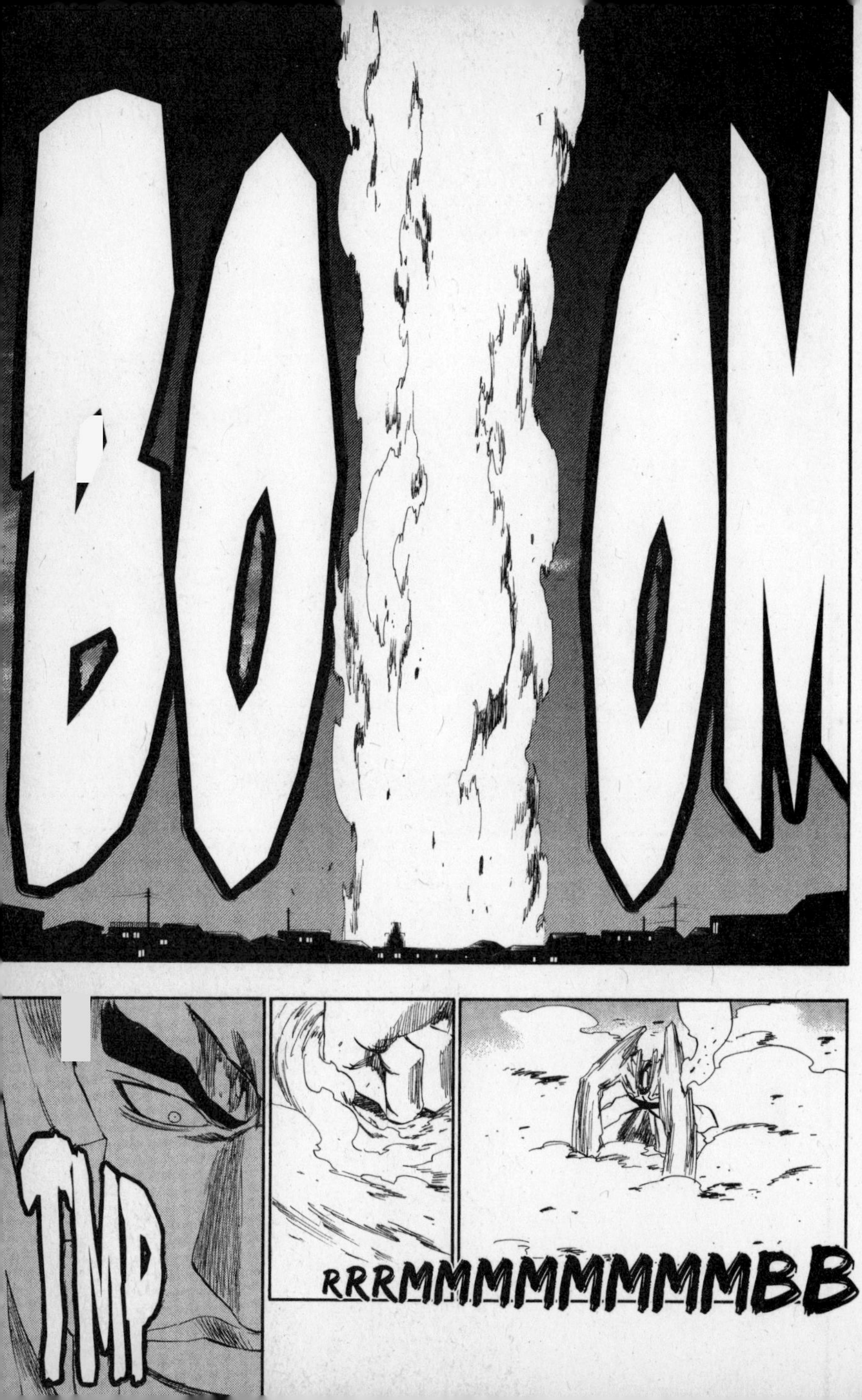
BOOM
RRRMMMMMMMMBB
TMP

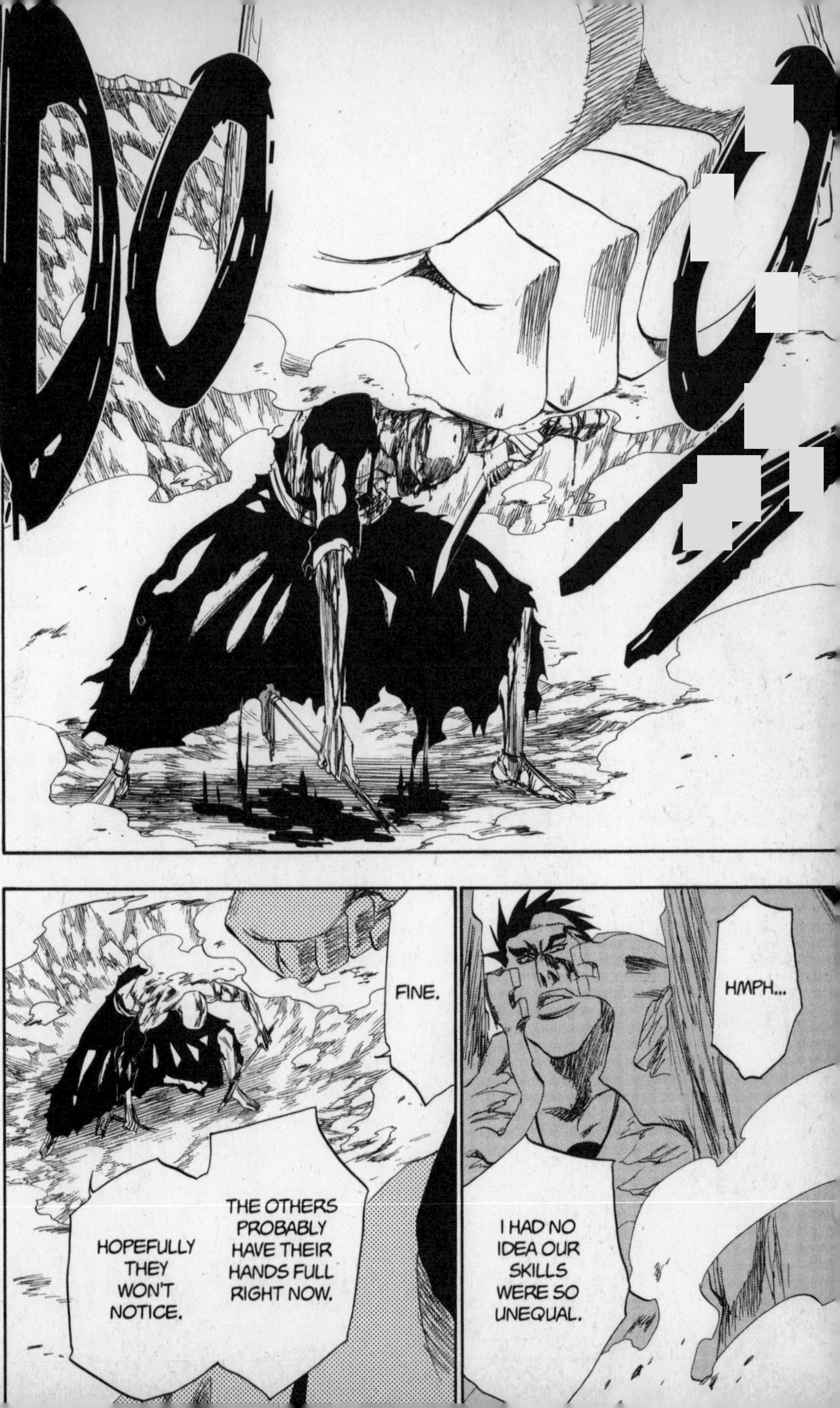
DO
HMPH...
I HAD NO IDEA OUR SKILLS WERE SO UNEQUAL.
FINE.
THE OTHERS PROBABLY HAVE THEIR HANDS FULL RIGHT NOW.
HOPEFULLY THEY WON'T NOTICE.

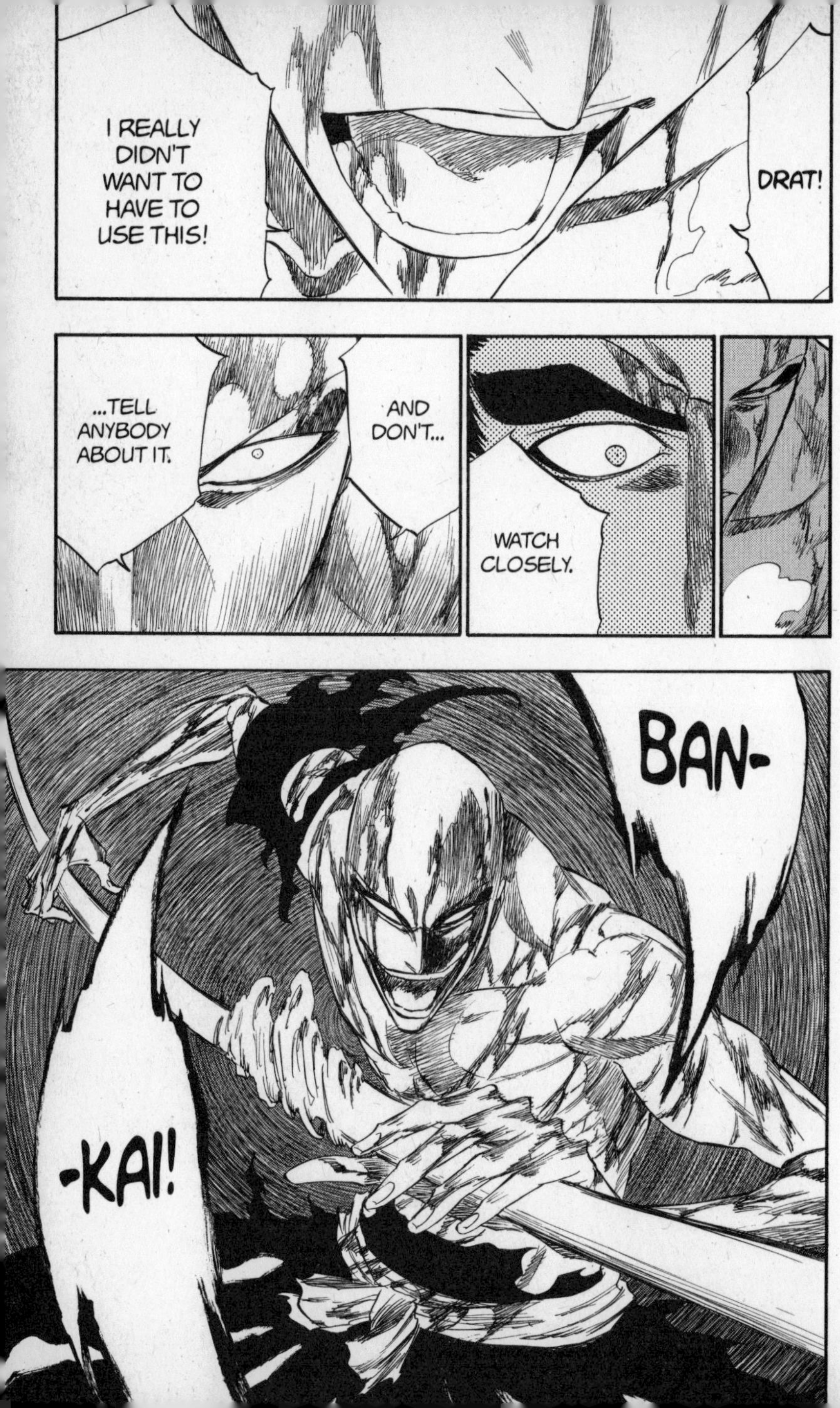
DRAT!
I REALLY DIDN'T WANT TO HAVE TO USE THIS!
WATCH CLOSELY.
AND DON'T...
...TELL ANYBODY ABOUT IT.
BAN-
-KAI!

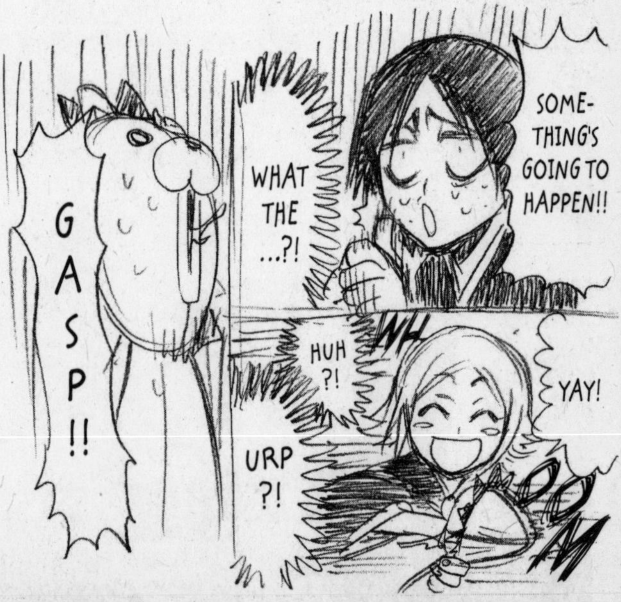
SOME-THING'S GOING TO HAPPEN!!
WHAT THE ...?!
YAY!
HUH ?!
URP ?!
DOOM
GASP!!

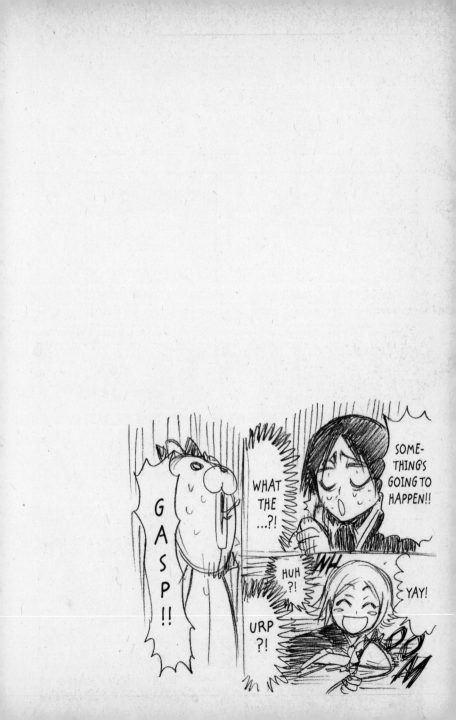

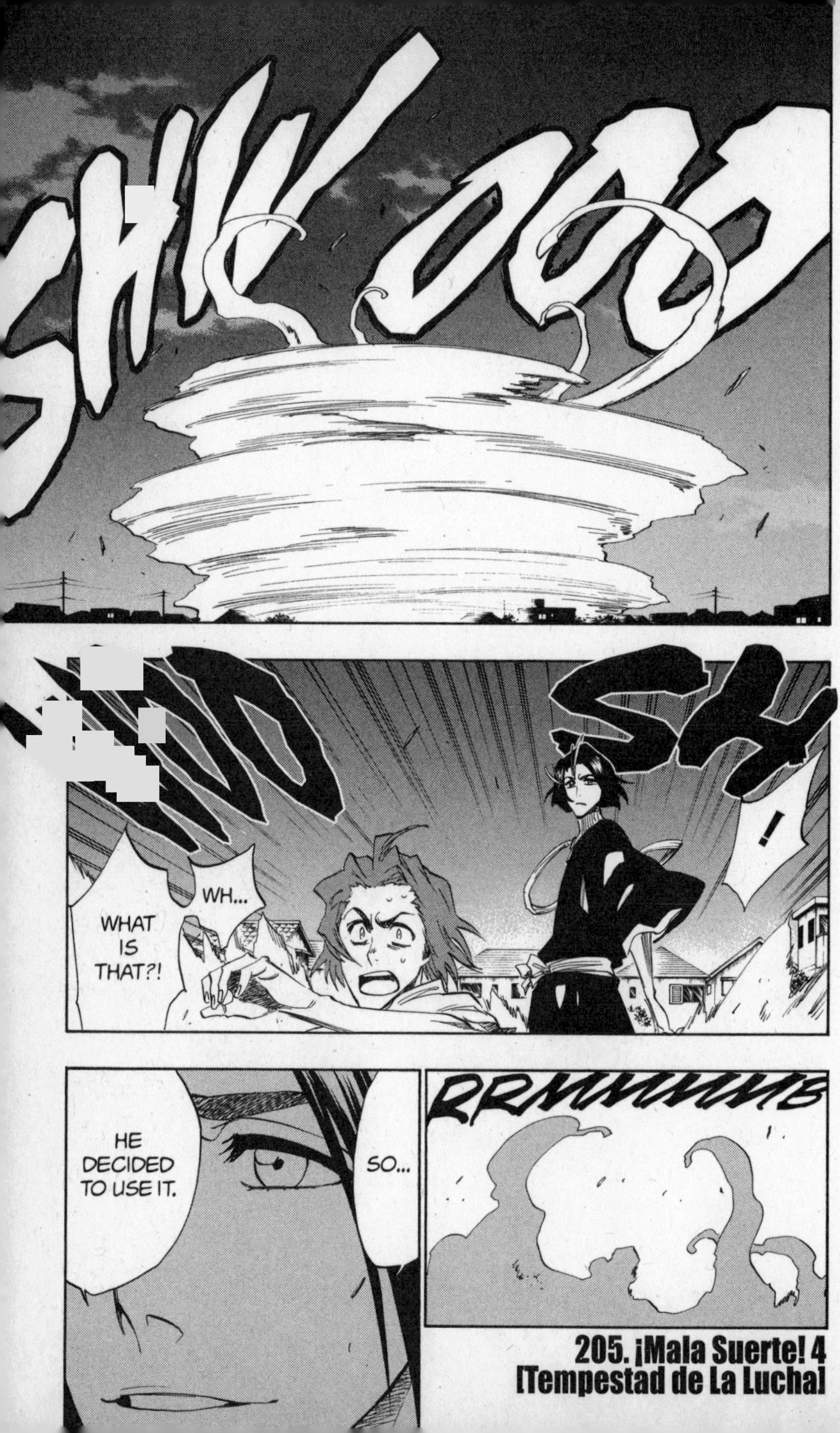
WH...
WHAT IS THAT?!
RRMMMMMB
SO...
HE DECIDED TO USE IT.

205. ¡Mala Suerte! 4 [Tempestad de La Lucha]

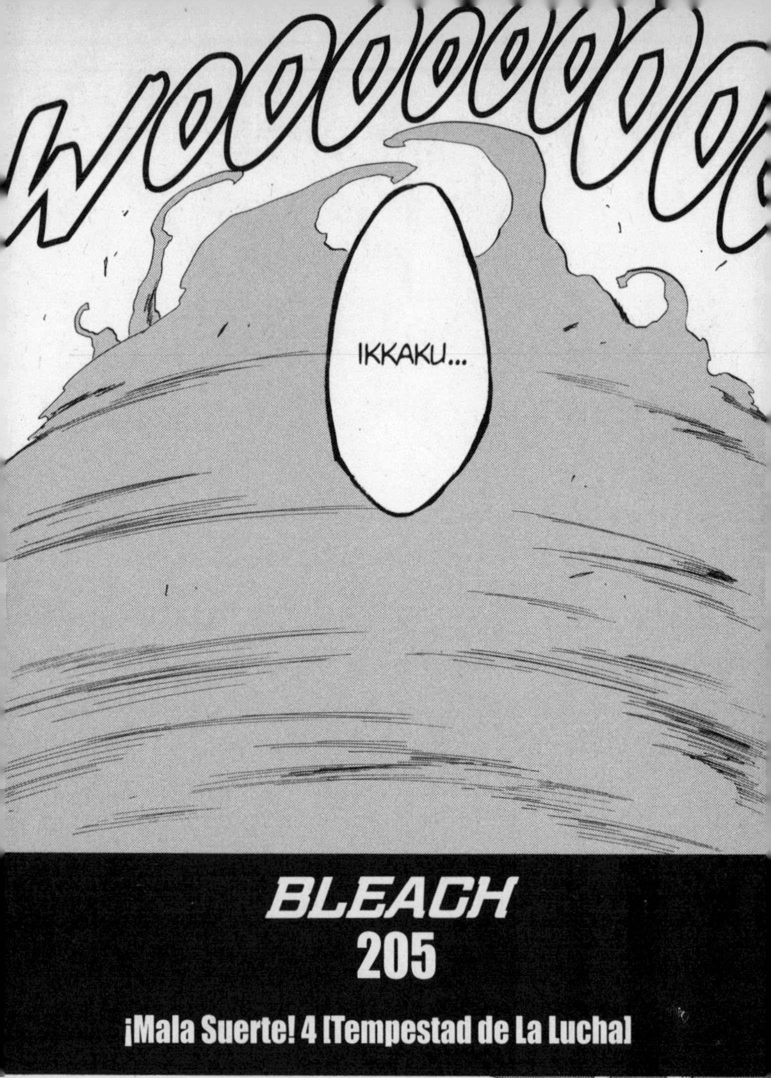
IKKAKU...

BLEACH
205
¡Mala Suerte! 4 [Tempestad de La Lucha]

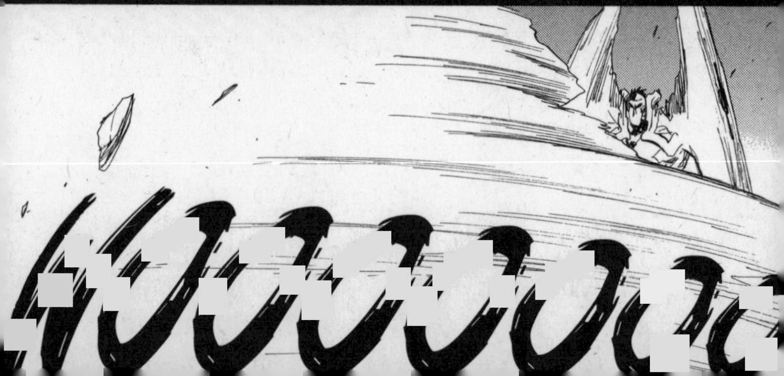

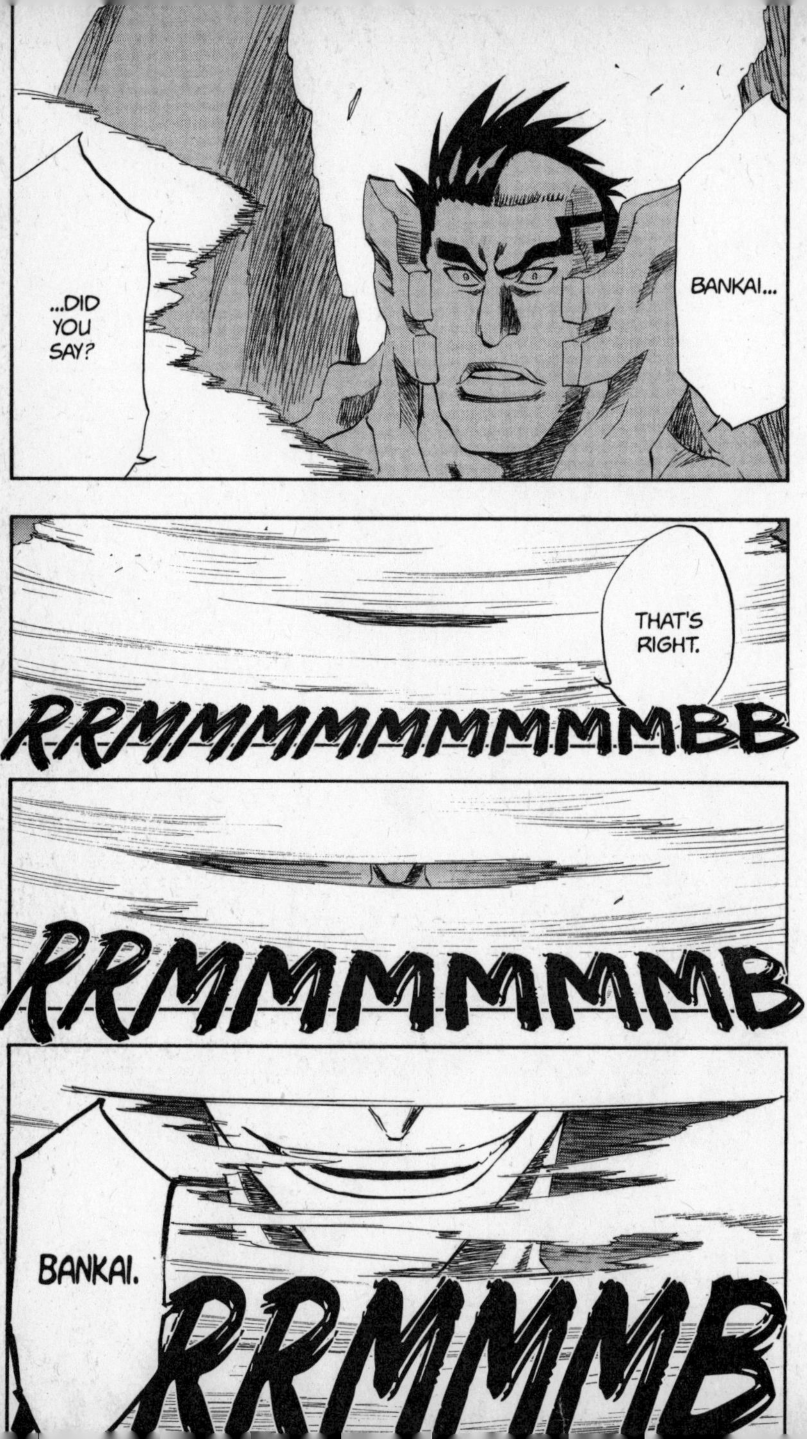
BANKAI...
...DID YOU SAY?
THAT'S RIGHT.
RRMMMMMMMMMMBB
RRMMMMMMB
BANKAI.
RRMMMMB

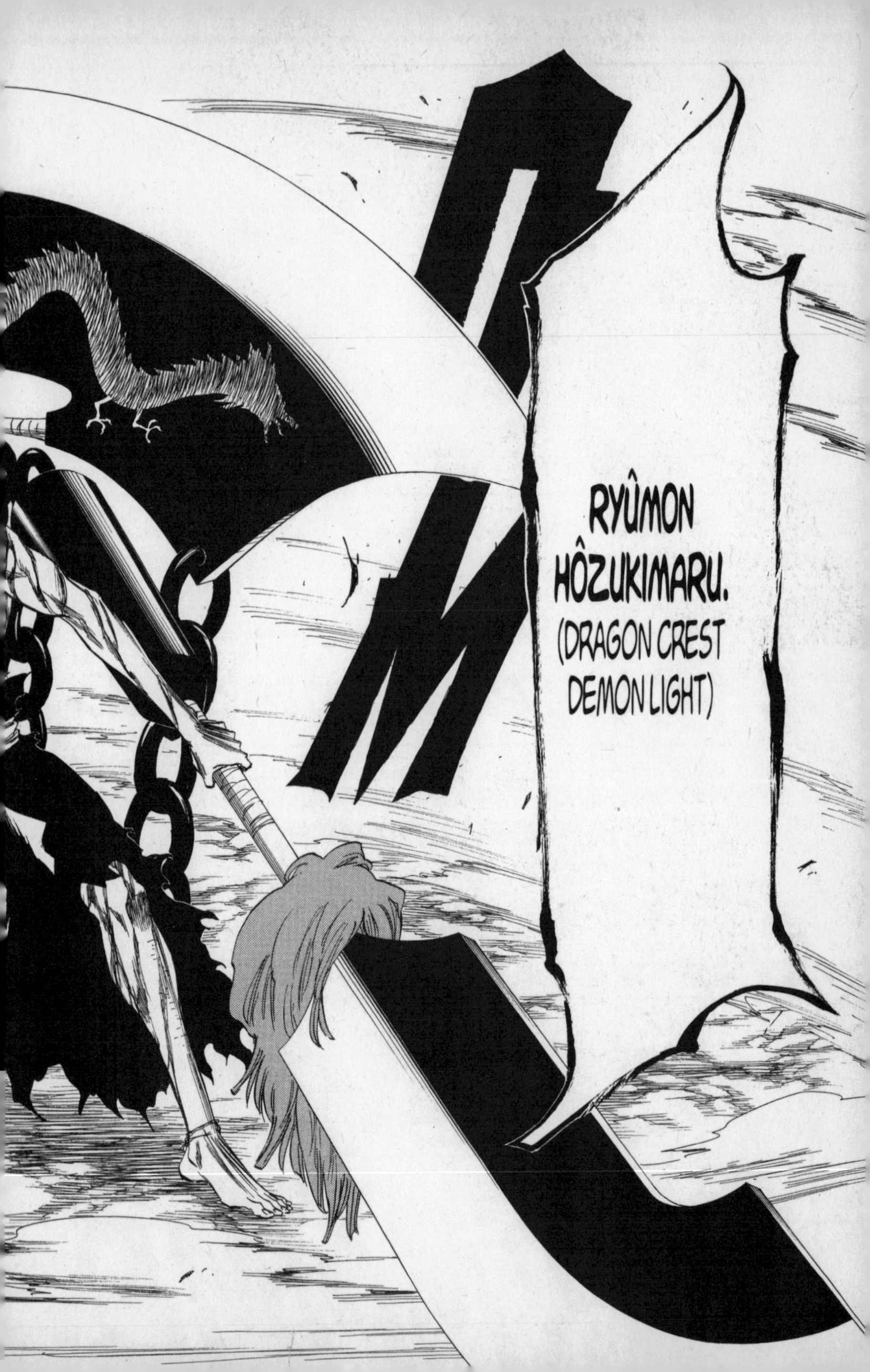
RYÛMON HÔZUKIMARU.
(DRAGON CREST DEMON LIGHT)

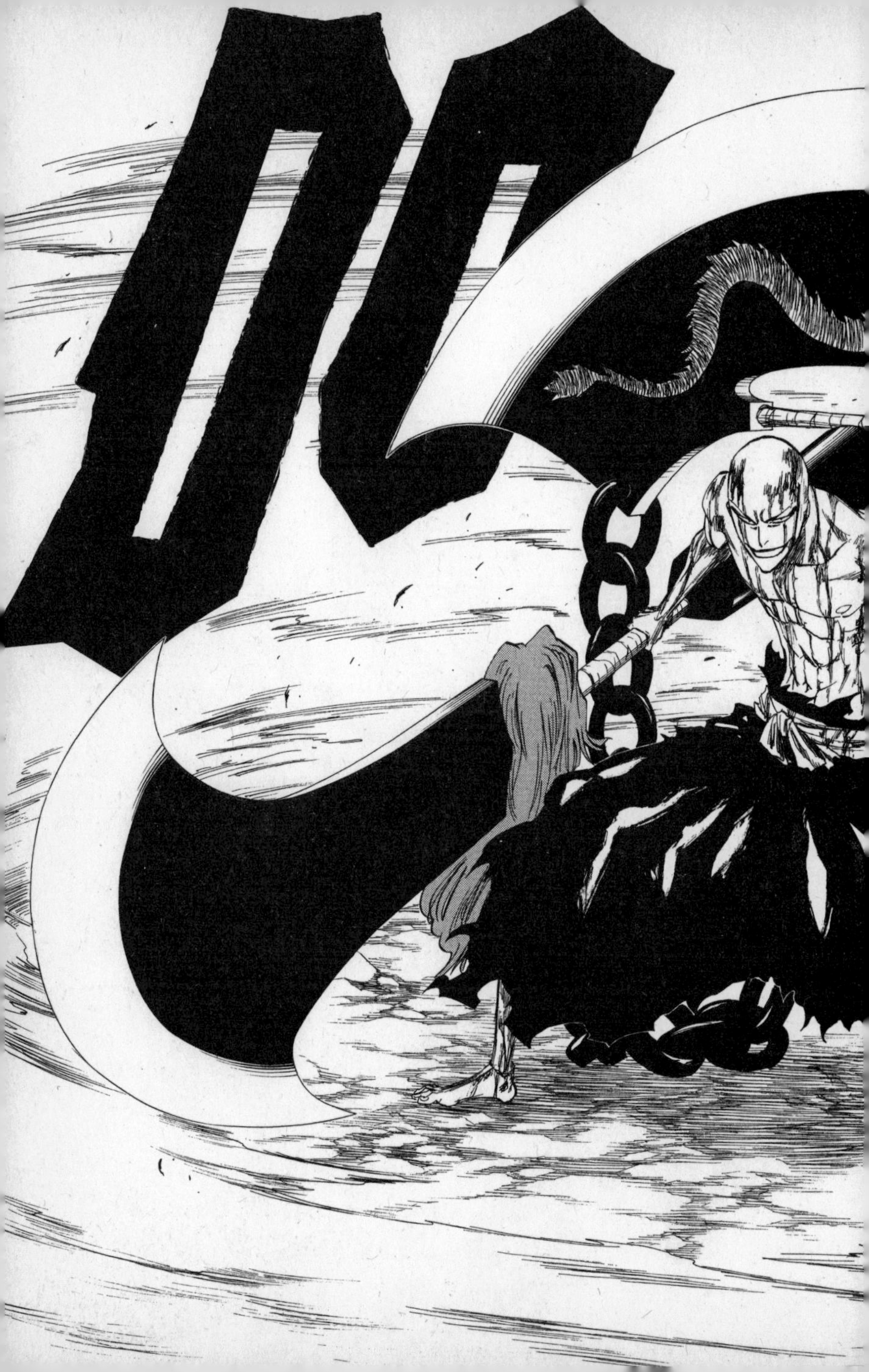

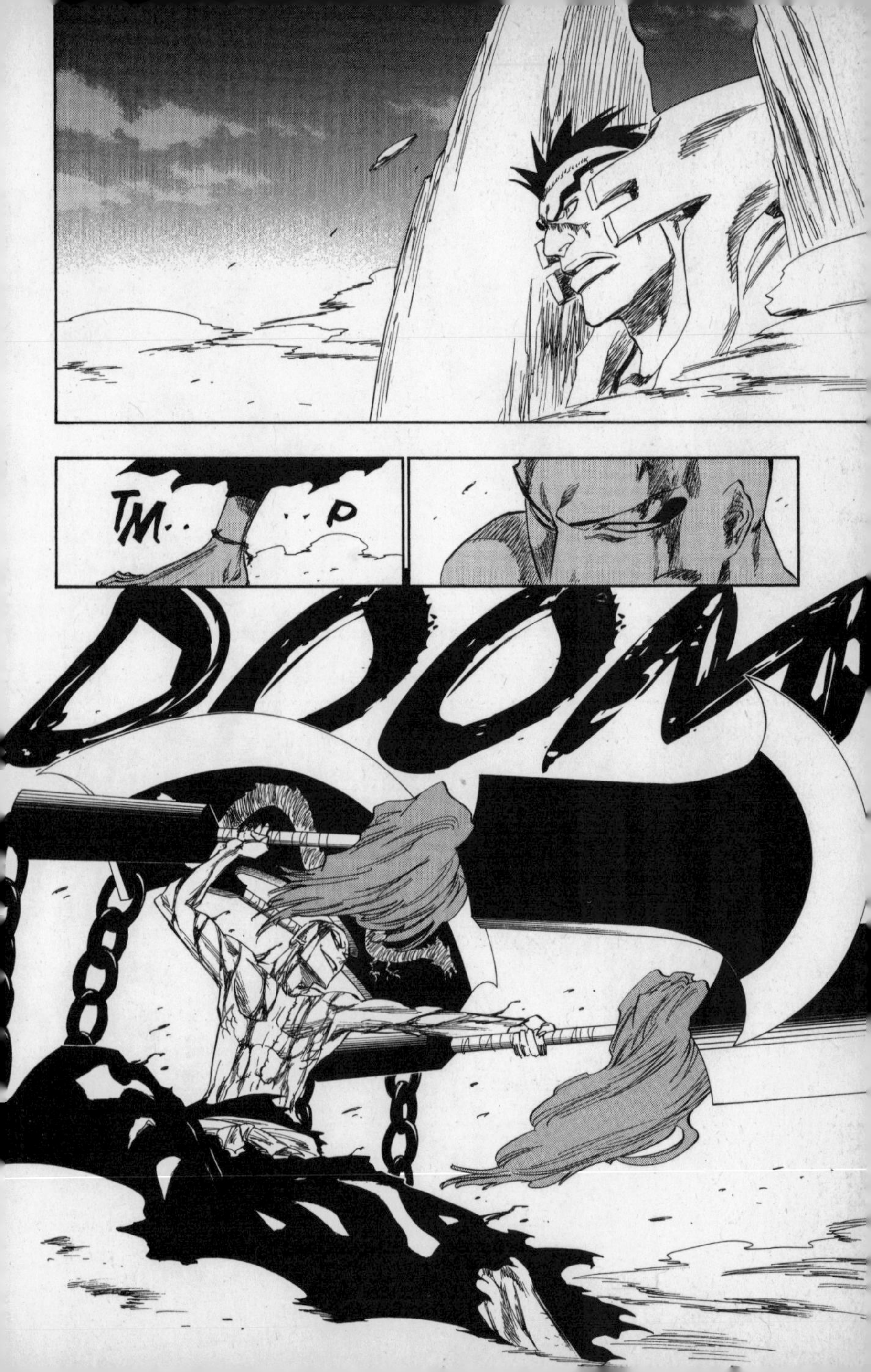
TM.. ..P
DOOM

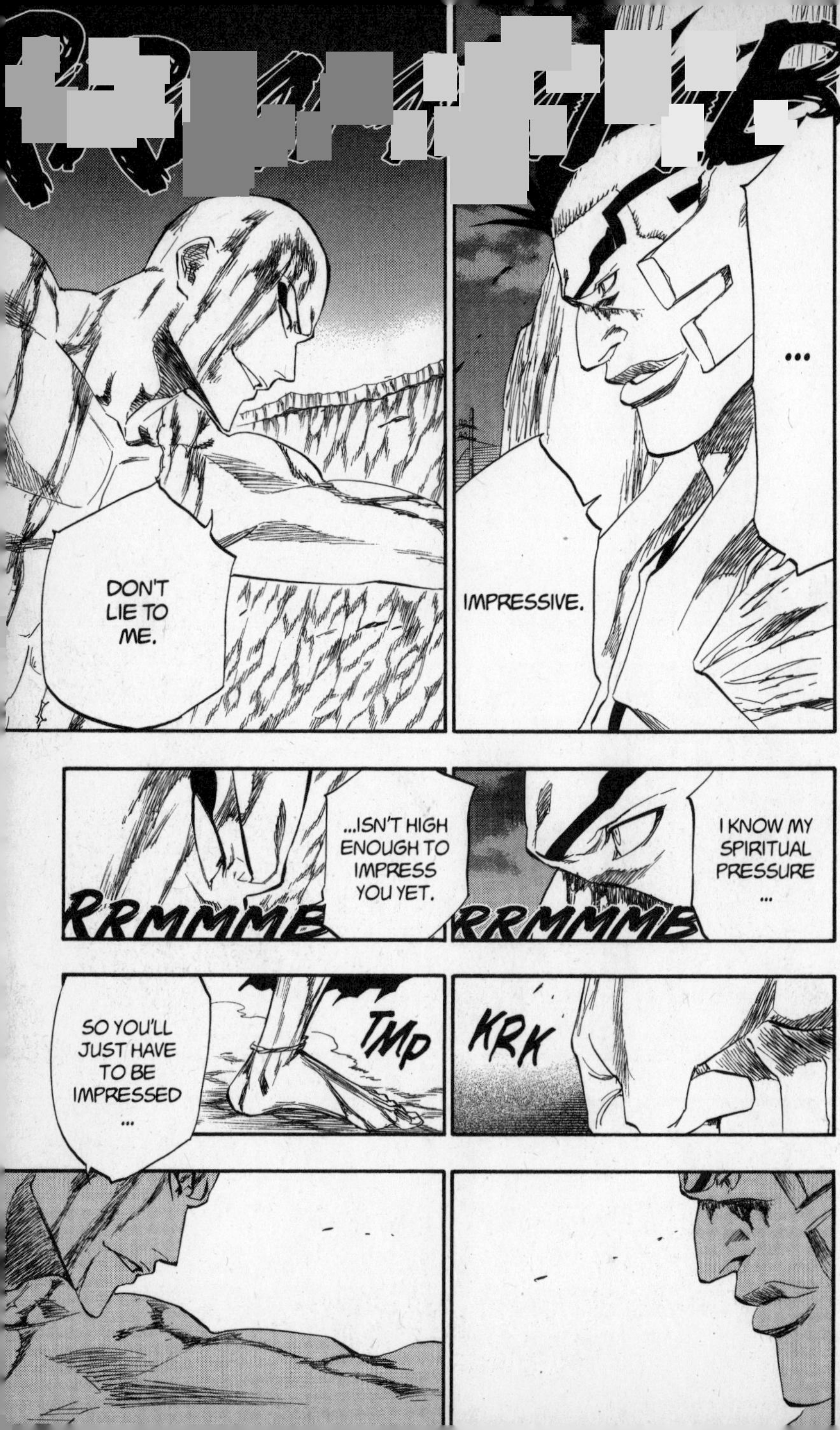
...
IMPRESSIVE.
DON'T LIE TO ME.
I KNOW MY SPIRITUAL PRESSURE ...
RRMMMB
...ISN'T HIGH ENOUGH TO IMPRESS YOU YET.
RRMMMB
KRK
TMP
SO YOU'LL JUST HAVE TO BE IMPRESSED ...

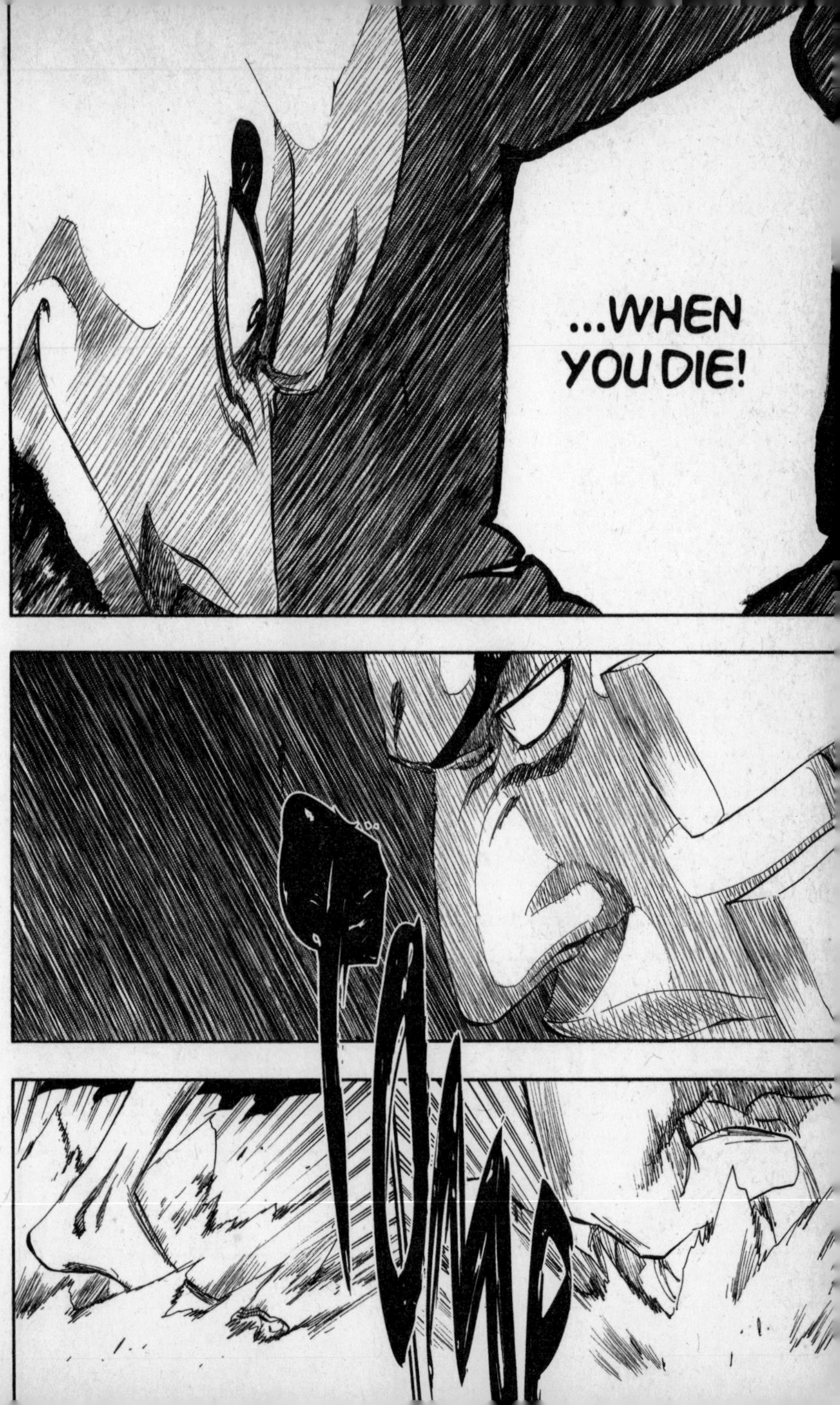
...WHEN YOU DIE!

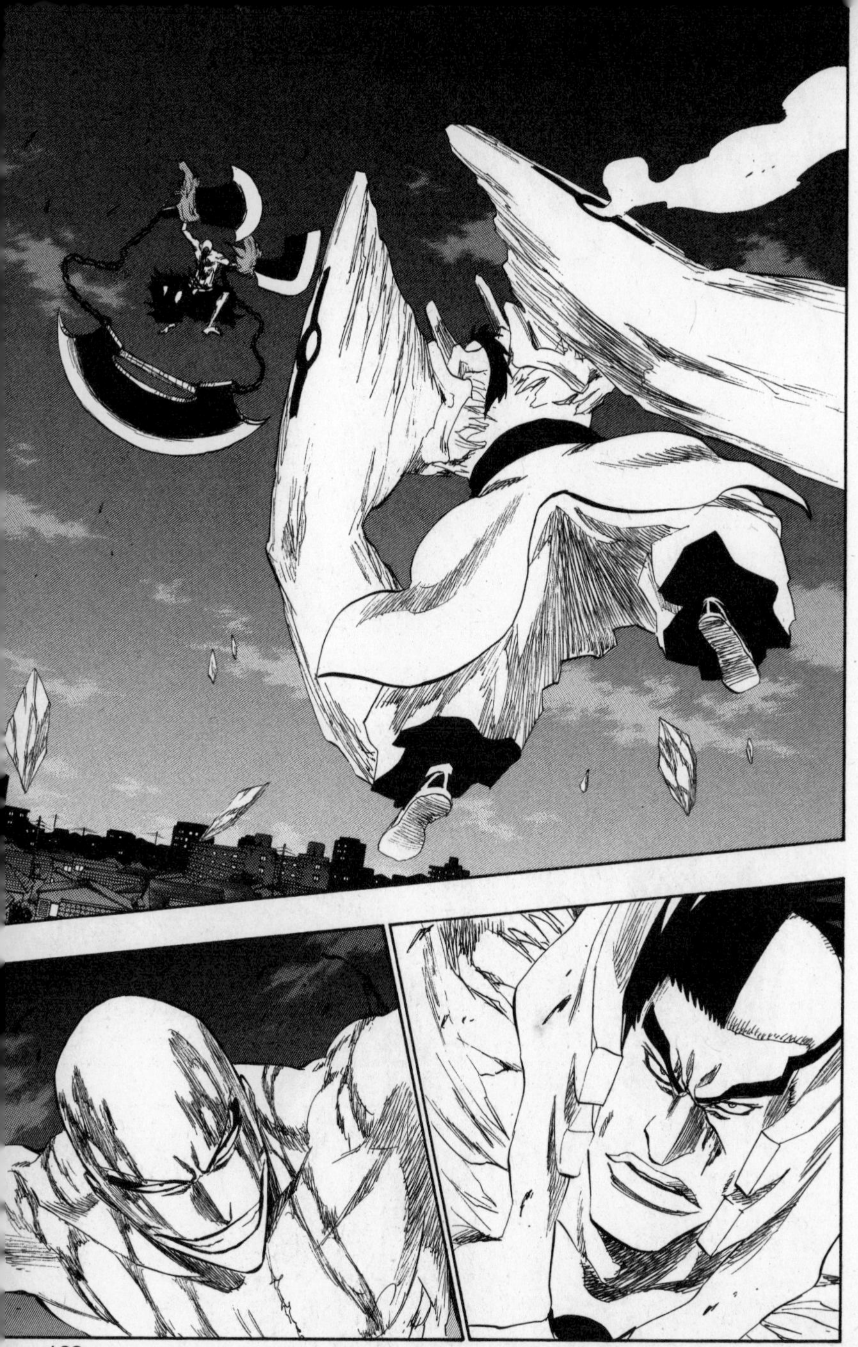

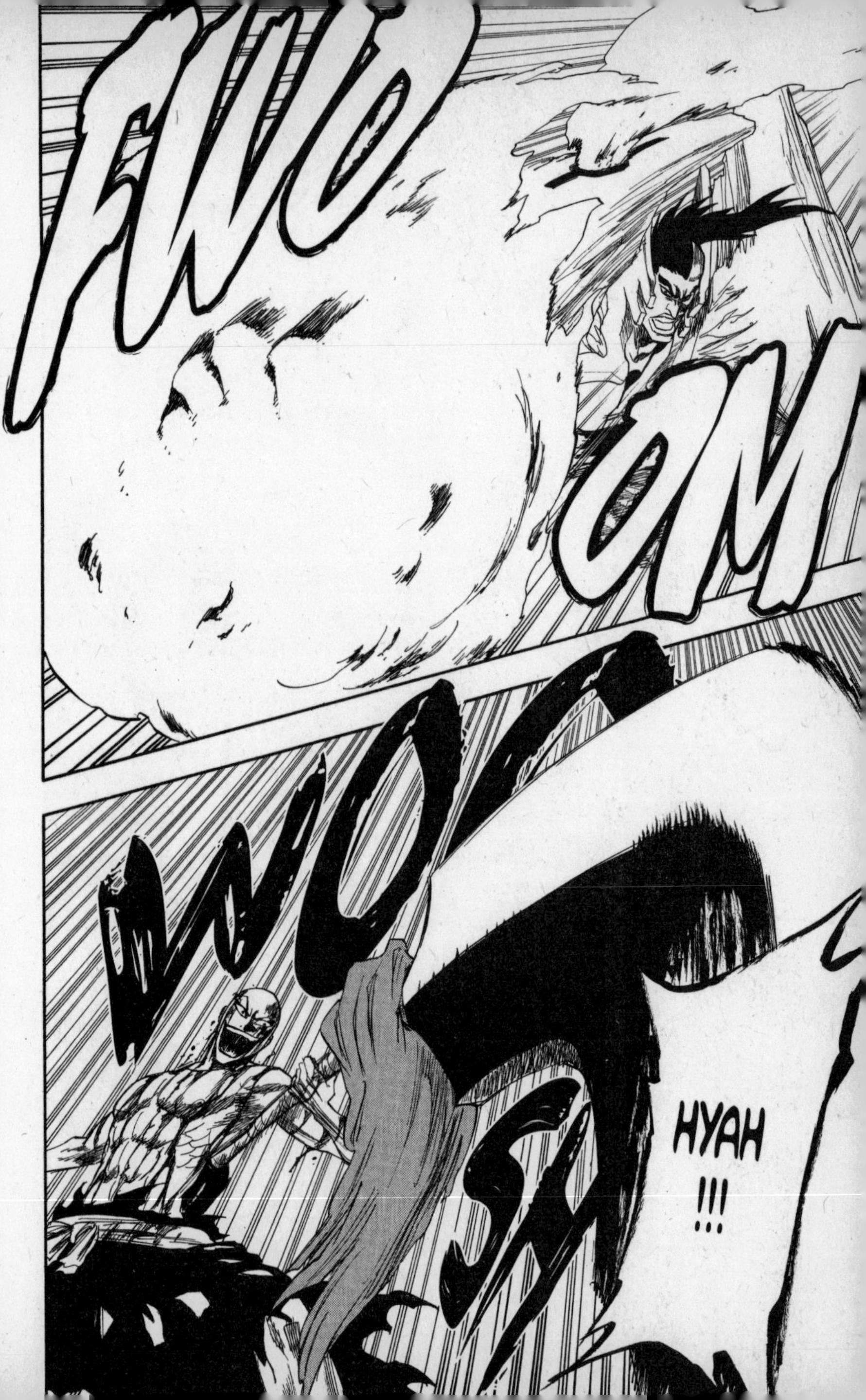
HYAH
!!!

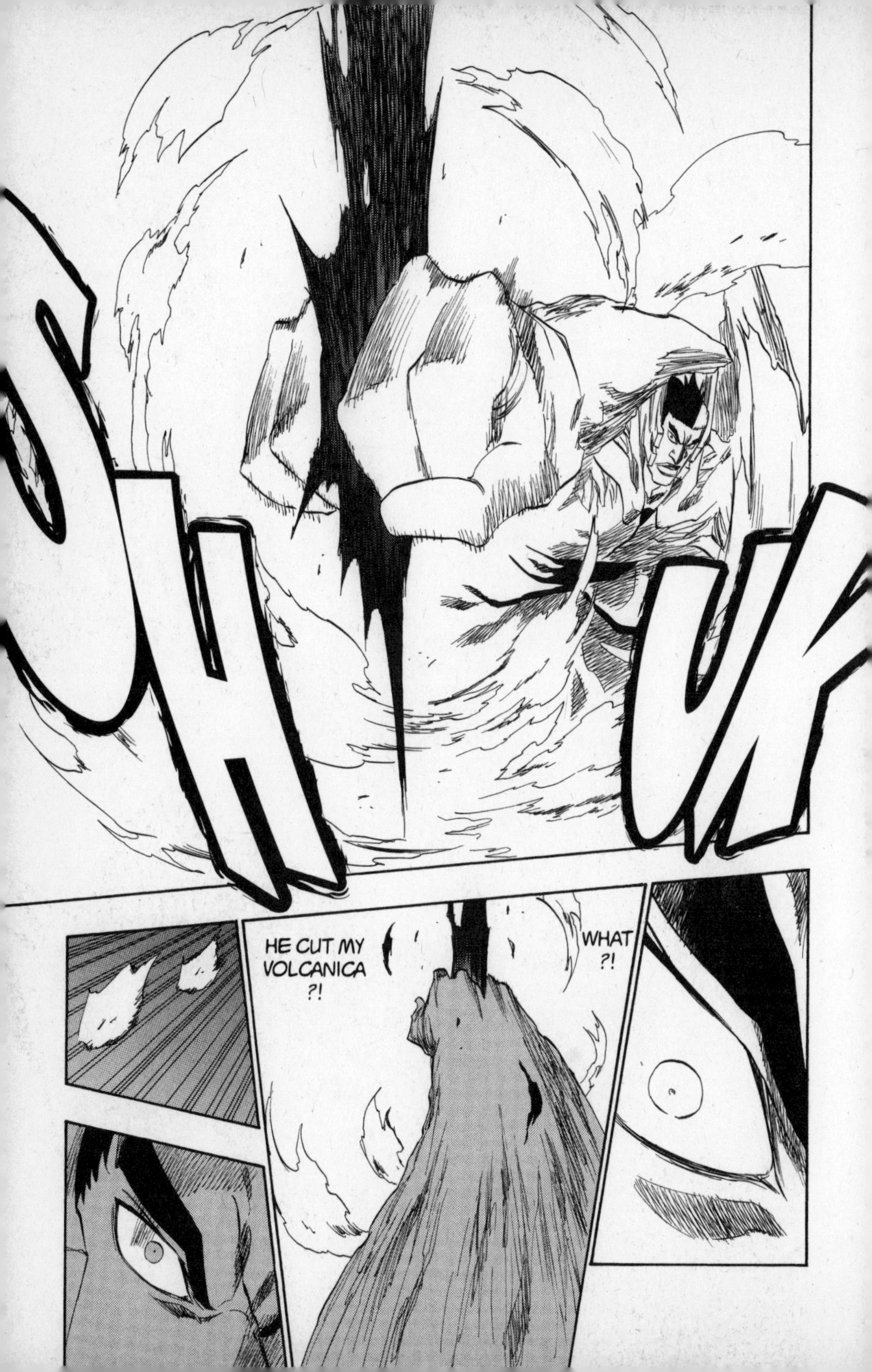
CHUK
WHAT?!
HE CUT MY VOLCANICA?!

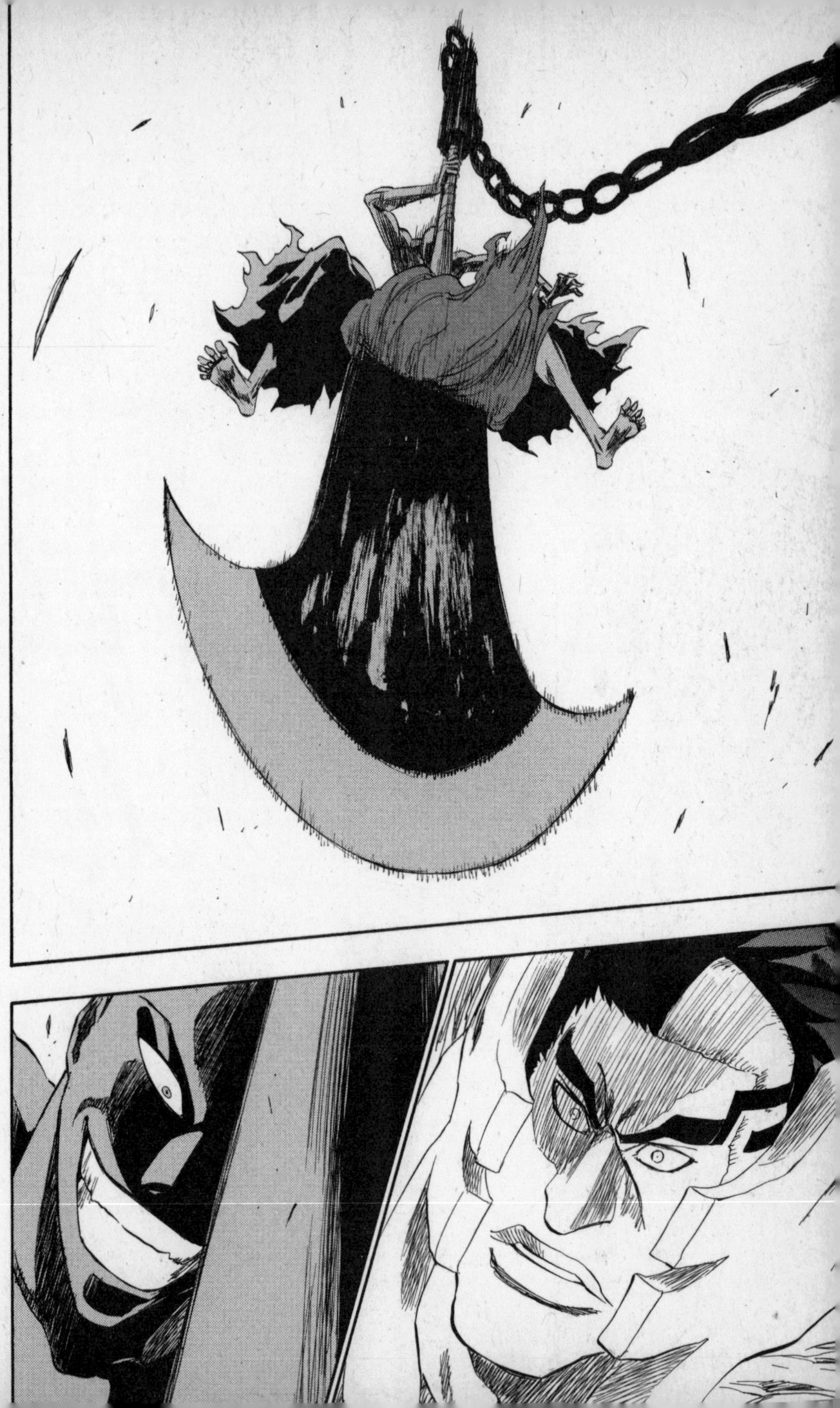

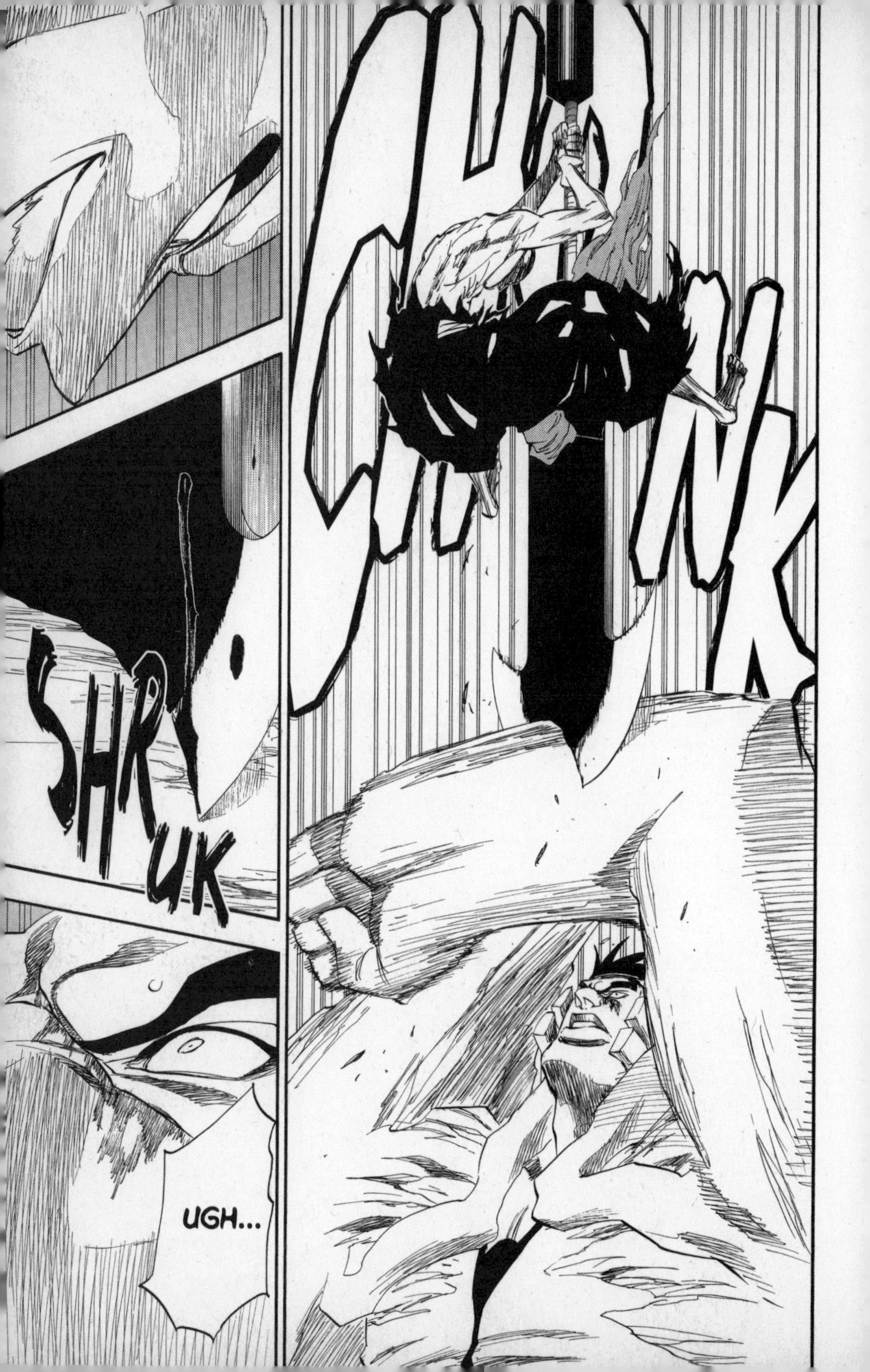
CHUNK
SHRUK
UGH...

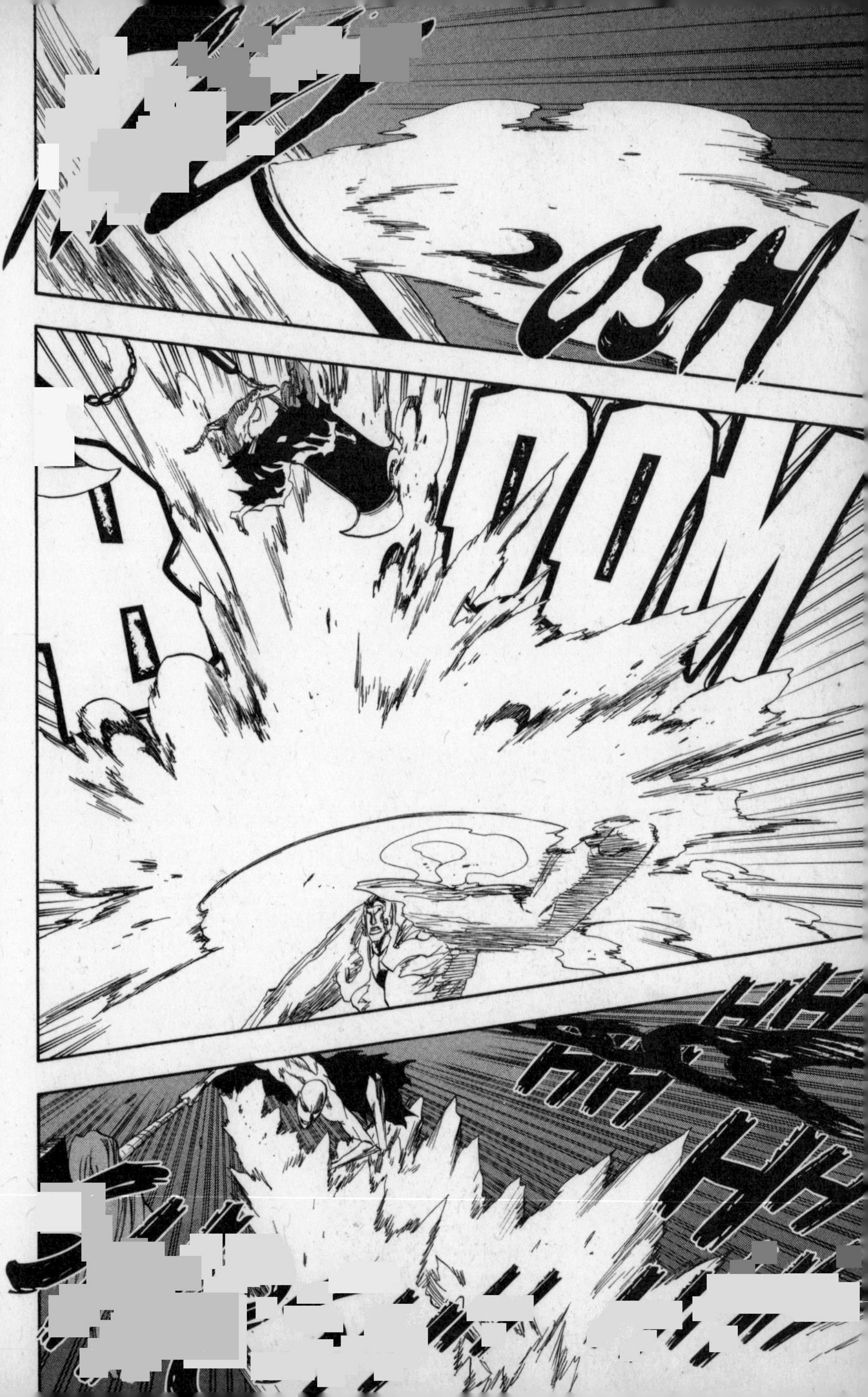
OSH
DOM

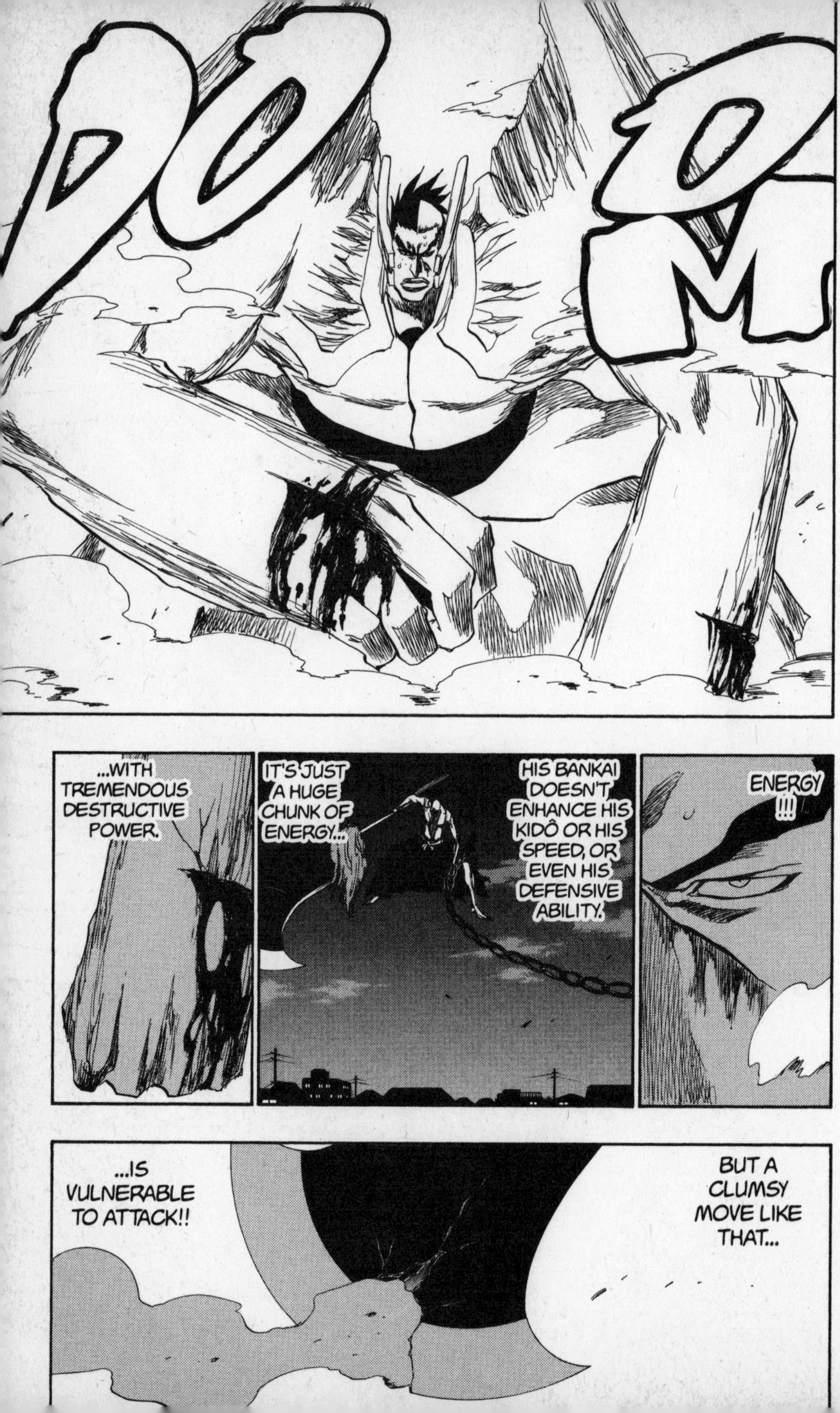
DOOM
ENERGY !!!
HIS BANKAI DOESN'T ENHANCE HIS KIDÔ OR HIS SPEED, OR EVEN HIS DEFENSIVE ABILITY.
IT'S JUST A HUGE CHUNK OF ENERGY...
...WITH TREMENDOUS DESTRUCTIVE POWER.
BUT A CLUMSY MOVE LIKE THAT...
...IS VULNERABLE TO ATTACK!!

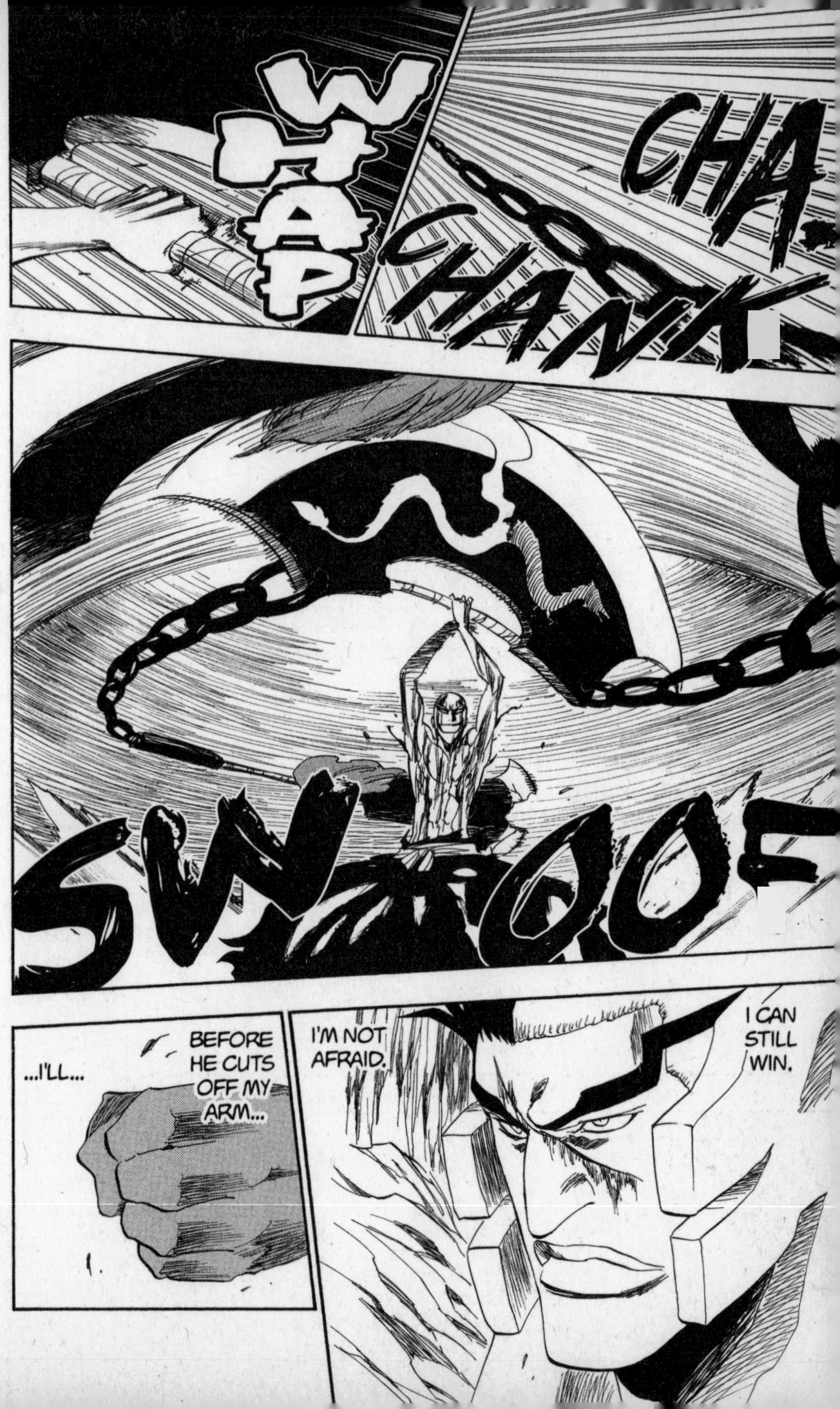
CHA CHANK
WHAP
SWOOF
I CAN STILL WIN.
I'M NOT AFRAID.
BEFORE HE CUTS OFF MY ARM...
...I'LL...

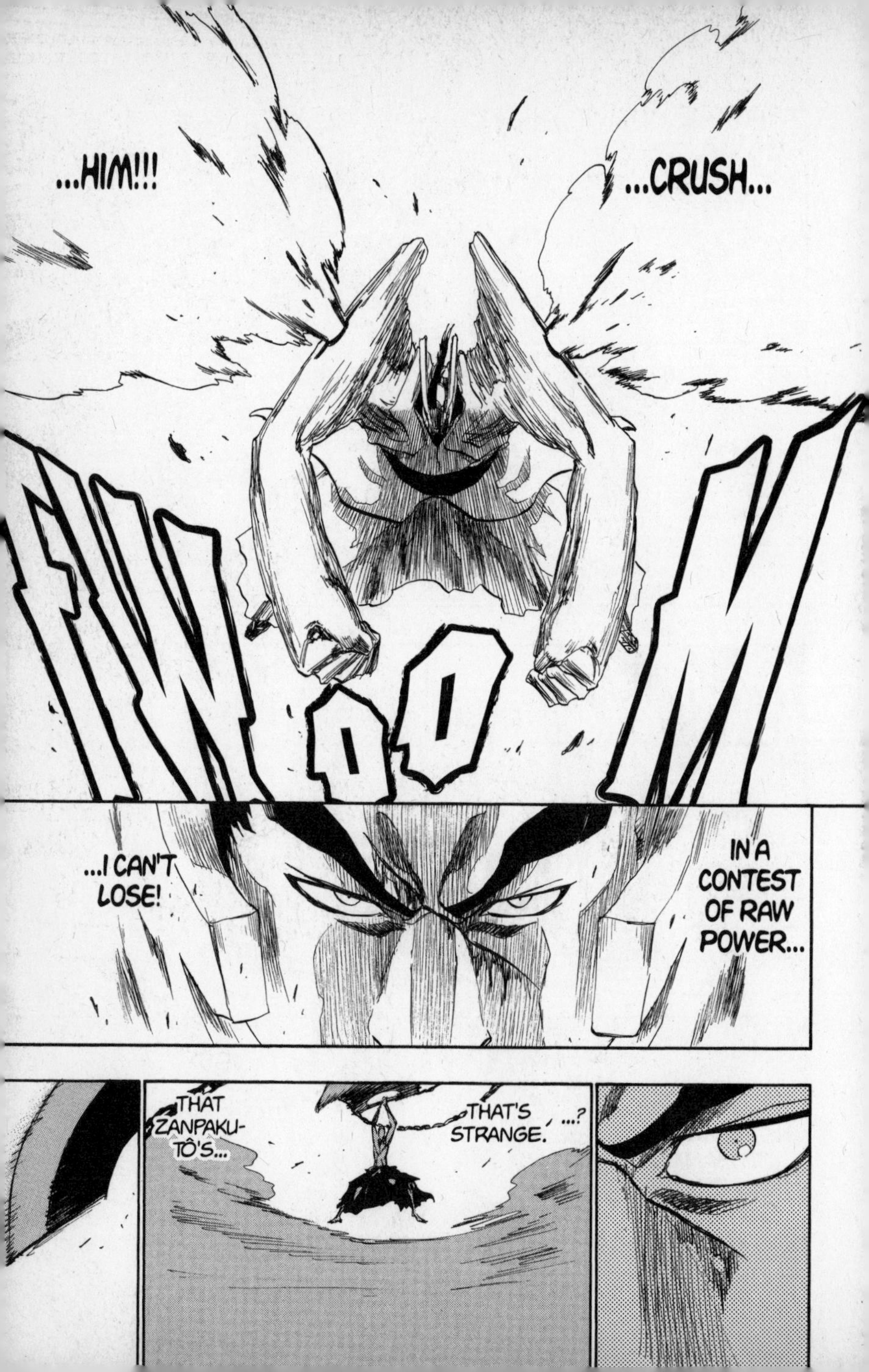
...CRUSH...
...HIM!!!
FWOOM
IN A CONTEST OF RAW POWER...
...I CAN'T LOSE!
...?
THAT'S STRANGE.
THAT ZANPAKU-TÔ'S...

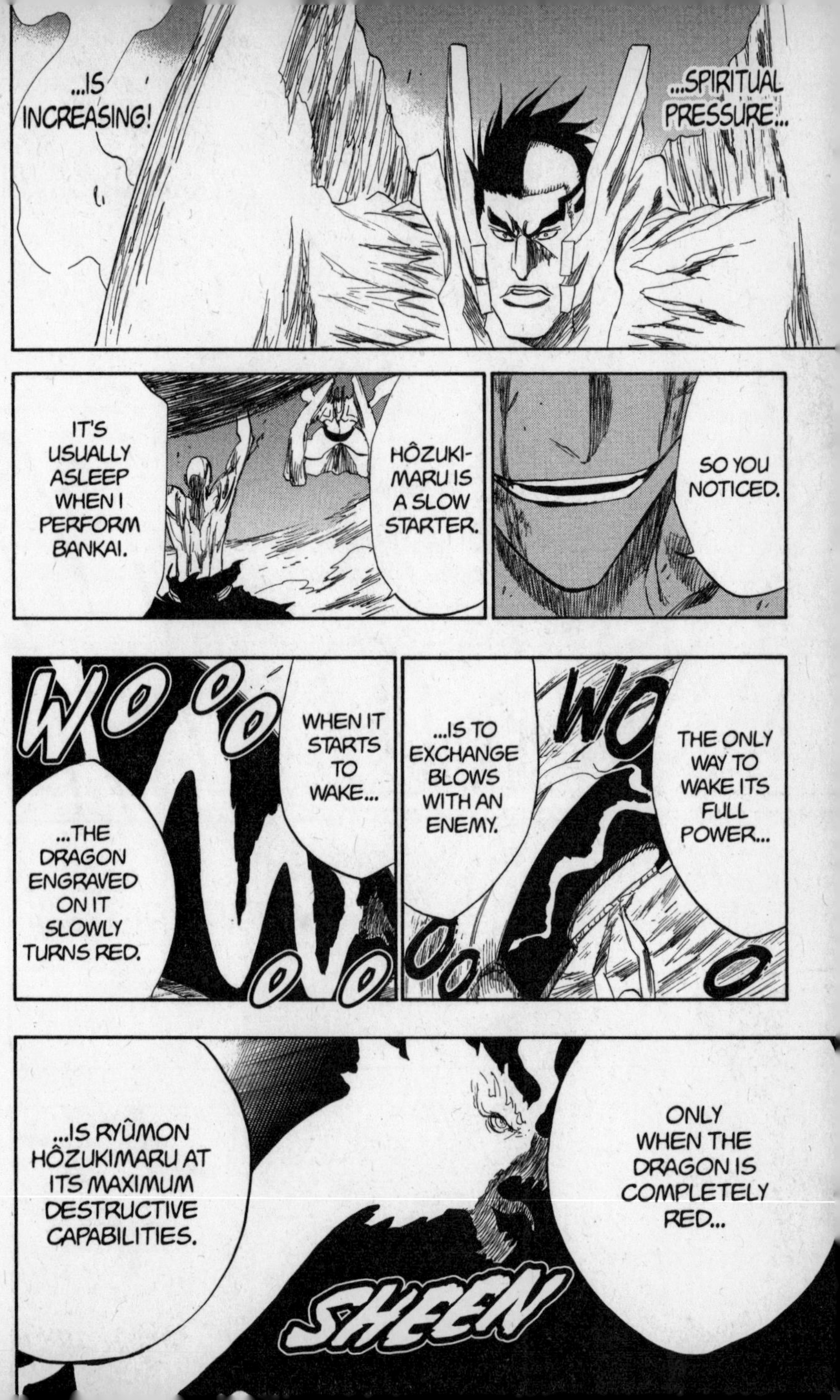
...SPIRITUAL PRESSURE...
...IS INCREASING!
SO YOU NOTICED.
HÔZUKI-MARU IS A SLOW STARTER.
IT'S USUALLY ASLEEP WHEN I PERFORM BANKAI.
THE ONLY WAY TO WAKE ITS FULL POWER...
WOOOO
...IS TO EXCHANGE BLOWS WITH AN ENEMY.
WHEN IT STARTS TO WAKE...
WOOOO
...THE DRAGON ENGRAVED ON IT SLOWLY TURNS RED.
ONLY WHEN THE DRAGON IS COMPLETELY RED...
...IS RYÛMON HÔZUKIMARU AT ITS MAXIMUM DESTRUCTIVE CAPABILITIES.
SHEEN

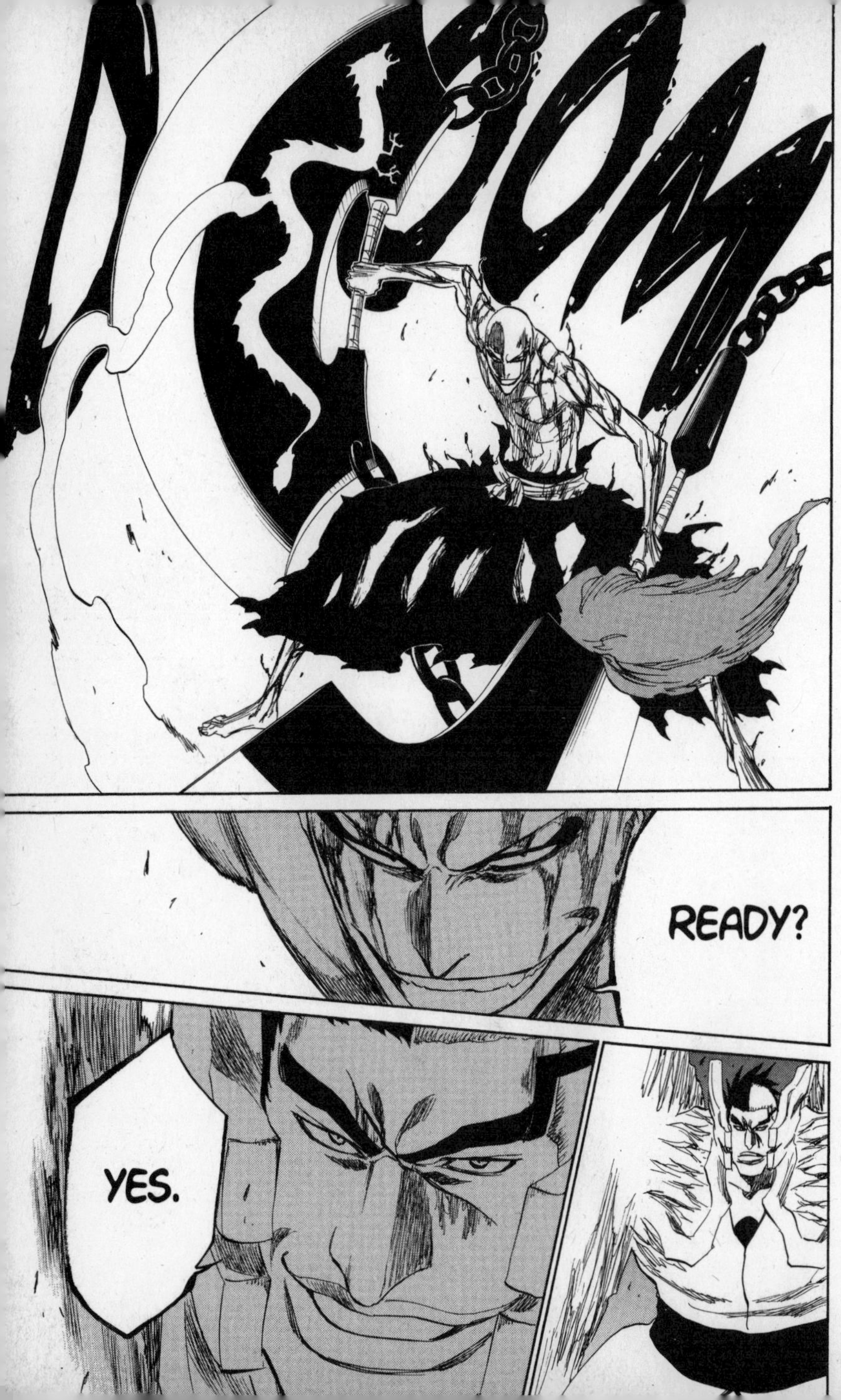
READY?
YES.

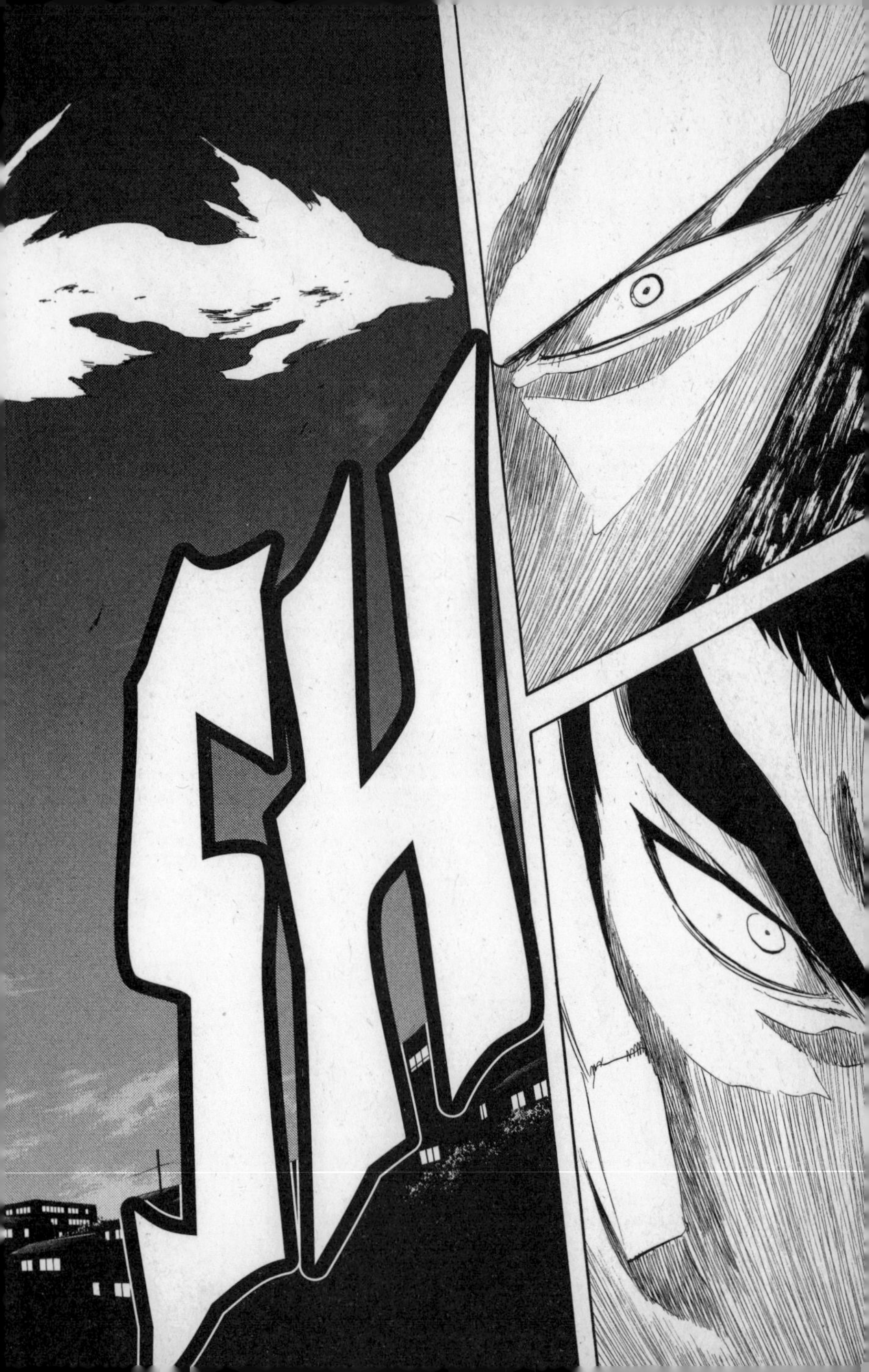

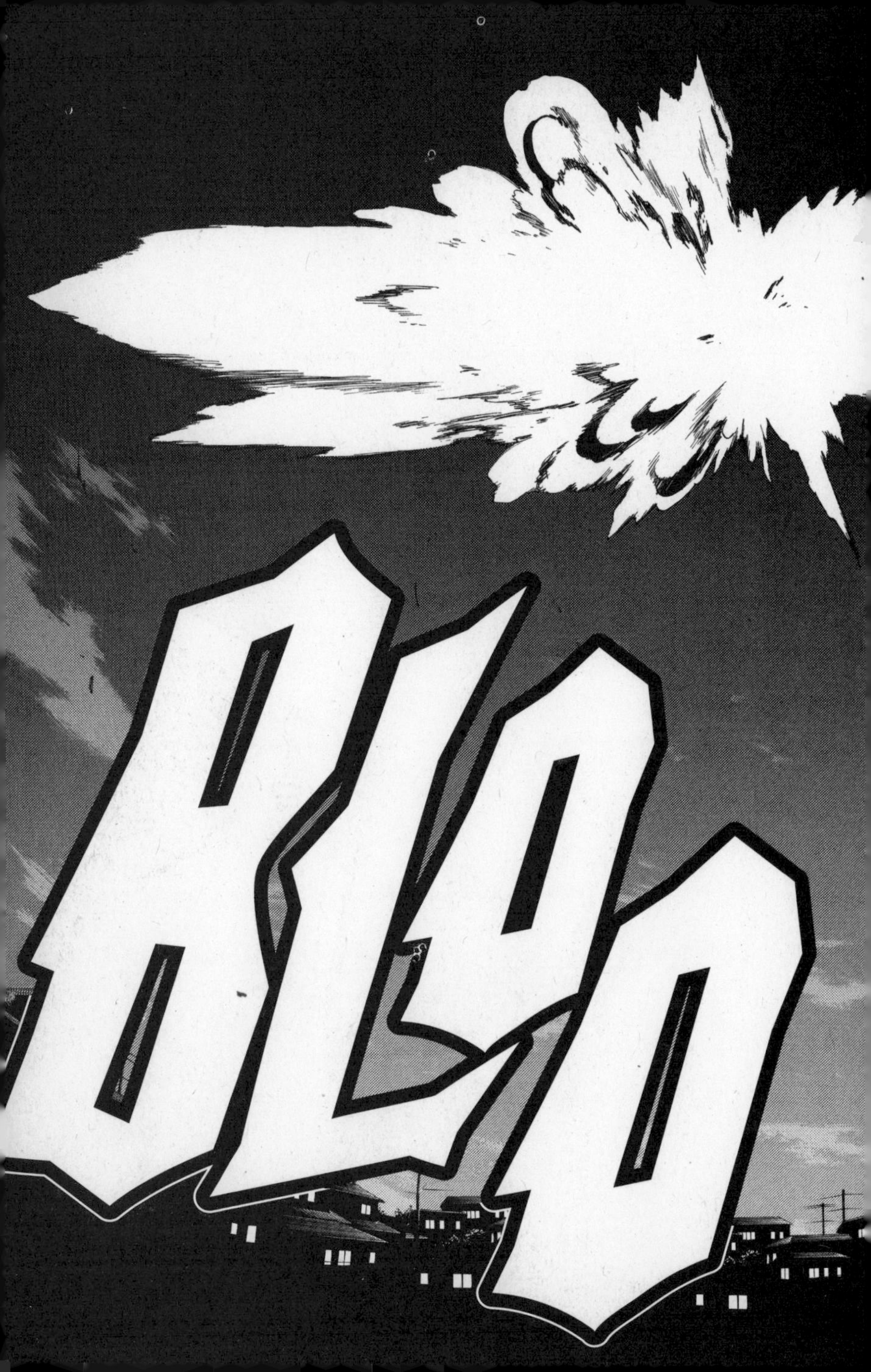

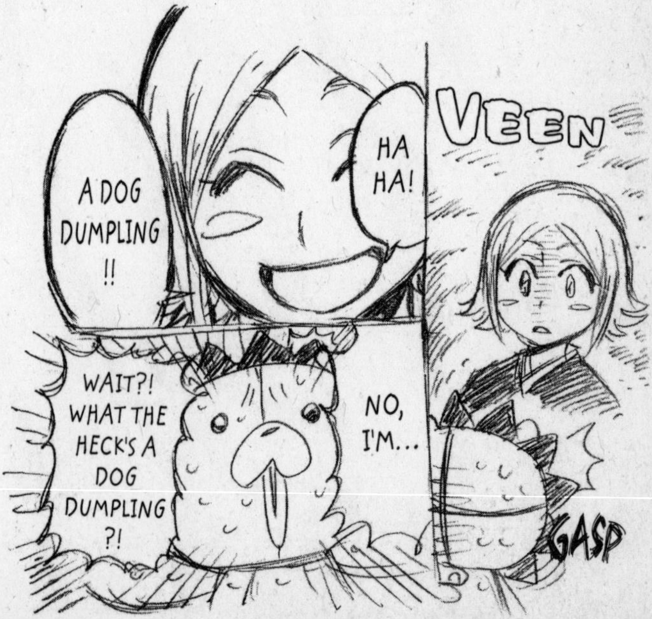
VEEN
GASP
HA HA!
A DOG DUMPLING !!
NO, I'M...
WAIT?! WHAT THE HECK'S A DOG DUMPLING ?!

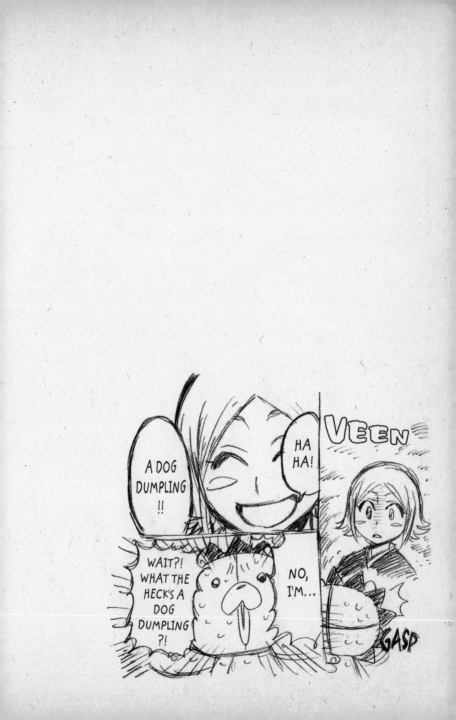

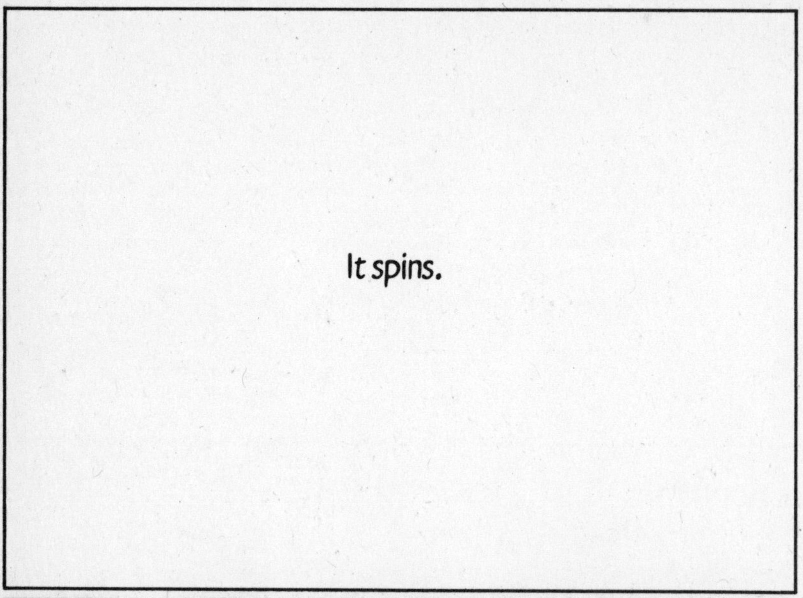
It spins.

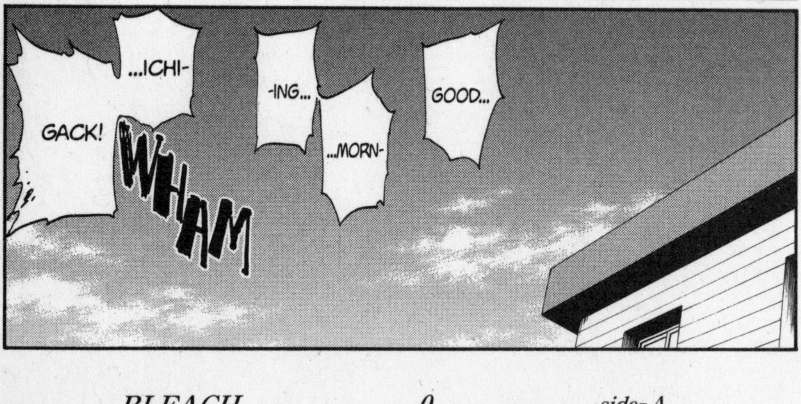
GOOD...
...MORN-
-ING...
...ICHI-
WHAM
GACK!

BLEACH *0* *side-A*

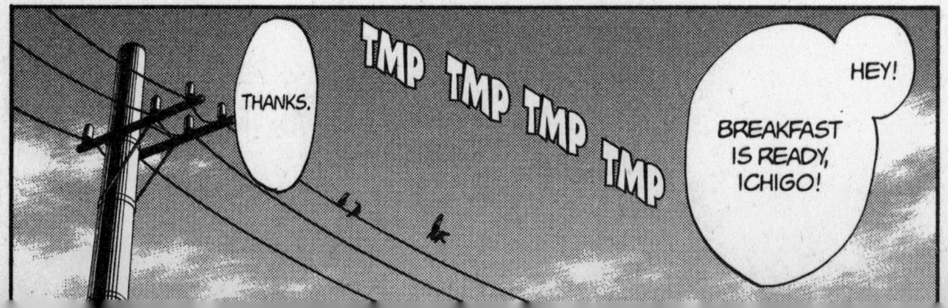
HEY! BREAKFAST IS READY, ICHIGO!
TMP TMP TMP TMP
THANKS.

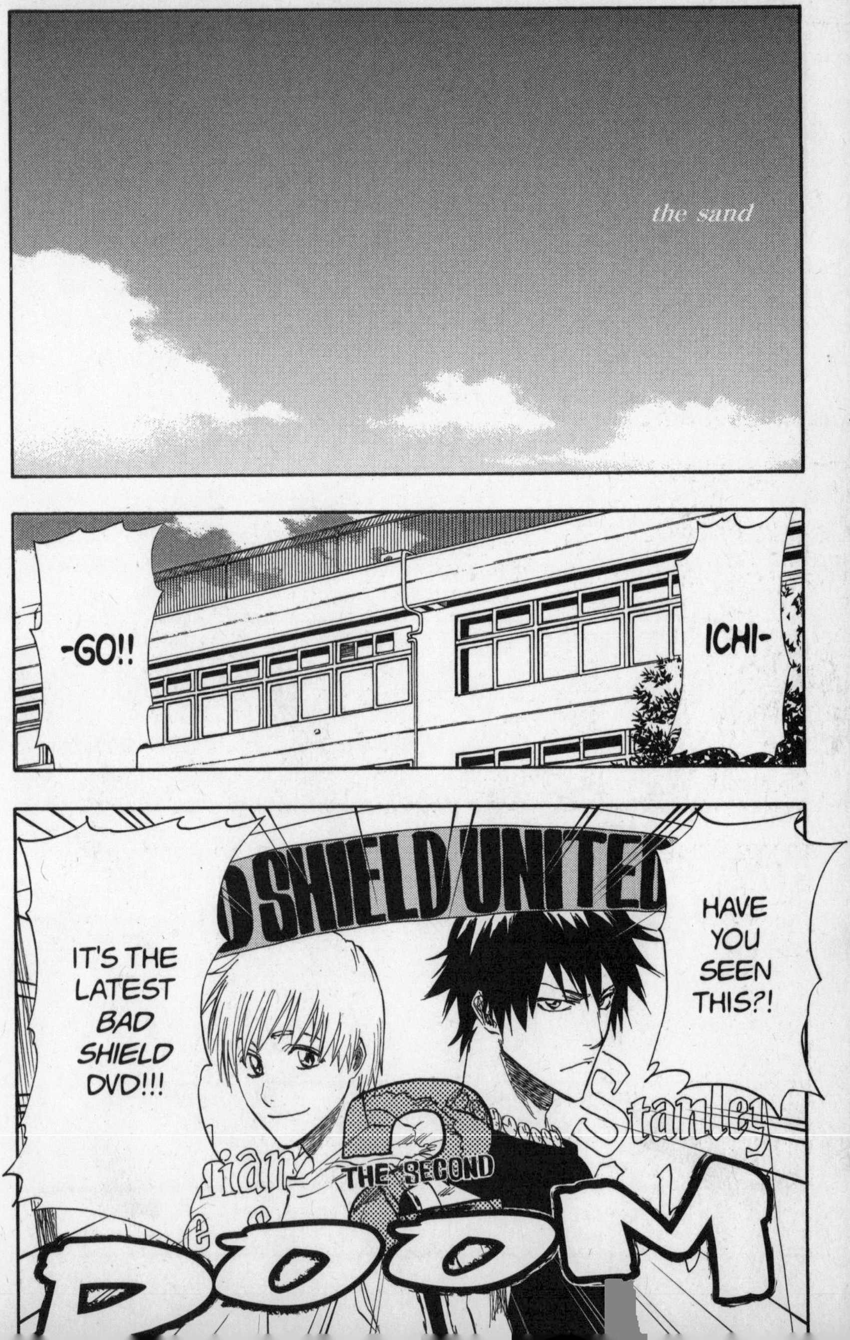
the sand
ICHI-
-GO!!
HAVE YOU SEEN THIS?!
IT'S THE LATEST BAD SHIELD DVD!!!
Stanley
THE SECOND
DOOM

READ THIS WAY

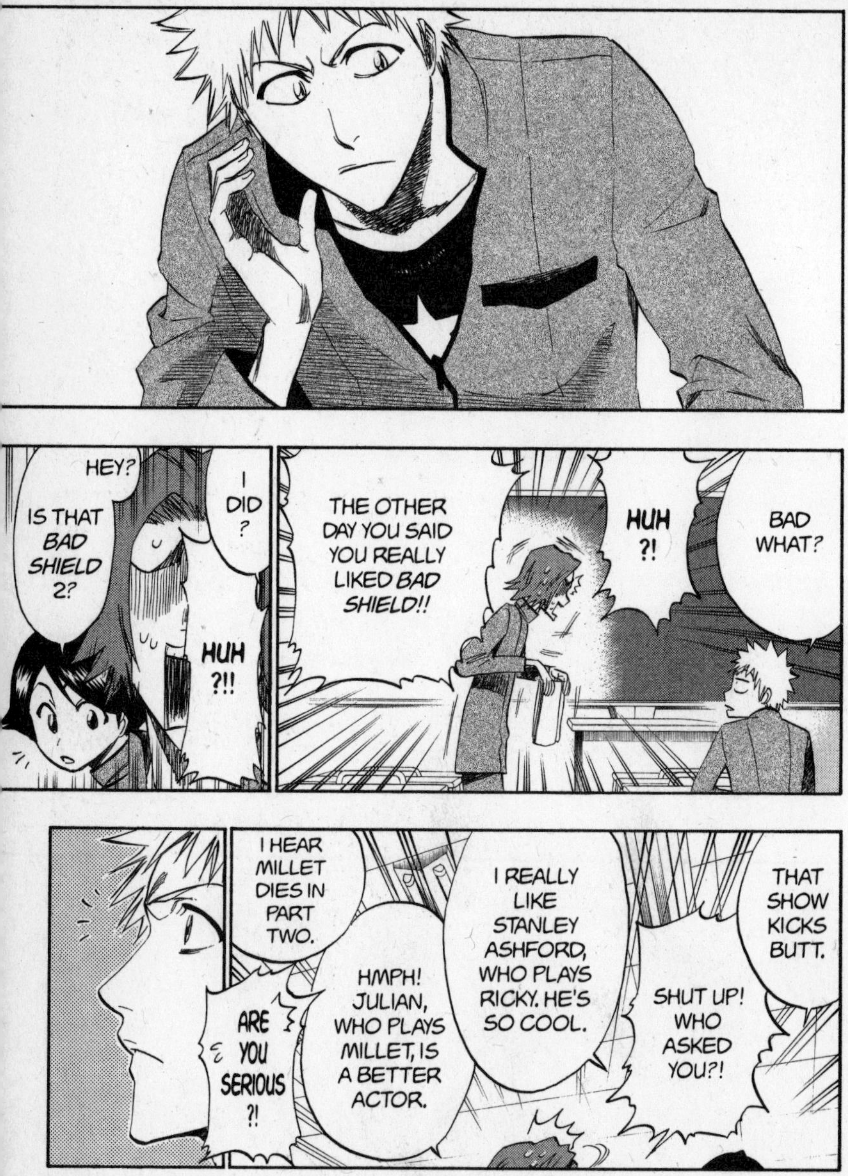
BAD WHAT?
HUH ?!
THE OTHER DAY YOU SAID YOU REALLY LIKED *BAD SHIELD*!!
I DID ?
HUH ?!!
HEY? IS THAT *BAD SHIELD* 2?
THAT SHOW KICKS BUTT.
SHUT UP! WHO ASKED YOU?!
I REALLY LIKE STANLEY ASHFORD, WHO PLAYS RICKY. HE'S SO COOL.
I HEAR MILLET DIES IN PART TWO.
HMPH! JULIAN, WHO PLAYS MILLET, IS A BETTER ACTOR.
ARE YOU SERIOUS ?!

The world changes.

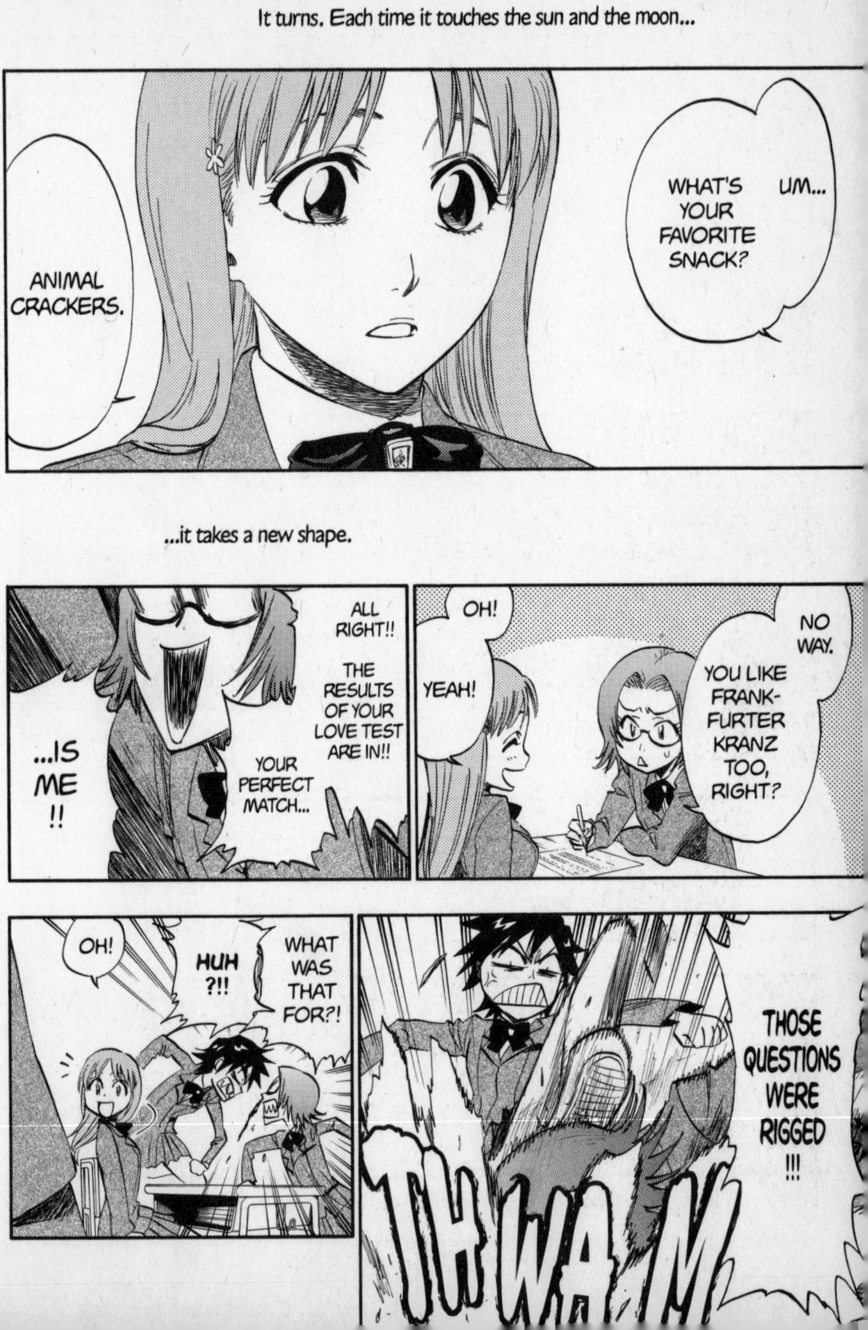
It turns. Each time it touches the sun and the moon...
UM...
WHAT'S YOUR FAVORITE SNACK?
ANIMAL CRACKERS.
...it takes a new shape.
NO WAY.
YOU LIKE FRANK-FURTER KRANZ TOO, RIGHT?
OH!
YEAH!
ALL RIGHT!! THE RESULTS OF YOUR LOVE TEST ARE IN!!
YOUR PERFECT MATCH...
...IS ME !!
THOSE QUESTIONS WERE RIGGED !!!
THWAM
WHAT WAS THAT FOR?!
HUH ?!!
OH!

READ THIS WAY

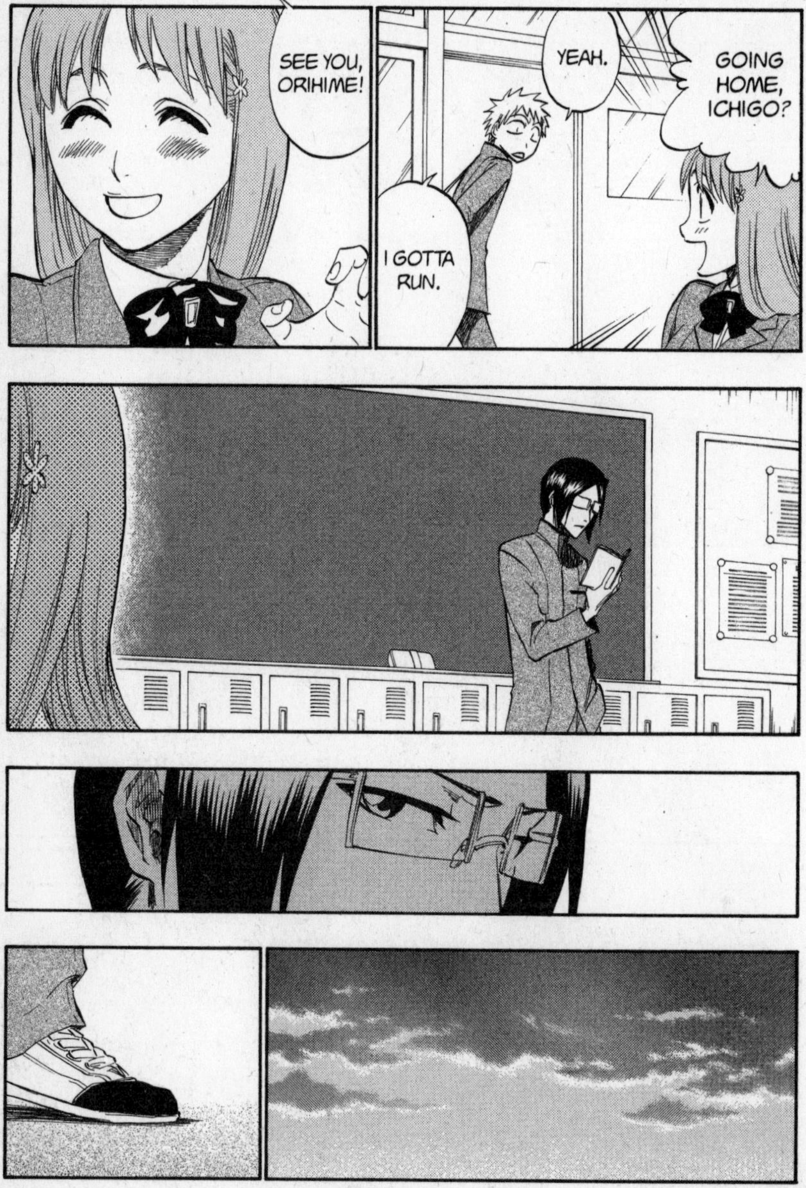
GOING HOME, ICHIGO?
YEAH.
I GOTTA RUN.
SEE YOU, ORIHIME!

The one thing that does not change...

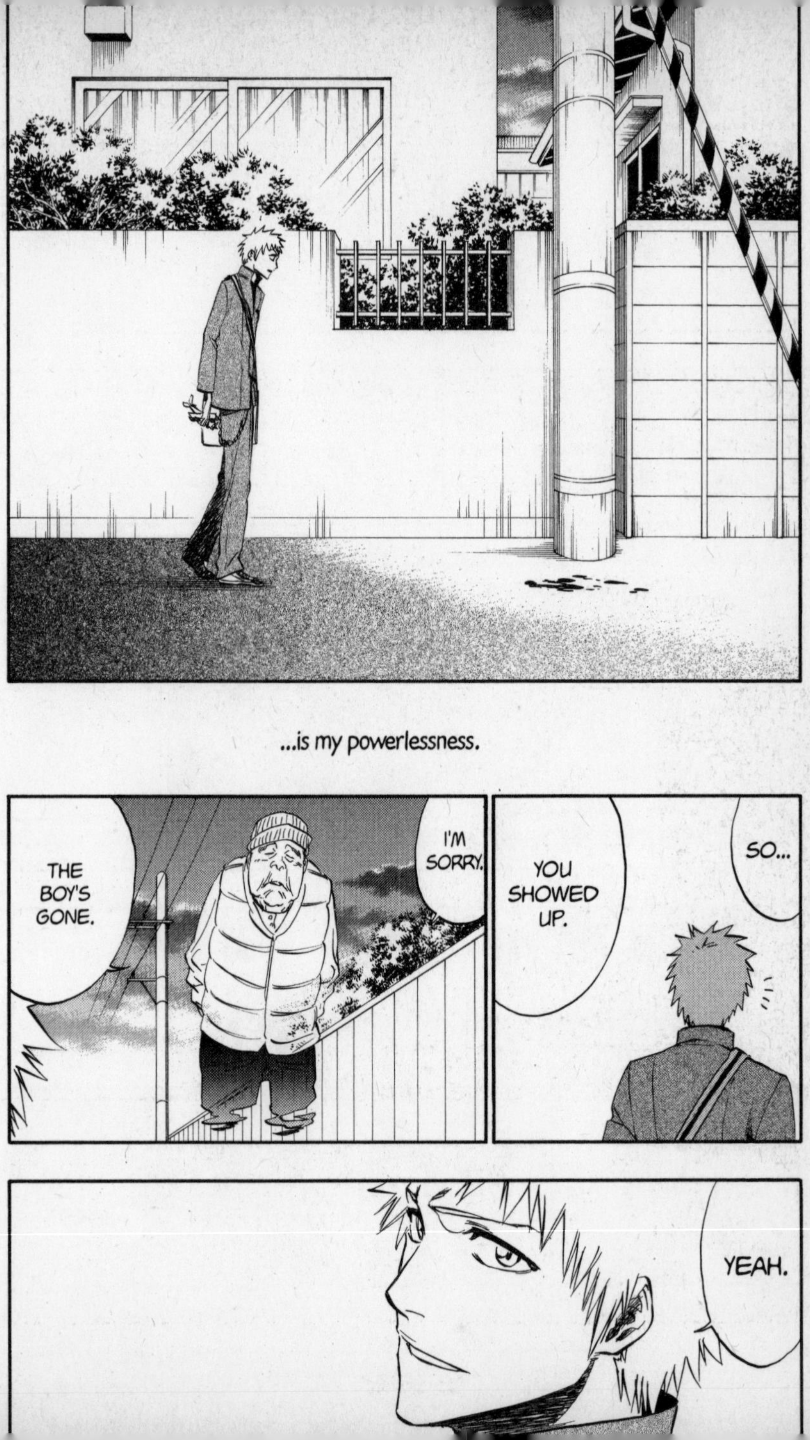
...is my powerlessness.
SO...
YOU SHOWED UP.
I'M SORRY.
THE BOY'S GONE.
YEAH.

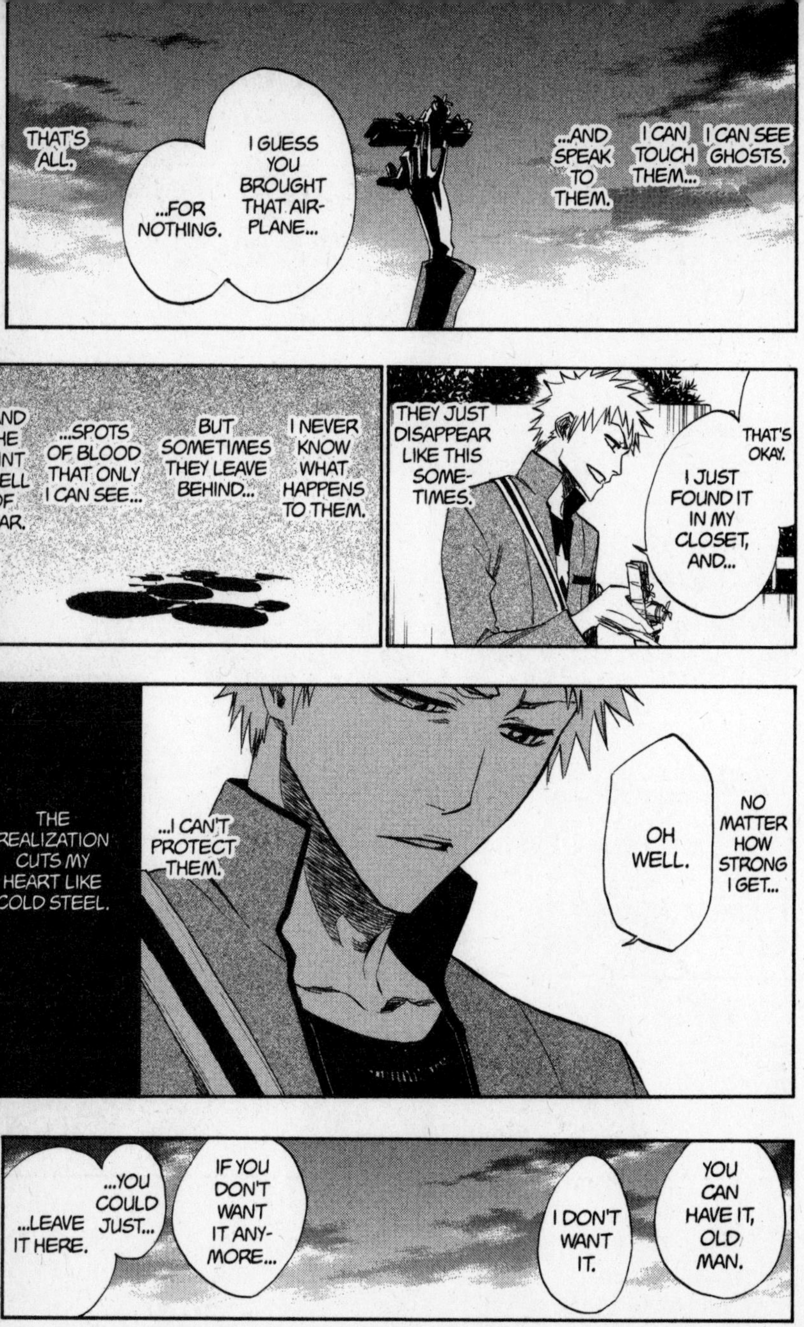
I CAN SEE GHOSTS.
I CAN TOUCH THEM...
...AND SPEAK TO THEM.
I GUESS YOU BROUGHT THAT AIR-PLANE...
...FOR NOTHING.
THAT'S ALL.
THAT'S OKAY.
I JUST FOUND IT IN MY CLOSET, AND...
THEY JUST DISAPPEAR LIKE THIS SOME-TIMES.
I NEVER KNOW WHAT HAPPENS TO THEM.
BUT SOMETIMES THEY LEAVE BEHIND...
...SPOTS OF BLOOD THAT ONLY I CAN SEE...
...AND THE FAINT SMELL OF FEAR.
NO MATTER HOW STRONG I GET...
OH WELL.
...I CAN'T PROTECT THEM.
THE REALIZATION CUTS MY HEART LIKE COLD STEEL.
YOU CAN HAVE IT, OLD MAN.
I DON'T WANT IT.
IF YOU DON'T WANT IT ANY-MORE...
...YOU COULD JUST...
...LEAVE IT HERE.

It's turning.

If fate is a millstone...

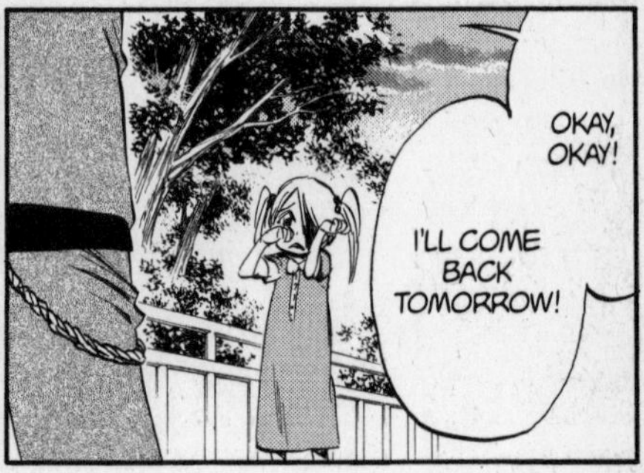
OKAY, OKAY!
I'LL COME BACK TOMORROW!

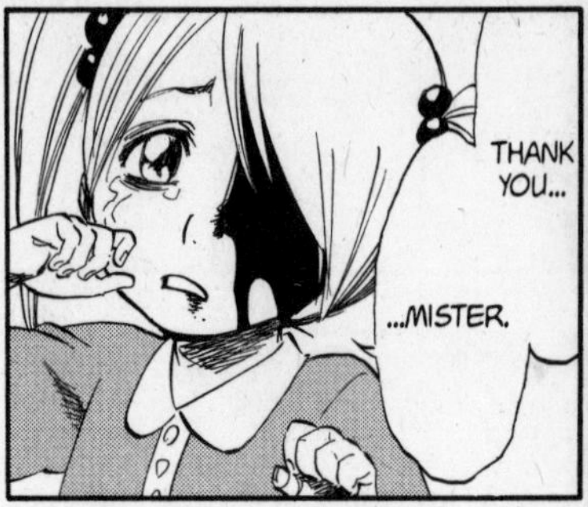
THANK YOU...
...MISTER.

...then we are the grist.

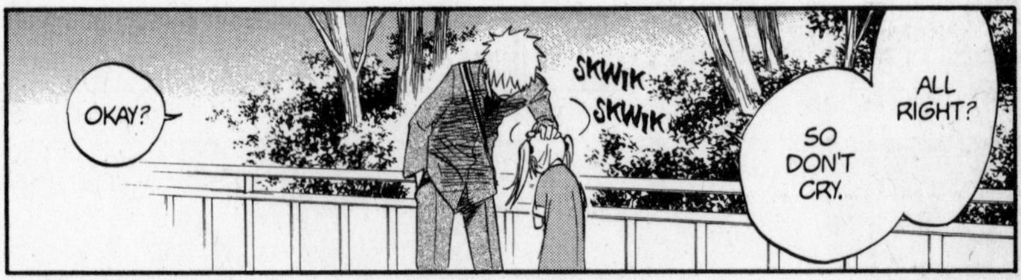
ALL RIGHT?
SO DON'T CRY.
SKWIK SKWIK
OKAY?

There is nothing we can do.

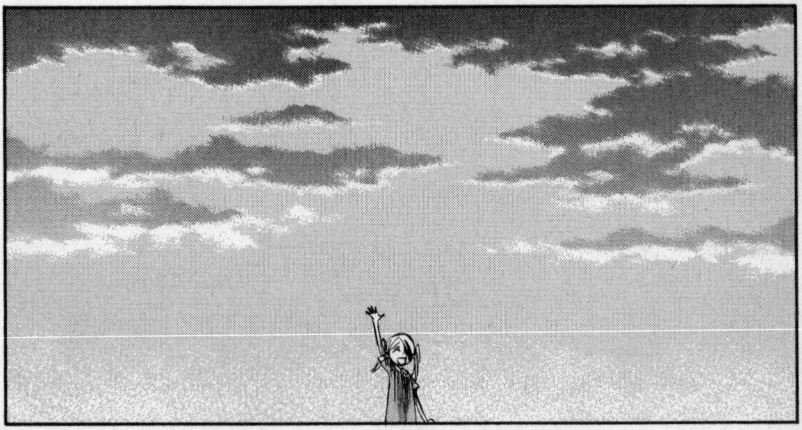

So I wish for strength.

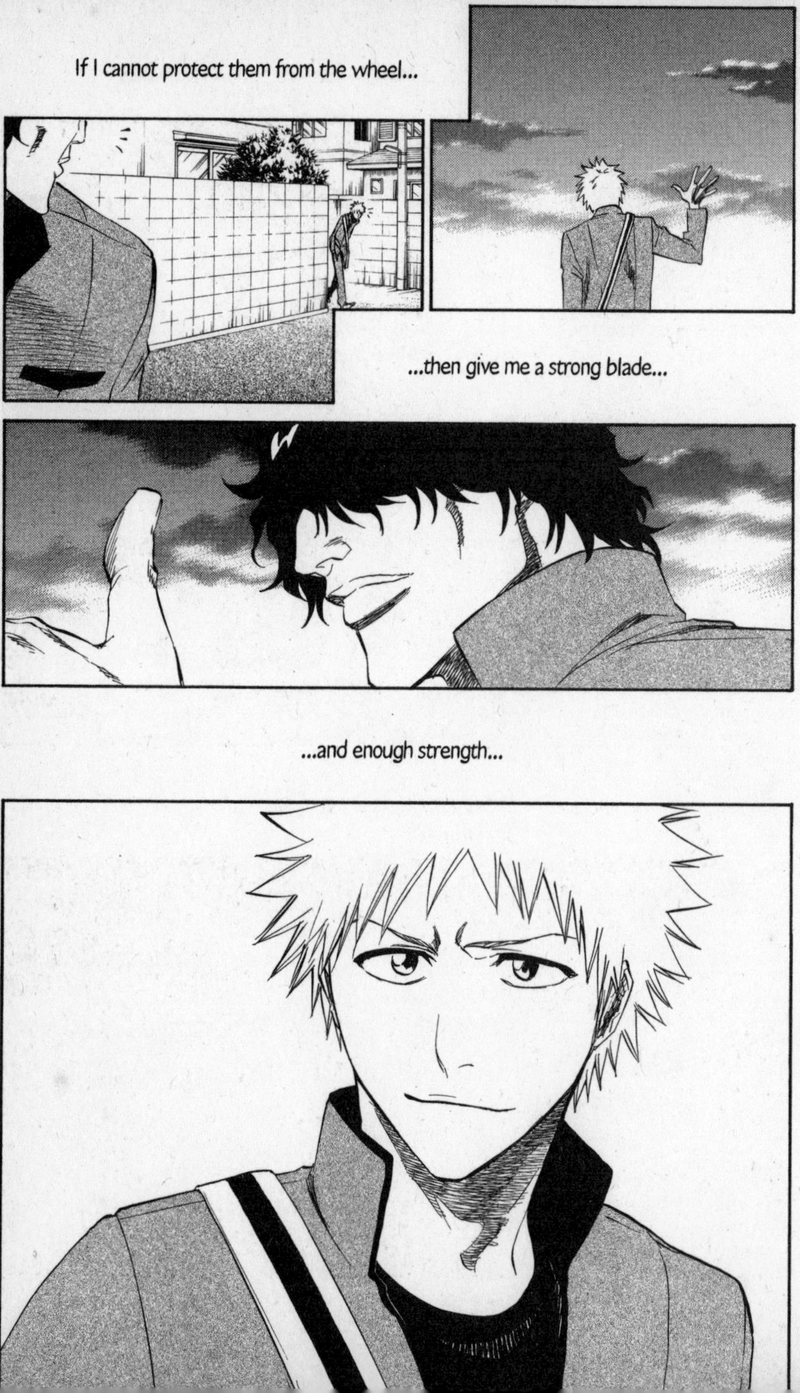
If I cannot protect them from the wheel...
...then give me a strong blade...
...and enough strength...

...TO
SHATTER
FATE.

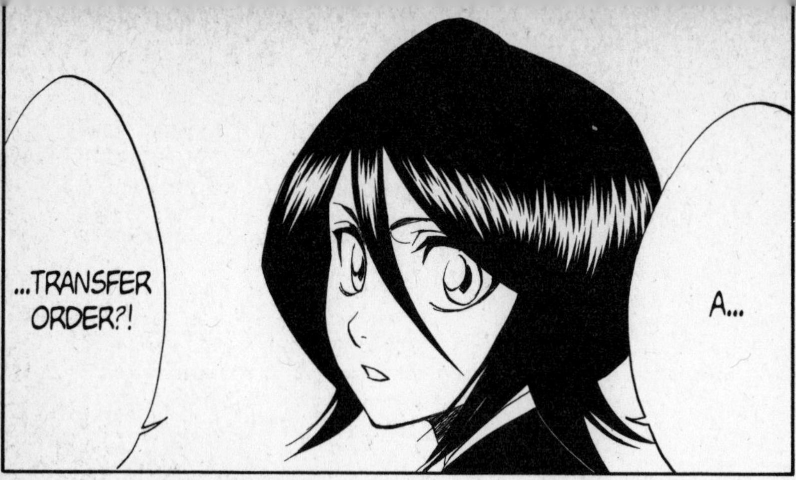
A...
...TRANSFER ORDER?!

BLEACH 0 side-B

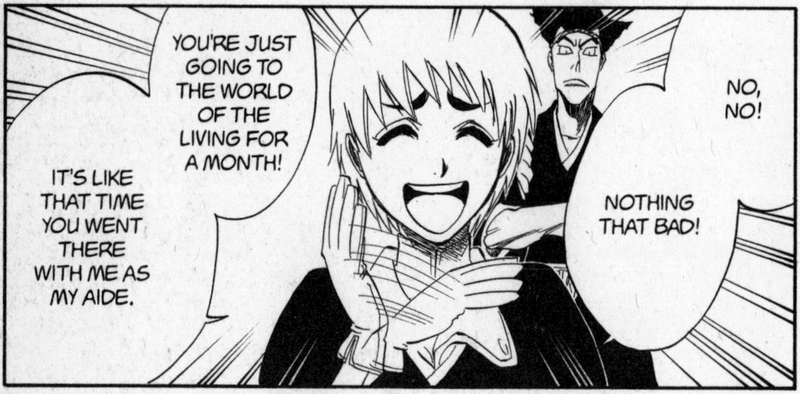
NO, NO!
NOTHING THAT BAD!
YOU'RE JUST GOING TO THE WORLD OF THE LIVING FOR A MONTH!
IT'S LIKE THAT TIME YOU WENT THERE WITH ME AS MY AIDE.

the rotator

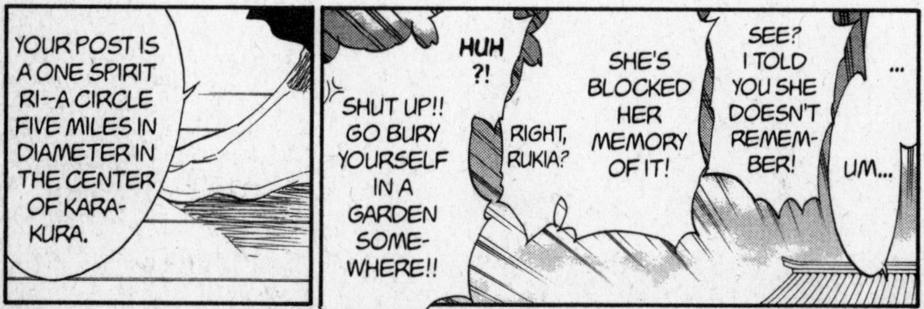
...
UM...
SEE? I TOLD YOU SHE DOESN'T REMEM-BER!
SHE'S BLOCKED HER MEMORY OF IT!
RIGHT, RUKIA?
HUH ?!
SHUT UP!! GO BURY YOURSELF IN A GARDEN SOME-WHERE!!
YOUR POST IS A ONE SPIRIT RI--A CIRCLE FIVE MILES IN DIAMETER IN THE CENTER OF KARA-KURA.

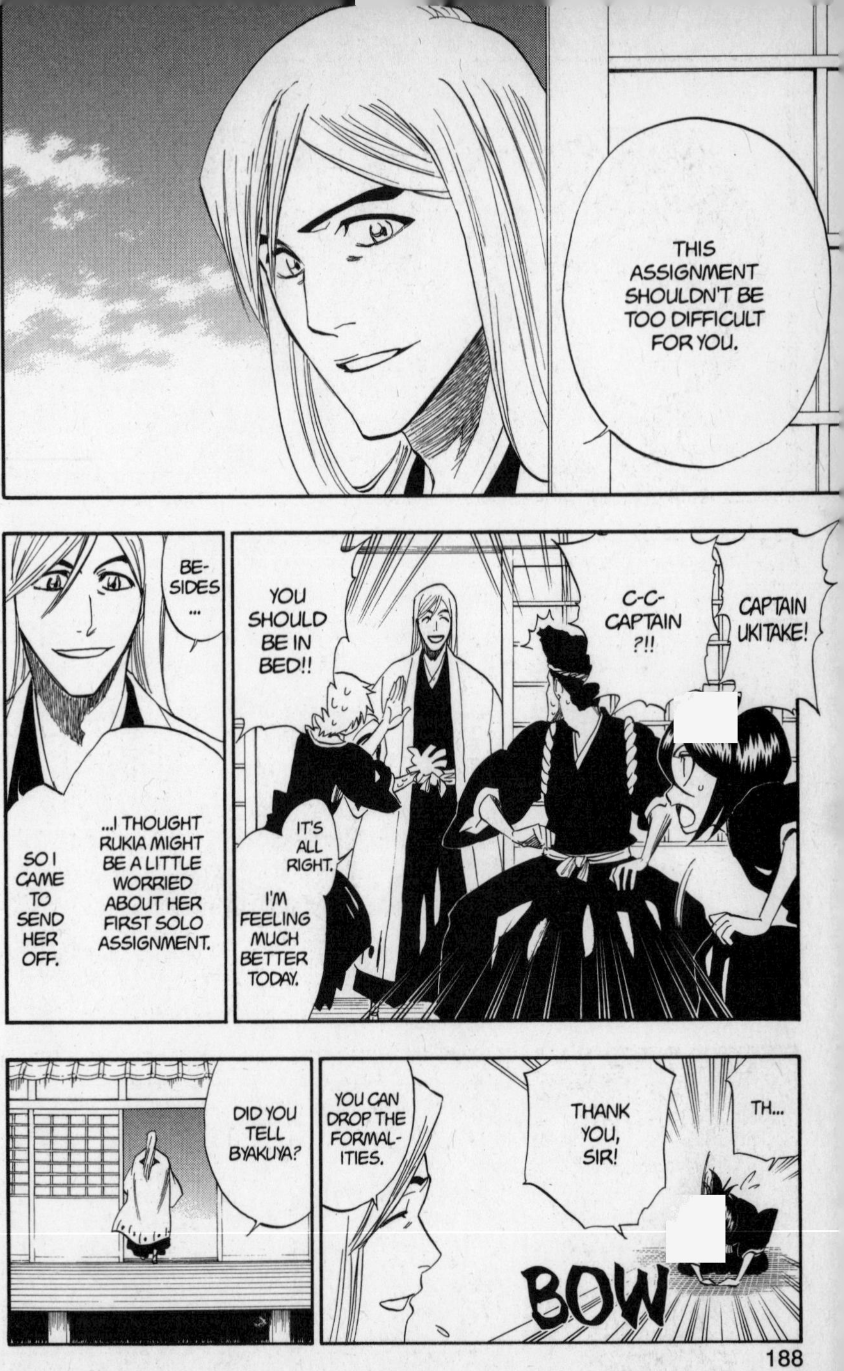
THIS ASSIGNMENT SHOULDN'T BE TOO DIFFICULT FOR YOU.
CAPTAIN UKITAKE!
C-C-CAPTAIN?!!
YOU SHOULD BE IN BED!!
IT'S ALL RIGHT.
I'M FEELING MUCH BETTER TODAY.
BE-SIDES...
...I THOUGHT RUKIA MIGHT BE A LITTLE WORRIED ABOUT HER FIRST SOLO ASSIGNMENT.
SO I CAME TO SEND HER OFF.
TH...
THANK YOU, SIR!
BOW
YOU CAN DROP THE FORMAL-ITIES.
DID YOU TELL BYAKUYA?

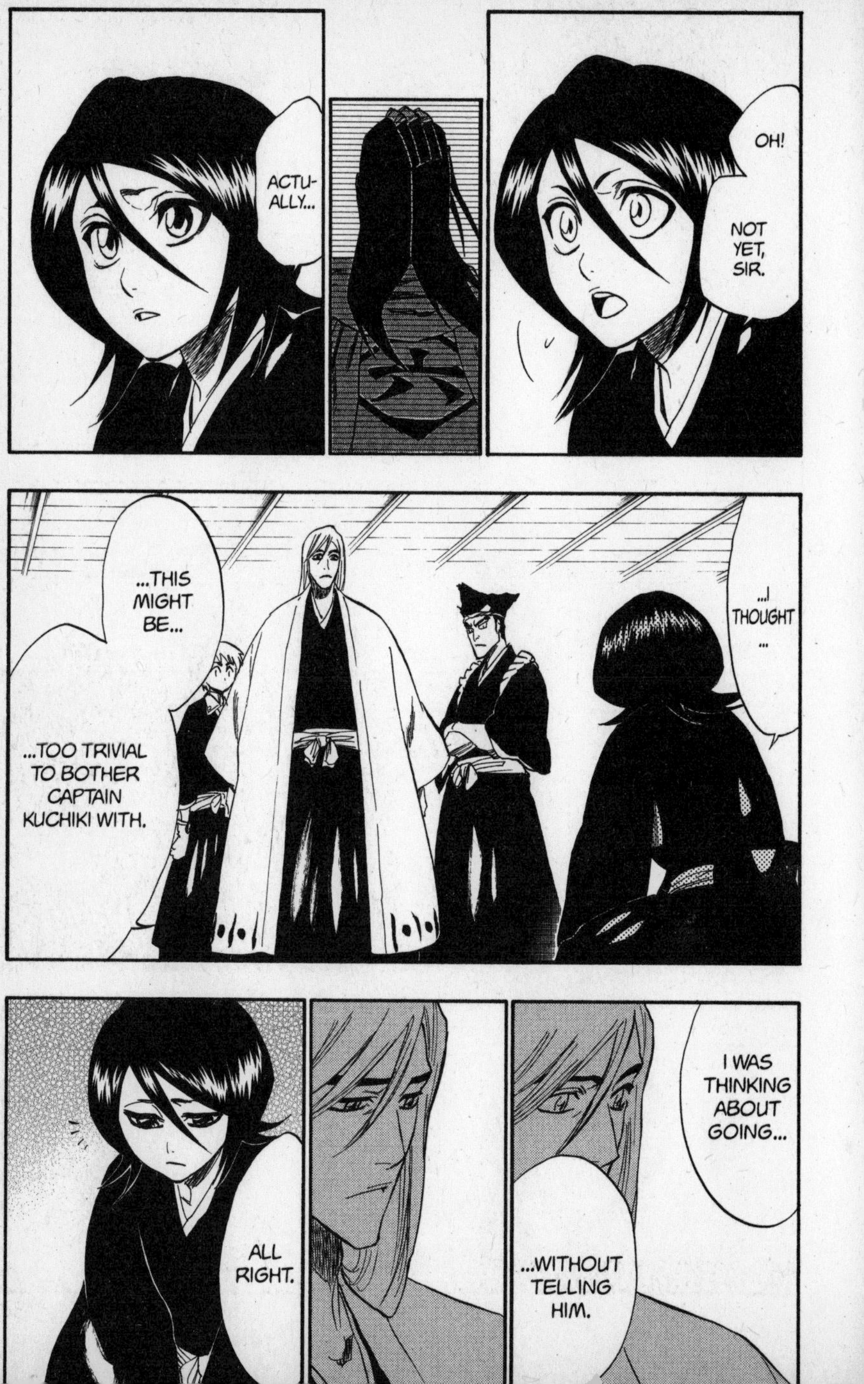
OH!
NOT YET, SIR.
ACTU-ALLY...
...I THOUGHT ...
...THIS MIGHT BE...
...TOO TRIVIAL TO BOTHER CAPTAIN KUCHIKI WITH.
I WAS THINKING ABOUT GOING...
...WITHOUT TELLING HIM.
ALL RIGHT.

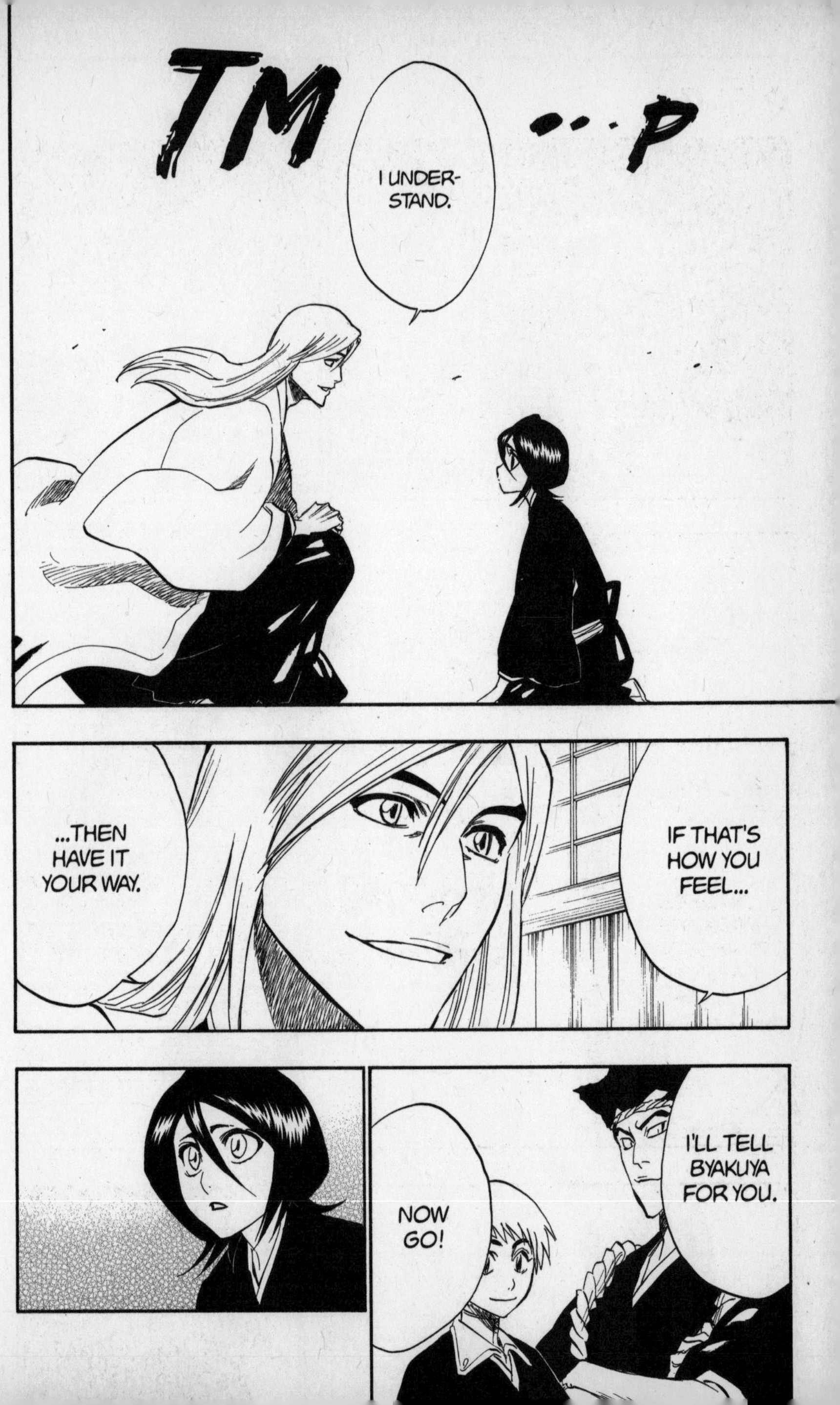

TM...P
I UNDER-STAND.
IF THAT'S HOW YOU FEEL...
...THEN HAVE IT YOUR WAY.
I'LL TELL BYAKUYA FOR YOU.
NOW GO!

READ THIS WAY

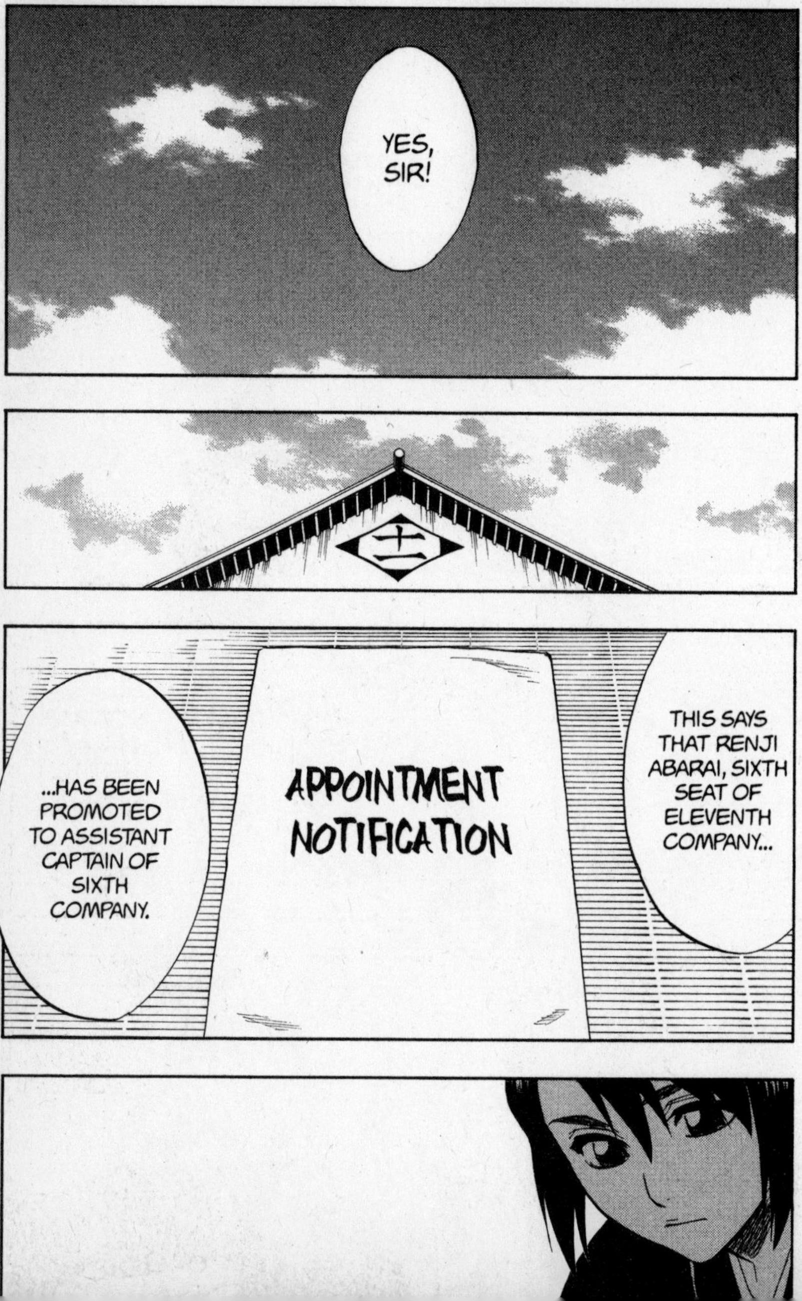
YES, SIR!
THIS SAYS THAT RENJI ABARAI, SIXTH SEAT OF ELEVENTH COMPANY...
APPOINTMENT NOTIFICATION
...HAS BEEN PROMOTED TO ASSISTANT CAPTAIN OF SIXTH COMPANY.

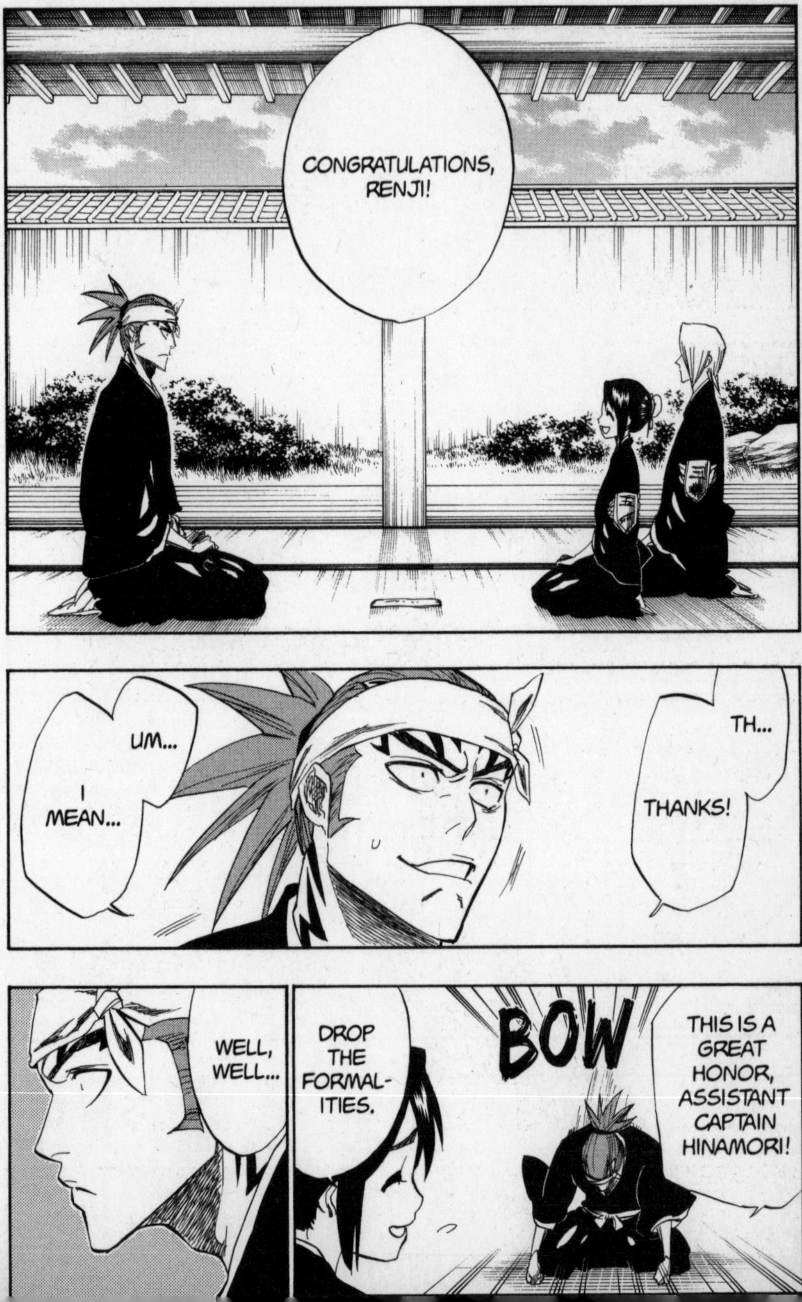
CONGRATULATIONS, RENJI!
TH... THANKS!
UM... I MEAN...
THIS IS A GREAT HONOR, ASSISTANT CAPTAIN HINAMORI!
BOW
DROP THE FORMAL-ITIES.
WELL, WELL...

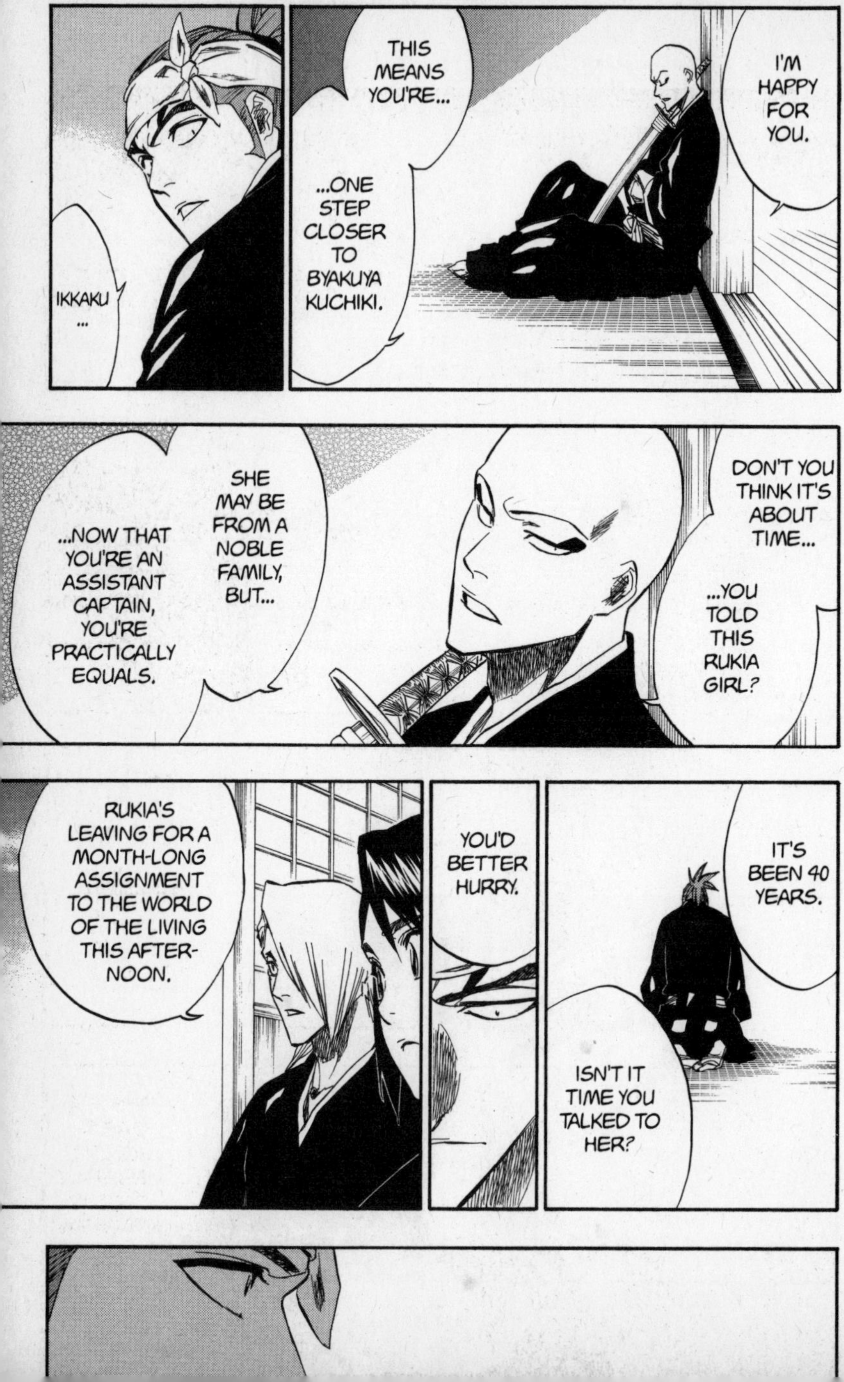
I'M HAPPY FOR YOU.
THIS MEANS YOU'RE...
...ONE STEP CLOSER TO BYAKUYA KUCHIKI.
IKKAKU ...
DON'T YOU THINK IT'S ABOUT TIME...
...YOU TOLD THIS RUKIA GIRL?
SHE MAY BE FROM A NOBLE FAMILY, BUT...
...NOW THAT YOU'RE AN ASSISTANT CAPTAIN, YOU'RE PRACTICALLY EQUALS.
IT'S BEEN 40 YEARS.
ISN'T IT TIME YOU TALKED TO HER?
YOU'D BETTER HURRY.
RUKIA'S LEAVING FOR A MONTH-LONG ASSIGNMENT TO THE WORLD OF THE LIVING THIS AFTER-NOON.

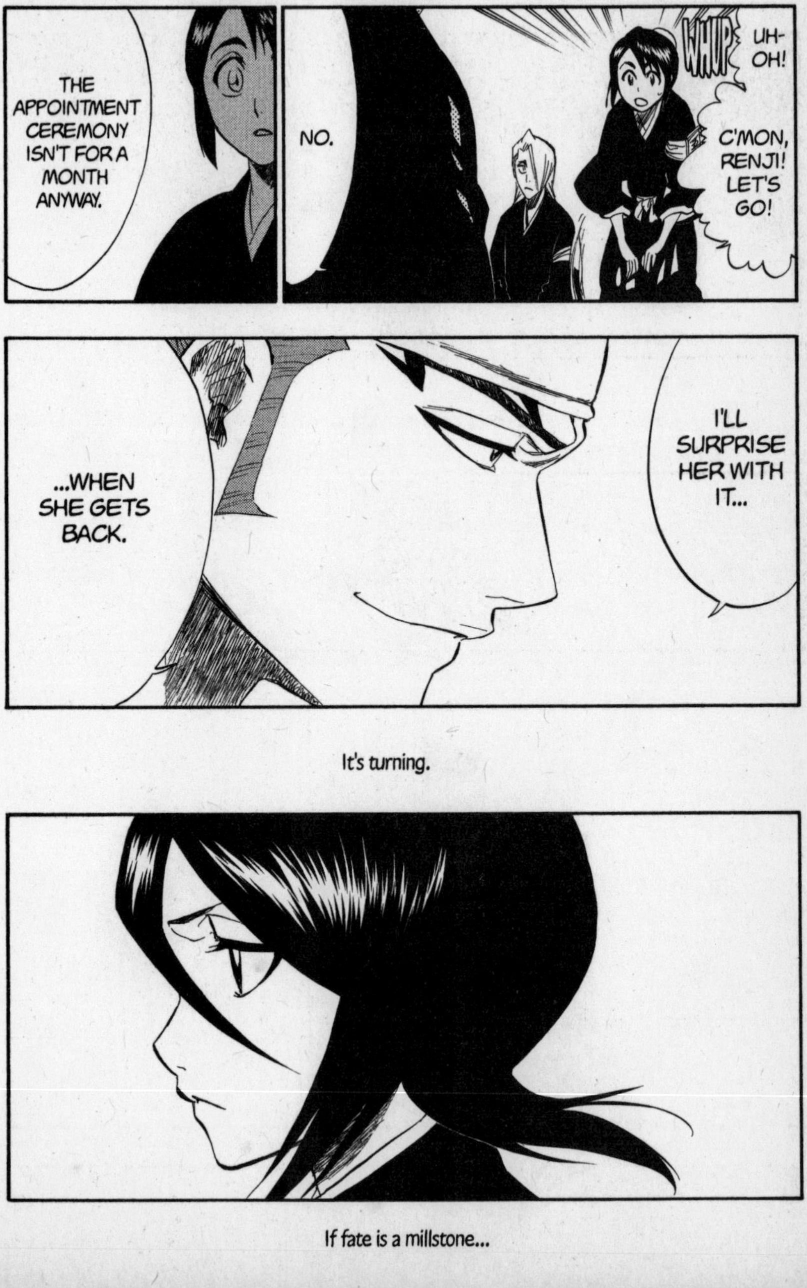
WHUP
UH-OH!
C'MON, RENJI! LET'S GO!
NO.
THE APPOINTMENT CEREMONY ISN'T FOR A MONTH ANYWAY.
I'LL SURPRISE HER WITH IT...
...WHEN SHE GETS BACK.
It's turning.
If fate is a millstone...

...we are the ones that make it turn.

We believe that the crushing wheel...

...is guided by an infallible power.

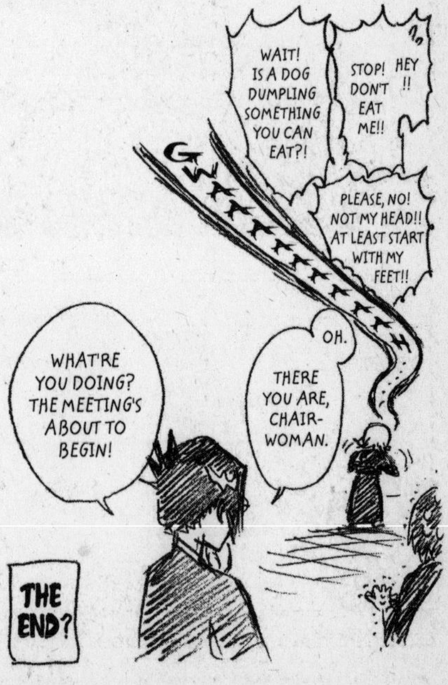
HEY !!
STOP! DON'T EAT ME!!
WAIT! IS A DOG DUMPLING SOMETHING YOU CAN EAT?!
PLEASE, NO! NOT MY HEAD!! AT LEAST START WITH MY FEET!!
OH.
THERE YOU ARE, CHAIR-WOMAN.
WHAT'RE YOU DOING? THE MEETING'S ABOUT TO BEGIN!
THE END?

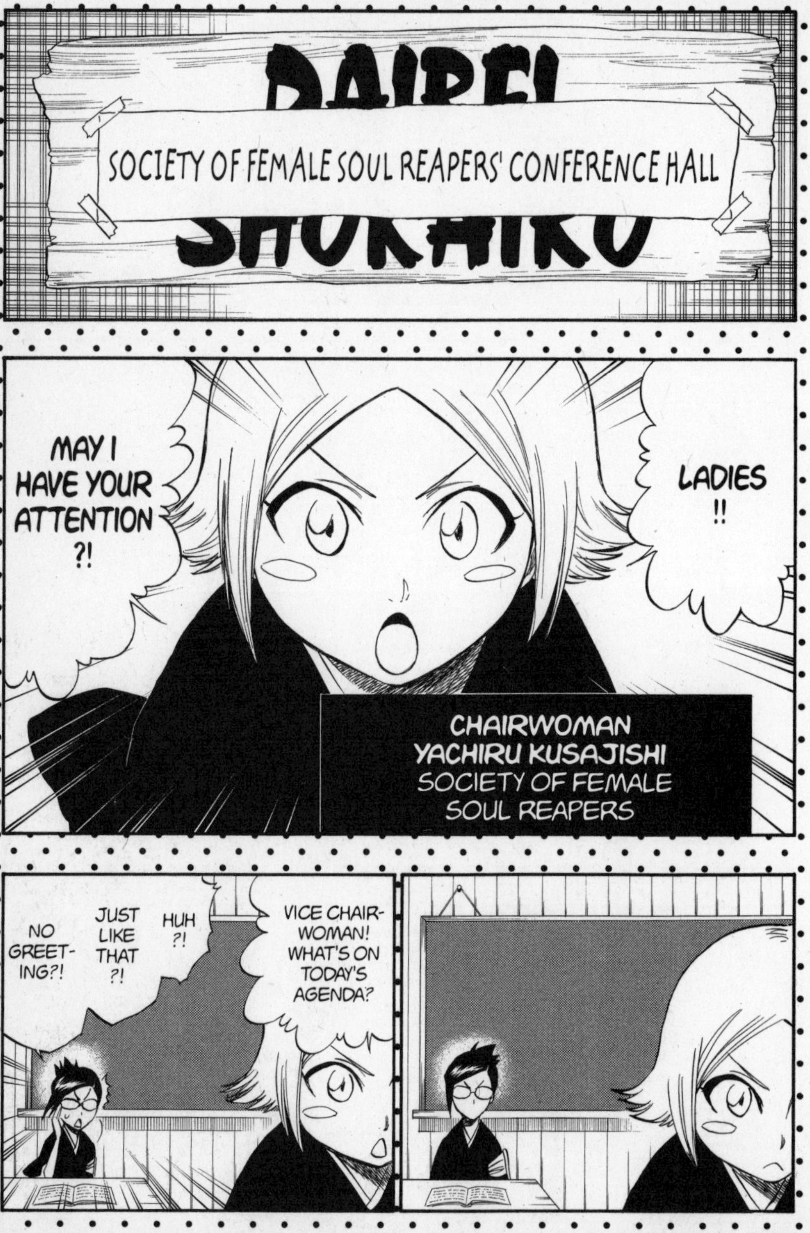
SOCIETY OF FEMALE SOUL REAPERS' CONFERENCE HALL
LADIES !!
MAY I HAVE YOUR ATTENTION ?!
CHAIRWOMAN YACHIRU KUSAJISHI SOCIETY OF FEMALE SOUL REAPERS
VICE CHAIR-WOMAN! WHAT'S ON TODAY'S AGENDA?
HUH ?!
JUST LIKE THAT ?!
NO GREET-ING?!

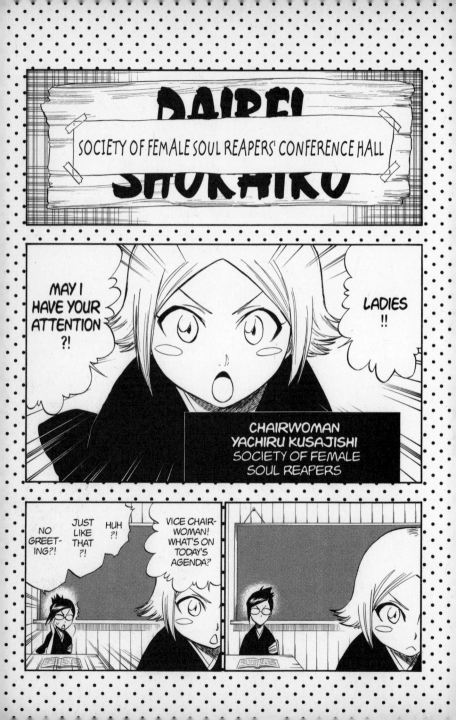

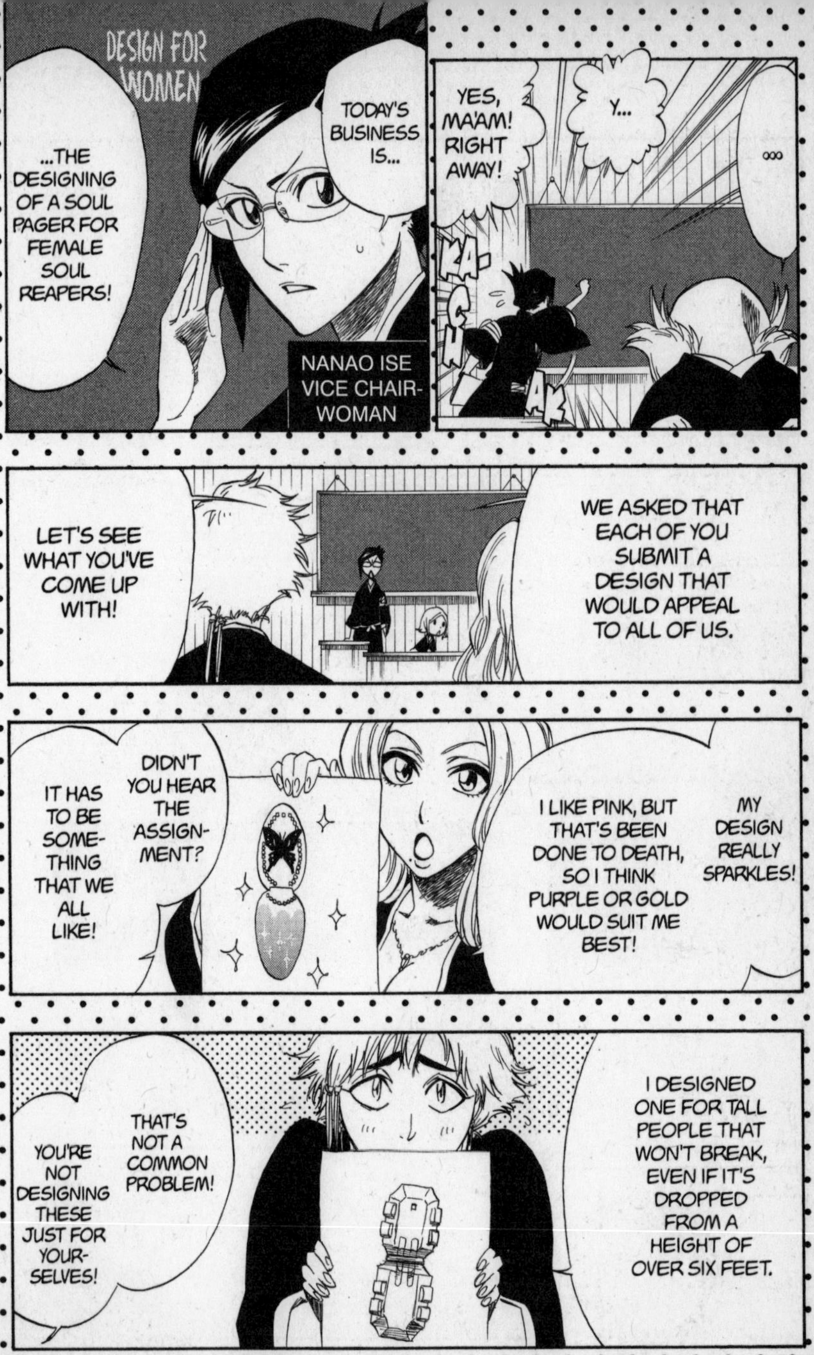
ooo
Y...
YES, MA'AM! RIGHT AWAY!
DESIGN FOR WOMEN
TODAY'S BUSINESS IS...
...THE DESIGNING OF A SOUL PAGER FOR FEMALE SOUL REAPERS!
NANAO ISE VICE CHAIR-WOMAN
WE ASKED THAT EACH OF YOU SUBMIT A DESIGN THAT WOULD APPEAL TO ALL OF US.
LET'S SEE WHAT YOU'VE COME UP WITH!
MY DESIGN REALLY SPARKLES!
I LIKE PINK, BUT THAT'S BEEN DONE TO DEATH, SO I THINK PURPLE OR GOLD WOULD SUIT ME BEST!
DIDN'T YOU HEAR THE ASSIGN-MENT?
IT HAS TO BE SOME-THING THAT WE ALL LIKE!
I DESIGNED ONE FOR TALL PEOPLE THAT WON'T BREAK, EVEN IF IT'S DROPPED FROM A HEIGHT OF OVER SIX FEET.
THAT'S NOT A COMMON PROBLEM!
YOU'RE NOT DESIGNING THESE JUST FOR YOUR-SELVES!

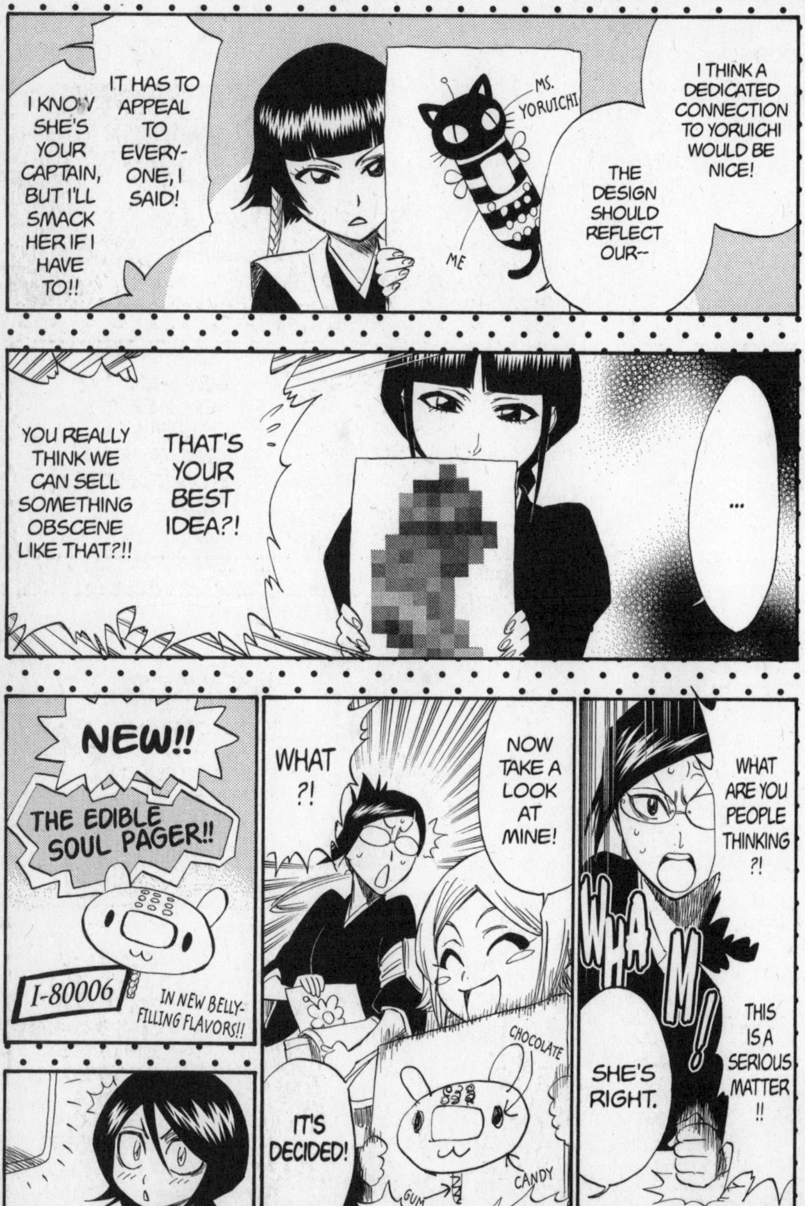
I THINK A DEDICATED CONNECTION TO YORUICHI WOULD BE NICE!
THE DESIGN SHOULD REFLECT OUR--
MS. YORUICHI
ME
IT HAS TO APPEAL TO EVERY-ONE, I SAID!
I KNOW SHE'S YOUR CAPTAIN, BUT I'LL SMACK HER IF I HAVE TO!!
...
THAT'S YOUR BEST IDEA?!
YOU REALLY THINK WE CAN SELL SOMETHING OBSCENE LIKE THAT?!!
WHAT ARE YOU PEOPLE THINKING?!
WHAM!
THIS IS A SERIOUS MATTER!!
SHE'S RIGHT.
NOW TAKE A LOOK AT MINE!
WHAT?!
CHOCOLATE
CANDY
GUM
IT'S DECIDED!
NEW!!
THE EDIBLE SOUL PAGER!!
I-80006
IN NEW BELLY-FILLING FLAVORS!!
OH!

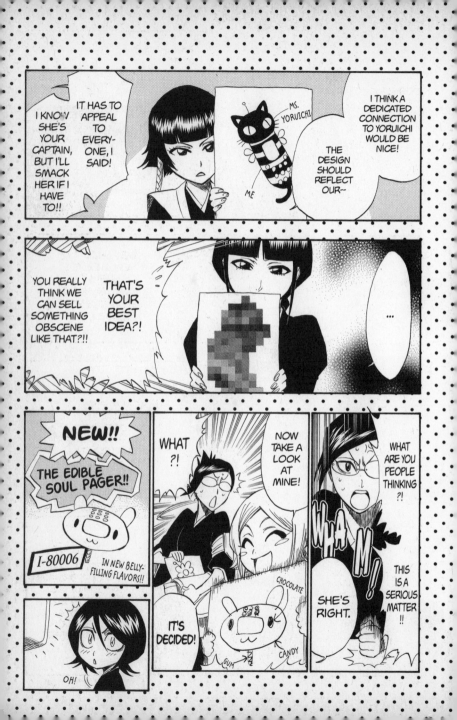

Next Volume Preview

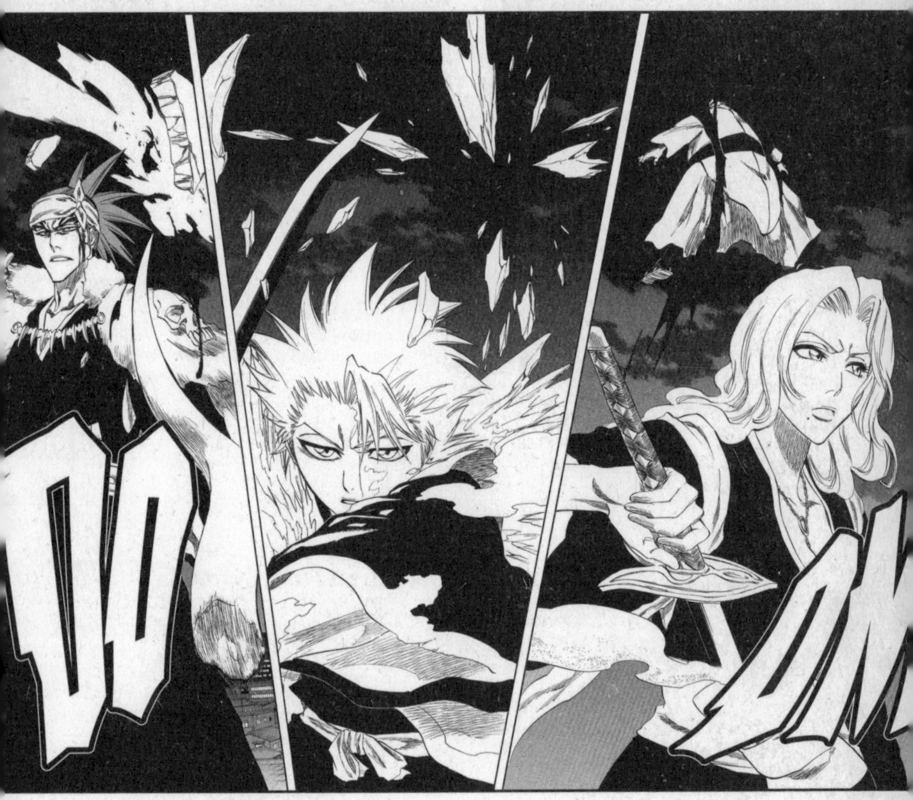

Ichigo and the Soul Reapers' fight with the Arrancars rages on, and even the kids from Urahara Shôten are joining in! The bad news is these aren't even the strongest Arrancars in Heuco Mundo, and they're still winning! The good news is the Soul Reapers have a surprise up their sleeves…

Read it first in SHONEN JUMP magazine!

$7.⁹⁹

MANGA
ON SALE NOW!

WHO IS BEHIND THE MYSTERIOUS HOSHIN PROJECT?

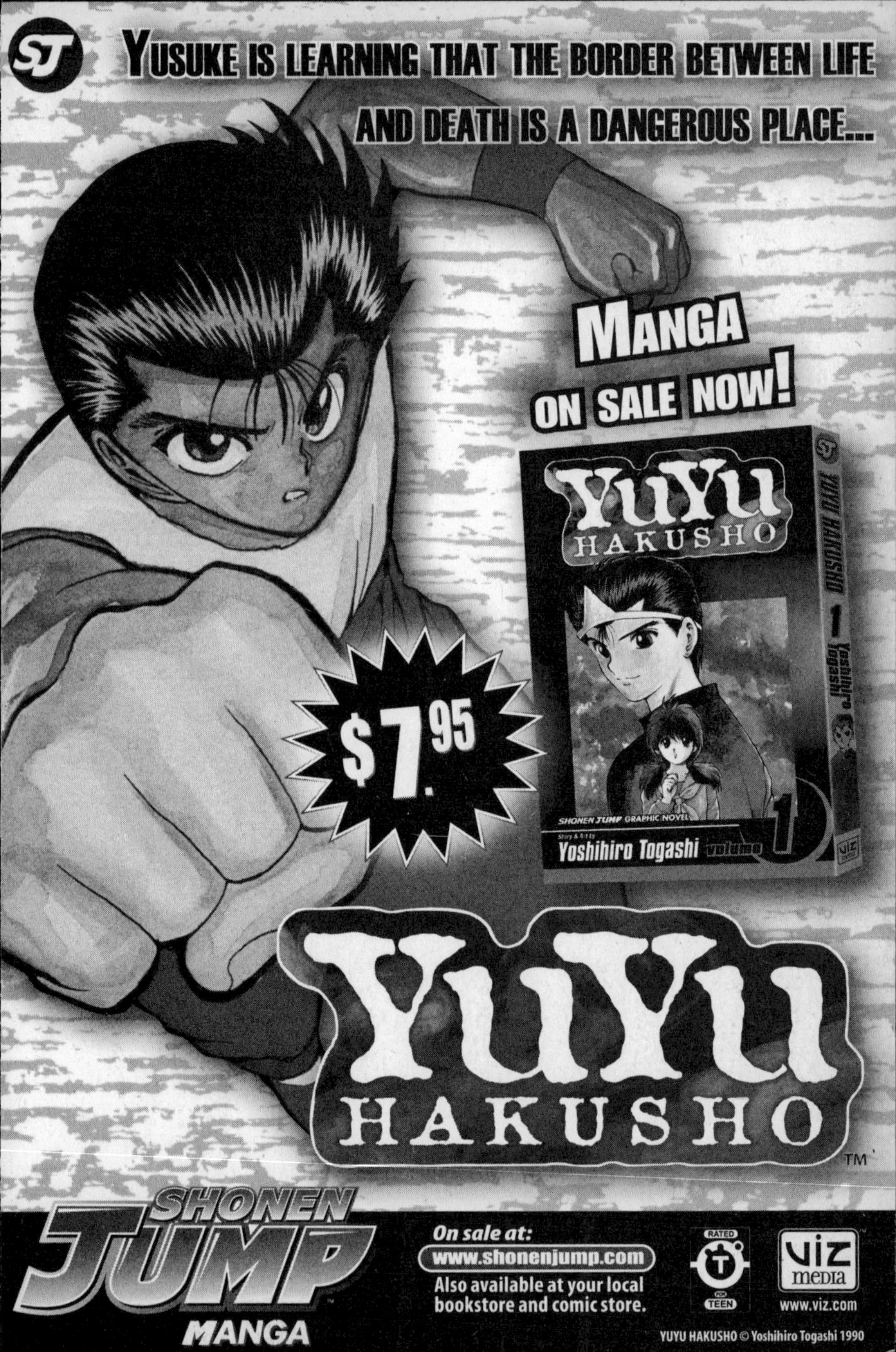

YUSUKE IS LEARNING THAT THE BORDER BETWEEN LIFE
AND DEATH IS A DANGEROUS PLACE...
MANGA
ON SALE NOW!
$7.95
YuYu HAKUSHO
SHONEN JUMP GRAPHIC NOVEL
Yoshihiro Togashi volume 1
YuYu HAKUSHO™
SHONEN JUMP MANGA
On sale at:
www.shonenjump.com
Also available at your local bookstore and comic store.
RATED T TEEN
viz media
www.viz.com
YUYU HAKUSHO © Yoshihiro Togashi 1990

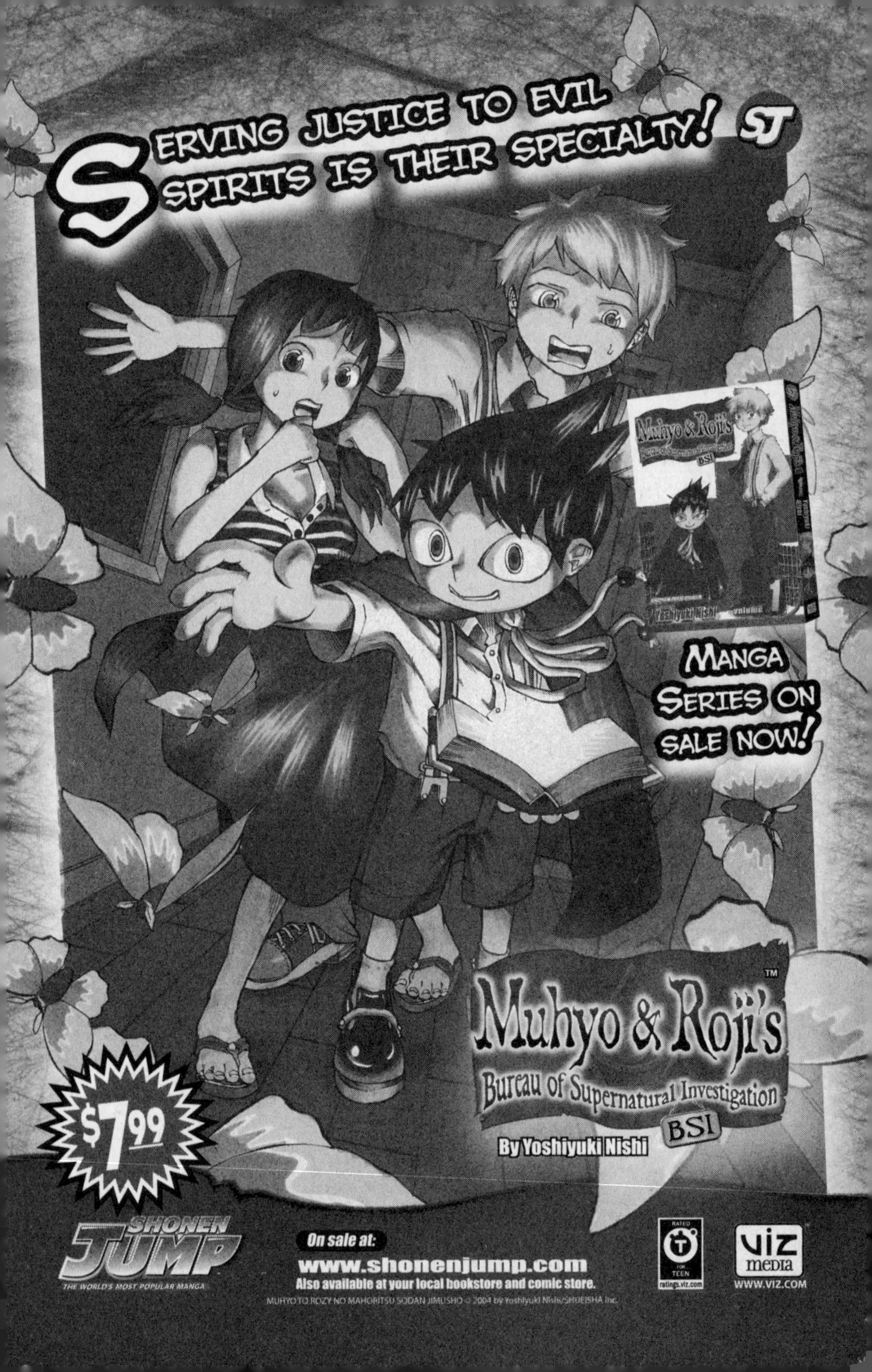
SERVING JUSTICE TO EVIL SPIRITS IS THEIR SPECIALTY!
SJ
Muhyo & Roji's Bureau of Supernatural Investigation BSI
volume 1
MANGA SERIES ON SALE NOW!
Muhyo & Roji's™
Bureau of Supernatural Investigation
BSI
By Yoshiyuki Nishi
$7.99
SHONEN JUMP
THE WORLD'S MOST POPULAR MANGA
On sale at:
www.shonenjump.com
Also available at your local bookstore and comic store.
RATED T FOR TEEN
ratings.viz.com
VIZ media
WWW.VIZ.COM
MUHYO TO ROZY NO MAHORITSU SODAN JIMUSHO © 2004 by Yoshiyuki Nishi/SHUEISHA Inc.

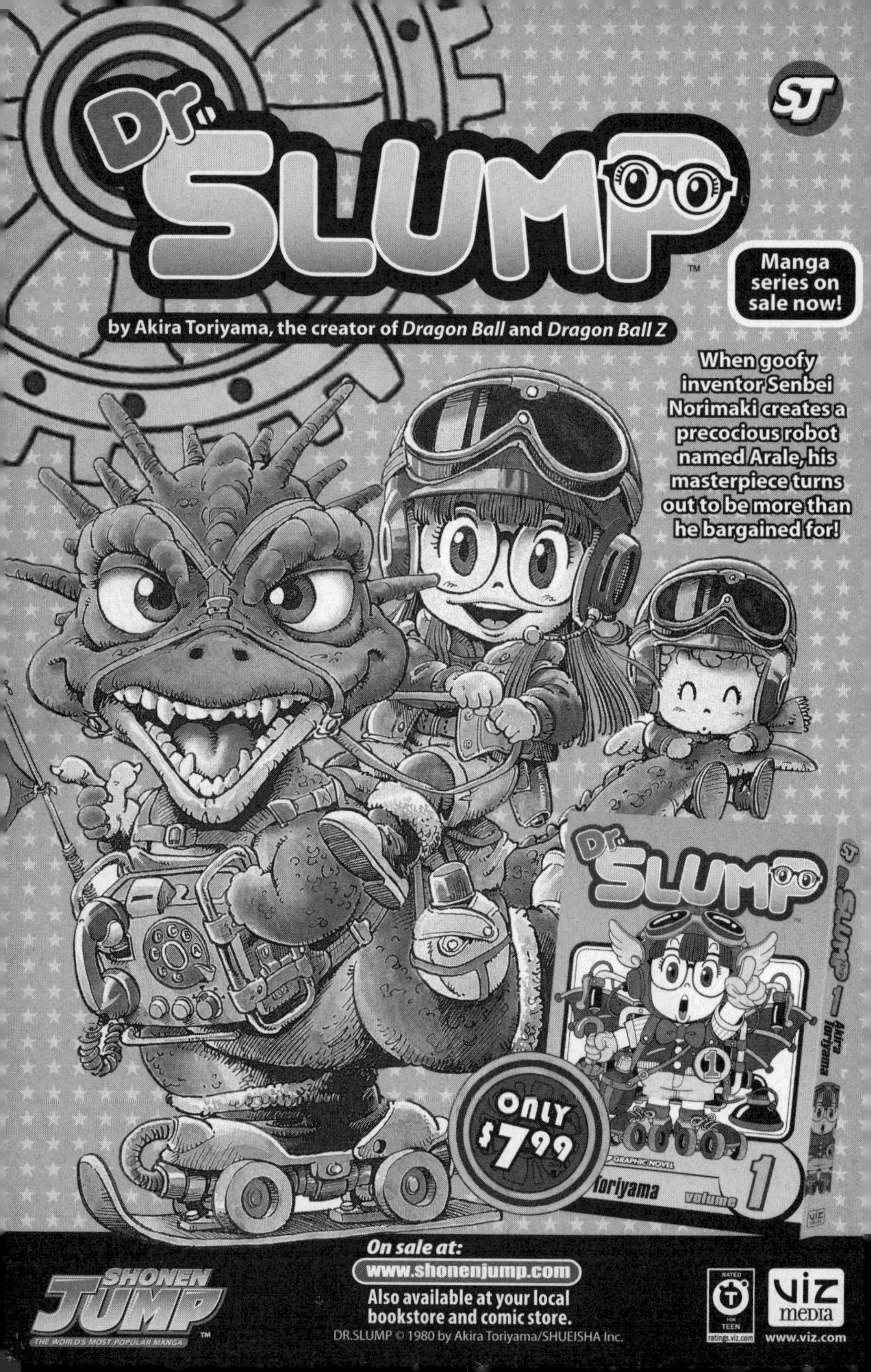
SJ
Dr. SLUMP™
Manga series on sale now!
by Akira Toriyama, the creator of Dragon Ball and Dragon Ball Z
When goofy inventor Senbei Norimaki creates a precocious robot named Arale, his masterpiece turns out to be more than he bargained for!
Dr. SLUMP
GRAPHIC NOVEL
Toriyama
volume 1
ONLY $7.99
On sale at:
www.shonenjump.com
Also available at your local bookstore and comic store.
DR.SLUMP © 1980 by Akira Toriyama/SHUEISHA Inc.
SHONEN JUMP™
THE WORLD'S MOST POPULAR MANGA
RATED T FOR TEEN
ratings.viz.com
VIZ media
www.viz.com

Tell us what you think about SHONEN JUMP manga!

Our survey is now available online.
Go to: **www.SHONENJUMP.com/mangasurvey**

Help us make our product offering better!

04/10